THE

CHRISTIAN

RETROSPECT AND REGISTER:

A SUMMARY OF

THE SCIENTIFIC, MORAL AND RELIGIOUS PROGRESS

OF THE

FIRST HALF OF THE XIXTH CENTURY.

BY ROBERT BAIRD.

THIRD EDITION.

NEW YORK:
PUBLISHED BY M. W. DODD,
BRICK CHURCH CHAPEL, CITY HALL SQUARE,
(OPPOSITE THE CITY HALL.)

1851.

INTRODUCTION.

In the early part of last winter, we were requested by a friend,* to engage to prepare annually, if the proper encouragement should be secured, a volume of some 400 duodecimo pages, which should contain a *resumé*, or summary, of all that relates to the Progress of the Kingdom of God in this world, as well as of what has a direct bearing on the most important interests of mankind.

After much reflection, and with no little reluctance, we agreed to undertake the task, and begin with the year 1851. This would have given us the entire year for the preparation of the first volume. But we had no sooner given our consent to attempt the work proposed than an earnest application was made to us to prepare a preliminary volume, which should give a review of what had been done during the first fifty years of this century. And, although it was extremely inconvenient for us to take upon

* Rev. John Beach, of Michigan, who has taken a great interest in the enterprise.

us such a work, situated as we were, and enjoying very imperfect health, we set about the enterprise in the early days of March, and (through God's blessing) we have been able to get through it. The reader will find that the work is divided into two Parts. The first relates to the progress of Mankind in what may, in a general sense, be called their MATERIAL INTERESTS. This portion of the volume is divided into eight chapters, and these again into sections.

For all of the Vth, VIth, VIIth and VIIIth chapters of this part of the book, the reader, as well as ourselves, is indebted to the Rev. Benjamin N. Martin, of Albany. They will be found admirably written, and all that could be desired in a work of this nature, and so limited in extent.

The second Part relates to what we have denominated the Progress in the MORAL AND RELIGIOUS INTERESTS which the world has made during the period under consideration.

It has been our aim to prepare a volume which might be read with interest and profit by all who desired to know something of the advance which has been made during the first half of the XIXth century in that which has a bearing upon the temporal well-being of the Human race, as well as in what relates to the enlargement of the kingdom of the Messiah. As the work has been written for popular use—for the benefit rather of those who have not time to read numerous and not easily found books, numerous reports of Societies, religious journals, etc.,—neither great detail, nor extended research, will be expected.

In the chapters relating to Science, the applications of Science, etc., all that could be attempted was to speak of those things which possess the most importance, and which are more easily understood by the ordinary reader.

The work is entirely Protestant in its character, and relates to the progress of Protestantism in the world,—for the author regards true Protestantism as identical, if not synonymous, with true Christianity.

It only remains to say that, from the nature of the case many movements to which some persons attach no little importance, could not be treated in this volume;—some because of their comparative want of merit; some because it is not clear that they have had, or will have, the influence which their advocates claim for them, upon the best interests, temporal or spiritual, of mankind; and some because the size of the volume would not allow of their being introduced. We trust, however, that whatever is of intrinsical importance in its nature, or has an effective bearing on the subjects treated in this work, will be here found set forth as fully as our limits would allow.

NEW YORK, *May 9th*, 1851.

CONTENTS.

PART I.

CHAPTER I.

CHAPTER II.

CHAPTER III.

CHAPTER IV.

CHAPTER V.

HISTORICAL SKETCH OF SCIENCE IN THE FIRST HALF OF THE NINETEENTH CENTURY.

CHAPTER VI.

APPLIED SCIENCE.

CHAPTER VII.

PROGRESS IN THE ARTS OF INTERCOMMUNICATION.

CHAPTER VIII.

SOCIAL PROGRESS IN THE FIRST HALF OF THE NINETEENTH CENTURY.

PART II.

CHAPTER I.

ENLARGEMENT OF CHRISTENDOM DURING THE FIRST HALF OF THE NINETEENTH CENTURY.

CHAPTER II.

PROGRESS OF RELIGIOUS LIBERTY.

CHAPTER III.

PROGRESS OF EVANGELICAL CHRISTIANITY.

CHAPTER IV.

SOCIETIES FOR THE DIFFUSION OF THE SCRIPTURES.

CHAPTER V.

SOCIETIES FOR THE CIRCULATION OF RELIGIOUS BOOKS.

CHAPTER VI.

SOCIETIES FOR HOME EVANGELIZATION.

CHAPTER VII.

SUNDAY-SCHOOL SOCIETIES.

CHAPTER VIII.

EDUCATIONAL SOCIETIES.

CHAPTER IX.

THE TEMPERANCE REFORMATION.

CHAPTER X.

CHAPTER XI.

CHAPTER XII.

CHAPTER XIII.

CHAPTER XXIII.

CHAPTER XXIV.

CHAPTER XXV.

CHAPTER XXVI.

CHAPTER XXVII.

CHAPTER XXVIII.

CHRISTIAN RETROSPECT AND REGISTER.

CHAPTER I.

POLITICAL CHANGES OF THE FIRST HALF OF THE NINETEENTH CENTURY.

THE close of the XVIIIth century left Europe in a state of extreme political agitation,—the influence of which was, in fact, felt in a greater or less degree, to the remotest boundaries of the Civilized World. The history of the last quarter of that century is unsurpassed in interest by that of any preceding period of equal length in the annals of Mankind. Within it occurred two Revolutions which will leave their impress upon the destinies of the human race in all coming time.

In the New World the Revolution of 1775–83,—itself one of the glorious fruits, as was the existence of the nation which it made free, of the Great Reformation of the XVIth century,—gave independence and a republican form of government to THE UNITED STATES OF NORTH AMERICA. In the Old World, the Revolution of 1789 in France,—which was, in some respects, an effect of that which had just occurred in the Western Hemisphere,—was the first of a great series of OVERTURNINGS in the nations, of which, no prophet has arisen to tell us either the number, the extent, or the duration. All Europe was convulsed to its centre. In that great struggle the Throne and the Altar went down together in the country where it commenced, to be followed in succession by the Triumvirate and the reign of Atheism, the Directory and the reign of Deism, the Consulate and the reign of Military Despotism.

Such was the state of things when the present century was about to open. On the North American Continent, with the exception of some unimportant collisions between the United States and the Aborigines, and a brief naval war between that country and France, which was coming to a close, all was quiet. Nor was South America agitated by war. The great countries on that Continent which were in the possession of nations of European origin, were submissive colonies of Spain and Portugal.

In Europe, France, which a few years previously had, with tremendous energy, driven the hostile armies that had invaded her territory from all quarters, but had afterwards lost ground almost everywhere through the incapacity of the men who were in power, was just entering upon her wonderful career of victory and of conquest. The "Man of Destiny," as he has been called, had returned from his romantic expedition to Egypt and the East, and the Revolution of 18th Brumaire (Nov. 9th, 1799) had made him First Consul, with Siéyes and Ducos as his colleagues. The influence of this change was magical. An effective government was speedily established, which restored order throughout all portions of that country; whilst abroad, her armies once more marched to victory in all directions. The battles of Montebello (June 10th), and Marengo (June 14th, 1800), reëstablished the overwhelming influence of the French in the northern and middle parts of Italy; whilst that of Hohenlinden, on the 3d of December following, opened Germany to the conqueror, and compelled the proud House of Hapsburg to accept the terms of peace which Napoleon dictated at the Treaty of Luneville.

SECTION I.

POLITICAL CHANGES IN EUROPE SINCE THE YEAR 1800.

THE aspect of Europe at the dawn of the present century was exceedingly various. In the Centre, Germany was reduced to the necessity of accepting the peace which was forced upon her at the Treaty (Feb., 1801) just named; whilst in the South, French domination was fast pressing the government of Naples to a state of desperation; and in the North, the thunders of British cannon at Copenhagen (April 2d), in conjunction with violence in the Palace of the Czars, dissolved "the Armed Neutrality." Nevertheless, the demand of Humanity for the cessation of the murderous strife which had convulsed that portion of the world for the preceding decade of years, was heard, and the Treaty of Amiens (March 27th, 1802) restored peace for a while to England, France, Spain and Holland.

But this happy period was of short duration. The war was renewed. Napoleon, who had been crowned Emperor of France (Dec. 2d, 1804), prepared to invade England. But he was soon compelled to adjourn the attempt, in order to look after Austria. The great victory of Austerlitz (Dec. 2d, 1805) again humbled Southern Germany; and the battles of Jena, Lübeck, Eylau and Friedland in 1806 and 1807 prostrated Northern Germany, and drove the Russians back to their own vast domain. England, by the victory of Trafalgar over the combined fleets of France and Spain (Oct. 21st, 1805), and the destruction of that of Denmark (Sept. 2d, 1807), secured her ascendency on the ocean. The Treaty of Tilsit (July 7th, 1807) gave a short-lived peace to a large portion of the Continent. At this epoch the sun of Napoleon was fast ascending to the zenith. For a little while not only France, but Italy, Spain, Holland, Germany, Poland, Russia—in a word, almost the entire Continent—was subject to his powerful will. But soon a dark and lowering cloud was seen in the horizon. A war began in Spain, which lasted five years, and ended with the expulsion of the French armies from that country. In 1809, Napoleon again invaded Austria, and by the battle of Wagram humbled for the fourth time the House of Hapsburg, and tore from the brow of Austria the proud laurels which her victories for three centuries, over the Turks and other nations on her borders, had placed there.

The disastrous invasion of Russia by France, in 1812, not only brought those two great powers into collision, but involved almost all Europe. The invasion of Germany by France in 1813, renewed the gigantic struggle, which was ended by the marching of the combined armies of Austria, Prussia, and Russia to the gates of Paris, the abdication of Buonaparte, and his exile in the Island of Elba. His escape from that island again arrayed all Europe in arms; but the "Reign of One Hundred Days" was ended by the decisive battle of Waterloo (June 18th, 1815), which sent Napoleon to St. Helena (where he died, May 5th, 1821), and eleven hundred thousand men, who were on their way to France, back to their homes.

Since 1815 Europe has seen no general wars. Attempts were made at Revolution in Italy in 1820, and the great Powers intervened in Spain, in that year, and by means of French armies suppressed the popular movement, abolished the Cortes and the Constitution, and restored the despotism of Ferdinand VIIth.

The Russians marched their victorious troops across the Balkan mountains to the gates of Adrianople, in the year 1828, and would have advanced them to the walls of Constantinople, if the other great Powers had consented. By this war Russia extended her border from the Pruth to the Danube.

The Revolution in Greece, one of the bloodiest in the annals of mankind, lasted from 1821 to 1828, and ended in the independence of that country. This result was greatly hastened by the battle of Navarino (Oct. 20th, 1827), by which the combined fleets of England, France, and Russia destroyed those of Turkey and Egypt.

In France a dynastic Revolution took place in July, 1830, by which the Duke of Orleans (Louis Philippe) was placed on the throne of Charles Xth. This was followed by a Revolution (Sept. 23d, 1830) in Belgium, by which that country was severed from Holland, with which it had been united since 1814.

An unfortunate attempt at Revolution in Poland was made in the autumn of that year, and after prodigies of valor had been displayed by its brave inhabitants, was completely suppressed in the year following.

In the year 1830, France conquered Algeria, and has maintained her dominion in that land—although it cost her a long war with Abd-el-kader.

After having thrown off in a great degree the authority of the Sultan, and conquered Syria, Mehemet Ali, Pasha of Egypt, prepared to invade Turkey. On the 25th of June, 1839, his son, Ibrahim Pasha, gained a decisive victory over the Turks at Nezib; but was compelled to retreat to Egypt, by the great Powers, who required both him and his father to return to their allegiance to the Sublime Porte.

In the year 1846 another attempt at Revolution was made in Poland,—chiefly in Gallicia, or Austrian Poland,—which had a most deplorable issue. More than sixteen hundred nobles were cruelly massacred by the peasants, or tenants, whom the Austrian Government, for the purpose of making a counter-revolution, incited to this infamous deed, by holding out to them the hope of gaining the possessions of these landed proprietors! Still more: the Government of Austria availed itself of the pretext which this unfortunate attempt afforded to persuade Russia and Prussia to agree to the annexation of the Republic of Cracow—lying between the Polish possessions of Russia, Austria, and Prussia, and containing 140,000 inhabitants—to the

Austrian Empire, in utter disregard of the Treaty of Vienna, by which the existence of that Republic was guaranteed not only by these three Powers, but also by England and France.

But the year 1848 was the most memorable of all in the first half of the XIXth century. A Revolution broke out at Paris (the 22d Feb.), which hurled Louis Philippe from the throne of France, overthrew the monarchy, and led to the substitution of a Republic in its place. This great and sudden movement precipitated vast changes in Italy and Germany, of whose near approach there had been, for three or four years, numerous and most unequivocal indications. In the former, every government seemed for a while to be on the point of becoming Constitutional. At one time there was the prospect that all the Italian Powers would make a united and effective effort to drive the Austrians out of Lombardy, and construct a Confederation of States in that long-oppressed country. The King of Sardinia, as being the only monarch, save the Pope, who was truly Italian by descent, put himself at the head of this movement—a task to which he was wholly unequal. Deserted by his allies, he was driven back from Lombardy, defeated at the battle of Novara (March 23d, 1849), and nothing but the intervention of France and England saved him from the loss of a portion of his own patrimonial possessions. Overwhelmed with defeat and disappointment, he abdicated his throne, and died of chagrin (July 28th, 1849), at the city of Oporto, in Portugal.

In the meanwhile, Pope Pius Ninth, who, during the first two years of his reign had inspired the Romans with the most sanguine hopes, refused to yield to the demands of the people for Italian nationality, a constituent assembly (to form a constitution), and a new ministry. But the Quirinal being surrounded by the people, and his prime minister, Sig. Rossi, having been assassinated, his Holiness was compelled to submit. A few days later (Nov. 24th, 1846,) he fled in the livery of a servant, to Gaeta, in the Kingdom of Naples. Upon his refusing to return, a Republic was proclaimed, with a Triumvirate at its head, of which Sig. Mazzini was the most prominent member. This Republic was overthrown by a French army (July 3d, 1849), under General Oudinot. The government was carried on by a Triumvirate of Cardinals until the Pope returned (April 12th, 1850) to the "Eternal City," from his sojourn in exile, at Gaeta and Portici, of more than fifteen months. For the present all has been lost—save the liberal ideas which many able newspapers diffused in Rome and throughout Italy, during the existence of the Republic, and, above all, the hidden influence of the thousands of copies of the Word of God which were circulated in Rome during the absence of his Holiness. The despotism of the darkest ages, together with its legitimate auxiliary, the Inquisition, has returned to the "City on the Seven Hills."

As might be expected, the reäction has extended over all Italy, and every vestige of the Constitutions which had been made, or were making at the close of 1848, had disappeared by the end of 1850, excepting in the Kingdom of Sardinia, where, we are happy to say, that a Constitution still exists, and is well administered under the sceptre of the young monarch, Victor Emanuel.

Revolutions broke forth almost simultaneously in Vienna and Berlin, which led to the most serious consequences, especially the former. The Hungarians, who had long been groaning under the intolerable oppressiveness of the Austrian rule, and who were prepared to act with promptitude, renewed and urged their just demands for the redress of their grievances, and for a more national and equal government. Their demands were at first yielded to through fear, by the imbecile Emperor Ferdinand, and afterwards the concession was retracted. This led to a bloody, and, to them in the end, disastrous war. Driving the Austrian and Croatian troops out of their country, they were about to carry their victorious arms into the hereditary dominions of the House of Hapsburg, and overthrow the Austrian Empire itself, when Russia intervened. With her overwhelming armies, aided by domestic treason, she annihilated, for the present, the hopes of Freedom in one of the fairest portions of Europe, whose brave inhabitants had, for two centuries and more, formed a rampart to protect Christendom and civilization against the Mohammedan fanaticism and fury of the Turks. And Kossuth, like Mazzini, was compelled to seek safety in exile.

In Prussia, a constitution was granted by Frederick William IVth, and is now in operation. And although Germany is still agitated, the issue will be, it is probable, that something like the Diet which Germany had from 1815 to 1848, will be restored, and that the influence of Austria and Prussia will be paramount in it.

The revolutionary movement of 1848,—which affected, in all, some seventeen states and countries, and which promised at one time to secure constitutional freedom to nearly all Europe, has almost completely subsided. And although the reäction has been more or less triumphant everywhere, we are far from holding the opinion that nothing has been gained for liberty. The nations have been made, to some extent, to know, from their recent failures, the true sources of their weakness, and how to overcome it. They have been taught that they have their political education to make; that it can be acquired only by painful experience; and that it is only through *suffering* that nations, as well as individuals, can be prepared for the acquisition, appreciation, and enjoyment of the greatest blessings. Above all, they have been made to see that in this great struggle for human rights, and a well-founded freedom, but little aid is to be expected from Rome on the one hand, or Infidelity on the other.

We will conclude this notice of the political changes which have occurred in Europe since the present century commenced, with the remark, that they have left it greatly changed in some respects. Norway now belongs to Sweden, Finland to Russia; the kingdoms of Poland and Hungary exist no more, the former being absorbed in Russia, and the latter in Austria; Germany consists of thirty-eight states, instead of 354, as it did two hundred years ago, or of eighty or ninety, as in the year 1800; Greece is now an independent kingdom; Malta and the Ionian Isles are under the government of England; Belgium is an independent constitutional monarchy, instead of being held by Austria, France or Spain; the Swiss Confederation embraces twenty-two Cantons, instead of nineteen, as it did in the latter part of the XVIIIth century. Europe now contains twenty Kingdoms, thirty-one Duchies, four Principalities, and nine Republics,—including the four Free Cities of Germany—in all sixty-four States. This is a great advance towards the reconstruction of the governments on the basis of *nationality*,—to which things have been tending for ages, and decidedly so during the last half-century.

SECTION II.

POLITICAL CHANGES IN THE REST OF THE EASTERN HEMISPHERE.

Asia.—The northern end of Asia, or the vast country of Siberia, was under the dominion of Russia at the commencement of the present century, nor has her dominion been much extended in that direction since. The war with Persia, in the year 1826, enlarged somewhat the Trans-Caucasian possessions of Russia. That with Khiva, a country lying eastward of the Caspian Sea, was unfavorable to the arms of Russia, and added little or nothing to her vast territories. The war with the Circassians in the Caucasus has been prosecuted for a long period; nor does its end appear to be near. In fact it would seem that Russia is in no great hurry to conquer that mountainous region, or she would prosecute the war with more vigor. As to Bokhara, an extensive region lying south-east of the Caspian Sea, and between the Russian Provinces south of the Caucasus and the Province of Affghanistan, if Russia has ever seriously thought of conquering that country, she has certainly kept her thoughts to herself. When she shall have effected that conquest, and England that of Affghanistan, then a collision, in Central Asia, between these two great Powers will not be far distant.

But while the political changes in Northern Asia have been neither great nor important, during the last fifty years, it has been far otherwise in the southern portion of that Continent. Within that period, the British empire in India has received vast increase, both as to extension and consolidation. The native princes have been very effectually subdued; the great provinces of the Punjaub and Scinde and others have been added within the last few years. The attempt to annex Affghanistan, in 1840, to their immense dominions in India was unfavorable to the English, and they were compelled to renounce, for the time at least, the enterprise. At this moment, there must be all of one hundred millions of people in India under the government of Great Britain, and fifteen or twenty millions on the confines, who are greatly under her influence. And this vast empire has grown to its present enormous extent from small beginnings within a period of one hundred and fifty years, and mainly since the commencement of the present century.

In the years 1840 and '41 a war took place between England and China, which ended in the latter being compelled to open five of her seaports to the English, and pay 21,000,000 dollars.

As to the other countries in Asia, with the exception of the conquest and temporary occupation of Syria by the late Pasha of Egypt, we know of no political changes worthy of note that have occurred during the present century.

Africa.—In the northern part of Africa political changes of much importance have occurred since the year 1800. The

Pashalic of Egypt has been converted into a hereditary monarchy, acknowledging a certain allegiance and subjection to the Sultan of Turkey. This was accomplished by Mehemet Ali, the grandfather of the present Pasha Abbas. That remarkable man annihilated the long-endured tyranny of the Mamelukes, and set about the reorganization of the administration of the country upon a more regular plan—extremely despotic, and yet embracing a considerable element of European civilization.

The Barbary Powers—as Tunis, Tripoli, Algiers, and Morocco were formerly called—have been compelled since this century commenced, and chiefly within the last twenty-five years, to abandon entirely their piratical habits. Nor do they now dare to exact tribute from Christian nations. Since the year 1830, Algiers, with its territory, has been in the hands of the French,—a state of things which has had a great influence upon the adjoining states.

England took the southern end of Africa, or Cape of Good Hope, from Holland in the year 1795, but restored it in 1802. In 1806 she took it again from the Dutch, and her claim was confirmed by the Congress of Vienna in 1814. Her possession of it seems to be permanently established, and under her government the population is gradually increasing by means of immigration from the British Isles. Civilization and Christianity are gradually penetrating northward into the interior, although great hindrance is experienced from the savage tribes.

At various points colonies, chiefly composed of free negroes from the United States, are planting along the western coast of Africa, north of the Equator, which promise at a future day to exert an important political, as well as moral and religious, influence upon that great but almost unknown continent.

The Insular portions of the Eastern Hemisphere.—Great Britain possesses the large islands of New Holland, Van Dieman's Land, and New Zealand, besides others of less importance, in the Southern Ocean, and a great emigration from her shores is annually making its way to them. Already there is a large population in them—probably not far from a quarter of a million—of Anglo-Saxon origin. Almost all this has taken place since the opening of the present century. Who can tell how great an influence the planting of these English colonies will have upon the destinies of the human race in that portion of our globe?

The Dutch still have the great and important islands of Java and Sumatra, and the half of Borneo,—England having given them up at the Treaty of Vienna. On many accounts this is to be deplored, for the Dutch cannot be compared with the English in capacity for planting and governing colonies; and above all, they do almost nothing towards introducing into their foreign possessions the knowledge of a pure Christianity, and of the happy institutions to which it gives existence.

There has been but little political change in the smaller islands of the Eastern Hemisphere. France has now the Society Islands and the Marquesas. In many of them a happy moral and social as well as religious change is going forward, through the labors of Protestant missionaries.

SECTION III.

POLITICAL CHANGES IN NORTH AMERICA DURING THE FIRST HALF OF THE NINETEENTH CENTURY.

United States.—At the commencement of this century, twenty-five years had passed since the people of the United States had risen and thrown off the yoke of England. The present Constitution,—formed in 1787, adopted by most of the States in 1788, become operative in 1789,—had been in existence eleven years. The limits of the country in the year 1800 were: the British possessions on the north; the province of New Brunswick, and the Atlantic, on the east; the Floridas and Louisiana, on the south; and the Mississippi River on the west. The number of the States was sixteen, namely, New Hampshire, Massachusetts, Vermont, Rhode Island, Connecticut, New York, New Jersey, Pennsylvania, Delaware, Maryland, Virginia, North Carolina, South Carolina, Georgia, Tennessee, and Kentucky. Three of these—Vermont, Tennessee, and Kentucky—had been formed after the independence of the other thirteen had been established. Besides these sixteen States, there was the great territory north of the Ohio and east of the Upper Mississippi River, an extensive territory lying west of Georgia, and the small district of Columbia. The entire area of the country was, at that epoch, estimated to embrace one million of square miles.

In the year 1803, the government of the United States purchased of France what was called Louisiana, or all that country bounded on the north by the British Possessions that lie west of Lake Superior; on the east by the Upper and Lower Mississippi, down to north lat. 31°, and then by the Pearl River; south by the Gulf of Mexico, Texas, New Mexico, and Upper California; and west by the Pacific Ocean. The price paid for this vast domain was $15,000,000. It was called the Louisiana territory, and its area was estimated at more than a million and a half of square miles.

In 1819, a treaty was made between Spain and the United States, by which the former ceded Florida to the latter for five millions of dollars, the sum at which the spoliations upon American commerce committed by Spanish vessels were estimated. Florida was taken possession of July 10, 1821. By this cession the United States acquired a territory of 57,750 square miles in extent.

In the year 1845, Texas was received as one of the United States, having established and maintained her independence of Mexico. As she claimed the Rio Grande as her western boundary, her entire area was estimated at 325,500 square miles.

And, finally, at the close of the late war with Mexico that country ceded to the United States, for the sum of twelve millions of dollars, and other considerations, New Mexico and Upper California, containing 526,078 square miles.

These several acquisitions of territory added to the original extent of the United States, would make its area to be 3,449,348 square miles. But by a treaty with England, made June 13, 1846, the northern boundary of Oregon, or that part of the Louisiana territory west of the Rocky Mountains, was made to lie on the 49th degree of north latitude, instead of 54 deg. 40 sec., as was originally claimed. This makes the area of the United States to be about *three millions and a quarter of square miles!* This is about 400,000 square miles less than the entire Continent of Europe. The United States now stretch from the Atlantic Ocean, on the east, to the Pacific, on the west, and from the Gulf of Mexico, on the south, to the British Possessions on the north. In point of extent it ranks next to the great Empire of Russia.

Since the commencement of the present century the following new States have been added, making the entire number of the States in the Union *thirty-one.*

Names.	Date of Admission.
Ohio,	Nov. 29, 1802.
Louisiana,	April 30, 1811.
Indiana,	Dec. 11, 1816.
Mississippi,	Dec. 10, 1817.
Illinois,	Dec. 3, 1819.
Alabama,	Dec. 14, 1819.
Maine,	March 16, 1820.
Missouri,	Aug. 10, 1820.
Arkansas,	June 15, 1836.
Michigan,	" "
Florida,	May 3, 1845.

Names.	Date of Admission.
Iowa, ...	May 3, 1845.
Texas, ...	Dec. 29, 1845.
Wisconsin, ...	May 29, 1848.
California, ...	Sept. 7, 1850.

The territories are: Minnesota (organized in 1849), Nebraska (unorganized), both lying east of the Rocky Mountains; Oregon (organized Aug. 2–13, 1848), west of those mountains; New Mexico and Utah (organized in Sept. 1850), and the district of Columbia.

The population of the United States was 3,929,327 in the year 1790; 5,305,925 in the year 1800; 7,239,814 in 1810; 9,638,131 in 1820; 12,866,920 in 1830; 17,100,572 in 1840; and not much short of 23,200,000 in 1850.

Within the United States there are, it is estimated, between 400,000 and 500,000 aborigines. In the year 1820, there were 2,247 Indians in New England; 5,184 in the State of New York; 47,783 north of the Ohio, and east of the Upper Mississippi; and 65,122 east of the Lower Mississippi,—in the States of Mississippi, Alabama, Florida, Georgia and Tennessee. About this time the government of the United States came to the conclusion, at the instance of some of the wisest and best men in the country, to remove all these people, as fast as it could be done, with their consent, to a territory west of the States of Arkansas and Missouri, which was to be their own without molestation. This it is proposed to do in order to place them beyond the limits of the organized States, and on lands claimed by no States. This great task has been almost accomplished. And large communities of the aborigines are there formed, having organized governments of their own, schools, academies, workshops, churches, etc., and other fruits of civilization. This is particularly the case with the Cherokees and Choctaws, and to some extent with the Creeks and some small tribes. It is possible that some of the aboriginal tribes may organize their governments after the fashion of the States, ask for admission into the Union, and become constituent parts of the United States.

The government of the United States, under the Constitution, has existed (at the time of this writing, March, 1851) nearly sixty-two years. There have been thirty-one Congresses—each elected for two years. And there have been thirteen Presidents.

Washington,	Van Buren,
John Adams,	Harrison,
Jefferson,	Tyler,
Madison,	Polk,
Monroe,	Taylor,
John Quincy Adams,	Fillmore, *now the incumbent.*
Jackson,	

Harrison was President for one month; his death placed Mr. Tyler in the chair for the remainder of the term. Taylor was President during sixteen months; his death placed Mr. Fillmore in the chair. All the Presidents of the United States have been men of respectable talents; some of them have possessed distinguished abilities; with one or two exceptions, they have been decided believers in Christianity, and regular attendants upon public worship, and friends to every good work; and some of them have been pious men. Thus far the nation has had no reason to feel mortified at the comparison of its Chief Magistrates with the rulers of any other people.

The United States have been happily preserved for near seventy years from the evils of dreadful and long-continued wars. In 1805, they had a short war with Tripoli. The arbitrary and unreasonable course of France and England in regard to neutral vessels, greatly injured the commerce of the United States, from 1800 till 1812, and finally brought on a war with the latter. This war was declared June 18th, 1812, and lasted between two and three years. The battles on land were none of them on a large scale. Those of Chippewa, Bridgewater, Fort Erie, Plattsburg, the Thames, and New Orleans were the most important. On the sea and on lakes Erie and Champlain the American arms gained some brilliant victories.

There was a war with Algiers of a few weeks' continuance in 1815; with the Creek Indians in 1814; with the Seminoles in 1818; with Black Hawk and his tribe in 1832; again with the Seminoles in 1839–44.

In April, 1846, hostilities commenced on the Rio Grande, between the United States and Mexico, and continued nearly two years. They were terminated by the Treaty of Guadaloupe-Hidalgo, Feb. 22d, 1848. The most noted of the battles fought were those of Palo Alto, Resaca de la Palma, Monterey, Buena Vista, Sacramento, Vera Cruz, Cerro Gordo, Contreras, Molino del Rey, Churubusco, Chepultepec, and Mexico.

The most remarkable domestic difficulties which the government of the United States has passed through within the last fifty years, were those growing out of Nullification in South Carolina (1832), Dorr's Rebellion in Rhode Island (1842). But these affairs were happily settled without loss of life. A few serious riots have occurred in Philadelphia, New York, Baltimore, and other places, anti-rent riots in the State of New York, etc., but they are not worthy of notice. When it is considered that the government of the United States is one of Public Opinion—sustained by the institutions and influence of Christianity—and not of Force, it is wonderful that so much order and tranquillity have prevailed, especially when the vast emigration from the Old World to our shores, and the character of the emigrants, are taken into view. We certainly are not without some serious apprehensions for the Future, and especially in view of some of the embarrassing questions now before the country: still, our hope is, that the God of our fathers will carry the nation safely through them all, and preserve us a united, prosperous, and happy people.

Changes in British Possessions in North America.—The Political Changes in this part of the North American Continent have not been great since the commencement of the present century. England's sway in that part of the world has not been disputed by any one, unless we may consider the attempts at invasion on the part of the United States, in 1812–15 in that light. In 1837 there was an Insurrection in Lower Canada, which extended to Upper Canada a few weeks later, but was speedily suppressed. In the autumn of 1838, another and more serious attempt at revolution was made in the vicinity of Montreal, but without success. These movements excited not a little sympathy in the United States, especially along the frontier, and several hundreds of volunteers hastened to help the insurgents. Much difficulty ensued, which demanded great prudence and forbearance on the part of the governments of England and the United States. About the same time troubles broke out on the "Disputed Territory" on the borders of Canada and the State of Maine. Happily, all these difficulties were arranged without the occurrence of collision between the two nations.

Several years ago Upper and Lower Canada were united, and have now but one Legislature. The government has been migratory—sometimes making Montreal the capital, sometimes Kingston, sometimes Toronto. We learn that it is likely to become permanently established at Quebec.

A good deal was said, a few years ago, about uniting the Canadas, New Brunswick, Nova Scotia, and the other British Possessions in North America under one Colonial Government; but nothing has yet been done towards the accomplishment of such a project. The population of these Possessions considerably exceeds two millions, and is steadily, and in some of them, —especially in Canada West,—even rapidly increasing. The

Home Government has done much of late years to promote internal improvements in the Canadas. The openings of lines of railroads from Portland and Boston to Montreal, and the great increase of steamboats on the Lakes and on the St. Lawrence, as well as the establishment of a line of steamers from Liverpool to Halifax, have all concurred to promote the prosperity of these countries.

Mexico and Central America.—These countries separated from Spain about the year 1820. Mexico now has an area of 1,100,000 square miles, and 7,661,919 inhabitants. The government is republican in form as well as in name. But faction has succeeded faction, and demagogue succeeded demagogue—from Iturbide (1822–24) to Santa Anna,—in the government of that beautiful but unhappy and unprosperous country. And there is little prospect of tranquillity and well-ordered government. It is said that the present President, Arista, has enlightened views on the subject of religious liberty, and is desirous of diminishing the enormous wealth and power of the Roman Catholic hierarchy in that country.

South of Mexico lies the country of Yucatan, which has usually been connected with Mexico, and sometimes separated from it. There is no well-settled government in it. The English possess the country called *Balize*, lying south of Yucatan, on the Gulf of Mexico. It has but a small population. West of this lies the country of Guatemala. South of this lie the countries of Honduras and San Salvador. Next comes Nicaragua, with the Mosquito Coast (on the east), and last of all there is Costa Rica. All these countries, excepting Yucatan, form part of what is called *Central America;* Guatemala, Honduras, San Salvador, Nicaragua, and Costa Rica claim to be considered Republics. But anarchy, civil war, and war with each other, have long made tranquillity and prosperity alike unknown in them.

The following tabular view gives the extent and population

of each of these countries, which are destined to an importance of which few have had a conception :—

Guatemala,	28,000	*sq. m.*,	935,000	*population.*
San Salvador,	24,000	"	363,000	"
Nicaragua,	40,000	"	400,000	"
Costa Rica,	23,000	"	198,000	"
Honduras,	81,000	"	308,000	"
Balize, *Eng. Province*,	62,740	"	3,000	"

SECTION IV.

POLITICAL CHANGES IN SOUTH AMERICA.

New Granada.—In 1819, New Granada, Venezuela, and the Presidency of Quito united and formed the Republic of Colombia. Simon Bolivar, the most distinguished of all the South American chiefs, was the first President. Venezuela withdrew from the union in 1828, and Quito in 1831—thus forming three republics instead of one.

New Granada has an area of 380,000 square miles, and a population of more than a million and a half. Upon the whole it is better governed, and more prosperous than almost any other country in South America. There is also a greater disposition to grant religious toleration than is found elsewhere on that Continent.

Venezuela.—This country has an area of 450,000 square miles, and a million of inhabitants. Caraccas is the capital. Since 1831, it has been independent of New Granada. J. T. Monagas is the present President. General Paez was the first President. A deadly hatred has long subsisted between these men, and has several times led to civil war. Paez is now in this country as an exile.

Ecuador, or Equator.—This country was formerly the Spanish Presidency of Quito, which is its chief city. It has been a republic since 1831, independent of New Granada. It has an area of 325,000 square miles, and 600,000 inhabitants.

Peru.—This country declared itself independent of Spain in the year 1821. After years of civil strife, the country has become more tranquil, and is better governed than it was. It has an area of 524,000 square miles, and a population of 1,373,000.

Bolivia.—This country was formerly called Upper Peru. Since 1824 it has been independent of Peru. Its area contains 318,000 square miles, and its population is estimated at 1,700,000. Like Peru, and almost all the South American Republics, Bolivia has been much troubled by factions.

Chili.—This country threw off the dominion of Spain in 1818. It is the smallest and best governed of the Republics of South America. It has an area of only 144,000 square miles, and a population of 1,200,000.

Buenos Ayres.—This country threw off the dominion of Spain in 1816, and in 1819 adopted a constitution much like that of the United States of North America. In 1826 it began to be called the Argentine Republic. In 1828 the confederation of States which formed this Republic was dissolved. Since 1830 this country has been governed by a despot of the name of Rosas, whose sway has been very tyrannical and sanguinary. The area of this Republic, if such it can now be called, is 728,000 square miles, and its population scarcely reaches 675,000.

Uruguay.—This country is also called the Oriental Republic. It is often called the Republic of Montevideo, from the name of its capital. This Republic has an area of 120,000 square miles, and its population is only 140,000. Rosas, the Dictator of Buenos Ayres, has long been trying to conquer this little State, but hitherto in vain. The rulers of this

Republic are quite disposed to be liberal on the subject of Religious Toleration.

Paraguay.—This country became a Republic in 1813, and separated from Spain. The next year a Dr. Francia made himself Dictator,—which office he held till his death in 1840,—at the age of eighty years. He was a most extraordinary man,—another Rosas,—and governed his country in the most despotic and cruel manner. The country is now governed by President Lopez. Its extent is 74,000 square miles, and its population about 250,000.

Brazil.—This country was under the government of Portugal till the year 1822. King John VI. having been driven from Lisbon in 1808, made Rio Janeiro his place of residence till 1821, when he returned to Portugal, leaving his son Don Pedro Prince Regent. The year following Brazil declared herself independent, and made Don Pedro emperor. In 1831 he abdicated in favor of his son, who reigns still under the title of Don Pedro II. Brazil is a constitutional monarchy, and in many respects the finest, as it is by far the largest, country in South America. Its area exceeds 2,300,000 square miles; its population is supposed to be about 7,500,000.

The Guianas.—In the north-eastern part of South America lie the following provinces—the only countries on that Continent which are subject to the dominion of any European country. Those belonging to France and Holland were, for a time, severed from the mother countries in the early part of this century, but have, since 1815, sustained their former relations.

British Guiana,	76,000	*sq. miles.*	96,500	*Inhabitants.*
Dutch Guiana,	36,000	"	6,500	"
French Guiana,	21,648	"	18,000	"

SECTION V.

WEST INDIES.

The only possessions which remain to Spain of all her once vast empire in the American Hemisphere are the islands of Cuba, Porto Rico, and some smaller ones which she held at the commencement of this century. In these islands no political, moral, or any other change has taken place, save the introduction of railroads in Cuba, and the running of a few steamers, and they mostly in the hands of foreigners, between these islands.

Nor have any political changes taken place, in the other islands, since the year 1800, save that England has increased hers by adding Trinidad and a few smaller ones. In 1835 England abolished slavery in her islands; and France did the same in 1848. By these acts more than one million of people of African origin obtained freedom and citizenship in the West India Islands. Denmark and Sweden have taken measures to secure the same blessings to their small islands. Long years of *transition* will be necessary to bring about the changes in character, occupation, enterprise, manners, trade, etc., which this great measure has rendered necessary and inevitable in West Indian society. A *feudal* state—a state in which the wealth, the property, is in the hands of the *few*, and the masses possess nothing but merely the means (food, raiment, and habitations) of living, is henceforth impossible. The aggregate of property will one day, however, be greater than in the days of slavery.

But the most remarkable political changes in the West Indies have occurred in Hayti, or St. Domingo. This island declared its independence in July 22, 1801, through the influence of Toussaint, a mulatto. It was recovered by the French the next year. Dessalines, a negro, next put himself at the head of the enslaved race, and ordered, by public proclamation (March 29, 1804), the massacre of all the whites. This monster was crowned King, under the name of Jacques I., Oct. 8, 1804, and died, by assassination, Sept. 21, 1805. Christophe, a negro, became President, in Feb. 1807, and was crowned Emperor with the title Henri I., in March, 1811. He reigned at Cape Francois, in the northern side of the island, and his empire was very small, whilst Pétion, a mulatto, ruled as President at Port-au-Prince, in the western side. Boyer, a mulatto, succeeded Pétion, in May, 1818. Upon the death of Christophe, in 1820, Boyer became President of the whole island. Upon his downfall in 1843, a state of anarchy or misgovernment ensued, which exists still. Souluque, a negro, the fourth President since Boyer, and elected March 2, 1847, caused himself to be proclaimed Emperor, Aug. 24, 1849. His absurd and oppressive course has caused the people of the Spanish, or eastern, end of the island to separate from the western, or French end, and set up a Provisional Government of their own. It is probable that this state of things will not last long, for the cruel and yet fantastic rule of his Imperial Majesty, Faustin I., is endured with great impatience. Nothing saves him but his large army of blacks.

Such is the brief notice which the limits of this work allow us to give of the Political Changes which have occurred during the last half-century in the Old and New Worlds. Such a sketch we have deemed appropriate to the nature and design of this work. It will enable the reader to get, with but little trouble, a *coup d'œil* of the changes which the world has undergone the last fifty years, so far as political government is concerned, as well as its present state.

CHAPTER II.

PROGRESS OF POLITICAL LIBERTY DURING THE FIRST HALF OF THE NINETEENTH CENTURY.

SECTION I.

EASTERN HEMISPHERE.

Europe.—At the commencement of this century the governments in Europe that had a constitutional form were the following:—Great Britain and Sweden, which were monarchies; and France, Holland, Switzerland, and the four free cities of Germany,—Hamburg, Lübeck, Bremen, and Frankfort-on-the-Main,—which were Republics. To these we must add the two very insignificant Republics of San Marino* in Italy, and Andorra in Spain.

The structure of the English Government, consisting of the Monarch and a Parliament of two Houses,—that of the Peers hereditary, and that of the Commons elective,—is too well known to need any notice in this work. It has undergone no essential change in its form during this century. The representation of the people in the House of Commons has been much modified, and the right of suffrage greatly conceded in all of the Three Kingdoms since the year 1830.

* San Marino embraces but 34 square miles, and has about 8,000 inhabitants. It has five villages, the central one of which is the most elevated. This little Republic is governed by a Senate of 300 members, and two Captains (Gonfalonieri), or Consuls, who are elected every three months.

The constitution of Sweden is old, and the structure of the government is quite too antiquated. The Diet, which formerly met every five years, now meets once in three years, at Stockholm, the modern capital of that country. This body consists of four Houses or Branches,—the Nobles, the Burgesses, the Clergy, and the Peasants. The first is hereditary, and the other three are elected by the clergy and people. The House of Nobles consists of nearly 1200 in number; that of the Burgesses or Representatives of the Cities and Towns, about eighty; that of the Clergy about seventy-five, including the Archbishop and eleven Bishops; and that of the Peasants or Farmers, about one hundred and forty. As they vote by Houses, each having one vote, and the votes of three Houses being necessary to the enactment of any law, legislation is necessarily a slow business in that country. An attempt was made a few months ago to modify the Diet, so as to have but two Houses, after the English form; but the project failed, although the King warmly recommended the measure. No House but that of the Burgesses voted in its favor,—another fact to prove, what indeed the whole history of Liberty has shown on every page, that it is from the inhabitants of the cities and large towns that the most enlightened appreciation of its value, and the most effective support of its claims, must be expected.

The Republic of Holland, a singular combination of the aristocratic and democratic elements, was in the last stages of its existence—having been nearly ruined by the French interference—at the commencement of this century. Shortly after this, it ended its career by giving place to the monarchy which Napoleon created for his brother Louis.

Switzerland was a collection of nineteen Republics in the year 1800, rather than one united and compact government—each Canton having its Syndics, its Small or Executive Council, and its Great Council or Legislative Assembly.

As to the Free Cities of Germany, they were extremely aristocratic in their organization—with their Syndics, Burgomasters and Senates, all elected for life—the two former bodies chosen by the Senate, and the Senate filling the vacancies in its own number.

As to France, it certainly had the form of a Republic in the year 1800, but was fast verging to a military despotism. And though she had had for eight years what was called a Republic, it is certain that the Executive Power, whether a Triumvirate, Directory, or Consulate, so completely overshadowed, during much of the time, the Legislative, as to make it manifest that the government was republican in name, rather than in reality.

It appears, then, that at the beginning of the present century there were but eleven governments in Europe that could with any propriety be said to have a constitutional form, or to enjoy any measure of liberty secured by written constitutions, and in the making of whose laws, and in the administration of whose affairs, the People had any influence whatever. There were two monarchies, and nine republics—two of the latter, however, almost too insignificant to deserve to be placed in the list. As to the rest of Europe, there was nothing whatever that deserved the name of constitutional or free government; for the concessions which some of the Princes of Germany, and even some of the Emperors, had made under the title of "Capitulations" and "Capitularies," by which certain rights were defined and guaranteed, certainly do not even approach to anything that merits the name of a Constitution.

Aisa and Africa.—Nor was there the least vestige of Liberty, or constitutional government of any denomination in the rest of the Eastern Hemisphere. With the exceptions just enumerated, despotism, unlimited dominion, prevailed everywhere in civilized and uncivilized countries in Eastern Christendom, and beyond it.

SECTION II.

WESTERN HEMISPHERE.

America.—And on this Western Hemisphere, with the noble exception of these United States and the British Provinces, there was nothing in the year 1800 that could be called free government. To the south of our happy country, the entire of America, so far as it was in the possession of civilized nations, was governed by European Powers, and chiefly by Spain and Portugal.

SECTION III.

PRESENT STATE OF THE WORLD.

WIDELY different, in this respect, is the state of things in both Europe and America at the present day.

In North America, we have these United States, now consisting of thirty-one commonwealths, organized, and members of the Union, and several territories, which are in process of preparation for entrance into it.

South of us are the Republics of Mexico, Guatemala, San Salvador, Honduras, Nicaragua, and Costa Rica. North of us are the British Provinces, which not only enjoy the blessing of English laws, but have their own Legislatures, chosen by the People, to which is committed the making of the laws that most concern their best interests and their happiness.

In South America there are nine Republics—New Granada, Venezuela, Ecuador, Peru, Bolivia, Chili, Buenos Ayres, Uruguay, and Paraguay—and one Constitutional Empire. We are not aware that the Guianas,—British, French, and Dutch,—have any legislative bodies, but they are all under European governments that are constitutional, and this is something.

It appears, then, that there are sixteen Republics on this Western Hemisphere—seven in North America, and nine in South America—one Constitutional Monarchy, and nine countries,—Canada, New Brunswick, Nova Scotia, Cape Breton, Newfoundland, the Balize, and the three Guianas,—which are under the rule of European governments, that have a constitutional form, and which extend to them a large amount of constitutional liberty. In fact, there is no civilized part of America, North or South, over which despotic sway is maintained, with the exception of that which is maintained by Russia, in the North-West (in which there are not more than six or eight thousand inhabitants who know anything of civilization), and the Spanish Islands in the West Indies.

It is true that in most of the Republics, south of our own, constitutional governments are far from being well established. There is much, very much, to be deplored in the state of things in Mexico, in Guatemala, San Salvador, Honduras, Nicaragua, Costa Rica, Venezuela, Buénos Ayres, and other Spanish Republics; but there is, in most of them, some progress, though very slow. In process of time, liberty will be better established. Education will advance, a purer Christianity will enter and prevail. The example of this country and other constitutional governments will become better known, more highly appreciated, and more successfully imitated.

And what shall we say of Europe, where only eleven constitutional governments, as we have just seen, existed at the commencement of this century? What a change has come over that part of the world within fifty years! The Revolution of 1830, in France, gave a great impulse to the cause of Liberty in the Old World; that of 1848, however, gave a far greater. The case now stands thus:—

CONSTITUTIONAL GOVERNMENTS.

Monarchies.

Great Britain,	Denmark,	Saxony,
Portugal,	Norway,	Bavaria,
Spain,	Sweden,	Würtemburg,
Holland,	Hanover	Sardinia,
Belgium,	Prussia,	Greece.

23 Duchies in Germany.

Republics.

France,	San Marino,
Switzerland,	Andorra, and
Ionian Isles,	4 Free Cities in Germany.

WITHOUT CONSTITUTIONS.

Monarchies.	*Duchies.*
Russia,	Tuscany,
Austria,	Parma,
States of the Church,	Modena,
Naples,	5 Duchies in Germany.
Turkey.	

Principalities.

Moldavia,	Servia,
Wallachia,	Monaco.

Making in all forty-seven Constitutional or Free Governments, and seventeen which have no constitutions,—in other words, are despotisms. Let us admit that there is much, very much wanting in the Constitutional Monarchies and in the Republics of Europe; that the amount of real Liberty in most of them is small; the rights and duties of the rulers and the ruled are not well defined, and that the people, in many countries, have not been educated to freedom and free governments. Yet we must rejoice that a beginning has been made, and we must believe that Liberty, though destined to meet many reverses, will advance, and in the end gain the victory over despotism in every form!

CHAPTER III.

PROGRESS OF EDUCATION—COMMON SCHOOLS—COLLEGES, ETC.—IN THE FIRST HALF OF THE NINETEENTH CFNTURY.

By no one fact is the first half of the XIXth Century more marked than the increased interest which the subject of education—especially that which concerns the masses, or what is called Popular Education—has excited in all those portions of the civilized world in which there is any real progress. Next to this ranks the interest taken in Secondary Schools, or Academies, as they are commonly called with us. Nor have the Colleges and Universities failed to share in the general educational movement.

SECTION I.

THE UNITED STATES.

The founders of the colonies which were planted in what is now called the United States,—with the exception of Maryland, Florida, and Louisiana,—were Protestants. And even the first-named scarcely deserves to be considered an exception, for it was not long till the Protestants became the majority in that colony, as they were from the first in all the other Anglo-Saxon colonies which laid the foundations of the nation. All those Protestant colonies felt the importance of promoting the education of the children and youth in the knowledge of letters, as well as in correct moral and religious principles. This was especially true of the Puritan colonies of New England. Massachusetts, as early as 1647, required by law that every township which had fifty householders should have a school-house and employ a teacher, and that such as had one thousand freeholders should have a Grammar-school. And from the first, schools were supported by a properly regulated taxation.

From that time forward the subject of education has received increasing attention, not only in the New England States, but throughout the whole country, and much has been done to extend the principle of having Common or Public Schools supported by State provision, especially since the commencement of this century. Not only have the Eastern or New England States systems of Public Schools, but New York, New Jersey, Ohio, Pennsylvania, Michigan, and Wisconsin have followed their example.* At no distant day the same thing will be true of Indiana, Illinois, Kentucky,† and some other states.

In the Southern States, owing to the country being more sparsely peopled in many cases, and to the peculiar state of society, the Governments have hitherto attempted little beyond the making of provision—in some cases quite liberal—for the education of poor white children.

We may safely say that education is a subject that has in-

* Massachusetts has a School Fund of $846,082; it increases at the rate of $30,000 per annum. Connecticut has a School Fund of $2,075,000. Maine has a small School Fund. In 1845 it amounted to $57,629, and has not increased much since. Vermont, New Hampshire, and Rhode Island depend wholly on taxation for the support of their schools. The State of New York has a School Fund of $2,170,514, and a Literary Fund of $265,306. New Jersey has a fund of $370,000, and Ohio $1,520,000. Pennsylvania appropriates annually from its Treasury the sum of $190,000, and the Townships raise $392,442 by taxation. Michigan has a fund which yields $30,000 annually for schools. Wisconsin has a fund which is expected to yield $106,878 this year—1851.

† Kentucky has a School Fund of $1,299,268. Delaware, Virginia, the Carolinas, and almost all the other Southern States do more or less for the education of the poor, but have no school system.

variably occupied the attention of the Legislatures of all our States, as one that is fundamental in importance. And every year the interest in this subject is increasing. In the States of Massachusetts, Connecticut, and New York excellent Normal Schools have been established, for the preparation of teachers, partly at the expense of the Government of those States, and partly through the munificence of individuals.*

Infant Schools were introduced into the United States in the year 1827, but have never been extensively established among us. They exist now chiefly as Sunday Schools for very small children.

Lancasterian Schools were for a time in considerable repute in some parts of the United States, but there is scarcely one to be found now. Schools on the plans of Pestalozzi and Fellenberg have never succeeded with us, because they were found not to accomplish what was promised, or to suit the manners of our people, or the state of American society. Manual Labor Schools, or schools in which young men can do something for their support by laboring a few hours daily, have been established at various places in the United States, and enjoyed some measure of success; but they have, with few exceptions, had a short-lived success.

In all the States a good deal has been done for Secondary Schools, or Academies; in many of which instruction in Latin and Greek, as well as in the higher branches of a good English education, is imparted. In many cases the State gives some aid towards the founding of such institutions. In some cases they owe their existence solely to private munificence.

* The late Hon. Edmund Dwight of Boston gave, in 1838, the sum of $10,000 to found one or more Normal Schools in Massachusetts. This led to the opening of three such institutions—at West Newton, Westfield, and Bridgewater. In 1849 the inhabitants of Berlin, in Connecticut, raised $16,000 for a Normal School in that place, which went into operation in 1850. The largest and most complete Normal School in the United States is the one in Albany, N. Y., established in 1844.

Within the last twenty-five years a great deal has been done to establish Female Seminaries, of a high order, in all parts of the United States. Probably there has been more progress in this branch of education than in any other in the whole country. These institutions are now to be found not only in the chief cities, but also in the large towns and villages. They are destined to exert an immense influence upon the best interests of the country. Two or three years spent in a good seminary of this class after she has acquired the elements of an education in the primary or common schools, seldom fail to have a great effect upon the mind, the character, and the manners of a young lady.

The Colleges of the United States have greatly increased within fifty years. At the beginning of this century there were scarcely twenty-five. There are now, it is believed, one hundred and twenty.

In 1801,	there was	1	Baptist	College,	now	13
" "	there were	2	Episcopal	"	"	10
" "	there was	1	Methodist	"	"	13
" "	there were	2	Roman Catholic	"	"	13
" "	there were	19	Cong. and Presb.	"	"	71

In the year 1801, there were,

In New England,	7	Colleges,	now	14
" Middle States,	6	"	"	22
" Southern States,	9	"	"	37
" Western States,	3	"	"	47

Many of these Colleges have been established within a very few years, and are but poorly endowed. In many cases the Professors are not men of much erudition. The libraries and apparatus of many of these Colleges are on a very limited scale. Some of the older Colleges are now beginning to be pretty well endowed. This is the case with Harvard University at Cambridge, Mass., and to some extent with Yale College, at New Haven, and the College of New Jersey, at Princeton, in that State, the University of Virginia, and some others.

As a general proposition, it may be affirmed that the education of a country will always correspond with the wants of that country. As intelligence advances among the people, it will demand an advance in the studies pursued in the Colleges and other seminaries of learning. There has been great progress in this respect during the last fifty years, and especially within the last twenty or twenty-five years.

Not only has the number of Colleges greatly increased since the year 1800, but there has been a remarkable progress in regard to what may be called professional Institutions. In former times, young men who desired to prepare themselves for the Pulpit or the Bar, or for the Medical Profession, were compelled to prosecute their studies under the direction of some distinguished minister of the Gospel, some able lawyer, or some eminent physician. Or at best, they might prosecute, to some extent, these studies with a Professor of a College. But at present there are forty-two Theological Institutions in this country, twelve Law Schools, and thirty-seven Medical Schools. All these seminaries, excepting three Medical Schools, have sprung up since the year 1800.

Of the Theological Seminaries, six are Congregational, fifteen Presbyterian, five Lutheran, two Dutch Reformed, one Methodist, three Episcopal, two Unitarian, and ten belong to the Baptist and other denominations. The Theological Seminary at Andover, opened in 1808, was the first that was established in the United States on the plan of having several professors.

Neither the number of Law Schools, nor of students in them, bears any comparison to the Theological and Medical Schools and their many pupils.

The Medical Schools have succeeded wonderfully. Those of Philadelphia,—where there are three or four,—have become quite celebrated, and are attended every winter by a very large number of young men. That city may now be ranked with Paris, Edinburgh, and Vienna, as one of the great seats of Medical knowledge.

The United States' Government supports only two schools,—one the Military Academy at West Point, the other the Naval Academy at Annapolis.

The former was projected in 1790 by General Knox, then Secretary of War, recommended by President Washington; went into operation in 1794, and was established at West Point in 1802. The law allows one cadet to be nominated by each Representative in Congress from his district, and ten by the President of the United States. This would require 243, but owing to the severity of the examinations, many are sent away every year, and the complement of cadets is never complete. There are thirty-two Professors and assistants. Each cadet receives $28 per month for his support. This institution costs the United States from $125,000 to $150,000 a-year.

The Naval Academy was founded in the year 1842. It has usually about sixty pupils, who are receiving a very thorough training from thirteen Professors and assistants. The institution costs the United States the sum of $28,200 per annum.

SECTION II.

OTHER COUNTRIES IN AMERICA.

We are not able to say as much in behalf of the progress of education in other parts of this Hemisphere.

In the British Possessions, to the north of us, there has certainly been an increasing interest in the subject of Education, and a growing attention to it. And yet there is no system of public schools established in any one of those possessions. There has been something done, especially in Canada, for the opening of Colleges and the advancement of education in Secondary Institutions.

In Mexico we cannot report that much progress has been made, and yet there has been some. Education among the masses is far from being what it is in the United States; nor are the Colleges and Universities advancing as fast as one could desire. The modes and subjects of instruction are quite behind the age.

The state of things in South America is various. In Chili, New Granada, and Venezuela, the Governments have done more to promote education than the others have done. There has been some advance in all the countries of South America, as well as in many of the West India Islands, since the commencement of this century,—enough to convince us that, with proper efforts and encouragement on the part of the Governments, the best interests of education would soon begin to make good progress among them all.

SECTION III.

THE EASTERN HEMISPHERE.

Europe.—The education of the masses may be said to be emphatically a subject of interest both to governments and philanthropists, only since the commencement of the present century. Whatever interest was felt in it in preceding times, was confined almost exclusively to the Churches, and especially to the Protestant Churches.

The first Public School System that was established in any country, in modern days, so far as we know, was that of Scotland, and this, in its present form, dates only from the year 1616. This system is a peculiar one. It provides for at least one school for each parish, to be supported out of a portion of the *tiends* or *tenths*, arising from certain lands which belonged in former times to the Roman Catholic Church, in Scotland.* There are not far short of one thousand parishes in Scotland. Most of them have but one school that is known by the name of "The Parish School," and supported from public funds. Some of the larger and more populous parishes have two or more schools which are supported by the parish. The other schools in each parish are supported on the voluntary principle, and just as if there were no parish schools.

The grand peculiarity of the Parish Schools in Scotland is the fact, that they are taught by men who have almost without exception received a university education, and are therefore capable of teaching Latin and Greek, as well as the higher branches of the Mathematics. They are in fact Classical as well as common English schools, and a large number of the youth who frequent them study Latin and Greek, and many of them go from them to the Universities. It is to this state of things that Scotland owes her great superiority over England and almost all other countries, in the number of her highly-educated sons. But this school system has not sprung up within the present century, and it is the only one in Europe that has not.

As to England and Wales, it is only within a few years that any attempt has been made to lay the foundations of a Public School System for the benefit of all classes. But little progress has as yet been made. Great difficulty has been encountered on account of the position in which ecclesiastical matters stand in that country. The Established Church has contended for a controlling influence over the proposed system of public schools, which the Dissenters do not deem to be proper. This is a difficulty which is sure to exist, to a greater or less degree, in every country where there is a national and overshadowing

* The Roman Catholic Church, it is believed, possessed in one way and another, through its churches, schools, convents, etc., one half of the lands in Scotland before the Reformation!

Church united to the State, and upheld by it. There is a vast amount of very gross popular ignorance in the mining and rural districts, as well as in the large cities and manufacturing towns of England. And if it had not been for the Sunday Schools, which have received their extensive establishment chiefly during the present century, we hardly know how the poorest classes of England could, in many places, have received any education at all.

Ireland has had, for the last seven or eight years, a Public School System, which is gradually establishing itself in the affections of the people, and gaining ground in all directions, notwithstanding the opposition which is so generally made by the hierarchy of Rome. This School System promises to be a great blessing to that long-neglected, misgoverned, and priest-ridden, but warm-hearted, gifted people.

On the Continent, the first great movement in the cause of popular education was made in Prussia, where a school system was commenced nearly forty years ago, and perfected by the late Monarch, that has been introduced into all parts of Germany, and even into the Germanic and Italian portion of the Austrian Empire. Frederick the Great had established some Normal Schools in Silesia,—and this is the only feature of the Prussian School System which does not owe its existence to the efforts of Frederick William III. This system is remarkably perfect in its details. The teachers are, for the most part, highly competent, the school-books have been prepared with great care, and there are legal provisions of such a nature as to ensure with almost entire certainty the attendance of the children. As we have just said, the Prussian School System is now established in all parts of Germany.

Holland has an excellent School System, which is, perhaps, too much under the influence of the Reformed Dutch Church to be entirely equal and fair towards all the denominations of Christians. M. Cousin, of France, has given a very interesting account of the School System of Holland as well as that of Prussia.

Denmark has likewise a very good system of Public Schools, and so have most of the Protestant Cantons of Switzerland.

France has only had a system of Primary Schools supported by law since the year 1833. It is modelled after the Prussian system in a good degree. M. Guizot, who was at that time the Minister of Public Instruction under the government of Louis Philippe, was the author of this great measure. Nearly sixty Normal Schools have been founded for the preparation of teachers, and about two thousand persons leave them every year to enter upon the business of teaching a school. The schools are aided partly by the departmental governments, and partly by the communes (or townships), whilst the teachers must receive a portion of their support from the parents of the children. The system is in the main a good one, or at least as good as could be expected in so short a time. It encounters many obstacles, one of which is the frequent change of Prefects of the Departments.

The Government of Belgium established the excellent School System of Prussia not long after the Revolution of 1830, which is producing good fruits. The Jesuits have given much trouble —first by opposing the scheme, and then, failing in that, by trying to gain an undue influence over the schools. The Government has not, however, been wanting in vigilance and impartiality.

The united Scandinavian kingdoms of Norway and Sweden have no system of Public Schools, but will have, it is probable, before long. Last year the enlightened Monarch of those countries sent a young Professor of Upsala to examine our School Systems, and report fully upon them, for the purpose of preparing the way for the introduction of a plan of Public Schools.

A great deal has been done n Russia, since the commencement of the present century, tc promote the education of the masses. In the year 1846, the Minister of Public Instruction informed us that the number of pupils in the schools on the Public Domains, together with those in the schools in the army, the students in the Colleges and Universities, the cadets (of whom there were nearly 10,000) in the twenty-four Military Schools, and those in the Naval was not far from half a million. This statement includes those only who belong to the educational establishments which are under the direction of the Minister of Public Instruction. The number of pupils in the private schools in Russia we have not been able to learn.

In Spain and Portugal little or nothing is doing by the Governments for the promotion of schools, although we believe that the subject has been somewhat agitated of late years.

In Italy, with the exception of Lombardy and Tuscany, there was nothing that could be called a System of Public Schools a few years ago. We are happy to say that the Government of Sardinia is taking hold of the question of Popular Education among its five millions of subjects with much zeal. It gives us great pleasure to state that in the Protestant community of the Waldenses, who have their "Mountain home" in that kingdom, an admirable School System has been brought into operation, greatly through the aid of British Christians, and especially of General Beckwith, which now consists of 1 College, 3 Grammar Schools, 8 Girls' Schools, 15 Parish Schools, and 127 Hamlet Schools,—in all 154; in which there are 4,820 pupils. The present Pope, at the commencement of his reign, showed a very laudable interest in the subject of popular education. We fear that his zeal has greatly diminished since the occurrences of 1848 and 1849. It is to be expected that his Holiness will henceforth prefer the old opinions and practice of the Holy See in education, as well as in political affairs.

It is interesting to see that even the Turkish Government is catching the spirit of the Age, and is talking of having a System of Public Schools in its empire,—a task which will demand all the energies of Reschid Pasha and the other ministers of Sultan Abdul-Medjid.

But in no country in Europe has the cause of Primary Education made more cheering progress than in the little kingdom of Greece, emerging as it is out of the ruin in which the Revolution of 1821–28 left it. When we were there, in 1846, there were nearly four hundred Primary Schools, four Gymnasia, and one University.* And although there was a great want of good school accommodations, and of books, slates, etc., it was in the highest degree cheering to see the great desire of the children and youth of that poor people to obtain an education. All this beautiful movement is the fruit of a few years of National Independence. The Government is doing much in behalf of the cause, and wealthy Greeks, residing for the most part out of the country—at Corfu, Trieste, Salonica, Smyrna, Constantinople, etc., —have done much for the land of their ancestors in this respect. They have given most liberally to found the Gymnasia, as well as the University, its Library, and its admirable Observatory.

From this survey, it appears that in Spain and Portugal, a large portion of Italy, Turkey, all the Austrian Empire, except the Germanic and Italian portions, and the entire Russian Empire, there is nothing which can be called a Public System of Primary Schools, and that Sweden and Norway are only beginning to move in behalf of this great and fundamental measure, the true basis of all national prosperity and of national freedom.

We can only add a few words respecting Secondary Instruction in Europe. Since the year 1800 much progress has been made in this direction also. In almost all countries in that part of the world, a good deal has been done to encourage higher schools and colleges. In Ireland the English Government has

* The University is at Athens, and has 26 Professors, and 250 students. Of the Gymnasia, one is in Athens, one in Chalcis, one at Patras, and one in Syra.

established several Colleges within a year or two, to which great opposition has been made by the Roman Catholic Hierarchy, under the pretext that the instruction which is given in them is infidel. This is Rome's usual position. In other words,—everything is infidel, or tends to infidelity, in the shape of instruction, which is not in her hands!

The London University, King's College, Durham University, and several Colleges among the Dissenters, have been opened in England since the commencement of the present century. In France almost everything in the shape of Higher Instruction, or Secondary Institutions, has been the work of the present century. In Belgium, one, if not more of the four Universities of that country has been founded during this century. The University of Christiania, in Norway, was founded several years after the commencement of this century—we believe about the year 1816.

The higher literary institutions of Germany, Austria, Russia, Spain, Portugal, Italy, and Turkey,* have undergone but little change since this century began. Those of Greece, as we have said, have sprung up since the Revolution of 1821–28, which liberated that country from the domination of the Turks.

Upon the whole, Education, Primary and Secondary, has made much progress in Europe since the XIXth century commenced.

SECTION IV.

ASIA AND AFRICA.

There is little to be said respecting the progress of Education in the rest of the Old World since the year 1800. The most interesting progress has been in India, in Ceylon, in some islands

* The most interesting literary institution in Turkey is the College at Bebek, on the Bosphorus, founded by the American Missionaries.

in the Pacific Ocean, in our American colonies along the western coast of Africa, in the founding of Mission Schools by Protestant Missionaries. Some of them are of a high grade, and even deserve the name of Colleges. These institutions ought to be dear to the heart of the philanthropist as well as the Christian, for such seminaries of learning will have a great bearing upon the progress of Christianity and Civilization in those countries.

Here we bring our remarks, respecting the Progress of Education in the first half of the XIXth century, to a close. It is necessarily brief, but it will probably suffice to give some conception of the progress which the world has made in this respect during the period under review.

CHAPTER IV.

FREEDOM OF THE PRESS—ITS PROGRESS—NEWSPAPERS AND OTHER FORMS OF PERIODICAL INFORMATION AND LITERATURE.

SECTION I.

AMERICA.

United States.—The liberty of the Press, so far as any action of the Government General or State is concerned, became as complete as it could be in the early part of this century. We are not aware that since the administration of Mr. Jefferson, which lasted from 1801 to 1809, any suit at law has been brought against any editor or any one else, native or foreign, by the United States Government. Nor are we informed of any prosecution of this nature having been made by the State Governments. The Government of this country—in other words, our political institutions—is too well founded in the hearts of the people, to make it necessary to notice anything which some noisy declaimer, or any hostile editor, whether conducting a paper for the use of Americans, or for the tens of thousands of unnaturalized foreigners who sojourn for a while among us, may be able to say or to publish. This fact demonstrates, on the one hand, the stability of our political government, and on the other, the wisdom of those who are intrusted with the task of carrying it on. It may be said, therefore, with truth, that the liberty of the Press is perfect among us,—as perfect as it can, probably, be made,—being restrained only by the laws which guarantee the rights of individuals and the demands of morality and propriety. As to the measures of the Government, General or State, and the principles and conduct of parties, they are subjects for unrestricted discussion; and so are the qualifications, and, to some extent, the characters of office-holders, and candidates for the suffrages of their fellow-citizens. There may be, and there often is, gross abuse of this almost unbounded freedom of the Press, but the evil is not without counteraction in divers ways, and especially through the very freedom in question. At all events, whatever may be the injury resulting from this freedom's occasionally degenerating into licentiousness, greater evils result, in every country that tries them, from attempts to prevent them by governmental interference with the Press.

NEWSPAPERS.

The United States, as might be expected from the great freedom of the Press which is enjoyed, is emphatically a newspaper-producing and newspaper-reading country. In the year 1800, there were, it is believed, about two hundred newspapers published in this country, of which seventeen were issued daily, seven three times a-week, thirty twice a-week, and the remainder once a-week. In 1810, there were three hundred and fifty-eight; in 1828, the number was eight hundred and two; in 1839, it was fifteen hundred and fifty-five; and in 1850, it is believed that it was not less than three thousand.

In 1800, there were sixty-five newspapers in the six New England States; in 1842, there were 223. The number in the Middle States, in 1800, was 74; in 1842, it was 513.

In the year 1842, the State of New York had 245 newspapers; Pennsylvania, 187; Ohio, 123; Massachusetts, 91; Indiana, 73; and Virginia, 51.

In 1850, there were 371 newspapers in the New England States, and in the State of New York, 460. Of the rest of the country we have not yet received the statistics.

For a long time the newspapers of this country were conducted in a very economical manner. The proprietor was often both editor and printer, and with the aid of an apprentice or two, and perhaps a journeyman occasionally, was enabled to get his small sheet, one half, and sometimes three fourth parts of which were occupied with advertisements, through the press once a week. And this is the case still with many of the papers published in the villages and country towns. But in the large cities, great papers have, of late years, sprung up, which require, especially those which are issued daily, a large number of compositors and pressmen, and one, two, and sometimes three or four editors and assistant-editors. And instead of publishing only items of news, domestic and foreign, they now often contain elaborate articles on almost all subjects, written with much talent, and furnished by editors or correspondents. A wonderful advance has been made within ten years even; whilst the difference between the newspapers published in our chief cities at present, and those which were published twenty-five years ago—to say nothing of fifty years ago—is immense. The employment, too, of travelling and stationary correspondents in the most important countries abroad, is a new feature in the conduct of the newspapers of this country, as well as of England, France, and Germany, which is of great importance, and of very recent origin.

In the early portion of the Colonial Era of what is now the United States, there was not one newspaper in the country. The first that was published was the "*Boston News-Letter*," commenced in 1704; the second was the "*Boston Gazette*," in 1719; the third was the "*American Weekly Mercury*," at Philadelphia, in the same year. The first newspaper published in the city of New York was the "*New York Gazette*," in 1725.

At the commencement of the American Revolution (1775), there were but 37 newspapers in all the colonies. It would seem that some of the Royal Governors looked upon the Press very much as do some of the despotic rulers of our day. Governor Berkley, of Virginia, in 1675, said: "I thank God that we have no free schools nor printing presses, and I hope that we shall not have any for a hundred years; for learning has brought disobedience, and heresy, and sects into the world, and printing has divulged them, and libelled governments. God keep us from both!" Lord Effingham, who was Governor of the same colony, in 1683, was ordered "to allow no person to use a printing press on any occasion whatever."

Newspapers are now made the vehicles of all sorts of intelligence. There are more than one hundred and twenty religious newspapers, it is believed, in the United States, almost all of which contain a considerable amount of secular and political news in a condensed form, whilst the greater part of their contents consists of news relating to the cause of Religion, at home and abroad. Periodicals of an octavo or quarto form, devoted to religious matters, existed long ago in this country and in Europe; but the first religious newspaper, it is maintained, of the form which has now become so common in this country, was published in Boston, in January, 1816, and was called the "*Boston Recorder*."* Since that day the number has increased very rapidly, until there are now, as has been stated, one hundred and twenty such journals. Some of these, such as the *New York Observer*, the *New York Evangelist*, the *Christian*

* This is the position of Mr. Sidney E. Morse, who was the editor of the *Boston Recorder*, at the time referred to, and who founded the *New York Observer*, in the year 1823. But although this may be true, so far as a first successful experiment of a plan may be, in some sense, a just claim to the invention, it is, nevertheless, unquestionably true, that a religious newspaper, conducted on the plan on which the *Boston Recorder* was published, was printed at Chilicothe, Ohio, by the late Rev. John Andrews, as early as 1815, if not earlier. In fact, Mr. Morse stands very much in the same relation to the Religious Newspapers that his excellent brother, the Professor, does to the Electric Telegraph, or as Mr. Fulton does to the Steamboat.

Advocate, the *Presbyterian*, the *New York Recorder*, the *Independent*, and many others, have a very wide circulation. It would probably be within the limits of the truth to say that the weekly issues of the Religious Newspaper Press exceed half a million copies. The influence of so many sheets, some of which contain matter enough to make a duodecimo volume of 150 or 160 pages, if not more, must be very great, sent abroad as they are to all parts of the land, and each of them containing, besides much religious news, many excellent articles, original or selected, on those doctrines and precepts of Christianity which are at once the foundation and the fruit of a holy life.

Besides Religious Newspapers, we have now a great number of papers devoted to the advocacy of many special measures and objects,—such as Temperance Papers, Anti-Slavery Papers, Moral Reform Papers, Agricultural Papers, Scientific Papers, Educational Papers, Anti-Masonic Papers, etc. Every great interest or movement has its own paper to serve as an organ by which its influence may be brought to bear upon the public mind. We know not the number of such papers, but it must be very great. Some of the Aborigines on our borders have newspapers in their own languages. This is the case with the Choctaws and Cherokees.

Although, as a general thing, the tone of the more respectable and well-conducted Newspaper Press is in the main decidedly salutary, it must be confessed that there is a class of papers, conducted with a certain degree of talent, and circulating among the less educated, and less wealthy, industrial ranks of society, which are exceedingly injurious to good morals. Some of them are published on the Sabbath, or circulated on that day. Quite a large number are published in foreign languages, especially the German, and are very hostile to everything that bears the mark of Christianity.*

* Some of the worst papers in this land are published in German, by men who seem to rejoice in pouring forth in the columns of such pa-

So great is the circulation of some of the daily newspapers in our chief cities, that presses driven by steam are now demanded to enable the conductors of them to supply the subscribers in reasonable time. By means of this great power, and by the use of Mr. Hoe's wonderful press, which can be made to throw off many thousands of sheets in an hour, the papers of the greatest circulation can be printed and sent forth, in the course of a few hours, every morning or evening. There is no department of art in the United States, in which greater progress has been made during the last 25 or 30 years than in that of printing, especially in printing newspapers with rapidity and facility.

MAGAZINES, REVIEWS, AND OTHER MONTHLY AND QUARTERLY PUBLICATIONS.

There were but few Monthly Publications of any description in the United States before the commencement of this century.* In 1810, it is estimated that there were twenty-six of this class of journals amongst us; in 1835, it is supposed that there were one hundred and forty; and in 1850, about one hundred and seventy-five.

Within a few years, some periodicals of this description have attained to a vast circulation in this country. *Graham's Magazine*, *Godey's Magazine*, *Sartain's Magazine* (all published in Philadelphia), and some others, have from 15,000 or 20,000 up to 30,000 or 40,000. They employ the pens of some of the most talented writers among us; but their contents are, for the most part, articles in prose and poetry of a light and popular, but not very instructive nature. They make no pretensions

pers, now that they have reached a land of political and religious liberty, their unmitigated hatred of everything like religion.

* *Aitkin's Pennsylvania Magazine*, the *American Museum* (from 1787 to 1792), the *American Monthly Magazine* (1745 to 1748), and *Massachusetts Magazine* (1784 to 1795) were the most noted.

to the character and claims of Reviews. This species of literature has wonderfully increased among us within the last twenty-five years, and especially within ten years.

Of secular and literary Monthly Reviews, properly so called, we have the *Knickerbocker*, the *Southern Literary Messenger*, *Hunt's Merchants' Magazine*, the *Christian Examiner*, the *American Review*, the *Democratic Review*, and a few others,—all of them highly creditable to the country.

Of Quarterly Reviews, whether literary or scientific, we have not many. The *North American Review*, commenced at Cambridge, in 1815, and *Silliman's Journal*, commenced at New Haven, in 1817, do honor to the country. The *American Quarterly Review* (from 1827 to 1837), and the *Southern Quarterly Review* (from 1828 to 1833), the former published at Philadelphia and the latter at Charleston, were for several years very ably conducted; but both had a short existence.* To these we may add the *Boston Quarterly Review* (Brownson's), *Massachusetts Quarterly*, and *Stryker's American Register*.

The Religious Quarterlies have developed no inconsiderable amount of talent, and their number has become quite respectable. The *Biblical Repertory*, published at Princeton, and commenced in 1824, the *American Biblical Repository*, commenced at Andover, in 1831, united with the *Quarterly Observer*, in 1833, with the *American Spectator*, in 1839, and with the *Bibliotheca Sacra* (an able critical, exegetical and literary Quarterly, which was published in Andover, from the year 1844), in 1850. The *New Englander* commenced in New Haven, in 1843, the *Christian Review*, the *Methodist Quarterly Review*, the *Mercersburg Review*, and some others, belong to this category.

* The *Southern Review* was revived in 1842; but though ably conducted, it is not what it was in the hands of the late talented and lamented Legare.

There is quite a number of able Medical and Law Journals, which are of much repute, and all of them, we believe, have sprung up since the commencement of this century.

Four of the great Quarterly Reviews of England,—the *London Quarterly Review*, the *Edinburgh Review*, the *Westminster Review*, the *North British Review*, together with *Blackwood's Magazine* (monthly), are republished in the United States. Besides this, there are such works as the *Eclectic Magazine*, *Harper's Magazine*, the *International Magazine* (and Littell's *Living Age*, *weekly*, may be included), which are either wholly, or nearly so, composed of articles selected from the British and other foreign Periodicals. For a long time the London *Christian Observer* was republished in the United States,—one of the best Religious Magazines the world has ever seen.

Taken in the widest sense of the phrase, the periodical literature of the United States, indigenous and foreign, is immense —embracing the Newspapers, and the Monthly and Quarterly Magazines and Reviews. The regular issues,—daily, tri-weekly, monthly,* and quarterly,—amount to several millions; and the entire number of copies, in the course of a year, must be many millions.

SECTION II.

OTHER PARTS OF AMERICA.

The increase of newspapers and other forms of periodical publication has been great, also, in other parts of the Western Hemisphere. This has been the case in the British Possessions,

* The Monthly Magazines and Papers published by the Religious Societies of the United States have a vast circulation,—amounting probably to not much less than half a million of copies each month. And all this has sprung up long since the commencement of the XIXth century.

north of the United States, as well as in those in the West India Islands. How great that increase has been we are not able to say with precision. It would not be hazardous, judging from such data as we have, to say that it has been four-fold, at least. And many of these colonial journals are edited with decided ability.

And although the number of newspapers and other periodicals published among the nations in America, North and South, which are of Latin origin (Spanish, Portuguese, and French), bears no comparison with that of those which are published among the people of Anglo-Saxon descent, it is, nevertheless, quite considerable, and cannot be overlooked. The number of newspapers published in Mexico, the States of Central America, Hayti, the Republics of South America, together with Brazil, is incomparably greater than it was at the commencement of this century. In fact, it was, at that epoch, almost nothing at all. Now it is considerable, and constantly, though not rapidly, increasing. This is indeed cheering, and gives hope for the future.

SECTION III.

EUROPE.

Great Britain and Ireland.—The Press having been long freed from all censorship in the British Realm, it may readily be supposed that its issues in all the forms of literature, occasional and periodical, in books, in pamphlets, and in sheets, would be exceedingly numerous. Heavy duties, in one form or another, operate as a great drawback, especially in the case of newspapers, on which there is a stamp-duty of one penny on each copy.

Newspapers.—The number of newspapers published in England before the commencement of the 18th century, was very inconsiderable. The first that was printed, although it bore but little resemblance to the newspapers of our day, was the "*Weekly Newes*," published by Nathaniel Butler, in 1622. The first paper that might be called a vehicle of general information, was established by Sir Roger L'Estrange, in 1663, and was called the *Public Intelligencer*. We have no means of knowing the number of newspapers in England in the year 1700. In the year 1713 stamps were first employed. In the year 1753, the number of stamps was only 7,411,757, in 1800, it was no more than 16,084,905; but in 1849, it was 76,569,285—a fact that demonstrates how rapidly the circulation of newspapers has augmented in the United Kingdom since the commencement of this century.

At the epoch last named (1849), the number of newspapers in Great Britain and Ireland was 603: namely, 160 in London, 282 in the counties of England and the Principality of Wales; 117 in Ireland, and 94 in Scotland. The number of advertisements, during that year, in the newspapers of the United Kingdom was 2,182,272, yielding to the crown a revenue of £158,-114 16*s*., or about $785,570.

Many of the newspapers published in the British Realm are edited with great talent. In this respect the *London Times* stands pre-eminent. In its columns constantly appear some of the finest specimens of a vigorous and ornate style to be found in the English language. The political influence of this paper is immense, and yet there is, sometimes, a sad want of honest principle, and of a reasonable, generous, and Christian spirit in its editorial columns. The *Morning Chronicle*, the *Herald*, the *Standard*, the *Daily News*, and others might be mentioned as journals conducted with singular ability. Many of the newspapers published in Edinburgh, Glasgow, Dublin, Belfast, Liverpool, Manchester, Birmingham, and other principal provincial cities and towns, display much editorial talent and skill, although far from being equal to the great papers of the GREAT METROPOLIS.

Periodical Publications.—The Periodical Literature of Great Britain and Ireland is very extensive, and has no rival in any land. The number of Monthlies and Quarterlies,—Literary, Theological, Legal, and Medical,—is very great, and many of them are conducted with ability. The *Edinburgh Review*, the *London Quarterly*, the *Westminster Review* (now united with the *Foreign Quarterly*), the *North British Review*, the *British Review*, the *Dublin Review*—all come into existence since the commencement of the XIXth century,—have contained some of the ablest essays on great questions in Literature, and Criticism, in Jurisprudence, Law, Science, and Art, to be found in the English language. Many of the Monthly Magazines and Reviews are conducted with scarcely less talent. The progress of England, in this great branch of Human Effort, during the last fifty years, has been incalculable, and that progress has had a most intimate connection with the best interests of Christianity.

The Continent.—The Freedom of the Press is very unequal in the different portions of the Continent. In those countries which possess the largest amount of political liberty, there is, as might be expected, the most freedom of the Press. The Protestant countries have more of both than those which are Papal.

Scandinavian Countries.—There is more political liberty in Norway than in any other kingdom on the Continent, and there the Press is unshackled. In 1840 there were about twenty newspapers published in that poor but interesting country, a few of which were *dailies*, and the others *weeklies*. Some of them, especially those in Christiania, the capital, are conducted by able men.* These newspapers have almost all sprung up since 1814.

* There is a newspaper published in Tromsöe, a village on a small island on the coast of Norway, in latitude 70°. There is no other newspaper in the world published so far north.

There are many newspapers in Sweden and Denmark, but the Press labors under considerable restrictions, especially in the former. There are, notwithstanding, some able and very independent journals in both those countries, and the number of newspapers has much increased within fifty years.

There is quite a number of Monthly and Quarterly Magazines and Literary Reviews in the Scandinavian Countries.

Holland.—The Press is in a good measure unshackled in the Kingdom of Holland, and newspapers and larger Periodical publications have greatly increased there since the year 1800. We are not able to give the number of either.

Germany.—There is much more freedom of the Press in the Free Cities, and in Prussia, and the other Protestant countries of Germany than in Bavaria, Austria, and the other Papal parts of that country. The Press is not, however, entirely free in any part of Germany, though it is under far less restraint than it was at the commencement of this century, or than it was even four or five years since. The number of newspapers has wonderfully increased within a few years, especially in Prussia, and it is surprising to see with what ability and courage political questions are discussed in their columns, which a few years ago they would not have dared to touch.

The number of Semi-Monthly, Monthly, and Quarterly publications in Germany, devoted to Literature, both Classical and Modern, to Science, Art, Theology, Law, Medicine, etc., is large and increasing. Until within a very few years, the German mind, for want of other subjects on which it might employ its energies, was shut up to the pursuits of Learning, both as a means of living and of enjoyment. But a very different day is coming, and has even now commenced to dawn.

France.—It is now a little more than sixty years since France began to talk of political liberty; but up to this day she has had but few intervals, and they very short, in which she has had anything like real constitutional freedom. The Press has, of course, shared the fortunes of the State. When there has been a moment of political liberty, the Press has flourished.

The first newspaper published in France was the *Gazette de France*, established in 1631. But the number was utterly insignificant before the great Revolution in 1789. Under the Directory, the Consulate, and the Empire, the Press was under great restraint. Nor was the state of things much better during the Restoration—from 1814 to 1830. In the reign of Louis Philippe the newspapers rapidly increased for a while, so that there were as many as 374 published in that country in the year 1832. But soon the conduct of the government became extremely oppressive. In utter violation of the *Charte*, or Constitution, of 1830, no less than 1,129 prosecutions were issued against publishers and writers for the public press, during this reign, the aggregate of whose punishment was 3,141 years of imprisonment, and fines to the amount of more than $1,300,000! The Revolution of 1848 flooded France with newspapers, but the Reaction and the Presidency of Louis Napoleon have swept many of them away. Still, the Press in France has great boldness and energy, and enjoys a large measure of liberty in comparison with its condition in the past.

France is far from excelling in great Periodicals in the shape of Reviews. Excepting some Monthlies, and bi-Monthlies, of which *la Revue des Deux Mondes* is the most important, and several Medical, Legal, Scientific, Agricultural, and Theological Magazines, she has nothing in this species of literature worthy of mention.

Spain and Portugal.—There is a great deal more liberty of the Press in both these countries than there was thirty years ago, or even twenty; and by consequence newspapers have greatly increased in number, and improved in character. Of the higher periodicals there are several in both.

Italy.—Excepting in the kingdom of Sardinia, it cannot be said that the Press now flourishes in Italy. In that kingdom, which enjoys a constitutional form of government, there is a large amount of freedom of the Press, and quite a number of ably conducted newspapers.

The Revolutions of 1848 opened the way for the sudden and extensive establishment of a great number of newspapers in Tuscany, in Piedmont, at Rome, and even in Naples and Sicily. But those halcyon days were but few, and have passed away. They will yet return to shed their happy influence upon the now excited and inquiring mind of Italy.

The higher periodical literature of Italy is not extensive; it is chiefly scientific and general,—not political.

Greece.—The little kingdom of Greece had, in 1846, when we were there, twenty-four newspapers, all, with one exception, published in the modern Greek. Eighteen of these newspapers were published at Athens, and six at Patras, Chalcis, Syra, and Napoli. Several of the papers published at Athens are daily ones, and most of them are conducted by able editors. They are quite equal in character and talent to ours. There is nothing in Greece more interesting than her Schools, Gymnasia, University, and Newspapers. The Greeks still "seek after wisdom."

Turkey.—There is nothing worthy of mention in the shape of newspapers and other periodicals in Turkey. One newspaper in French, and not more than one in Turkish, constitute the entire of this species of literature in Turkey in Europe.

Russia.—There is a considerable number of newspapers in the Russian Empire, probably as many as 150; but they are under a very rigid censorship. Their contents, beyond the official announcements of the government, its ukases, etc., consist of items of intelligence of what is going on in foreign lands, but so stated as not to inculcate anything dangerous to the state of things in that empire.

There are several periodical works, relating chiefly to Science and Art, Agriculture, etc.

SECTION IV.

ASIA, AFRICA, AND THE ISLANDS OF THE EASTERN HEMISPHERE.

THERE is not much to be said respecting the progress of Periodical Publications in the other parts of the Eastern Hemisphere, but that little is interesting.

Asia.—India, under British sway, begins to learn to appreciate newspapers, and several have sprung up there, published in the languages of the native population. This movement will exert a vast influence for good or for evil—for the former, we doubt not—as the Future will soon demonstrate. Some of these native newspapers are conducted with much talent, we are told, and are read with great avidity. Among those which are conducted by natives under Christian influence, the *Samachar Darpun* is one of the most able. They will furnish an admirable medium for discussing the nature, evidences, and claims of Christianity, before the people of Hindostan. Already, indeed, the work has commenced; nor will it cease till the Truth has triumphed over all opposition.

There are several English journals published in India and Ceylon, and one or two monthly magazines. We will name only the *Calcutta Christian Observer*, published monthly, under the united direction of all the Protestant missionaries; the *Calcutta Review*, which appears quarterly, edited chiefly by Dr. Duff, of the Scottish Free Church Mission; and the *Friend of India*, a weekly publication of great interest, under the care of Mr. Marshman, a son of the former excellent missionary of that name.

The English and American Missionaries in China published formerly a valuable monthly magazine, called the *Indo-Chinese Gleaner*, which was read extensively by the English and American residents and sojourners in the several sea-ports, in which

Europeans and Americans are now allowed to trade with the natives. It now exists under the title of the *Chinese Repository.*

Africa.—There are English newspapers published at the Cape of Good Hope, and French journals published in Algiers, in the northern extremity of that continent. Whilst on the western coast there are newspapers published, in the English language, in Liberia, in Sierra Leone, and at Cape Palmas, for the benefit of the colonies planting in those places. All this is the result of movements commenced since the beginning of the present century.

Islands in the Pacific and Indian Oceans.—We know not how many newspapers in the Dutch language are published in Java and other parts of Netherlands India, but we suppose that there are not many.

There are several newspapers published among the English colonies in New Holland, Van Dieman's Land, and New Zealand; and the number is increasing.

Several newspapers are also published at the Sandwich Islands, edited by the missionaries and others, whose influence is extensive among the many foreigners residing in those islands, as well as among the native population. And this, too, is one of the evidences, as it is one of the fruits, of the Progress which has characterized the last fifty years.

In concluding this survey of the advance of the Press during the First Half of the XIXth century, we cannot but remark that it has been wonderful. How greatly have the means been increased, within the short period of fifty years, of diffusing knowledge on all subjects that concern Humanity, both in relation to this life and to that which is to come! There are, probably, four or five times as many of these cheap vehicles of information, which we call newspapers, in the world as there were in the year 1800. This is, indeed, a great progress. The grandest obstacle in the way of imparting the Gospel to mankind, and of promoting their best interests even in this world, is IGNORANCE. And the more that facilities for dispelling it and for diffusing knowledge among the human race, become increased and made to bear upon all classes, the more certainly will the Kingdom of our Lord be promoted.

We shall now advance to the consideration of the progress of Science, in many of its branches, during the last fifty years.

4

CHAPTER V.

HISTORICAL SKETCH OF SCIENCE IN THE FIRST HALF OF THE NINETEENTH CENTURY.

THE Scientific history of the first half of the nineteenth century is exceedingly various and extended. In no department has science been altogether stationary; each previous form of knowledge has pushed its path further out into the wide unknown. Many branches of Science entirely unknown before, have been created within this period. Meteorology, Electro-Chemistry, Geology, Physical Geography—belong exclusively to it. The relations between all the various departments of Science have become much more prominent and distinct. The applications of Science, to practical and useful ends, are innumerable and remarkable. The development has already become so great, that the want of some general guide has everywhere been felt; and Cuvier in France, Whewell in England, and the gentlemen of the British Association, have offered histories of recent progress, which afford us one principal means of preparing the sketch which we now proceed to offer.

SECTION I.

ASTRONOMY.

THE progress of Astronomy was not distinguished by any very remarkable discoveries for some time after the commencement of the present century. At the beginning of that period several important instruments were coming into use—as the

English theodolite and the French repeating circle—the principal part of the Mécanique Céleste was published; and the theory of perturbations was beginning to be well understood.

The Observatory at Greenwich was the only one at which regular observations were then systematically made; and a mass of these was accumulating which surpassed all others known in accuracy and value. A great number of observatories, however, have since been established; and many periodical publications now make their observations accessible. One of the latter was commenced by Zach, in 1800, which contributed greatly to the progress of Science—and especially in respect to the small planets.

In 1832 there were thirty-five well-furnished observatories in Europe: of which six were in the British Isles, two in France, one in Switzerland, seven in Italy, one in Norway, one in Denmark, ten in Germany, and several in Poland and Russia. The East India Company has established two in India, and one in St. Helena; private enterprise has erected and furnished one in New South Wales.

Several have since been added to this number, in Russia, Belgium, Spain, and Greece.

In America there was, in 1832, but one observatory,—that of Yale College. Since then, however, most of our literary institutions have sought to provide them. Among these, Harvard College maintains an honorable distinction; its instruments being upon a level with the highest refinements of mechanical skill in this department. Two observatories of very high grade have been founded by the government—those at West Point and at Washington. Several of our cities, Philadelphia, Brooklyn, and particularly Cincinnati, have established similar institutions of great promise. The whole number of American Observatories is stated by Prof. Loomis, at fifteen.

The progress of Astronomy during the past half-century has been stimulated by a large number of societies; and is chronicled in a great many periodicals devoted to this subject, as well as in many papers, both European and American, in scientific journals of a general character.

Astronomy has owed much of the interest and success with which its latest discoveries have been prosecuted, to the improvement which has been gradually effected in the construction of instruments. The first Mural circle was erected at Greenwich in 1812—and its introduction marks a new epoch in the science. Motion is now given by clock-work to the largest instruments; by which the same star may be kept constantly in the field of view. Achromatic lenses, which formerly could not be made of any considerable dimensions, have since been constructed by Fraunhofer of nine inches diameter,—later by Cauchoix of eleven or twelve,—and still later by Merz & Mahler of Munich, of fifteen. These instruments, especially the first-named, may not be more powerful than the great telescopes of the Herschells; yet, their diffusion has greatly promoted scientific discovery.

At the beginning of the period under review, the only good catalogue of stars, according to Prof. Airy, was that of Dr. Maskelyne. Since that period, many eminent astronomers have greatly multiplied the number of the stars, whose positions, as fundamental points of measurement for others, have been determined. New investigations of refraction, made by the most distinguished men, have introduced an accuracy unknown before, into this branch of the Science. Tables have been computed and published by numerous authors for determining the places and figures of the sun and moon, and the planets and their satellites.

At the beginning of the century, the only bodies recognized as belonging to the Solar System were the Sun, seven planets, with their satellites, and Halley's Comet. On January 1st, 1801, Piazzi discovered the planet Ceres,—in 1802, Olbers detected a second of these bodies, Pallas,—in 1804 Harding detected a third, Juno,—and in 1807, Olbers again distinguished himself by discovering Vesta. These discoveries attracted great attention, and their orbits and perturbations were speedily computed. The interest awakened by them arose in part from the fact that the existence of a planet at that distance from the Sun, had long been suspected; and it was greatly increased by a suggestion early offered by Olbers, that they might be fragments of one original body. It was by investigations growing out of this hypothesis that the last of the four was discovered.

Many observations were made in order to detect any other bodies which might exist in the vicinity of these, but with no success; and after 1816, the search was generally abandoned. In 1845, however, another was discovered,—and the zeal of discovery revived. Since that time six new planets have been detected in this portion of the heavens. They are all much inferior in size to the four previously ascertained, and the discovery is doubtless due to the multiplication of instruments and of observers. The present number of the certainly ascertained Asteroids is thirteen; two more, however, are very recently announced.

An eighth satellite of Saturn was discovered, in 1848, by Mr. Bond, of the Harvard Observatory; and the satellites of Uranus, which had not been seen since Sir William Herschell's discovery of them, are now again found and computed. A third ring of Saturn has also been detected.

One of the most interesting chapters of astronomical discovery relates to the theory of comets. Before the present century, little was known of their true character; and only a single comet, Halley's, was fully ascertained to belong permanently to the solar system. With the introduction of improved methods for the determination of cometary orbits, a new impulse was given to the observation of these bodies; and in 1819, Encke ascertained that a comet recently observed could revolve only in an ellipse of short period. His first computations gave 1310 days as the period of a revolution. The interest awakened by this announcement was intense; and very great attention was at once given to the subject. It was soon found that the orbit of the new comet agreed with one which had been observed before, and the identity of the two was fully established.

A new question, however, immediately arose. The orbit now observed was perceptibly less than on the previous occasions of its appearance, and the difference could not be accounted for, except by supposing the existence, throughout the planetary spaces, of a resisting medium. The return of the body was most anxiously watched, in the hope that it would settle this interesting point; and at its return, in 1829, the general opinion seemed to be that there could be no mistake about the reality, or the magnitude, of the resistance which it had experienced. This is, however, the only body that has fully indicated such a resisting medium to us; and its indications do not extend beyond the orbit of Mercury.

A great number of comets has since been observed and computed; of which several have been discovered within the last ten years—two of them in America.

The latter part of the past half-century has, however, witnessed the attainment of some results scarcely inferior in brilliancy and greatness to any others that astronomical history records. Among these the discovery of another planet is, perhaps, the most remarkable achievement. The perturbations of the most remote of the known planets of our system, Uranus, had long attracted the attention of observers, and in 1840 they were thoroughly computed by Bessel, who declared that without the supposition of an additional planet, yet more distant, they were inexplicable. The problem was to find this disturbing body; a problem which the highest authority, Professor Airy, pronounced utterly hopeless till after several successive revolutions of Uranus. It was, however, attempted, the position of the unknown planet was fixed upon, and its mass and apparent size determined, upon purely theoretical grounds; and the first examination of its calculated place disclosed the reality of its existence. This discovery has been held to indicate the correctness of our astronomical theories, the minute certainty of our knowledge of the planetary motions, and the perfection of our instruments of observation, and has won for its author, Le Verrier, immortal renown.

The knowledge of the fixed stars, too, has greatly increased. At the beginning of the century, the only accurate knowledge of double stars was contained in the papers of the elder Herschel, who discovered, in 1803, the fact of their revolution, and subsequently enlarged greatly his catalogue of them. Many more were observed by Struve and Bessel; but the most accurate measurements of such bodies are due to Sir John Herschel's labors in 1830. The belief that some law of attraction connected these remarkable bodies, led to many efforts to compute their periods; of which that of the last-named gentleman was by far the most remarkable and useful. The computations rendered possible by this method, have fairly resulted in extending the Newtonian law of gravitation across the immeasurable distance, as it then seemed, which separates the planetary from the sidereal systems.

The step, however, which has given to Astronomy its greatest extension, is the determination of the parallax of the fixed stars. By this term is meant the apparent change of position, which a distant body undergoes, from a change in the position of the observer. Hitherto no such change of the point of observation produced the smallest perceptible effect upon any one of the fixed stars. Even the vast change of position which the different places of the earth in its orbit, at different seasons, involves, has seemed to produce no corresponding alteration in the relative positions of the stars. At length, however, such a change has been detected. A series of observations by Bessel, in 1837–40, determined the position of one of the fixed stars to be decidedly different in January from that which it occupied in June. His observations determined the distance of the star to be 592,000 times the radius of the earth's orbit.

This successful attempt to bring the Solar System into relation with the stars, awakened the highest interest among astronomers. Henderson, of Edinburgh, soon ascertained a similar parallax in another star; and Dr. Peters, of Pultowa, has extended the list, and verified Bessel's results. This great discovery may now be considered as established, and the vast field to which it belongs is open to the improved observation of the age.

Another achievement is the verification of Sir William Herschel's opinion, in respect to the motion of the Solar System in space. A comparison of the motions of those stars, which were best ascertained, suggested to him the idea that the Sun was moving toward a point in the constellation Hercules. A more careful examination of a greater number of stars, and by several most competent observers, seems to establish this result, and to indicate, that the Solar System moves through space with a velocity about one fourth of that of the earth in its orbit. Whether this motion is rectilinear or orbital, whether the stars participate in it, and what is the grand centre of it, can hardly yet be decided. Prof. Madler, of Dorpat, has discussed these problems, and reached definite conclusions. He marks the star known as Alcyone in the centre of the Pleiades, as the true and grand central sun of the whole system. He has even reached some indication of the time in which our Sun revolves in this vast orbit—18 millions of years; but his conclusions are yet involved in too much doubt to permit us to rely upon them.

In the resolution of nebulæ, astronomy has advanced to a field of observation yet more remote. The elder Herschel observed, with his vast reflecting telescopes, many of these remarkable bodies; 500 were enumerated in a single paper, and the number was greatly increased in 1811 and in 1817. The chief improvement in this particular has been achieved by the Earl of Rosse, whose gigantic telescope of twice the size of Herschel's, has revealed the character of many of these singular bodies, and shown them to be distant groups of distinct stars. A great number of nebulæ have been thus resolved: though others yet retain their indistinct and hazy outline under all appliances, and remain problems for future solution.

The elaborate, various, and complicated processes of computation and observation through which such discoveries have been achieved, it is impossible to indicate. Many hundreds of stars—some thousands even, have been determined with precision, as points of reference for smaller ones; and of these 50,000 are recorded in the observations of Delalande alone. The record of a single year's observation at the National Observatory at Washington, will give 12,000 to 15,000 stars, most of them unknown to any existing catalogue; and the plan contemplates the exact record of every star, down to those of the tenth magnitude. Concerted observations of astronomers at different positions, bring the whole heavens under constant inspection; and the advanced state of Astronomical Science, and the improved and powerful character of the instruments employed, authorize the hope of a rapid and wide extension of knowledge in this, the most advanced department, of Physical Science.

SECTION II.

OPTICS.

At the beginning of this century the Newtonian theory of light—the *emission* theory, as it is called—was in the ascendant. It owed its acceptance to the personal influence of its great author; and did not rest on any accurate basis of experiment. During the period under review several facts have been brought to light which enable us to test this, in connection with the rival theory of *undulations.*

The theory of undulations was adopted by Dr. Young, in 1801–3, as explaining the phenomena of diffraction; and in 1815, Fresnel in France coincided with this view. In 1809, Young explained double refraction upon the same hypothesis.

The polarization of light was subjected to an elaborate mathematical examination by Fresnel, in 1820; and a subsequent theoretical examination of the laws of internal reflection, disclosed the very unexpected consequence of a *circular* polarization. This extraordinary result was immediately after verified by experiment, and produoed a deep impression of the truth of that theory.

The phenomena of dipolarization were discovered by Arago, in 1811, and reduced subsequently by Fresnel, from the theory which has served to explain so many of these otherwise inexplicable facts.

The coincidence of that theory with so many of the great optical laws, has produced a strong tendency among philosophers of the present day, to its general adoption. It is, however, still somewhat dubious; and the very recondite character of the facts themselves do not seem to promise any very speedy settlement of the question. The comprehensive character of this theory, the facility with which it has explained, and the correctness with which it has predicted, the curious phenomena of this science, have given it a higher rank among physical theories than any which has been proposed since Newton's theory of gravitation, with which it is classed by philosophers of high repute. Mr. Whewell does not consider it either in generality or in certainty, of an order inferior to that of this celebrated hypothesis.

SECTION III.

METEOROLOGY.

This science which has for its objects the phenomena of the atmosphere, has assumed its present form entirely within the present century. At the beginning of that period it was characterized by two prominent circumstances,—one the possession of the most important instruments of observation, the barometer, thermometer, hygrometer, &c.; and the other, the recent determination of the uniform composition of the atmosphere at all accessible heights, and in all countries.

Numberless observations have been made with each of these instruments, to determine the variations of temperature, humidity, &c., of particular places, and to ascertain the laws of the atmospheric changes throughout the earth. In some places these observations have been made hourly for long periods of time. Observations of this kind for a period of two years in Scotland, were discussed by Dr. Brewster, in 1827.

Many attempts have been made to ascertain the laws of terrestrial heat. The subject has been investigated mathematically by the French philosophers, with their accustomed zeal. Several important problems have been earnestly discussed, such as the specific heats of different substances—the proper heat of the earth, &c.

Among the most interesting of these results, may be mentioned the conclusions, that equal volumes of the different gases have the same specific heat—that no appreciable change of temperature in the Italian climate, has taken place for two hundred years—that the earth has a proper heat of its own,—that its temperature, at a given depth below the surface, is invariable at all seasons, and increases with each succeeding increase of depth.

To Dr. Dalton the world is indebted for some experiments which have ascertained the dew-point, or the temperature at which dew begins to be deposited. He has also determined the composition of the air to be the result of a mechanical mixture, and not of a chemical combination, of its gaseous elements.

The law which governs the amounts of rain falling in different districts of the earth, has been in some degree ascertained. Arago, in 1824–5, traced its regular decrease from the Equator to the poles. On the Malabar coast 123 inches is the annual amount, which is reduced in lat. 60° to 17 inches. Annual amounts have been ascertained in other places far surpassing this: at Paramaribo, 229 inches,—in the Western Ghauts, south of Bombay, 300 inches.

The phenomena of dew were ascertained by a beautiful series of experiments, in 1814, by Dr. Wells, in England. He succeeded in connecting them with temperature as their cause, modified by the conducting power of the body on which moisture is deposited. The theory thus established speedily afforded a solution of all the phenomena.

An ingenious classification of clouds into *cirrus*, *cumulus*, and *stratus*, (corresponding to feather-cloud,—heap-cloud,—and layer cloud, in German,) with their different combinations, was proposed in 1803, by Mr. Howard. It has been generally accepted, and gives great precision to descriptions of atmospheric phenomena.

At the beginning of our period there was no general theory of Winds and Storms; and the want of such a theory was much felt. Since then, however, the general laws of the wind have, in some most important respects, been ascertained. The constant winds of the tropics have been shown to be owing to regular changes of temperature;—the land and sea breezes to the diurnal variations,—the monsoons, to the changes of the seasons,—and the trade-winds, to the difference of climate between the equatorial and polar regions.

A very interesting investigation has recently been conducted by several eminent men, into the nature of the great American Storms, which has already thrown much light upon this subject. Until a very late period they were supposed to be merely gales of wind, moving at a high velocity, and in a straight line. Mr. Redfield, of New York, suggested that they were rotary, and adduced many observations on the great Atlantic Storms, which seemed strongly to sustain this view. It was adopted by Col. Reid, of the British army, and supported by his very numerous observations upon storms in the East and West Indies. A different theory has been advocated by Prof. Espy, who maintains, on similar grounds of fact, and upon established principles of science, that the direction of the wind in such storms, instead of being rotary, is convergent towards a center. The opinions of scientific men are yet divided on the subject; and the discussion has developed some very interesting laws in respect to the causes, motions, and extent of such phenomena.

Many observations have enabled us to ascertain the mean direction of the wind at particular points. Farther investigations in this direction have been undertaken by Lieut. Maury of the Washington Observatory, who has ascertained, from a very extended comparison of the records of numerous ships, that certain winds prevail within given limits much more regularly than had been supposed. The investigation promises great advantages to mariners, as they may select the paths in which a favorable wind is most generally found; and some important results of this kind have, it is believed, been already attained.

Meteorological observations are now made with great regularity and constancy, and over very wide areas. Two of our principal States, New York and Pennsylvania, have recently established stations for this purpose throughout their whole extent. The character of the questions now open, and the number and zeal of observers, give promise of results of high scientific interest, and of great practical value.

SECTION IV.

GEOGRAPHY.

The last century was characterized by a very active spirit of geographical discovery, extending over nearly the whole of that period. While the Russian navigators (among whom Behring stands conspicuous) achieved the exploration of the north-eastern parts of Asia, and the seas between the Asiatic and the American coasts, the other European nations traversed, with similar aims, the vast Pacific. The voyages of De Bougainville and La Perouse, under the auspices of the French government, and especially Cook's well-known voyages, together with numerous other and less conspicuous adventures of the same kind, had made known the general distribution of the great lands and oceans of the globe. The discovery of New Holland, in 1770, by Cook, is the most remarkable achievement of this kind. The unknown portions of the Russian Empire had been illustrated, in some degree, by the efforts of Pallas and others, in the employ of that government; while many others had contributed to extend the knowledge of other portions of the earth. Among these Bruce in Abyssinia, Niebuhr in Arabia and Egypt, Park in Central Africa, and Mackenzie in North America, were particularly distinguished. Through the labors of such adventurers, the general surface of the earth was, at the close of the last century, delineated with considerable exactness, and in some detail.

The subsequent fifty years have extended such explorations in almost every direction, and with many most important results. A very great portion of the Arctic coast of North America has been successfully explored and delineated by successive expeditions of the British government for the discovery of a North West Passage to the Pacific. The names of Ross, Parry, and Franklin will be long memorable in the annals of discovery in this field, each of them having commanded several distinct expeditions of this kind. At the present time, the first-named of these gentlemen yet battles with the tempest and the ice of those rigorous regions in an effort to discover and relieve the last-named, now absent and unheard of for a period of five years and eight months. In this humane undertaking no less than four distinct expeditions are now engaged in company with this veteran commander. Of these one is American, and one French, and two have been sent out by the devoted exertions which have immortalized the name of Lady Franklin.

Upon the continent of America, the Columbia River discovered a year or two earlier, was, with the Missouri, explored by Lewis and Clark in 1804–5.

The sources of the Mississippi were examined in 1805 by Pike, and in 1819–20, through the St. Peters to the Rocky Mountains, by Long.

The investigations of Humboldt, in 1800–4, resulted in a much more accurate knowledge of some portions of South America and Mexico; while the southern extremity of the continent and its south-western shore have been carefully surveyed by a British expedition of discovery conducted in the Beagle,—a survey which has disclosed many important facts in various departments of science.

The western coast of North America was carefully examined through nearly its whole extent by the United States Exploring Expedition under Capt. Wilkes.

The interior geography of the continent has been recently elucidated by the explorations of Lieutenant Fremont. His first expedition (in 1842) terminated at Fremont's Peak, near the South Pass,—two points which mark the highest elevation and the lowest depression of the great chain of the Rocky Mountains. His second (1843–4) found its theatre west of that range in Oregon and Northern California, and disclosed the existence and character of the great Salt Lake. His third resulted in the discovery of that remarkable peculiarity of the interior of Northern California—the great basin—an area of 500 miles in diameter, and from 4000 to 5000 feet in height, with its own system of lakes and rivers. It disclosed, too, the singular characteristics of the Sierra Nevada, with its fertile valleys on the Pacific slope, and its arid and sterile regions on the east. These explorations fill up a vast chasm in the geography of the continent, and connected with Capt. Wilkes's survey of the mouth of the Columbia, present an accurate view of the continent from the Mississippi River to the Pacific Ocean.

The great Australian continent is yet but very imperfectly known. The whole central portion of it is still enveloped in mystery. At the visit of the United States Exploring Expedition, it had been examined through only one fourth part of its extent from the coast. A recent German traveller, from whose exploration much information was expected, has now been absent for a period of three years; and, at the latest accounts, an expedition was just preparing to set out from Singapore in search of him.

In Africa, the explorations of Park had brought to light the existence of a great river, whose probable course formed, for twenty years, a problem of very difficult solution, in prosecution of which that dauntless adventurer soon after lost his life. The successful determination of this question was finally achieved by Lander, in 1830.

In 1822, Denham and Clapperton extensively explored Northern Africa. To the latter is due the honor of being the first European who ever traversed that continent from the Bight of Benin to the Mediterranean. At a later day the Niger was explored, and its course determined, for a distance of two thousand miles from the point where Park first saw it, in 1805, to its mouth.

The travels of Major Laing, in 1826, of Caille, in 1828, and of numerous others, have given us some definite knowledge of the geography, productions, and populations of this region so long unknown. Much, however, yet remains to be ascertained, and scientific observers are busy in exploration. A German expedition, under the direction of the Prussian government, is conducted by Bath and Overweg; and is expected to increase materially our knowledge, both geographical and scientific, of this interesting country.

Oriental lands have been the scene of many researches and discoveries, within the period of which we write.

Within the five years subsequent to 1812, Burckhardt traversed Syria, Arabia, Egypt, and Nubia; and through his extraordinary diligence and attainments, enriched and enlarged our knowledge with a vast amount of important information.

In 1838–39, Dr. Robinson made his very elaborate researches upon the regions of Sinai and Palestine. His labors have given a new impulse to such studies, and determined some very interesting questions of Biblical history. Our present ample knowledge of the geography of Palestine proper, is due entirely to his full and accurate observations. The subsequent examination, by Lieut. Lynch, of the United States Navy, of the Jordan and the Dead Sea, has given to the world its first reliable and precise knowledge of these localities; and has furnished an important contribution to the elucidation of the inspired narrative. His observations ascertained the region of the Dead Sea to be the lowest portion of the earth's surface.

The vast field of Asiatic Russia was explored by Humboldt, throughout its central part, in 1837 to 1842, in a tour which extended along the great Altai range, to the confines of China. He has since given to the world the scientific results of his tour. Still more recently, Ermand, a distinguished naturalist, has examined the northern portion of Asia, and his published journal is full of valuable information upon the population, productions, trade, and natural history of those regions.

Different Scientific expeditions fitted out by the principal European governments, as well as by our own, have greatly contributed to extend geographical science. A vast number of the most important positions, on distant and scarcely accessible shores, have been thus examined. Numerous islands and groups in the vast Pacific,—the coasts of Central and South America,—prominent channels in the China and Indian Seas,—the Arctic and Antarctic extremities of the globe,—have all been more or less carefully delineated. Three such expeditions, French, English, and American, made nearly simultaneous discoveries, of the great Antarctic continent, in 1840.

Missionary enterprise has accomplished many results of the same kind. English and French Protestant Missionaries have enlarged our knowledge of the interior of Southern Africa. American Missionaries have, in some degree, explored its equatorial region from the west; and Gobat has materially elucidated Abyssinia. Some very important observations in Turkey and Persia, and in the Archipelagos of Malaysia and Polynesia are due to the same source: while very numerous contributions of a less striking kind have aided to swell the sum of such knowledge in reference to the many remote and unknown localities to which these heralds of the cross have penetrated.

SECTION V.

PHYSICAL GEOGRAPHY.

The vast number and variety of facts ascertained by so extended and minute a survey of the earth's surface, could not fail to suggest many striking views of a general kind. Heat and moisture were found to be distributed very variously; and the law which governs the distribution assumed a deep interest. Different altitudes and exposures of the earth's surface stood connected with results of the highest consequence to the organized tribes. Many peculiarities, too, of distribution, and varieties of color and form in the organic world, demanded for their explanation a reference to some cause. The investigation of facts and questions, as are here involved, gave rise to Physical Geography as a science.

In this philosophical geography the great ocean beds have been classified—the marine currents determined—the ocean depths sounded, and the heights and length of the mountain-chains measured or computed. The high table-lands—the vast lowlands—the slopes and valleys which everywhere determine the distribution of animals and plants,—all have received a careful survey. The warm and fertile regions which beget population, and the frigid and arid districts which repel it—the mountain ridges and iron-bound coasts which forbid communication—the level plains and tranquil seas which facilitate it—all these have been traced in their influence upon the history of the animal tribes, and of the human race.

Some of the most valuable of the observations which have promoted its progress, are due to the labors of Alexander Humboldt. His journey through a great part of tropical and subtropical America, was undertaken upon a scale on which no private scientific expedition had ever before been planned. The enlarged views and high attainments of himself and his colleague, Bonpland, gave a value to his survey of nature in those lands, which no similar work had possessed, and which few have since attained. It is to his efforts that we principally owe the determination of the magnetic equator, and of many of the Isothermal lines which have since become well established, and are of the highest scientific value.

The science has been carried onward to a far higher point by Ritter and Steffens, in tracing the relations of the organic and moral history of the earth to its physical conformation. The great geographical work of the former surpasses every other in comprehensiveness of detail, and in originality of observation. Ten large octavo volumes had been published in 1846, of his geography, in its relations with nature and history; and yet only Asia and Africa had been completed. His maps are standard works over the world for their accuracy.

To Berghaus is due the praise of having furnished the finest physical Atlas of the Earth which has yet appeared. It has served as the basis of a very elaborate work of the same kind, which has been published by Professor Johnson, of England. His maps, too, of Asia and Africa possess the highest value.

To the moral relations which arise out of the earth's configuration much attention is now directed. Humboldt has himself contributed some important thoughts to the subject in a recent publication, the "Cosmos;" and his pupil, Prof. Guyot, has developed some striking and important aspects of the divine Providence over human history in this connection. This most interesting field has but recently opened, and each extension of the natural history of the different regions of the earth now promises to contribute something to our understanding of the designs of Providence.

SECTION VI.

GENERAL CHEMISTRY—ELECTRICITY.

It is now about a century since observation had so far detected the prominent phenomena of Electricity, as to show its claims to scientific investigation, and the interest which attended the study. Electrical *attraction* had been long known; but it was not till the beginning of the last century that electrical *repulsion* was observed and investigated by Dufay, in France. At about the same period the distinction between conductors and non-conductors was established by Grey, in England. If we add to these the discovery of the different *kinds* of electricity—vitreous and resinous—and the curious fact of the electric shock as given by the Leyden jar, we shall have before us the science of electricity as it was one century since. The chief peculiarity of this last fact was, that electricity was shown to be capable of transmission through a considerable number of persons, and to a very great distance, without any appreciable interval of time.

Philosophers began at once to speculate and to experiment with much interest upon these circumstances, and among these the name of Franklin acquired great distinction by his clear and satisfactory explanations of these electrical phenomena. Electricity by induction, and the identity of electricity with lightning, were soon after ascertained.

Subsequent investigation sought to develop a theory of electricity to ascertain the causes and the laws of these phenomena. Epinus of Petersburg, and Coulomb in France, two of the most eminent philosophers of the last century, labored to determine, by the most careful mathematical calculation, the results of different theories. The first adopted the theory of one fluid,—the latter that of two. Coulomb's theory has been calculated to its results with the utmost precision and detail, and shows a most striking coincidence with the facts of observation; yet in consequence, perhaps, of the highly abstruse character of his reasonings, it was not generally received. The law, however, that the force of electrical attraction varies inversely as the square of the distance, his calculations satisfactorily established.

Since the present century, the improved methods of mathematical investigation, which Laplace had invented for calculating astronomical problems, rendered a higher application possible of mathematics to electricity. In 1801, Biot determined thus the distribution of electricity upon the surface of a spheroid with great exactness. In 1811, Poisson calculated another of the problems to which many of Coulomb's experiments were referable, with very striking results of conformity. Still later, in 1836, Mosotti, of Turin, has calculated with equal profoundness and precision, the mathematical results of the opposite theory of Epinus, of a single fluid. As his results display not merely an accordance with observed facts, but open before us some remarkable general views of the nature of the mechanical forces of cohesion, gravitation, &c., they have awakened much interest, and scientific opinion is yet divided upon the question of one or two fluids. Mosotti found that the particles of the electrical fluid would, upon his theory, at the smallest distances repel each other—at greater distances the repulsion would vanish, while at all perceptible distances they would attract each other with a force inversely as the square of the distance. There would thus be a certain point at which the attraction and the repulsion would precisely balance each other, and constitute a stable equilibrium between the particles; and this, he suggests, may be the circumstance on which the physical structure of bodies depends. So comprehensive a generalization has been felt to be worthy of careful inquiry, and at this point the two electrical theories now rest.

At the same time the tendency of speculation in reference to the other imponderable agents, light and heat, is strongly to discard altogether the idea of a material fluid, and this tendency may, perhaps, affect the theories of electricity also. However this may be, the formulæ thus elaborately calculated will stand as expressions for the laws which govern the distribution and action of electrical forces.

SECTION VII.

GENERAL CHEMISTRY—MAGNETISM.

The history of magnetism bears a general resemblance to that of electricity, and many of the same persons were employed in the two trains of research. The general fact of magnetic attraction was known to the ancients; and it was early ascertained that magnets have poles, of which the similar ones attract, and the opposite ones repel, each other. The discovery of terrestrial magnetism and of the compass, marks a grand advance of knowledge on this subject; and by the seventeenth century several other facts of much interest were developed; those, for instance, of the dip, and of the local and diurnal variations of the magnetic needle. The laws of this variation were first carefully investigated by Halley, under the auspices of William and Mary.

General magnetic theories were proposed in the last century, by the same eminent men who discussed the two hypotheses of Electricity, Epinus and Coulomb; and their theories bore a similar relation to each other. The former adopted the idea of one magnetic fluid manifesting itself by excess and defect; the latter, that of two distinct fluids. Coulomb first ascertained that here also the law of the force is that of the inverse square, in opposition to the opinion of Newton, who imagined it to be inversely as the cube of the distance. Some other important laws are due to his investigations, to which his invention of the torsion balance chiefly contributed. The calculations to which he submitted his theory developed some results of an important kind, which experiment subsequently confirmed.

Within the present century the highest processes of mathematical analysis have been applied to this subject, by Biot, in 1811, and by Poisson in 1824. The result has been the attainment of the law which regulates the distribution of the magnetic fluid on an elliptical spheroid, by the former; and general expressions for the attractions and repulsions of a body of any form whatever, by the latter. Previously, however, Barlow had experimentally ascertained some remarkable facts, and obtained some important rules for determining the amount of the variation of the needle. He discovered that sensible magnetism resided only in the surface of bodies; and that a thin shell of iron produced as much effect as a solid ball of the same diameter. He was enabled, too, to correct the deviation of the needle, which is caused by the iron fastenings of a vessel, by placing a small plate of iron in a counteracting position near the compass—a happy improvement in the use of that instrument. His experiments and formulæ, are deemed to give a strong confirmation to the theory of Coulomb; of which Barlow's was only a novel aspect.

Terrestrial magnetism has been largely indebted to the elaborate observations of Humboldt, who successfully established the line round the earth, at which the needle does not dip—termed the magnetic equator. Biot's analysis of Humboldt's observations led him to the conclusion, that the earth, as a magnet, may be regarded as having its poles near its centre. Captain Ross, in his second Arctic voyage, reached the spot where one of these poles is indicated, the dip there being so great that the needle stood absolutely in a vertical position.

Hansteen showed that the observations compel us to suppose that there are four of these poles; two in the Northern, and two in the Southern hemisphere; and that instead of being stationary, they move with different velocities, and in different directions. "This curious collection of facts," Prof. Whewell observes, "awaits the hand of future theorists, when the ripeness of time shall invite them to the task."

A more recent analysis, by Gauss, of the whole body of magnetic observations has introduced yet another distinction, which materially elucidates the problem. He shows that there is but one magnetic *pole*, properly so called, in each hemisphere, characterized by the vertical dip of the needle, though each hemisphere contains two magnetic *foci* of intensity. One of these is in North America, and the other, somewhat less intense, in Siberia.

As the identity of magnetic and electrical actions have been already ascertained, the question of the reality of a material magnetic fluid is involved in much doubt. The history of the discovery of this connecting link belongs to the next branch of the subject.

SECTION VIII.

GENERAL CHEMISTRY—GALVANISM.

Three successive discoveries in this branch of general chemistry characterize, according to Cuvier, the principal epochs of its earlier stage. Of these, the first was its effect upon the animal system—discovered by Galvani, at Bologna, in 1790,—the second, its nature and origin, demonstrated by Volta, another Italian professor, in 1794; and the third, its remarkable chemical properties, discovered by Davy and Nicholson.

Galvani's discovery of muscular motion by electricity, came at a period when electrical science was almost stationary, and consequently excited great notice. As the cause was supposed to be a peculiar kind of electricity residing in the muscles of animals, it gave rise to many experiments, and to much speculation.

It was Volta, however, who ascertained philosophically the conditions of its origin. He found that the electricity sprang from the simple contact of two metals; and that the muscular contractions which Galvani had observed, were only the ordinary effects of that fluid. He soon after discovered a method of accumulating this electricity, the influence of which is similar to that of the Leyden phial in common electricity. By a great multiplication of the number of metallic plates, separated by wet pasteboard, he found the two electricities developed at the two ends respectively, of the pile thus formed. He proved that all the attractions and repulsions of the Leyden jar could be thus obtained; and ascertained that the pile resembled the action of such a jar, feebly charged, and constantly renewing its charge. He found, too, that by this continued action the most remarkable chemical changes were produced; many substances being rapidly decomposed under its influence. By enlarging the *size* of the plates, a great power of producing heat was developed, while a vast power of decomposition resulted from a similar increase of their *number*. These effects were severally ascribed to the different states of the electric fluid—the former to its *quantity*, and the latter to its *intensity*—distinctions which have since assumed a high importance, and been much more fully investigated.

The attempts to connect magnetism with electricity, which had nearly died away, were, in the year 1820, suddenly and vigorously revived by Oersted, of Copenhagen, who then announced the discovery, that the needle suffers a decided change from proximity to the conducting wire of a voltaic circuit. It very unexpectedly appeared, that the needle tends to assume a position at right angles to the wire. This singular fact greatly stimulated scientific inquiry; many observers soon corroborated the statement, and added new facts to those which Oersted had observed in electro-magnetism. Among these Ampère was prominent, who immediately inferred, and soon afterward proved, that the earth, considered as a magnet, must, and does, affect the position of the voltaic wire. He advanced rapidly to a general theory of the subject, which implied that the voltaic wires must attract and repel each other. This conclusion was immediately tested and verified by experiment, and the laws of the attractions and repulsions ascertained with ingenuity.

Another singular fact was brought to light by Faraday, in 1821,—that this force would cause a revolution in either of the two bodies, the magnetic needle or the voltaic wire, about the other; a fact which again gave rise to several curious inquiries. It was soon ascertained that this force, so peculiar in its direction, followed the law of all similar forces, in being inversely as the square of the distance.

As the needle assumed a position at right angles to the wire, it might be supposed either that the wire was a collection of transverse needles, or that the magnetic needle was a bundle of transverse wires. In either case they would assume toward each other the positions thus indicated. Ampère adopted the latter of these suppositions, in opposition to most of the philosophers; and succeeded, not without some complex calculations, in explaining by means of it all the classes of phenomena which have been mentioned. The theory was for some time contested, particularly by Biot, who had adopted a different view; but in a succession of papers presented to the French Academy, and extending through a period of nearly two years, Ampère vindicated his theory from all objection, and satisfactorily established its exclusive conformity to the various facts.

In 1832 a brilliant career of discovery was commenced by Faraday. From the moment that magnetism had been proved to be a particular form of electrical action it had seemed practicable to produce electricity by magnetism; and an experiment of Arago's had even seemed to involve this effect. The revolution of a conducting-plate acted upon a magnet in its neighborhood. Following this suggestion, Faraday succeeded, after some futile endeavors, in detecting a momentary effect in a neighboring wire, at the moments at which a voltaic circuit was formed or broken, and thus established magneto-electric *induction.* Simplifying the arrangements, he soon ascertained other important laws; and finally, that the earth itself might supply the place of a magnet, and that the mere motion of a wire would, in appropriate circumstances, produce a temporary electric current. The various and peculiar facts which he had discovered, he soon succeeded in reducing to a general law, by referring the position and motion of the wire to magnetic *curves,* which go from one pole of the magnet to the other. The general view in which he has united these various discoveries, is regarded as forming a most important step in the progress of this science.

The subsequent history of these sciences, merges into that of chemistry proper, under which head we shall again refer to them.

SECTION IX.

CHEMISTRY PROPER.

During the last century the chemistry of aëriform bodies formed a principal subject of chemical investigation, and it was through these investigations that the chief discoveries of the earlier portions of that century were made. In 1755, Black, at Glasgow, showed that the gases formed constituent elements of solid and fluid bodies. In 1766, Cavendish pointed out the peculiar properties of hydrogen gas, or, as it was then called, inflammable air. In 1774, Priestley discovered oxygen, and at about the same period nitrogen, and some other gases. Finally, in 1782, the brilliant experiments of Cavendish determined the composition of water, and visibly combined the two gaseous elements in the fluid form,—a result which was received with general assent and admiration.

During this period, however, the general theory of chemistry was that known as the phlogistic theory, which supposed combustion to take place by the extrication of an invisible substance, termed phlogiston, from the burning body. However erroneous this theory may have been, it is generally now regarded as having formed a most important step in the progress of chemistry, and from its adoption by Stahl, a German chemist, and its promulgation in 1718, it enjoyed a wide and almost universal acceptance.

At length, however, as continued investigation extended the body of known facts, the insufficiency of the theory became apparent, and the necessity of some other began to be felt. The nomenclature, too, of the science was altogether empirical and grotesque in itself, and inadequate to the exigencies of the occasion, when the facts to be classified, and the objects to be named, had become very numerous. A new nomenclature was proposed, in 1781, and was fully executed by an association of French chemists, in 1787, which introduced great clearness and connection into the facts of chemistry. In 1789, Lavoisier gave to the world a treatise, in which the new nomenclature and the new theory of *oxygen* were fully explained, and applied to the whole body of the facts then known. A great degree of mathematical accuracy had been already introduced into chemical investigations, particularly by Bergman, in his mineral analyses,—by Priestley in his experiments upon the gases,—or, as they were then called, airs,—and especially by Cavendish. The beautiful experiments and happy explanations of Lavoisier commended the new system to the delight and acceptance of the scientific world; and, though opposed by some of the eminent chemists of the day, it soon secured a general adoption. Priestley, however, in the last year of the past century, was yet earnestly combating it, and never adopted either the scientific nomenclature, or the new theory of combustion.

From this time the science made most rapid advances. Many new elements came successively to light. The number of known metals, in 1789, was seventeen; of which *platina* had been but recently discovered, and another, *uranium*, was detected in that year. The year 1795 witnessed the discovery of *titanium*, and 1798 that of *tellurium;* while, in 1797, Vauquelin made the brilliant discovery of *chromium*. *Columbium* was drawn from a mineral of the United States in 1802; *cerium* was ascertained in 1801; four others of quite remarkable character were detected in crude platinum, in 1805 and 1806. The list of elementary metallic substances ran up soon to twenty-seven or eight.

Several new earths were discovered, during the same period. Five were known in 1789, and by the end of the century four more were added to the number.

The mineral acids became known in the course of the eighteenth century; but the animal and vegetable acids were by no means as well ascertained. Soon, however, under the influence of the new systems, a very great number of these were brought to light and carefully discriminated.

The various elements, acids, &c., thus discovered formed, of course, even in their simplest combinations, a very great number of substances, which afforded to chemical investigation a vast field of inquiry and research. The determination of the respective quantities of the acid and of the base in the various salts, required very long researches, especially in the case of the metallic salts, which have been very carefully investigated, and with many results of great utility in the arts. The same investigation was necessary to determine the precise amounts of the different elements of each of the gases, while the different products, both solid and fluid, of the animal organizations, demanded numerous and laborious analyses, and offered in return many novel and interesting results.

At about the same period an English chemist, Dalton, achieved a grand advance in this science by the discovery of the atomic theory. Some of the principles involved in it had been suggested before, but had nowhere acquired due prominence. The essential points of this theory are three :—"That elements combine by weight in *definite* proportions; that these determining proportions operate *reciprocally;* and that when, between the same elements, several combining proportions occur, they are related as *multiples.*" The last of these principles was entirely new to the scientific world, and even the first had but shortly before been called in question by Berthollet. The discovery was soon generally admitted, and was received with great admiration.

The theory received, immediately upon its introduction into France, an important modification. It was ascertained by Gay Lussac, that the gases combine *by volume*, in very simple and definite proportions. With this modification it has received a universal currency, and has been esteemed for the definiteness and precision which it has introduced into the science,—a remarkable and most important step in its progress.

One of the most beautiful discoveries of the present century, was the reduction by Davy, in 1807, of the fixed alkalies, soda, and potash, to a metallic base. It had been suspected that these were compound bodies, since the time of Berthollet's successful analysis of the volatile alkali, but all attempts to decompose them had proved vain, up to the period of Cuvier's Report on the Natural Sciences, in 1808, in which they are still classed as elementary. The value of this beautiful discovery lay not merely in the knowledge which it afforded of the alkaline metals themselves, but in the new laws which it revealed, and in the new field which it opened,—at once enlarging the domain, and correcting the principles, of science.

This discovery was shortly after followed by several others of a similar kind; the effect of which was to concentrate the attention of the chemical world upon the investigations and views from which they had resulted. Davy had been for some time engaged upon experiments designed to illustrate the relations between chemistry and some forms of galvanic and electrical action; and it was in pursuance of the theoretical views which he entertained upon these subjects, that these discoveries had been made.

The decomposition of water by electricity, had been observed in 1800; and in 1806, Davy announced his great discovery, that "The combinations and decompositions by electricity, were referable to the law of electrical attractions and repulsions;" and advanced the theory, that chemical and electrical attractions were due to the same cause. This beautiful generalization is regarded as one of the great events in the scientific history of this period; and it was immediately recognized as such all over Europe. The author of it received the distinguished honor of a prize of 3,000 francs, authorized by Napoleon, and awarded by the French Institute, for the best experiments on the galvanic fluid, though the two nations were at this period in fierce hostility.

This theory of Davy, at first put forth in terms much too general to satisfy the demands of science, received its full confirmation from the researches of Faraday. By a long series of experimental investigations, he established a principle, through which the definite measurement of the quantity of electrical forces became practicable. By the application of this method he succeeded in obtaining for each elementary substance, a number which represented the relative amount of its decomposition—or in other words, its "electro-chemical equivalent."

The proportion of these numbers was found, upon inquiry, to coincide with the atomic weights of the Daltonian theory. The result of these investigations was the complete establishment of the great law which Davy had suggested—the identity of electrical and chemical action; the widest and most comprehensive generalization to which chemistry has yet attained.

Since Davy's discovery of Potassium, in 1807, almost all the earths and alkalies have been resolved into metallic bases, though some have conceived that the base of silica is more analogous to carbon. The position, therefore, of this substance is yet somewhat doubtful.

The unrestricted statement of the theory of Lavoisier, that acids were formed in *all* instances by combination with oxygen, was soon called in question; and an important modification was suggested simultaneously by Davy, and by several of the French chemists. In 1812, an experiment was performed by the former, in the presence of several eminent philosophers at Edinburgh, the result of which was to satisfy them that muriatic acid was not so constituted. A new view of that subject has, in consequence, been since taken by most chemists; and that acid is regarded as a combination of hydrogen, with a peculiar principle, called chlorine. The existence of one such acid suggested inquiry in respect to others; and several are now recognized as probably possessing a similar constitution. Four important principles, chlorine, iodine, bromine, and fluorine, are now classed as analogous, among the elements of chemistry, though the last of these has not yet been separately obtained.

The number of elementary substances was reported, in 1837, by Prof. Whewell, to be fifty-three; since then, writers on chemistry enumerate fifty-five, and some substances which are yet but imperfectly known, carry it to not less than sixty.

A vast amount of chemical research has been expended in the formation and analysis of salts. Some idea of the extent of these researches may be formed from the fact, that more than two thousand compounds of this kind have been described or indicated, a great proportion of which have been largely investigated.

More recently the attention of chemists has been extensively devoted to the ananlysis of organic products. Many of the results of the earlier inquirers of the present century, having proved inaccurate, numerous attempts have been made to improve the methods of vegetable analysis, so as to secure more constant and exact results. Through these improvements, the existence of a very great number of vegetable acids has been ascertained. In 1832, they were set down at eighty-two in number. The list of vegetable alkalies included, at the same time, no less than thirty-three.

The merit of the first great discovery of this kind is due to Serturner, whose remarkable discovery in opium of morphine, a vegetable alkali, to which the soporific qualities of that drug are owing, took place at Edinburgh, in 1805, and led the way to a train of discoveries to which much of our knowledge in this branch is owing. He was followed by Pellétier and Caventon, who soon after discovered strychnine, and detected quinine, the active principle of Peruvian bark, in 1820.

Many important points, in respect to the nature of these proximate principles, are yet involved in much doubt. It is impossible yet to say whether they are or are not binary compounds—whether the alkalies do, or do not, contain ammonia—and, in some instances, whether they really exist in the substances from which they are derived, or are formed by the lengthened processes by means of which they are obtained.

Other vegetable principles, possessing neither alkaline nor acid properties, have been extracted from a great variety of substances. Of these, twelve are described as coloring matters;—eighteen as gums, resins, &c.;—and thirty-seven as indifferent principles—neither acid nor alkaline. Besides which there is a vast variety of vegetable oils, many of which are not characterized by properties sufficiently distinct to make their differences easily intelligible. Many of these substances have been found capable of most important and extensive application in the useful arts; and others have proved of the highest value in medicine.

In Animal chemistry similar researches have been instituted into the composition of the various products of the animal economy, with results, however, less numerous. The number of proximate principles yet discovered is materially smaller. Animal chemistry has been chiefly studied in connection with physiology; and most of the investigations have had reference to the healthy or diseased functions of the human system. The various products and tissues of the system have been carefully examined. The blood, the bile, milk, albumen, fat, &c., have each been the subject of careful and extended researches. Of acid principles, twenty, and of indifferent and alkaline, thirty-four, were, in 1832, reported, as well characterized, and established, to the British Association; besides a considerable number which were yet involved in some obscurity. At that period the fatty bodies were the only ones which had been thoroughly investigated; and the name of Chevreul was honorably distinguished in their investigation.

The great number of specific principles thus established, involving a very wide extension of our knowledge of the chemistry of animal and vegetable organization, has necessarily led to much both of reasoning and of research in these departments. Questions of the highest interest could not fail to be suggested, as soon as any specific knowledge was obtained of the nature and the variety of the products of animal and vegetable life. The characteristics of these peculiar compounds,—the sources from which they were derived,—the processes by which they were elaborated,—the ends which they subserved in the organization that produced them,—these and numerous other problems of the same kind tasked the ingenuity and the resources of the chemical philosophers to the utmost. The whole great mystery of organic life, with its numerous and remarkable phenomena of respiration, nutrition, digestion,—of growth and decay,—of combination and decomposition,—demanded elucidation at the hand of this advanced science, which had already penetrated to so many of the secrets of nature.

Among philosophers who have attempted the solution of such problems, none has achieved greater distinction than Liebig. His observations, which have been prosecuted with the highest enthusiasm, have combined great acuteness of research with an uncommon spirit of philosophical generalization. Some of the most remarkable instances of philosophical deduction, which the recent history of science records, are to be found in his speculations in organic chemistry. Thus, the capacity which chemical action in a given substance had been observed, in some instances, to possess of impressing itself upon other bodies, and originating a similar action in them, has received in his hands a generalization of the widest kind; and the universal law which he has sought thus to establish, furnishes an explanation of many phenomena hitherto inexplicable. The pernicious influence of malaria and of putrid substances,—the contagion of diseases and the action of some kinds of poisons,—are, upon this theory, explained with great simplicity, and made to assume the character of phenomena determined by one comprehensive law. His theory, too, of animal heat and of respiration, which regards these phenomena, as results of the change of the iron in the blood from one to the other of its oxides in the lungs, and back again in the capillaries to its previous form, is regarded as a beautiful application of the deductive method, completely explaining these mysterious phenomena. Upon the validity of these speculations chemical science has not yet fully pronounced, though there seems to be a strong disposition to impose considerable limitations upon Liebig's statements of the fundamental facts of his philosophy.

The extent to which subsequent investigation may carry these modifications of his theories, it is, of course, impossible to conjecture; but there seems little reason to doubt that in many important respects his views will long be regarded as beautiful examples of scientific research which have extended the domain of known chemical laws over some of the widest, most complicated, and most interesting phenomena of organized nature.

It is impossible to convey any idea within the brief limits to which this sketch must be confined of the vast amount of observation and thought to which these various discoveries are owing. It has been a prominent subject of investigation in every intelligent community. England, France, Germany, Sweden, Italy, have all contributed to its development, nor has our own country been without distinction in this brilliant career of discovery. In each of these nations a host of ardent observers has labored assiduously in the cultivation of this field. Countless analyses and experiments have been demanded for the discovery of each new substance; and every discovery has required for its verification processes equally elaborate and extended. The research has involved a degree of accuracy which nothing but the most patient toil could have attained, and which, but a very short time since, would have seemed incredible. A new notation for the description by brief formulæ of the constantly-increasing number of new organic and mineral compounds has been invented by Berzelius, and, with some modifications from the German chemists, is now rapidly coming into use. Investigation has already ascertained, by numerous and oft-repeated experiment, the precise composition of almost every product of animal, or of vegetable life. The wood,—the bark,—the leaves, —the fruits of each species of cultivated plants,—nay, of every variety at every period of the year, and at every stage of its growth,—have been analyzed and recorded. Each tissue of the animal system,—the bones,—the muscles, — the brain,—the blood,—each fluid secreted or excreted in the animal economy,—each healthy and each diseased product of organic life,—has been thousands of times analyzed, and the analysis verified by countless observations.

Whatever may become of recent theories, the vast body of facts which chemistry has already accumulated, must remain, together with many of the established laws of a general kind, to form the starting point for future observers. With such materials, advanced to such a state of generalization as chemistry now unquestionably possesses, the highest general views cannot be very remote, and we may anticipate a speedy solution of those mysterious phenomena of animal and vegetable life which are open to physical investigation, the attainment of which seems now the aim of chemical science in the future.

SECTION X.

MINERALOGY.

As mineralogy is peculiarly a science of classification, its progress must be measured essentially by the systems of classification which have been adopted. The first of these had been offered by Werner in the last century, and recognized almost exclusively the external characters of minerals, as its basis. In the discrimination of minerals by differences of color, weight, hardness, &c., this school gained great distinction, and furnished materials of great value for future use.

The constancy of the angles of crystallization had, however, impressed several minds during this period; and finally Haüy, a French mineralogist, proposed, in 1801, his system of crystallography. He discovered the importance of cleavage, and the laws by which secondary forms are derived from more fundamental ones. He developed these principles into a detailed system, described a vast number of secondary forms, which he deduced by mathematical processes from the primary ones, and examined the whole mineral kingdom in accordance with these views. He showed that the crystalline angles are the criteria of substances; and distinguished baryta and stontia, and identified the beryl and the emerald, before their chemical composition had been ascertained. His lectures were eagerly heard by great numbers in Paris; and his views were speedily disseminated throughout the world, and earnestly pursued by many observers.

The system received a modification from Weissul, who proposed a system of crystals, to which each individual might be referred. This theory regarded the crystal as disposed about an axis. This step constituted a real improvement, and soon found confirmation from another quarter. The optical properties of crystals, double refraction and dipolarization, were ascertained by Sir D. Brewster to sustain a relation to these systems of crystallization; and the distinction was thenceforth established as an important law (which farther discovery has confirmed), that the geometrical symmetry corresponds with the optical properties of crystals.

While these investigations were going on in crystallography, another system was in formation, which took the chemical composition as its basis, and arranged in the same class all minerals which were found to be chemically alike. The necessity for a new system arose from the fact now discovered, that the same angle of crystallization sometimes characterizes different substances; and that what might be assigned by its crystallization to one class of substances, was in reality wholly different. The explanation of this fact is due to Mitscherlich, who showed that one substance may sometimes accurately replace another in the composition of a mineral, assuming precisely the same crystalline form. This discovery of Isomorphism he promulgated in 1822.

Berzelius had, before this, constructed his system of purely chemical characters, in which each substance was classed on the principle of its chemical proportions, and particularly with reference to electro-chemical properties. He arranged all minerals according to the electro-chemical character of their elements, and the elements themselves as electro-positive or electro-negative in different degrees. But the same results followed his system,—it was found impossible to conform all mineral substances to it, and Berzelius himself gave up the theory, and attempted another. In this all were arranged according to the same class of agencies, but wholly with reference to the electro-negative element. Instead of classing together all varieties of iron or of copper, all the *sulphurets*, all the *oxides*, &c., were united.

The result, however, both of this and of other attempts of the same kind, was unsuccessful; and the science now rests upon a mixed method, in which all the characters of these various systems are employed for distinguishing minerals. This method is of course very complex, and involves in each instance questions of chemical composition—physical character—and crystalline form. The mass of mineral species has now become very great, and is continually increasing, and the difficulty of discrimination in doubtful cases is by no means small. But each of the systems we have mentioned has contributed essentially to our means of knowledge, and together they furnish a valuable approximation to a complete system.

SECTION XI.

GEOLOGY.

It was at the beginning of the XVIth century that geological facts first awakened attention and inquiry; and within the next two hundred years they had accumulated to a considerable number, especially in Italy, and had given rise to much speculation. During the latter part of the XVIIIth century a variety of theories had been proposed for the explanation of such facts as were then known—theories which serve at present only to indicate to what an extent the wonder and curiosity of inquirers had been awakened. Buffon had proposed a theory which found advocates till the close of that century. The two Bertrands had originated others in Switzerland and France; and several theorizers in England and Germany had obtained similar distinction by the same means. These theories were of a character the most visionary and capricious. The first, regarded our earth as having been struck off from the sun, while in a heated state, by a comet—another, as having been originally a mass of ice—and upon each of them the few established facts were explained, by calling in any agencies which might seem adequate to such effects.

Other observers, however, as Saussure in the Alps, and Pallas in Siberia, confined themselves to the collection of facts, and accumulated materials which have proved of great value to their successors. At the close of that century, the interest of the scientific world was concentrated upon two theories which long divided the suffrages of the learned. Werner, a Professor in Saxony, contended that all rocks were deposited by water, and this was known as the Neptunian theory; while in Scotland, Hutton taught that the unstratified rocks had been deposited in a melted state, and his theory was designated accordingly as the Plutonian. The latter of these views has, with important modifications, been adopted by most subsequent geologists; yet to Werner is due the credit of having extended correct general views of the distinctions of classification of strata. In 1793, an Englishman, William Smith, achieved a great advance in geology by his classification of the strata of some portions of his country; and in 1815 he gave to the world a survey of England, in which the strata were discriminated by their organic remains. During this period many of the most ingenious minds were devoting themselves to similar researches. In 1807 the formation of the London Geological Society took place,—an association which has materially and most honorably connected its name with the subsequent progress of Geology in England.

In the mean time the study of fossils was pursued with great genius and enthusiasm in various countries. Lamarck and Defrance determined the fossil shells in the neighborhood of Paris, and in 1811, the memorable work of Cuvier and Brogniart, "On the Environs of Paris," constituted an epoch in geological science. Cuvier's discovery of many species of vertebrated animals in the basin of Paris, some of them of immense size and of the most extraordinary character, stimulated naturalists throughout Europe to more extended examinations of the tertiary strata, from which they have since reaped an ample harvest of most important facts. The restoration of more than forty species of extinct quadrupeds, principally of the pachydermata, attests the extent and the success of his labors.

Another most remarkable group of animals,—the Saurian,—was brought to light principally by the geologists of England. In 1816, Sir Everard Home ascertained that, among the fossil remains of England, were some which it was impossible to arrange with any known class of animals. The animal thus referred to was named the *Ichthyosaurus*, as intermediate between fishes and lizards. Another still more nearly approaching the lizard, was discovered by Conybeare, in 1821, and named *Plesiosaurus*. These were marine genera. At a somewhat later day, Dr. Buckland designated another, and a terrestrial genus, as the *Megalosaurus*, and, finally, Dr. Mantell brought to light the most gigantic of them all—the *Iguanodon*—a herbivorous reptile of nearly 100 feet in length. There are now at least eighty species of these fossil reptiles known, many of them of immense size and some of extraordinary character. They have been divided by Dr. Buckland into four groups,—the Marine, Terrestrial, Amphibious, and Flying Reptiles.

The curiosity and wonder excited by such a series of discoveries greatly stimulated the ardor of inquirers, and a great number of observers now pursued investigations, which had proved so fruitful of novel and brilliant results. Many of the most acute and philosophical minds of the age have been, and still are, engaged in efforts to solve the problems which geology offers to our examination. The investigations of Agassiz upon the fossil fish, published in two separate works in Neuchatel, in 1834, and in England, in 1835, have resulted in a new and admirable classification of that branch of physical science. More recently the observations of the same gentleman upon the glaciers of Switzerland and the erratic blocks, have opened a new field of investigation in the *ice* period.

The fossil plants were first fully investigated by Brogniart. The number of species which he had ascertained, in 1836, amounted to 527, which have since increased to about two thousand. As a large proportion of plants would disappear during the process of fossilization, fungi, mosses, &c., the aggregate, it is supposed, may have approached the existing number. One half of the whole are contained in the caroniferous series, before the great herbivorous quadrupeds existed.

The earliest well-characterized plants hitherto ascertained are coniferous trees at the base of the old red sandstone. Their discovery is due to the protracted investigations of Hugh Miller, in a field, whose fruitfulness he had the merit of discovering.

The species of fossil fish number about two thousand. They have grown to this number under the hand of Prof. Agassiz. The number which Cuvier had distinguished amounted to only ninety-two.

The depth of British strata investigated and found to be fossiliferous was estimated, in 1840, at six and a half miles. Prof. Rogers, of Pennsylvania, estimated the American strata below the coal as of much greater thickness than the European.

Many important questions, which have arisen during the course of these investigations, have been successfully solved. Among these no single one was attended with greater difficulty than that of determining the equivalence of the strata of different regions, a work which required the most careful examination of the fossil remains of distant formations. The identity of the compact marbles of Italy and Greece, with the loose limestones which form the Oolitic series of England, was pointed out by Dr. Buckland, in 1820, and his view has since been fully confirmed. The determination of hundreds of shells by most skilful conchologists was requisite to decide the position of some of the calcareous beds of Germany as compared with the formations of Great Britain.

More recently, however, this effort has been so far extended that the general system of the rocks is now universally agreed upon, and is understood over the whole of Europe, and of eastern North America. In more distant countries, however, the equivalence of strata with those already known is more doubtful, though investigation is rapidly enlarging our knowledge in every direction. Humboldt has labored to extend the doctrine of geological equivalence, as shown in the rocks of Europe, to those of the Andes.

The equivalence of the strata of New York with those of Europe and northern Asia was determined, in 1846, by M. de

Verneuil, who determined the fact that no country offers so complete and uninterrupted a development of the Devonian system as this State.

Geological science has been greatly indebted for its progress to the accurate surveys which various governments have ordered. The surveys of the European coast, undertaken for military and commercial purposes, have furnished opportunity of geological observation also. Extended geological investigations have been accomplished of all the more important European countries.

American geology has been greatly indebted to the same aid. The several States have almost universally instituted surveys for economical as well as scientific purposes. Among the most distinguished of these are those of Massachusetts, which were made, in 1833, by Prof. Hitchcock, and New York, which were undertaken, in 1836, by several gentlemen of scientific distinction, and contemplated a general survey of the Natural History of the State.

The United States Government has had geological surveys made of some extended regions of the interior of the country; and the Exploring Expedition, under Captain Wilkes, has made a most valuable contribution to science in this branch, in the work of Professor Dana.

There are in every department of geology questions of great interest awaiting their solution. M. de Beaumont has suggested a theory of the contemporaneous elevation of parallel mountain-chains, which has attracted much attention. More recently, a different view has been taken, which attributes them to the contraction of the earth's crust.

Among the more interesting points which are regarded as settled, may be mentioned the very recent appearance of man upon the globe, and the termination of creation with the formation of man, as no single species can be shown to have originated since this modern period.

The highest authorities agree in denying the possibility of the transmutation of lower into higher forms of organic life, and generally in affirming the diffusion of each species from a single point throughout its whole range.

Two theories at present divide the geological world, in respect to the method and the agencies by which the earth's changes have been produced. One view attributes the phenomena to the violent action of causes not now equally influential; the other, represented by Lyell, to the long-continued action of causes such as those which are now raising the Scandinavian peninsula. Facts at present are not sufficiently numerous to authorize any confident conclusion.

SECTION XII.

BOTANY.

The principal fact which has characterized the history of Botany during the present century, is the acceptance of the natural system of arrangement. Previously, the prevailing method was that of Linnæus, to whom all departments of natural history owed very great obligations for the specific names—the precision of language—and the comprehensive method which he introduced into them. His system was founded upon the number and position of the reproductive organs of plants, and introduced an arrangement which was highly convenient for reference, but altogether artificial.

Botanists still looked, therefore, for some system which should group plants not merely according to a given number of stamens, but in harmony with the higher affinities which prevail in nature. Such a system was proposed by De Jussieu, in 1789.

The principle of this system is the estimation of organs according to their importance. We observe some groups in which certain organs are constantly present; and finding that the organs which are constant in one family are constant also in the others, these are assumed as of higher consequence than more variable organs. Arranging upon this principle, we reach a classification identical with the natural relations in which plants stand to each other. An illustration of this process, and of its results, is afforded by the distinction adopted in all the natural systems between Monocotyledonous and Dicotyledonous plants. In the former it is found that the wood is developed toward the inside, in the latter, upon the outside of the tree. The distinction corresponds, therefore, to a grand fact in the organization of the plant.

This system was yet farther developed by a Swiss botanist, De Candolle, who showed that this method affords a guide to the knowledge of the properties of medicinal plants.

It has since been widely adopted, and is at present the fundamental principle of botany.

The science has extended with every year, till it embraces a vast number of species. Exploration in every part of the globe has been, and still is, adding to the catalogue. Some idea of its growth may be formed, from the statement, that a century since, Linnæus enumerated 7,300 species, which were increased in his second edition to 8,800. In 1808, the number had reached 30,000; in 1830 it was more than 50,000; and in 1850 they amounted to not less than 120,000.

The floras of Europe, together with those of many distant portions of the earth, were undergoing at the beginning of this century careful examination. This has been continued till beautiful and extensive works have been published, describing and picturing the whole body of European, and a vast number of foreign plants. Brown brought to England, in 1805, as many as 4,000 species of Australian plants. Humboldt discovered a vast number in Mexico and Peru. Brazil has been examined by many naturalists—the East and West Indies—

Bengal, Sumatra, Java, Abyssinia, China—all have been subjected to repeated inspection by eminent and laborious men.

By means of this extended investigation, botanists have been able to divide the surface of the earth into a number of districts, which show with some accuracy, the general distribution of plants. De Candolle established 20 botanical regions, which Martius, of Munich, has extended to 51; of these, 5 are in Europe, 11 in Africa, 13 in Asia, 3 in New Holland, 4 in North, and 8 in South America, besides a number more limited in extent. Humboldt gives the following view of the distribution of plants, both as to height and latitude:

The equatorial zone is the region of palms and bananas.

The tropical, of tree-ferns and figs.

The subtropical, of myrtles and laurels.

The warm temperate, of evergreen trees.

The cold temperate, of deciduous trees.

The subarctic, of pines.

The arctic, of rhododendrons.

The polar, of alpine plants.

The three great classes of plants are, the *cryptogamia*, fungi, mosses, &c., whose flowers are invisible, and which are the lowest in organization; the *monocotyledonous*, as grasses and ferns, and the *dicotyledonous*, or flowering plants—the most numerous, and the highest in organization. The first class characterizes the vegetation of high latitudes; the second flourishes in the tropical regions; while the third has its chief development in the temperate zones.

The flora of tropical America is the richest of the world; Europe has about half the number of species; Asia less than Europe; Australia, still less; and Africa, fewer vegetable productions than any equal area of the globe. Wherever the species of plants are generally identical in different countries, it is proved by Prof. E. Forbes that the regions were once connected. The agents of the diffusion of plants are currents of water, winds, birds, quadrupeds, and man. The cryptogamia, whose minute seeds, sometimes invisible, are transported by the winds, enjoy the widest diffusion, while very few dicotyledonous plants are common to two distant countries, and in many instances their diffusion can be traced with the highest probability to the causes above mentioned.

SECTION XIII.

ZOOLOGY.

The progress of Zoology within the present century is mainly due to the grand impulse given by Cuvier. Previously the general system of Linnæus was adopted, which failed to distinguish a natural order. The great epoch is the appearance of the *Regne Animal*, or Animal Kingdom of Cuvier, in 1817. Since that period naturalists have felt themselves in the true path of nature, in treading in the steps which his genius indicated.

Lamarck divided all animals into vertebrate and invertebrate, the general analogies of the former class being sufficiently obvious. But the latter it was reserved for Cuvier to illustrate. He separated early this class into several, instead of dividing them, as Linnæus had done, into two,—insects and worms. In 1801, Cuvier distinguished a class of the latter, which have red blood, and finally, in 1812, he distributed the invertebrates into three classes, each co-ordinate to the branch formed by the vertebrata. This classification marks them :—

The Vertebrata—Characterized by a spine and skull, with lateral appendages, which enclose the viscera and support the muscles.

The Mollusca—With muscles attached to the skin, and no bony skeletons, embracing shell-fish, cuttle-fish, &c.

The Articulata—Consisting of insects, lobsters, &c., characterized by a head and a number of successive portions of the body *jointed* together.

The Radiata—Comprising the zoophytes, in which the members radiate from a central axis. This system was fully developed, in 1817, in the "Regne Animal," and has since been universally adopted.

The animals being thus reduced to four general types, naturalists have, in some instances, sought to simplify the result and bring all animals of each class to a single type. Such views, however, have hitherto failed to secure any general concurrence, and Cuvier to the last resisted the attempt. Prof. Oken, in 1807, labored to resolve the skull into vertebræ, and with some success, for many naturalists adopted and carried out his views, and both Cuvier and Owen countenanced the effort. It is supposed by Whewell to have been fully acquiesced in by the best physiologists; but it has recently been very vigorously attacked by Hugh Miller, and on grounds which, if they are not decisive against the theory, bring up the question at least for renewed discussion.

Vertebrata.—The different classes of this grand division have been very largely investigated, and the number has greatly increased in every department.

Among the mammalia, the 300 species of Buffon had grown, in1826, to 700, as estimated by M. Desmarets. We have now 207 described by Bachman, in North America alone. Africa, India, and South America are constantly sending us new ones. In their distribution the quadrupeds of the southern extremities of the continents differ far more widely from each other than those of the northern; while the Polar animals of all the continents are identical in species.

There are 480 species of mammalia peculiar to the American continent, scarcely one of which is capable of easy and useful domestication. Asia has 288, among which occur almost all the domesticated animals.

Herpetology.—The Reptiles have been distinguished into four conspicuous natural groups. Their numbers are far greater as we approach the tropics, and they form a principal characteristic of the American continent. Their range is generally limited, and the species are not numerous.

Ornithology.—In ornithology, the extreme beauty and very wide range of many species have made them the subjects of much study. Six natural orders are easily discriminated. Many naturalists, as Vaillant in Africa, and Temminck in South America, have, with great assiduity, penetrated the wildest and least accessible regions to observe the species of these lands. The ornithology, too, of Europe and North America has been elucidated by names too familiar to require any mention.

The wide range of many birds is interesting as throwing light upon the general problem of the distribution of animals. It is found that the species of birds which, for the purpose of rearing their young, annually visit the Polar regions, where the different continents approach each other, are identical in Europe, Asia, and America. Of the others, which are confined to lower latitudes, none are identical on opposite sides of the ocean.

Great attention has been given to the anatomy of the vocal organs, so remarkable in this class.

The number of ascertained species is about 6000.

Ichthyology.—In ichthyology materials had accumulated greatly at the close of the last century, and Bloch, in a great work on the plan of Linnæus, attempted to systematize them. He was unsuccessful, however, in his arrangement, and Cuvier was the first to indicate a philosophical path in this department. His grand distinction is taken from the character of the skeleton, and he makes two classes, the bony or osseous, and the cartilaginous fish. The characteristics of the orders have been taken from the jaws, gills, and fins.

This classification was in part rejected by M. Agassiz, who, in forming a new system, founded the distinctions of it upon the scales alone, and made four orders, not coincident with any previous division. This system has peculiar advantages in geology, as in many instances only the bony scales have been preserved.

It enables us to assert general propositions of a very striking kind, such, for instance, as that only the two first are found geologically below the chalk, and has, for geological purposes, very great merit. It was at first doubted whether this was a true natural method, but naturalists very generally adopt at present some, at least, of the distinctions which belong to it, and appreciate the system very highly.

The number of species of fish is certainly increasing with the investigation of distant seas. The European species number about 650, of which 210 are fresh-water species, and the remainder marine—60 of these go up the rivers to spawn.

Some remarkable peculiarities have been ascertained in respect to the depth at which they live; and several distinct zones of depth are now discriminated, each having its own class of fish. Their distribution is limited; most large lakes have peculiar species: and many tropical rivers. The different continents and oceans possess species entirely distinct; and the rivers and lakes of remote regions rarely possess the same.

The species already ascertained amount to about ten thousand.

Mollusca.—The class of mollusca have undergone very careful and extended examination during the present century. The attention bestowed upon this class arises not so much from their inherent beauty or interest, as from the abundance of their fossil remains, and the value of their shells in determining the relative ages of the strata in which they occur.

The divisions of Linnæus in this department were few and imperfect, and his genera were subsequently greatly subdivided and increased in number, by Lamarck. More recently the system itself has been greatly changed. The shell, or external skeleton is no longer made the basis of classification, since it was found that this principle classed together animals whose structure and habits were entirely distinct. The organization of the animal itself furnishes now the basis of a system which bears the mark of Cuvier's master hand.

The existing species numbered about 6,000 in 1840, and more are continually coming to light.

Radiata.—The remaining branch of zoology, the radiata, has been perhaps less investigated than either of the others. Recently, however, it has begun to receive more attention. The corals have been arranged anew by Prof. Dana, of the United States Exploring Expedition, in his Report, and a vast number of new species added, many more indeed than were previously known. M. Agassiz, too, is engaged in an investigation of them in our Atlantic waters, and on the Florida coast.

Articulata.—This branch of natural history has been greatly indebted to Cuvier's arrangement, which was subsequently carried out by several naturalists of distinction. Latreille developed an admirable natural system, in which the group is separated into the three great families of crustacea, arachnides, and insecta.

Anatomical investigation has alone rendered this division practicable; and it is incredible to what an extent this branch of study has been carried. The anatomy of a single caterpillar occupied Lyonnet ten years; and Strauss ascertained 494 muscles, 24 pair of nerves, and 300 pieces of the outer envelope, in a cockchafer, of an inch in length. Cuvier stated that, in 1827, naturalists were already becoming frightened at the vast number of species in entomology. They numbered then 50,000, and some thirty years were thought requisite for a minute acquaintance with even their external forms. Now the number is raised to 300,000,—by far the largest in any department of science, and it is impossible to tell where the increase will end.

It will be perceived, from the brief sketch that we have presented, that scientific investigation has been active and earnest in every year of the half-century just past. Philosophical knowledge has advanced in every direction, and in many branches in directions previously inconceivable. Amid movements so extended and so peculiar, it must be a question of deep interest to the Christian: "How is all this accumulation of knowledge to bear upon the religious faith of the world?" To this, it is believed, an answer may be given more favorable and with greater confidence than in respect to any similar development in previous ages. Vast as the body of science now is, it is in almost every great department thoroughly Christian in its radical principles, and in the sincerest and deepest convictions of those by whose labors it has been formed. There is no greater name, and there are no higher achievements in modern science, than those of Cuvier; and his highest efforts were made under the control and by the inspiration of a belief in an intelligent and beneficent God. The principle of all his astonishing restorations was, that each peculiarity of an animal form was designed to subserve an end to enable it to fulfil what he designated as "the conditions of its existence:" and for the scientific validity and value of this principle he strenuously contended against the opposing school of St. Hilaire, who refused to allow the principle of final causes. His achievements have vindicated his method, and shown that the belief of an all-wise Author of Nature lies at the bottom of all sound scientific investigation.

The eminent leaders of science in other lands have shared this belief, and no highly distinguished name among the students of nature seeks now to place Science in conflict with Revelation. The vast array of facts and laws which make up science as it is, Christianity has already so far assimilated to itself, that no apprehension is now felt in respect to the issue of any debated questions in their bearing upon either the Evangelical or the Mosaic history. Nay, many among the most ardent and conspicuous cultivators of science count it among their highest duties and delights to reconcile all apparently conflicting developments of Science and of Faith, and pursue their investigations to promote at once the happiness of man and the glory of God.

Starting from such principles and moving for such ends, science could not fail to create results of the highest interest and moment in practical life, and these, it will be our endeavor to sketch, in the next two or three chapters.

SECTION XIV.

MORAL ASPECTS OF SCIENCE.

The history of science presents an aspect towards religious truth which contrasts very strongly with that which it wore in the last century. Much that was most eminent in the science of that age presented itself in the attitude of open hostility to Revelation. "Astronomical records have been fabricated or misrepresented," says a writer,* at the beginning of this century, "for the purpose of discrediting the sacred chronology; the natural history of the earth and man investigated to disprove the Scripture; Chemistry, to find Materialism and deny a first cause; and Moral and Political Philosophy to strike at evangelical truth." It was characterized, not exclusively indeed, but in very great part as "an age of infidel Philosophy."

The more complete and scientific form which knowledge has taken, in our day, has totally reversed the character of science in this respect. More extended investigation has harmonized many seeming discrepancies, and science in every branch proffers support to the Gospel in its relations to nature and history. The materialism of former days has given place to a more spiritual philosophy, and atheism and infidelity find, when undisguised, few reputable advocates. Ethnology and ethnography, the natural history of the human race and of human language, already indicate the original connection of all the languages,

* Dr. Miller, in his Retrospect.

and the original unity of all the varieties of mankind. Moral sentiment assumes a far higher place in the philosophical speculations which are current with the present generation.

Geology,—the most comprehensive of all the modern sciences, and also perhaps the most popular, which, in the crude state in which it was a century ago, offered many objections to the Bible, has decided many such questions in favor of revealed truth,—has been carried to its present height by names as eminent for their Christian faith as for their scientific attainments, —and interests some of its most ardent votaries in efforts to establish a yet more complete harmony with the Word of God. Even the scientific speculations, which are hostile to Scripture, are seldom presented as such. The hold which the Bible has at length gained upon the mass of each great class of society forbids such writers to indulge the hope of any speedy acceptance of views which are seen to be at variance with it.

Such an achievement as this Christianity has never before accomplished in this field. The body of science has already become very vast. Many conclusions are firmly established, and many minds in the most distant moral conditions are ceaselessly philosophizing on the facts thus ascertained. The thorough Christianizing of such a development of human thought, extending over the whole field of man and nature, is wonderful. Much remains yet to be accomplished; but Christians can approach the task, however great it may be, or may become, with the confidence derived from numberless victories in the same field. The promise is as hopeful for the future as the progress has been great in the past. From this progress there is reason to hope that all real truth shall yet vindicate and sustain Divine Truth; that all the science and the wisdom of the world shall do homage to the infinite wisdom and knowledge of God, and that all the benevolence and humanity of society shall acknowledge their obligations to that love of God in the Gospel, which is their only efficient source.

CHAPTER VI.

APPLIED SCIENCE.

SECTION I.

MEDICINE.

In none of the practical applications of science have greater improvements been effected in the course of the period under review than in Medicine. Until the concluding years of the last century medicine was disfigured by theories of a kind altogether unscientific, which referred the phenomena of life and disease to "animal spirits," "humors," &c. This tendency gave place to a more just system of observation and reasoning in which many eminent minds participated, among whom Cullen and Hunter were particularly distinguished.

Chemistry has wrought important changes in medical practice; it has enabled the physician to obtain the active principle of a vegetable substance in a more condensed form—an effect exemplified in morphine, quinine, and strychnine, &c. Metallic preparations, too, are now obtained with far more ease and certainty; and the recent methods enable us to combine them without impairing, and even so as to increase, their activity. Iodine was discovered in 1813, and bromine in 1826, and both were brought into use in France.

To Liebig and the German chemists we are indebted for much valuable information in respect to the changes which take place in the blood and air in many important vital actions, such as the change of venous into arterial blood, the phenomena of respiration, the maintenance of heat, &c.

One of the earliest and most distinct improvements of this era, is the elucidation of those fundamental questions in Physiology relating to the theory of disease, which has been furnished by investigating the causes of sudden death. The first clear and precise information on these points is due to the labors of Bichat. He referred all the causes of death to the brain, the lungs, and the heart,—designating these organs as the Tripod of life. Though it is seldom in disease that life ceases in so simple a manner as in the instances of violent death, yet the scientific treatment of disease has owed much to the clear ideas thus obtained in Pathology. It is now fully understood, that all causes of sudden death act by arresting the flow of arterial blood through the system.

In physiology a host of ardent laborers have furnished most important additions to science. Andral, Wagner, and Jones have investigated with success, the blood in different states of health and disease. The vital action of the heart has been elucidated by Hope, Williams, and others; while the processes of nutrition, secretion, &c., have received important illustration from the experiments of Dutrochet. Much light has been thrown upon the ultimate structure of organic substances, particularly in respect to the general tendency of substances which are the result of vital action to assume the form of globules, or cells.

In the anatomy of disease some great improvements have been effected, which have afforded materials for more correct reasoning upon the nature of diseases, and given increased precision to the rules of medical practice. The investigation of *organic* diseases, or those dependent upon permanent alterations of structure, has been fruitful of useful results, as the knowledge of their predisposing and exciting causes affords a means of often preventing their occurrence. This remark is strikingly illustrated by the ingenious application of acoustics for determining diseases of the chest, which we owe to Laennec. He originated *auscultation*,—a method in which these diseases are discriminated with great certainty, by means of the sounds of the organs of the thorax. This method, though carried very far by the inventor of it, has been greatly improved since. The name of an American, Dr. Jackson, of Boston, is honorably connected with perhaps the most important addition to it,—the discovery of one of the earliest indications of consumption.

Our own country has furnished a number of the observers to whose labors the advance of medical science has been owing. Hosack, Physick, Dewees, Chapman, Horner, Warren, have contributed in an important degree to its progress. The introduction of anæsthetic agents into surgical operations took place in Boston, in 1846. The first surgical operation upon a patient rendered thus insensible to pain, was performed by Dr. J. C. Warren, Oct. 17, 1846. The discovery gave a great impulse to investigation in this direction, and a new agent was discovered by Simpson, of Edinburgh, in 1847, to possess the same property of producing temporary insensibility—chloroform. It is now generally adopted in such operations in preference to the sulphuric ether originally employed. The chloroform is itself an original American discovery, which was brought into medical use as a diffusible stimulant, by Prof. Silliman, of New Haven, before its accurate determination by the French chemist, Dumas, in 1835.

There have been a number of particular improvements in medical science within this period, limited in their scope, but exceedingly important. Among these is the general acceptance of vaccination, which, though proposed in 1798, by Jenner, came into general use not till some years later. Its universal prevalence has banished from every well-regulated community one of the most dreadful of diseases. The United States Government has widely disseminated it among the Indian tribes of the continent; and American Missionaries have introduced it successfully into the remote East Indies, at quite a recent day.

Another of these improvements consists in the new treatment of Insanity. This consists in the substitution of uniform kindness for bolts and bars—in moral restraint instead of stripes and fetters—in surrounding the patient with new and pleasing associations, &c. A great number of important facts have been ascertained which facilitate the cure of the disease; such as the early symptoms, the distinctions between the different kinds of insanity, the causes which induced it, &c. Under the extended observation and improved methods of the new system, the number of cures has increased from 30 per cent., which was nearly the average number at the commencement of this century, to more than 60, in our best institutions. The very early attention to the disease promises yet happier results than these; as in some instances 82½ per cent. of *recent* cases have been restored to mental health.

The frequency of insanity is found to bear a direct ratio to the advancement of civilization; it is always greater in the more cultivated communities. While it is in most instances attributable to some form of moral disorder, of sin, the religious sentiment is sometimes closely connected with it; a circumstance which has led some persons to believe that religion is to be considered a frequent cause of it. That this view is erroneous is evident from two facts: one, that a legitimate and judicious influence of the gospel is an essential means of recovery; the other, that M. Esquirol, the highest French authority, referring to its increased frequency after the wild changes of their First Revolution, says, "The changes in our *moral sentiments* and habits have produced more instances of madness than all our political calamities." The moral restraints of a sound and efficient religious training has thus been determined to constitute one of the most important preventives of insanity, in the grandest series of experiments which society has yet witnessed.

Medicine has owed its improvement to the co-operation of a great number of laborers in many lands. France, Germany Italy, England, our own country, each has contributed a host of writers and observers, whose united efforts have amassed a very great body of facts. Among these the French philosophers are more eminent in pathology, in pharmaceutical chemistry, and in anatomy. The Germans are chiefly distinguished in physiology and anatomy, and more recently in organic chemistry. The English, and with them our own physicians, in medical practice. There are fewer useless articles retained, and more decision judgment and success in the use of remedies, in the American and English practice than among any other class of physicians.

The progress of medical science displays some very gratifying results. We observe a constant increase in the average term of human life, which is attributable in great part to such improvements. The annual average of deaths, too, has been constantly diminishing for 150 to 200 years. The following table will indicate briefly this result:—

The proportion of deaths was annually,

In England,	1690,	as 1 to 33.	In	1848,	as	1 to 47.
" France,	1776,	" 1 " 25.	"	1848,	"	1 " 42.
" Germany,	1778,	" 1 " 32.	"	1848,	"	1 " 42.
" London,	1690,	" 1 " 24.	"	1844,	"	1 " 44.
" Paris,	1650,	" 1 " 25.	"	1820,	"	1 " 32.

The same result is strikingly indicated by a recent statement of Baron Dupin made to the French Academy, in respect to the mortality of children during the first five years of life. At the end of the XVIIIth century only 5,832, out of 10,000 survived five years, on a general average; whereas, in 1850, 7,292, out of even the *least favored* classes, reach the sixth year. In the first half of the last century only 6,695 out of 10,000 attained that age from the more fortunate classes.

It must not be supposed, that the whole of such improvement is due to the control of active disease. On the contrary, a large proportion of it undoubtedly arises from the improved knowledge of the causes of disease, and the conditions of health; and disease is thus prevented perhaps as often as it is cured.

Medical schools have contributed greatly both to the creation and to the diffusion of juster views in this department. The English institutions could scarcely be said to afford the means of a complete medical education, till the establishment of the London University, and the King's College. In our own country such institutions have multiplied with great—perhaps *too* great rapidity. The one or two which existed at the beginning of this century, have increased to more than thirty.

Medical publications have become quite numerous, and embody a vast amount of facts and reasonings of high value. Those of Paris are particularly distinguished; while London is excelled in this respect by both Edinburgh and Dublin.

The history of medical improvement during the period under review presents some striking moral lessons. The occurrence of the yellow fever at the close of the last century in our northern ports, and its dreadful prevalence during the first quarter of this century in Spain; the occurrence of the cholera in 1832–4, and again in 1848; the diseases connected with the famine of 1846–7 in Ireland, and with the vast emigration that was consequent upon it,—all point with very great directness and force to the importance of the moral condition of a people to their physical health and prosperity. In respect to the first-named of these diseases, a memoir read to the French Academy, by Audouard, presents a striking view of the origin of that terrible pestilence. The author, who had witnessed the last two epidemics of yellow fever in Spain, in 1821, at Barcelona and the *Port du Passage*, inferred the origination of this disorder from the filth generated in the holds of crowded slave-ships, and afterwards subjected to the heat of the sun. This suggestion was made to the authorities of those ports, in 1824, and the strict guard which has since been maintained in all the ports of Spain, against vessels which had been engaged in that trade, has prevented its recurrence there since that date. In twenty-eight years previous this scourge had carried off 140,000 of the inhabitants, and the single great epidemic of 1800, 60,000 in Andalusia alone. The northern states of this union have been almost exempt from it since the prohibition of the slave trade. Should this view of the subject be correct, how terrible a retribution has this monstrous wrong inflicted upon the Christian communities which tolerated and practised the African slave trade!

The cholera, too, in its repeated visits, gives new demonstration of the physical importance and value of sound morals, and humane social arrangements. It has prevailed in every community in exact proportion to the degradation, physical and moral, which it found there. Wherever the ordinary laws of health in respect to cleanliness, diet, and exposure were seriously violated, there the disease found victims; and wherever the crowded haunts of vice added to these violations of moral law, in intemperance and licentiousness, there it almost depopulated the locality. The errors and vices of society show thus their fatal influence upon social prosperity and welfare. The generation of disease in depraved and degraded vicinities afflicts, with something of similar force, the more elevated neighborhoods around, and shows us how great an interest the wealthy and favored classes have in the moral and social improvement of the destitute and wretched. Both must prosper, and both must suffer in sympathy with each other.

The woes of Ireland point, with equal distinctness, to the moral condition of the people as their most efficient cause. Doubtless, oppressive civil and social arrangements have had much influence; but even these have derived their power in great part from the extremely rapid multiplication of an ignorant and debased population, one million of whom have perished within a few years. The moral elevation which refuses to assume the responsibilities of the conjugal and parental character without some adequate provision in prospect—without some home and some assured support—would have saved Ireland from her heaviest sufferings. On every hand we are assured by the progress of events, that each form of wrong and each indulgence of human depravity works its bitter retribution of suffering upon the offending people that perpetrates or connives at it. Providence is more and more displaying the importance in all the disclosures of history of man's moral nature,—the existence and the evil of human depravity—and the priceless value of that Gospel which furnishes our only means of combating and subduing sin, and its indispensable necessity to the temporal as well as the eternal benefit of mankind.

SECTION II.

AGRICULTURE.

Agriculture constitutes another prominent application of the sciences so important in medicine. Both relate to living objects, and chemistry and physiology, not to speak of other branches of science, occupy the front rank among the causes which it is important to understand in each.

Much thought had been bestowed by the beginning of our era upon the general facts of agriculture,—principally, however, in the way of simple observation. Very little had then been done, or even attempted in the investigation of causes, or even of the less obvious laws of agricultural phenomena.

Attention had been attracted to the value of particular varieties of animals, as the Merino sheep and the hornless cow; but such varieties were few. Varieties of fruits and vegetables were better known. Some analyses of woods and grains of various kinds were made early in this century; but the imperfection of vegetable chemistry rendered them necessarily defective. The principles on which plants are nourished were almost unknown, and the practice of renovating soils by fallowing;—that is, by leaving the soil unoccupied to recover from its exhaustion—was almost universal among practical agriculturists.

One of the earliest scientific efforts for the improvement of agriculture was made by Sir H. Davy, who delivered a course of lectures annually, from 1802 to 1812, before the Board of Agriculture. They were published in 1814, and contain much that is still deemed valuable. He investigated vegetable chemistry and physiology, and made some useful analyses of soils, manures, &c., and also to some extent of the ashes of plants. The low state of this department of knowledge in the early part of this century may be judged from the fact, that this was the only work upon agricultural chemistry which was published in England in a period of forty years. The importance of ammonia to the growth of plants was at that time unknown, and Davy speaks of its use as probably efficacious in repelling insects. The value of nitrogen, too, was not discovered till a later day. Yet his work contains many valuable records of experiment and observation, some of which were on quite an extended scale.

The progress of chemical analysis has established a great distinction between the organic and the inorganic substances of which all plants are composed. The former are the compounds formed by the agency of living organs,—the latter are generally of earthy or mineral substances. The organic portion amounts generally to from 75 to 99 per cent. of their whole weight in the dry state. It consists almost exclusively of *four* elements in various states of combination,—carbon, oxygen, hydrogen, and nitrogen. Of *living* plants oxygen is found to constitute one half the weight. In the dry state, carbon approaches one half the whole weight; oxygen one third; hydrogen amounts to 20 per cent.; and nitrogen to about 2 per cent. The combinations of these elements in various proportions form a very numerous body of organic compounds, on the investigation of which great labor has been bestowed. We have already specified these results under the head of chemistry.

The great predominance in amount of these organic substances, and the very small proportion of the incombustible and mineral elements, for a long time led to an erroneous estimate of the importance of the latter. It was long supposed that the substances remaining after the organic portion of the plant had been burned away, were, doubtless, derived from the soil accidentally, and were too inconsiderable to affect materially either the growth or luxuriance of the plant itself. Careful and repeated experiments, however, showed that the quantity and the quality of this ash were nearly identical in the same species of plant, however various the soil might be, and that the ash of one species was separated by a marked and constant distinction of its elements from that of every other.

This view of the constancy of the inorganic portion of plants has shed new light upon every branch of agriculture. The establishment of it is due to Sprengel. It explains the relation which subsists between the nature of the crop and the chemical composition of the soil, the manner in which some crops impoverish land, and some manures enrich it, and showing that the plant is nourished in part by these mineral substances, it suggests numerous and most valuable agricultural processes.

This development of the general nature of the inorganic composition of plants has led to a vast number of analyses of vegetable products. Each of the cereal grains has been thus examined, and its mineral elements ascertained with the nicety which results from oft-repeated and exact experiments. The grains of different soils, and of different varieties of the various parts of the plant—the straw, the husk, the grain—the wood of our different kinds of fruit and forest trees—in all stages of its growth and from all parts of the tree—these have been the subjects of innumerable analyses. The result has been the discovery of the exact mineral composition of these substances, and a knowledge of the ingredients which require to be supplied to the soil to enable it to produce freely any desired crop. In consequence of these discoveries, it is now practicable to calculate accurately the amount of any mineral substance removed from an acre of land by any particular crop, and to ascertain thus what kind and amount of manure must be supplied to the soil to maintain its capacity. Such at least are the views of Prof. Johnson, though other British authorities place by no means so high an estimate upon these discoveries of the inorganic constituents of plants. The mineral manures, prepared and patented by Liebig, to afford by slow decomposition the supply which crops require, failed to answer the very high expectations which had been formed of their value.

Since the discovery of the chemical constitution of plants, agricultural science has been advancing with great rapidity. Animal chemistry, too, and physiology have been brought into striking and beautiful relations with agriculture.

One of the most interesting of these is the discovery of Liebig, that the flesh of animals is not formed in the process of digesting food, but exists antecedently in the food itself. The albumen, gluten, and casein, which chemistry detects in our cultivated grains, are identical in composition with the principle of the muscular fibre.

The discovery of a large proportion of nitrogen in fibrin or animal muscle has led to a different appreciation of the articles of food in which this element abounds, and this again has given a new value to the various articles which supply nitrogen as a manure.

The progress of knowledge in this respect is remarkable. In 1814, Davy pronounced fallowing altogether useless; but experience confirmed the common belief of its advantage. Later, De Candolle supposed that the roots of a plant might excrete some substances injurious to the same crop if immediately repeated, but useful to others, and that these latter might prepare the former again. This, however, is without any support from careful observation. It is now ascertained that the ammonia of the atmosphere is brought down by the rain, and absorbed by porous soils; that this is one of the principal fertilizers; and that the benefit of this restorative process can, by a judicious application of our knowledge of the chemistry of plants, be attained without the loss of a single season.

Such investigations have been prosecuted with great interest by several eminent chemists, among whom we may mention Boursingault and Payen in France, Mulder in Holland, Liebig in Germany, and Johnston, Kane, and Anderson in England. The results of their labors have been in many instances of marked value, and have raised greatly the general average of returns from agricultural labor in Europe. It is estimated, by Sir J. Sinclair and Radcliffe, that on lands long cultivated, and now renovated by the new agriculture, the average production is as follows:—

	Wheat.	Oats.	Potatoes.	
In England, per acre, .	28,	58,	350	bushels.
" Scotland, " .	32,	56,	400	"
" Flanders, " .	32,	52,	350	"

The average of American production on old lands is greatly inferior. It is estimated that in Duchess and Columbia counties of New York, the corresponding amounts are 15 bushels of wheat, 30 of oats, and 150 of potatoes. A very recent and exact census, however, of Seneca county, indicates a decided improvement,—the average of the wheat crop being 20 bushels to the acre, and the better class of farms reaching 25 bushels.

At the present time there is every indication of most rapid improvement. The public mind in Europe and America is becoming very fully alive to the importance of Agricultural Education. Almost every European country has established schools of instruction in scientific and practical agriculture. They amount now to 22 superior institutions, 54 intermediary, and 14 connected with universities, besides some hundreds of primary schools devoted to this branch. Two of our Legislatures have taken up the subject, and plans are under consideration for efficient institutions in New York and Massachusetts, to be supported by the State. Probably four fifths of the European institutions have come into existence within the last seven years.

The numerous agricultural societies which now exist have diffused intelligence, and awakened interest on this subject very widely. The field of science involved in intelligent agricultural labors is very extensive. Besides the chemical and physiological investigations of which we have spoken, geology must pronounce upon the soil, physical geography upon the climate, and natural history in its various branches must indicate the characters of the plants, animals, insects, &c., with which agriculture has to do. The subject has already attracted attention in several of our institutions of learning,—and when institutions of high grade shall be devoted to instruction and investigation on this subject, we may hope for a more general diffusion of education, and an elevation of the agricultural community, as well as a more profitable working of the soil.

It is one of the hopeful indications of our age, that society is becoming aware of the pecuniary loss which is inevitably connected with an ignorant and degraded state of the laboring population. The value of intelligence and thought—of the elevated character and sound morality which these alone can diffuse through the masses of a State, is beginning to be deeply felt. This public appreciation of the value of education has received both a new impulse and a new direction from the recent discoveries in agriculture. The superiority of skilled and instructed labor is now widely acknowledged; and this fact promises to awaken an interest in public education in those secluded rural districts, into which other influences do not easily penetrate. The scientific aspect which practical agriculture is daily more and more assuming, supplies a new impulse to the cause of education among the class which must ever be the most numerous and influential, as well as, perhaps, the least accessible in any State.

SECTION III.

APPLIED SCIENCE: TELEGRAPHS.

Another of the prominent applications of science is found in the modern system of telegraphic communication. The discovery of electro-magnetism, and the development of a class of phenomena which obviously were capable of being used as signals from points somewhat distant, created a very general interest in such an application of them. Many inquirers were soon engaged upon the problem thus set before them. Some doubts however yet hung over the subject at one or two points. It was doubtful, for instance, whether the phenomena observed in the laboratory could be relied upon when the apparatus should become very extended. This question suggested itself to Barlow, who undertook some experiments for the purpose of determining it. He satisfied himself that with a length of 200 feet of wire in his galvanic circuit, the power was dissipated so rapidly as to preclude the probability of using it for telegraphic purposes at any distance. His account of these experiments was published in the Edinburgh Philosophical Journal for 1825.

His conclusions were re-examined by Prof. Henry, now of

Washington, who succeeded in obtaining an opposite result. He announced in Silliman's Journal for 1831, that the magnetic action of a current is not diminished by passing through a long wire; and that this fact "is directly applicable to Mr. Barlow's project of forming a telegraph," &c. Prof. H. also determined that with a long wire a battery of a number of plates was necessary to give projectile force; the neglect of which had probably occasioned Barlow's error.

These facts being established, the ingenuity of many inventive minds was tasked to contrive some practical application of them; and the result has been the invention of several systems of telegraphing, which have already come into extensive use. Prof. Morse was engaged in such efforts as early as 1832; and the English system of Cooke and Wheatstone was formed not long after.

Oersted's experiments in electro-magnetism, disclosed several phenomena of that subject which might be employed for distant communications. The fact was ascertained, for instance, that the passage of the galvanic current, through a wire extending from one to the other of the poles of a battery, deflects a magnetic needle placed near, and parallel, to it, into a position at right angles to the wire. It was found too that the direction of the poles of the magnetic needle is decided by the direction of the current in the wire, and that the north pole of the magnet could thus be made to turn either to the East or the West, at the will of the operator. Two needles thus arranged constitute the indicating apparatus of the English telegraph. An operator controlling a galvanic battery in London, deflects, by means of a wire extending to Edinburgh, a needle at the latter station; and the different combinations of two such needles constitute a conventional alphabet. To call the attention of the correspondent at a distant station, another application of the same agent is made to ring a bell. The instrument however does not form any permanent record of the messages transmitted through it.

In this respect it is altogether inferior to the several American systems, each of which accomplishes this desideratum.

By far the most simple and practical system, however, is that of Prof. Morse. This was perfected in 1838 and 1839, and brought into use by aid of an appropriation from Congress, in 1843. It employs a different property of the electro-magnetic fluid. The passage of an electric current through a coil of wire, communicates magnetism to a piece of soft iron in the center of that coil,—an effect which instantly ceases upon the interruption of the current. Thus a coil of wire in New York properly connected with a battery in Philadelphia constitutes a piece of iron placed within the coil, a magnet; and causes it to attract a small bar of iron near it. This latter is connected with a lever, by which as often as the bar is attracted a steel point is pressed upon a strip of paper which is moved past it by machinery at a regular rate. Dots and lines are thus impressed upon the paper which constitute a permanent record of the communication.

A modification of this apparatus has been devised which gives it great efficiency. The power derived from the original battery, distant perhaps 100 miles from the spot where the communication is to be recorded, is in great part lost from the imperfect insulation of the wires through which it passes; and the residue is too weak to impress the characters with sufficient force upon the paper register. To remedy this inconvenience the main battery is combined at each receiving station with another, which performs the work of registering. The local battery is worked by the main battery; which latter is confined to the office of closing and breaking a galvanic circuit. This requires only so small an expenditure of power that a single main battery is able to complete the circuits of a great many local ones, on a long line of communication, and thus to record the same message in many distinct places at a single transmission. This valuable improvement was patented by Davy, an English inventor in 1839. Though not much employed in that country it is very extensively used in our own; and contributes greatly to the superior efficacy of the American Telegraphs.

Other applications of the same power have been employed for the same purpose. One of these depends upon electro-chemical, instead of electro-magnetic, agency. The electric current has the power of decomposing certain salts. In this system of telegraphing, it is caused to pass through a fabric chemically prepared in accordance with this property. The decomposition of the salt, at the precise point where the current passes through it, is indicated with surprising distinctness, by an instantaneous change of color. This principle, which is that employed in Bain's telegraph, formed also a part of Davy's patent. The beautiful arrangement through which the communication is, in this system, recorded by the spiral movement of a wire upon a circular disk, is believed to be due to Prof. Mitchell, of Cincinnati.

One of the most finished and elegant inventions for this purpose, is that of House's *printing* telegraph. In this, the ordinary letters of the alphabet are arranged on the circumference of a wheel, to which a very rapid motion is given, by means of condensed air. The electric agency interrupts the revolution, at the will of the operator of a distant station; and the letter which he thus selects is instantly printed, by an ingenious mechanical arrangement. The machinery, though extremely ingenious, is yet somewhat complicated, and of course, liable to some derangements. It operates, however, with great celerity,—distinctly printing, when working at the maximum rate, 3,000 words an hour. It is in use upon three main lines, extending from New York to Boston, Buffalo, and Philadelphia. Other lines are in progress in numerous directions; and among them one from New York to St. Louis.

The lines upon which Morse's instruments are used, extend almost over the whole country, and connect all the principal towns of the Union. Their total length is about 15,000 miles;

and they extend without interruption, from Halifax to New Orleans, and thence to Galena, and to New York again.

In no other country do telegraphs reach the same extent, and in no other are they in such free and constant use. In England there are about 2,000 miles of telegraph, and the cost of its erection is stated to be £150 per mile. The cost of the American lines is only one fifth of this amount. The high cost, together with the slower working of the English system, which does not exceed 1,200 words per hour, makes it more expensive than ours. The limited distances, too, of that country, the rapidity of railroad communication, and the cheapness and swiftness of the mail, render it less important to them. One of its chief uses, indeed, in England, is for railroad signals, which are rendered necessary by the extreme speed at which their express trains travel. In many instances, an explicit provision is inserted by the government, in the charter of a railroad company, requiring the construction of a telegraph upon the line, for such purposes. Some of those roads it would be absolutely impossible to operate without it. The cost of messages in England is from 8 to 16 cents per word; the cost in America is from 2 to 10 cents a word. This maximum rate pays for the transmission of messages from New York to New Orleans.

This great cheapness of communication leads to a very extended employment of the telegraph. Reports of the state of the market are daily exchanged between the great cities and the interior towns; foreign news is telegraphed, on the arrival of each steamer, from Boston or New York, to Washington and New Orleans; important proceedings of Congress are instantly despatched to every part of the country. Such despatches are generally paid for by associations of the newspapers of each city. In this way the President's annual message has been telegraphed at once to 17 distinct stations, on the line of 325 miles from New York to Buffalo; and more recently, from Philadelphia to St. Louis and Galena—with only the interval of half an hour. Communications of public interest are constantly traversing these extended wires. The exigencies, too, which arise out of the commercial transactions, and domestic relations, of individuals, require this rapid intercourse between distant points, and afford constant occupation to several distinct lines.

In Prussia, some 1400 miles of electric telegraph are in operation. The wire is there generally enclosed in tubes, and buried in the ground, some of that portion which was exposed having been destroyed by the populace in the recent political disturbances. It is first protected by a coat of gutta percha, which affords the most perfect insulation of the wires yet attainable. In England the whole telegraphic system of the country is monopolized by a single company. In America many private companies are occupied in working the various lines. On the continent of Europe the governments either retain the apparatus in their own hands, or rigidly superintend and control its operation. The statistics of European telegraphs are scarcely accessible yet in this country. The instruments generally used there are those of Prof. Morse.

The same general system of arrangements has been applied with great success to the determination of some important scientific questions. The instantaneous transmission of intelligence enables observers at two distant points to communicate with each other absolutely at the same instant; and this circumstance obviously affords the means of signalizing at distant points the precise moment at which any astronomical fact takes place. The transit of a star over the meridian at Boston can be signalized in New York at the very moment of its occurrence; and its subsequent transit, a few minutes later, over the meridian of the latter place affords another opportunity of comparing the two. By very numerous comparisons of this kind the differences of longitude of many of our principal cities have been determined with a degree of accuracy unattainable by any methods previously known. The astronomical observatories of Washington, Philadelphia, New York, and Cambridge, were connected by telegraphic arrangements, and their relative positions thus ascertained, in 1847 and 1848. Within the two years subsequent to these, the same system has been extended as far as Cincinnati and Charleston.

An astronomical clock invented by Dr. Locke, of Cincinnati, which acts upon the same principles of electro-magnetism, gives great facility to sidereal observations. A telegraphic communication being effected between several stations, the clock breaks and closes a galvanic circuit simultaneously in them all. The beats of the clock can be thus observed at all the stations, and the occurrence of any astronomical event simultaneously recorded. The extreme rapidity with which the record can be made, permits the observer to register many more observations within the same time than before. Prof. Loomis considers the value of a year's labor with the telegraphic system of recording to be seven-fold that of the former method.

Arrangements have also been devised for regulating by similar means the public clocks of a city. Such a plan invented by Mr. Speed, of Detroit, makes all the public clocks mark the hours with absolute uniformity. By similar means the clocks of any number of railway termini in a city, or at distant stations, may be brought to a uniform time; and a clock for purposes of this kind has been patented by Bain.

The period is yet too short,—seven years only having elapsed since the first successful telegraph was established,—for any full disclosure of the moral influence of this strange and remarkable class of phenomena. It has given a stimulus and a certainty to commercial operations, and facilitates and extends trade. Already it serves as a most important auxiliary in the administration of justice, and in consequence of its active and far-reaching agency, crime has fewer chances of escaping punishment.

But the applications of this power are yet only in their commencement. The report of the Patent Office announces the forthcoming of numerous inventions which will multiply its agency, and we cannot doubt that the next half-century will enrol electricity in its various forms among the active promoters of the civilization and welfare of mankind.

CHAPTER VII.

PROGRESS IN THE ARTS OF INTERCOMMUNICATION.

SECTION I.

STEAM NAVIGATION.

THE arts of locomotion have attained a development which seems as much as any other peculiarity characteristic of the present age. The first great improvement of this kind was the introduction of steamboats.

At various periods in the last century, efforts were made to apply the power of this recently discovered agent to the purposes of transportation by water; and the names of Hull in 1737—Miller, in 1787—and Symington, in 1801—who were the chief English experimenters, and of Evans, in 1768—Fitch, in 1784—and Rumsey, in 1785, equally distinguished in America, will ever deserve honorable mention.

The practical application of steam for this purpose however it was reserved for Fulton to achieve; and his boat, the Clermont, made the first trip on the waters of the Hudson in 1807, since which time steam navigation has never ceased. Though the idea was familiar long before his time, Fulton is undoubtedly entitled to the full credit of having perfectly accomplished this end, and that too in the face of the general distrust and contempt which the failure of all previous attempts had cast upon the enterprise. The first voyage, which was made to Albany in 32 hours, having demonstrated the triumph of perseverance and skill over obstacles so long insurmountable, Fulton proceeded to construct other boats, under a monopoly from the State of New York for the navigation by steam of her waters. Improvements were rapidly effected in the construction and working of these boats, until river navigation reached on this original theatre of its success a point which is perhaps not far below its absolute climax. The boats of the Hudson have been from the first hour, the models of such navigation on the Atlantic rivers. Their size and power have constantly increased till they now reach a length of 375 feet with a breadth of 35; and attain an average speed of 18 miles per hour, which is capable of being increased to 20 or 22 miles. The newest of these boats, the New World, has a cylinder of 76 inches in diameter and fifteen feet stroke; it is worked with 40 lbs. pressure in the boiler with the steam cut off at half stroke. The wheels are forty-five feet in diameter, and make sixteen revolutions per minute. According to Dr. Lardner's calculations, she may be estimated at 2,640 horse power.

The new invention possessed a most striking applicability to the wants of the new world in which it originated; and spread rapidly throughout the country. The Atlantic streams were soon alive with vessels; and the great lakes of the North began to be traversed by them. Ere long the steam paddle vexed the waters of the Mississippi and its tributaries; and penetrated into the vast and silent forests of the mighty West, at once the product and the precursor of the civilization which providence had prepared for them. The first boat on the Western waters was built by Fulton at Pittsburgh, in 1812. The Mississippi was first navigated by steam in 1815; and 28 days were required for the voyage from New Orleans to Cincinnati. The first steamboat on the Missouri was in 1817.

The aggregate number of steamboats is now estimated at 2000, and their aggregate capacity at 500,000 tons. They have pushed their way almost to the remotest navigable rivers of the continent, bearing population and commerce with them. Since the Mexican war, the Rio Grande has steamboats—since the California discoveries the Lake Nicaragua is provided with one, for the transportation of passengers across from ocean to ocean. They have been recently introduced into South American waters, from this country.

In October 1849 the first steamboat began her trips upon the inland waters of California; by the close of the next year they numbered 47—varying from 20 to 800 tons each.

The invention thus achieved in America, was speedily imported into England; and boats were soon established upon the principal rivers and coasts of Great Britain. The first was the Comet, which plied for passengers upon the Clyde in 1811. It was some time however before they were adopted upon the continent of Europe. It was not till 1816 that steamboats sailed up the Seine to Paris. The first steamboats constructed in France were built by American enterprise; and plied upon the Garonne, in 1818. In 1822 steam navigation was established upon the Loire, and a year or two earlier upon the lake of Geneva. It has continued to spread till every European river and every European sea, is traversed now by steam.

The maritime character of the British waters soon impressed a change upon their steam navigation, and the *Steamship* was the result. That which had, in America, been adapted and confined to the tranquil and extended rivers of this continent, now took a new adaptation, and expanded to oceanic navigation. The first steamship crossed the Irish Channel in 1818. Lines of steam-packets soon crossed the channels which separate England from Ireland and France; and a very extended system of Sea Steamers gradually connected Great Britain with every part of Europe. The first steam-vessel crossed the channel from Brighton to Havre, in 1816.

When this system had become tolerably complete, the question of crossing the Atlantic by steam, naturally suggested itself. At first the enterprise was doubtful, and to many it seemed impossible; but vessels were constructed to test the practicability of such an enterprise. In 1838, two steam-vessels, the Sirius, of Cork, and the Great Western, of Liverpool, left England for a voyage across the Atlantic. The purpose and the time of their departure was known in New York; and watchers on this side the Atlantic, who remembered the first voyage of "Fulton's Folly," hailed with delight, the dim smoke in the distance, which announced the success of the undertaking. Both vessels arrived on the 23d of April, after voyages respectively, of 18 and 15 days. This achievement signalized the first year of the reign of Victoria.

The navigation companies of Great Britain immediately ventured upon experiments for the improvement of their steam-vessels; and a gradual and almost constant success has attended the effort. The fate of the President, in 1841, of which no tidings reached either shore, and the wreck of the Great Britain, on the Irish coast, were painful and significant drawbacks; but, in the hands of Mr. Cunard, the Atlantic mail service of the British government has attained a regularity, a speed, and a safety, altogether wonderful. France and America have followed in the same career of progress. Steam-ships form part of every well-appointed navy; and the most distant shores of the earth are now visited by them. The East India Company's steamers connect all the important ports of British India with Suez. The latest English extension of the system is, from Great Britain to the Cape of Good Hope; while the Pacific shores are traversed by the American steamers. At the close of 1850, two steamships connected San Francisco with Oregon—and eleven with Panama; while thirty noble vessels linked New York with the ports of Europe, the West Indies, our Southern States, and Central America. The first American line plied to Southampton and Bremen; and the second, consisting of vessels of 300 feet long, 3,000 tons burthen, and 1,000 horse-power—

the largest, most powerful, and it is believed, the swiftest to be found in the world, connect New York and Liverpool.

Steamships have been built in England for many of the European governments, and in 1849, one was fitted out at Portsmouth, for the Pacha of Egypt. Others have been constructed in America, for the South American and Russian governments. While steam frigates of many nations occasionally cross the ocean, no regular trans-Atlantic line has been established, except those of the British and American governments, for the transmission of the mails between the two continents. These are owned by private companies, but commanded by naval officers, and are paid at a high rate for the mail service which they render. The Cunard line receives £145,000 per annum, for forty-four voyages, carrying a mail each week, except during four winter months, when it is carried once a fortnight. The Collins line receives from the United States government $383,000 per annum, for twenty voyages. These rival lines made many of their best passages in 1850 in 10 to 11 days, and their very shortest, in something less than 10 days, from port to port, across the Atlantic.

The number of British steam-vessels, in 1848, was 1,253, of 168,000 tons burthen,—one tenth of which amount was built in that year. Thirty-one sea-steamers, amounting to 42,000 tons burthen, were either wholly or partially built in our own country during the year 1850. Propellers have been recently introduced into steam-navigation, and are gaining much favor. The first very successful trial of them, was in the steamship Archimedes; and after many other attempts, the Ericson propeller was satisfactorily employed in the United States steamship, Princeton. Though not generally employed for steamships, this is becoming a favorite method of propelling boats on our inland waters. There are eight lines of propellers, numbering 22 vessels, in New York alone, besides many upon the other

Atlantic waters, and the great lakes. On the Mississippi high-pressure boats are employed exclusively.

SECTION II.

RAILROADS.

The modern railroad dates from the opening of the Liverpool and Manchester line in 1830; and is due, like so many of the modern triumphs of combined skill, capital, and enterprise, entirely to England. The advantages of the level roadway had been fully foreseen and could be definitely calculated; it had even been experimentally tested; but the value of steam as a moving power was yet undiscovered. While some deemed it impossible to use any other than stationary engines for the draught of loaded cars, others spent a vast amount of labor and ingenuity in contriving methods by which the engine might be made to move upon the rails. It was generally believed that the smooth and hard surface of the narrow rail would not allow sufficient adhesion to the wheel to enable it to draw any considerable weight; and plans, which now seem exceedingly curious, were devised to accomplish motion in some other mode. The most remarkable was one which proposed to move the car by means of iron feet, and limbs, which moved with ludicrous resemblance to the human knee. A reward however was offered by the company for the best method of applying steam power; and the mechanical skill of English engineers, gave to the world the Locomotive engine. This improvement was achieved by the distinguished engineer Robert Stevenson in 1829; and its chief peculiarity consisted in the tubular arrangement of the flues that traverse the boiler—an arrangement which has since come into universal adoption.

At this period, though high anticipations had been formed, there was no adequate idea of the amount of traffic which would pass over such a road; nor of the speed at which it would require to be transported. The rails were therefore deemed to be of ample strength at 35 lbs. the yard; and the engine and tender weighed 7½ tons. The traffic however, soon increased beyond all estimate; the possible velocity exceeded all previous expectation; and the demand of the public for augmented speed constrained every exertion to attain it. This however required an increased power, and the engines rose rapidly to 10, 12, and 15 tons. The appetite for speed continued to increase; and now one company in England owns 36 engines weighing with their tenders 40 tons each. One engine in that country weighs with its tender full freighted, about 60 tons. The average rate of speed attained in 1831 was 17 miles per hour; it gradually increased till in 1848 it was 30 miles. The speed of the fastest trains, which in 1831 was 24 miles, in 1848 was on one line 40 miles, and on two others 50 miles, per hour. In 1831 the average weight of a goods train was 52 tons—in 1848 it varied from 160 to 176 tons.

The number of trains has within the same period, and in the same country, increased from 150 to 250 per cent.; the weight of the engines increased 114 per cent.; the weight of the carriages 30 per cent.; the average speed 90, and the average weight of the trains 350 per cent.

For such increased work the rails originally employed were found totally inadequate; they were therefore taken up, and replaced by others of 62 and 65 lbs. per yard. These have since given place to yet heavier ones; 72 and 75 lbs. have been employed; and the latest rails laid down in England reach 80 lbs. and some, even 92 lbs. per yard.

The number of trains passing over the English railroads has become very great: upon the Grand Junction line it was in 1849, 38 daily; upon the London and Birmingham, 44; and upon the Liverpool and Manchester it reached 90 trains per lay.

The extreme speed of the fastest trains is not unfrequently 75 miles per hour; though it is believed that in no country except Great Britain has such a velocity been reached. According to the experiments of Dr. Hutton, the velocity of a cannon ball is 300 miles per hour—only four times as great.

The success which attended the early efforts at railway locomotion led to an immediate and rapid extension of the system throughout Great Britain. This has continued to the present time,—at some periods with a most extraordinary rapidity. The number of miles open for traffic on the 1st January, 1849, according to a report of the royal commissioners amounted to 5,007 miles; of which there were in England 3,918,—in Scotland 728,—and in Ireland 361 miles. The following table will indicate the rate at which the construction of railroads has advanced within the seven years extending from 1843 to 1849 inclusive.

	Number of miles open Jan. 1.	Miles opened during the year.
1843	1857	95
1844	1952	196
1845	2148	293
1846	2441	595
1847	3036	780
1848	3816	1191
1849	5007	

On the 1st Jan., 1849, there were in process of construction 2160 miles, the greater part of which was of course completed within that year.

The whole amount of railways authorized by Parliament up to that day was 12,012 miles; of which 5007 were open for traffic,—2160 in process of construction,—and 4800 yet to be commenced. Of this last amount, the commissioners deemed that nearly one half would never be built. If 2800 of this

4800 miles should be soon constructed, the total extent of the English railway system would be nearly 10,000 miles. Their present extent cannot be less than 6000.

Upon the construction of these roads, it appears by a parliamentary return that £200,000,000 had been actually expended; of which £156,500,000 had been paid in as capital, and £43,600,000 had been obtained as loans. To complete 2400 miles more would require an addition of £75,000,000; so that an extent of 9500 to 10,000 miles will have absorbed the sum of £275,000,000 to £300,000,000.

The average cost has been already £30,500 per mile; and, as many allowances must yet be made for unfinished roads included in this estimate, the aggregate will, it is supposed by Dr. Lardner, equal £40,000 per running mile.

The dividends upon these enormous investments have not, in some instances, been as great as it was expected that they would be, though the better class of them are sufficiently productive to pay very well. Ten of the principal lines paid, in the first six months of 1849, an average dividend of £3. 8*s.* 6*d.* per cent., and this is, perhaps, a fair indication of the average rate of the whole.

The total number of English companies amounted, in 1848, to 170; and the whole number of persons employed upon the roads was, upon those open for traffic, 52,680;—upon those in process of construction, 188,000. The total annual revenue of British railways is estimated at not less than £12,000,000,—a greater sum than the annual revenue of many important States.

The number of passengers transported by this vast system of communications is, of course, immense. The number, in 1843, was 23,468,000. The annual increase has varied from one sixth to one third, till, in 1848, it amounted in all to 58,000,000; and, by the close of 1850, to more than 60,000,000. The average distance travelled was, by first class passengers, 27 miles; by second class, 16; and by third class,

14 miles. The daily average number of passengers has increased, within the same period, from 64,000 to 160,000.

The average rate of fare, as compared with the coaches previously employed, is computed at about two fifths of the amount. The whole saving in time, expenses and fare, upon such a number of passengers is estimated at not less than £17,000,000 in two years.

The success of railway transportation on the Liverpool and Manchester line stimulated American enterprise to the earliest effort in this direction, which was made out of Great Britain. Several lines were projected between our principal cities, which were soon constructed and tested.

A very few years sufficed to bring it into practical operation in New England and New York, and, once commenced, the progress of the system was extremely rapid. As early as the year 1843, there were more than 4000 miles of railroad in operation, before any European country,—even before Great Britain itself,—possessed such communication to any similar extent.

In the year 1830, there were some short roads in existence, amounting to about 176 miles in length. They were worked, however, by horses. Steam power was first introduced upon the Mohawk and Hudson Road, in the year 1833. By the close of 1840, there were in operation 2380 miles, costing $70,000,000; in 1845, 3650 miles, costing $111,550,000; and in 1848, there were 5258 miles, at a cost of $153,420,000. At the close of 1849, there were in operation 8797 miles, at an aggregate cost of $286,500,000. The average cost is not far from $32,000 per mile.

The very great cheapness of the American roads as compared with the English, has led many to imagine that their structure is inferior, and that they must rapidly deteriorate; but this is regarded as an error.

The annual deterioration beyond ordinary repairs is less upon well-constructed roads than *one* per cent. on the capital. The cheapness of these lines is due to several circumstances, such as the following:—an entire exemption from parliamentary expenses in obtaining a charter,—the moderate cost of land,—the low rate of legal expenses,—and the facts that our lines are generally surface lines,—without expensive cuttings, viaducts, &c., and with single tracks, except where business requires them to be double. The average rate of fare is nearly 5 cents per mile; though in the Northern States it is generally materially less than this. In no case, in the State of New York, does the average rate for transportation of different classes of passengers exceed 3¼ cents—generally it is less than three cents.

The extent of railway lines in the different sections of the country, was in July, 1850, nearly as follows:—

	Miles.
In New England, ...	2465
In the Middle States, ...	2510
In the Southern States, ...	1549
In the Western States, ...	1053

Of these sums 1049 miles were in Massachusetts, 1306 in New York, 635 in Georgia, and 390 in Ohio; these states standing highest in the several divisions. During the last six months, nearly one thousand miles have been brought into use, principally in the West; and the extension continues with perhaps yet greater rapidity than this.

The main coast line extends fully one thousand miles from Portland, Me., to Wilmington, N. C., with a single break on the line of the Potomac from Washington to Fredericksburg, Va.—about 40 miles.

The principal northern cities are all centres of railway communication. Boston, New York, Philadelphia, and Baltimore, are all connected with each other by main lines,—each has numerous local lines around it,—and each is rapidly opening communications with the great interior of the continent. Boston is connected by lines now in complete operation with Ogdensburgh, on the St. Lawrence, a distance of some 400 miles; and by Albany, with Lake Erie at Buffalo, a distance of 525 miles. New York is rapidly connecting with Montreal, and with Lake Erie at Dunkirk—though the lines are not yet complete. Philadelphia and Baltimore are aiming to connect with the Ohio; and Charleston and Savannah with the Mississippi. The latter link is complete from these two cities to the Tennessee river, a distance of about 400 miles from the coast. No road of any extent has yet been completed west of the Mississippi.

The remarkable adaptation of the Western continent to railroad communication has suggested many great enterprises of this kind. The connection of the Eastern cities with the upper Mississippi is fast approaching completion; the connection of the Gulf of Mexico and the great lakes by way of Mobile and Chicago is seriously contemplated, and is now under survey, along the valley of the Mississippi, while all these immense projects are thrown into the shade by the proposed Pacific railroad of Mr. Whitney. In this it is suggested to cross the continent, and connect the two oceans—an enterprise so vast that nothing but the whole value of the soil through which it passes could profitably complete it. The position of the government of this country is now such that the gift of these lands will accomplish the construction of the mightiest and most valuable industrial work, which ever human hands achieved, or human genius planned. This highway of the world's traffic may be left a legacy to the generations of the future, that will forever claim their admiration and their gratitude for the generation whose noble foresight planned, and whose wise economy secured it. How long shall its construction be delayed and jeoparded by indifference and neglect?

After the English experiments had demonstrated the value

of the railroad system, Belgium was the first European country to adopt it. The impulse given to Belgium by her attainment of independence stimulated her government to a grand project, which the commercial necessities of the country, now cut off from the mouth of the Scheldt, the natural outlet of its commerce, seemed to require. It was accordingly proposed to construct two great lines, which should intersect each other at Malines; and each branch of which was to connect by side lines with the principal places near its route. The project was announced in May, 1834, and was received with such enthusiasm by the people, that the work was commenced on the 1st of June of the same year. In 1840, there were 190 miles open; in 1841, 212 miles; in 1842, 246 miles; in 1843, 300 miles; in 1844, 347 miles—the whole distance of the original plain.

These roads have been constructed entirely by the government, through a commission empowered to take all necessary steps for the purpose. They are of especial note, as the government has put forth annually the most complete and satisfactory report of their management yet published by any nation. Through these reports a great variety of very important questions relating to the economy of railways have been more fully elucidated than by any other statistics of this subject.

The total cost of these roads is about $31,500,000; and the average cost per mile $90,000. Their average speed is 18 miles per hour including stops—and 25 miles their running speed.

France was the next to appropriate the system, though not without a considerable interval. In 1837 a small line was completed by a private company from Paris to St. Germain, 13 miles. This circumstance, together with the rapid progress of the English roads, constrained the government to take up the subject; and a commission was appointed to devise a system of roads for France. A report was prepared in 1838, looking to a comprehensive system for the whole country; and based on the principle that the government should construct the great lines, and leave the smaller ones to private companies. Some change however took place in the public mind on this point; a long delay occurred before the question could be settled; and in the interval private companies came forward and offered to execute some of the most important. Under these auspices the work was undertaken; and by the joint action of the government and of stock companies it has advanced to a considerable extent.

In 1842 a new system of lines was proposed in the Chamber of Deputies, and was adopted as the basis of the French works. By this plan seven principal roads were determined upon—radiating from Paris—the first leading to the Belgian frontier,—the second to one of the channel ports,—the third, to one of the Atlantic ports,—the fourth and fifth to the Spanish frontier of Bordeaux, and Perpignan,—the sixth to the Mediterranean by Marseilles,—the seventh to the Rhine by Strasbourg. Two other great lines were also fixed upon—from Marseilles one to Bordeaux—the other by Lyons to the Rhine.

This system has been in part carried out. The total length of road projected is 3,573 miles, of which 1,722 miles are open for traffic, and 1,274 are in construction: 577 miles remain to be commenced.

A very extended system of roads has been projected in the German States. In the north of Germany including Prussia, Hanover and Saxony, there are already in operation a great number, covering with a close net-work of railways a tract of country 400 miles in length from East to West, and 200 miles in depth from North to South. Of this system Berlin is the great centre; and seven great lines radiate from it in all directions.

Another great system with this, follows the four principal valleys of Germany south into Switzerland and Austria. It is designed to lead the main lines across the Alps, and connect thus the Baltic and the German Ocean on the North, with the Mediterranean and the Adriatic, by Turin and Genoa—Verona and Venice—Vienna and Trieste. The latter alone of these communications is yet completed; and by means of it the traveller crosses Europe from Hamburg to the Adriatic in 60 hours. Numerous independent lines intersect Germany in every direction; and branch roads extend to and from every considerable city.

These roads are constructed very much upon the model of the American, with high gradients, numerous curves, and a single track. Their cost has been about $65,000 per mile; and the whole amount invested in them is not far below $70,000,000. There were 5,342 miles open in 1849, and 800 miles more in process of construction. In Prussia they have been constructed almost entirely by private companies, with some government aid,—in Austria and in Southern Germany, generally by the government, which exercises also a very rigid supervision of them. In 1850, the different German governments owned 1500 miles of railway.

Russia is projecting a vast system of railroads, consisting of five principal lines. The only one of these yet in operation is that from Cracow to Warsaw; which is to be completed to St. Petersburg, a distance of 683 miles. The only one at present actively prosecuted is that connecting the two capitals of St. Petersburg and Moscow—a distance of 450 miles. This is constructing under the supervision of Americans, and at the expense of the Emperor's government.

In Spain, a single line of 18 miles in length, connecting Barcelona with Mataro, is all that has been constructed. In Italy, several small roads exist, of which the principal is that from Venice to Vicenza, 40 miles. None yet exists in any part of the Papal States; but there are several small ones in the vicinity of Naples, and also in Lombardy, Sardinia, and Tuscany. The total length of the Italian roads is about 150 miles.

The influence of such systems of communication as we have described, it would be difficult to exaggerate. They form one of the most marked, important, recent, and therefore, characteristic, elements of the civilization of our age. They indicate its progress with greater truth than at first sight appears. Not only do they facilitate communication, but they hold a most important relation to the whole capital, and productive industry, of a people. Many articles of great use have no commercial value, from the impossibility of transporting them—thus, ice at mid winter is of no value in New England, its value depends upon the means of preserving it. The tropical fruits are of value only within the limited distance to which they can be transported in a sound state; every extension of that distance increases in a corresponding degree, the value of such articles. The fish of the coasts acquire a new value when they can be carried far into the interior; and the game of the interior wilds, when it can be brought down to the coast. Such facilities of transport, therefore, give an increased value to the whole productions of an extended region; and tend thus to the rapid multiplication of capital, and stimulus of industry.

The great cities no longer depend for their daily supplies upon the little ring of land immediately around them; distant tracts daily send milk, butter, fruit, and vegetables—remote districts supply fuel and food to the great centres. The agriculture of a whole State becomes, in consequence, more valuable. Cumbrous articles from the forest and the mine, which were valueless before, receive a new value from the opening of any avenue of trade which gives them access to a market. The wilderness is penetrated, the forest is felled, the mine is sunk, because now the timber and metal can be sold at a profit. Thus populations settle on the mountain-side, and civilization subdues the primeval wild.

The total amount of Railways constructed and in progress, in Europe, in 1848, was about 20,000 miles—of which nearly half was in Great Britain. An amount equal to that of Great Britain might be set down very safely for our own country.

Two thirds, therefore, of the railways, and almost the whole of the Oceanic steam navigation, of the world, which is applicable to commercial purposes, were in the hands of these two nations. A similar proportion of the capital which such traffic creates, must centre in their marts, and go to increase their efficiency and their influence.

Within the first half of 1849, one thousand miles of road were brought into use in the United States. This rate of increase would indicate a growth which, in the course of ten years will make the American roads equal in length to the whole of those existing in the rest of the world. In England then, and especially in our own land, wealth, trade, and the social advancement and political influence which they beget, are to find their chief places of abode in the half-century to come. In these Protestant lands, these lands distinguished among Protestant lands, for their evangelical faith and zeal—the means of influence are to accumulate and abound. Can there be a doubt that He who does his will among the host of heaven, and the inhabitants of the earth, is furnishing to Protestant Faith and Puritan Piety, the means of moulding the generations that are to come? Is not Providence affording us the means of stamping our own peculiarities of mind and character upon the less earnest and active nations which we have left so far behind us in social development, and whose backwardness in this respect only indicates that yet more ruinous state of spiritual depression out of which the defects of their civilization arise?

CHAPTER VIII.

SOCIAL PROGRESS IN THE FIRST HALF OF THE NINETEENTH CENTURY.

SECTION I.

HISTORY OF JURISPRUDENCE.

The progress of jurisprudence, during the past half-century, constitutes one of the most marked phases of social improvement. Changes so radical, so wise, and so humane, have never before been witnessed, save only in the divine Institution of the Hebrew code.

During the last century, there was little activity in the reform of legislative enactments; indeed in many cases the tendency seemed retrograde. In England, where alone there was any freedom of remonstrance and reform, the public mind seemed almost satisfied with the attainment of constitutional liberty; and the national energies were devoted almost exclusively to the physical and external advancement, which formed so marked a characteristic of that era. Political abuses were without number,—the press was greatly at the mercy of the government,—criminal law tended only to increased cruelty,—the prisons were in a shameful condition,—education was nowhere to be obtained by the masses,—and capital punishments were multiplied with a dreadful frequency, and a most criminal indifference. One hundred and sixty offences were by law punishable with death! Yet the most eminent legal and political writers of that period, Paley and Blackstone, thought it not unworthy of them to vindicate such jurisprudence.

The first writer who seriously proposed the general reform of this system, was the celebrated Bentham. Possessing the keenest powers of reasoning, and a most extraordinary memory, he gave himself to unwearied labor to become acquainted with the ancient and the modern systems alike. His eminent attainments were controlled by a humane and benevolent spirit; and for fifty years, from 1780 to 1830, his publications led the way in the improvement of legal science. They were translated into French by Dumont the Genevan, and gained a very wide circulation in France and throughout Europe, where indeed some of them were first published.

One great reform in the last century England owed to the labors of Erskine. In several brilliant efforts, and at considerable personal sacrifice, he assailed the principle of constructive treason; and by his courage, devotion, and eloquence, he obtained a revisal of the rule which forbade juries to decide upon the question of a law in suits for libel: only since that period has the English press been absolutely free. This principle is esteemed of so much value that it has recently been embodied in the new constitution of the State of New York.

The principles developed by Bentham were assiduously spread through England by his followers—among whom Mr. James Mill and Dr. Bowring were conspicuous. In Parliament, Romilly, Mackintosh, and Brougham labored to incorporate them into the legislation of that country. The effort was both a difficult and a protracted one.

Romilly introduced in 1808 a bill repealing the law which made it a capital crime to steal from the person anything of the value of twelvepence; and succeeded in carrying this, and another enactment of a similar kind, through Parliament. But his avowal of an intention to attempt, however cautiously, a general reform of the penal code, awakened the utmost alarm and hostility, and he was forced for the time to abandon the design. In 1811 he succeeded in abolishing capital punishment in cases in which soldiers and sailors were found begging without regular certificates of discharge. He subsequently exposed many, and corrected some, of the endless abuses of the Court of Chancery.

In 1819, Sir James Mackintosh, as chairman of a committee for the revision of the penal law, brought in six bills abolishing the punishment of death in certain cases of forgery, robbery, and larceny, and for other important amendments; but the effort was again a vain one. Not disheartened, the same accomplished statesman introduced in 1823 resolutions looking to a reform yet more thorough; and though these were formally defeated, the growing sentiment of the nation in favor of such reform compelled the government to undertake the same work, and soon a measure was enacted abolishing the death penalty in some fifty instances.

In the year 1828, Brougham delivered his memorable speech in the House of Commons on "The Present State of the Law." It assailed the system of civil procedure, and exposed unsparingly the delays, abuses, defects, and the consequent vexations and oppressions of this remedial portion of the law; and suggested measures for their removal and correction. The result was the appointment of two commissions of inquiry,—one into the state of the common law,—the other into the condition of real property. Upon these commissions twelve of the ablest lawyers of the kingdom labored; with what success may be understood from the fact that in 1840, Lord Brougham stated that out of sixty most important defects which that speech pointed out, fifty-five had been effectually remedied.

A few years later a third commission was appointed, to which the thorough reform and codification of the criminal law were referred; and very numerous improvements in the penal code through the last fifteen years, attest the extent and value of their labors. The reports of these three commissions have displayed great learning and ability, have introduced radical and beneficent changes into the English law, and have been studied and quoted in our own country as of the highest authority and value.

The progress of legal reform constitutes one of the most interesting chapters in the recent history of France. During the last century, until the Revolution, the legal system of that country stood in urgent need of a reconstruction. The Roman or civil law was universal throughout the country; but its chief application was to the regulation of contracts. The rights of property in married people, and the tenures of landed property, varied in the different parts of the kingdom; and numerous local customs prevailed with the force of law in every community. Feudal rights, too, remained in such numbers and of such a character as to be greatly vexatious and oppressive to the mass of the nation; a circumstance which was one of the causes of the violence of the Revolution. But such was the attachment of the higher classes to these feudal privileges, and such the prejudices of the people in favor of their local laws, that any general and just system was impossible while society retained the form it then had. These numerous and perplexing systems continued therefore till the grand change in French society at the close of the last century. The South was more under the sway of the Roman, the North, of the German law. Of the particular systems of law prevailing in the great feudal Provinces, that of Normandy was the most important, as it became after the conquest the basis of the feudal law of England; the next was that of the city of Paris.

When the frantic violence of the Revolution had trampled down all the hereditary rights and institutions of the nation, a renovation of the system became possible. Napoleon, seven months after his elevation to the consulate in 1799, on his return from the brilliant campaign of Marengo, named a commission of four eminent French jurisconsults to whom the work was

8

entrusted. In seven months more their task was completed and printed, March 15, 1801.

It was first submitted to all the courts of Appeal of France; and when reported upon by them, it was taken up in the Council of State, where it was debated in Napoleon's presence at length; and where it received some modifications from himself. 'In March, 1804, it was promulgated.

It consists of six distinct parts,—1st, the civil code; 2d, the code of civil procedure; 3d, the code of commerce; 4th, that of criminal procedure; 5th, the penal code; 6th, that of woods and forests. The latter is, from the wants of a country denuded of its forests by long occupancy, a matter of much more concern with the European nations than with us.

This system of laws received the name of the *Code Napoleon*, and was regarded by him as his chief gift to France. It equalized the administration of law throughout that country, upon a basis of justice and wisdom. It established courts of commerce for the speedy settlement of disputes between mercantile men; and introduced the trial by jury,—though without the obnoxious rule (which goes so far to annul the benefits of that institution among us) of requiring unanimity in order to a verdict.

At the Restoration the code was untouched, though its name was changed. It has since received various modifications, of which the chief respected the article permitting divorces.

This was the first great effort in that direction which modern history records. Austria and Prussia had made some attempts at systematizing their laws in the last century, but with little result. A code was put in force by the former in 1786, in Gallicia; and after many improvements it was extended to Lombardy and Venice in 1815. But the constitution of the state—fiscal rights—feudal and local privileges—the army—commerce—and the Jews were exempt from its application. This constitutes it is believed at the present day the Austrian code.

In Spain a code of commerce was promulgated by Ferdinand VII. in 1829. Before that time a variety of royal ordinances, and of local usages, perplexed commerce in the Spanish ports. The Cortes in 1822 decreed the formation of both criminal and civil codes; the former was suppressed, and the latter very imperfectly executed, by the government in 1836.

The code Napoleon being based upon the civil law, has naturally attracted great attention in all those nations whose jurisprudence rested on the same foundation. It has accordingly become the model of legal reform throughout a great part of Europe. Prussia, Sardinia, Geneva, and the Sicilies, have formed similar systems; and Russia is taking steps in the same direction. On this continent it was early copied in the codes of Hayti and Louisiana; both of which communities had derived their laws from the same origin. More recently Brazil moulded its jurisprudence into a similar form.

It is gratifying to witness this extension throughout so many of the modern nations, of a system so far in advance, both in its methods, and its principles, of all the legislation which had preceded it. The uniform and high appreciation in which it has been held furnishes an assurance of its ultimate prevalence in all the civil law countries of the world. It is an example of the good which a wise and kind Providence ever brings out of evil, that this lasting benefit of Society should have had its source in the revolution which for a time threatened the overthrow of all institutions. It suggests, too, the thought that revolutionary violence is sometimes less destructive and hopeless than it seems, when we find what reforms grow out of those dark hours, and how permanent, and universal, is the good, when the evil has passed away.

Simultaneous with the legal reforms to which we have referred, in Great Britain, was a series of progressive movements second in importance to none which history records in the progress of British freedom. One of these was the important measure of Catholic Emancipation. This term denotes the removal of the restrictions under which persons of that Faith were laid. The first great movement in this direction took place, in 1793, when Catholics were allowed the elective franchise, and were permitted to hold office, and to bear commissions in the army and navy. They were, however, still excluded from the three highest grades of the service, from thirty public offices, and from Parliament,—principally by two statutes known as the Corporation and Test Acts, and were still legally liable to various severe and degrading conditions.

The Legislative Union of Great Britain and Ireland took place in 1801, and the Catholics commenced from that period a series of movements designed to effect the removal of these restrictions. Under Pitt's administration, all Parliamentary action was prevented by the hostility of the king to any such changes. In 1822, a motion of Canning's for Catholic Relief passed the House of Commons, but was lost in the House of Lords; and the same fate befell similar measures introduced in 1825 and 1827.

Public opinion, however, was rapidly coming round to the approval of such a bill, and the Catholic voice was earnestly demanding it. At length the government found that it could not safely be longer withheld. The bill was finally advocated by Sir Robert Peel, and passed under the administration of the Duke of Wellington. By this law Catholics were made eligible to all offices except those of Lord Chancellor, Lord Lieutenant of Ireland, Commissioner of the Church of Scotland, and Regent of the Kingdom; and from presentations, courts, and offices connected with the Established Church. The year 1829 witnessed this termination of a series of measures long the reproach of the British name, and the scandal of her Protestant freedom; and the statute book of England bears no longer any penal enactments, nor with the single exception of the exclusion of the

Jews from Parliament, does it impose any civil disabilities upon its subjects on account of their religious belief.

Another of these important measures was that known as the Reform Bill. The constitution of the House of Commons had been unchanged for a period of six hundred years. In this period places formerly populous had become deserted, and great cities had sprung up on desolate moors; but the latter were unrepresented, and the former retained all their original importance on the rolls of Parliament. In one of these ruinous places, which acquired an immortality in the discussions of the Reform Bill, a recent writer observes,—"Not a tenement had been seen there since Columbus discovered America." Yet old Sarum had its representative, while cities, where the commerce of the world had centered, were unknown within the walls of Parliament. This mockery of representation had long scandalized the liberal and reforming spirit of this century, and the French Revolution, of 1830, breathed a new impulse into the progressive party, which expressed itself in a general and urgent demand for a reformation of Parliament. The Duke of Wellington and Sir R. Peel resisted the measure, but were driven from office. Earl Grey, with a liberal ministry, undertook the government, and Lord J. Russell introduced a bill into Parliament for a reform. It became the signal for a conflict such as had not agitated the country since the Revolution. The King was obliged to dissolve the Parliament and appeal to the people in an election. In the new Parliament the bill was passed by a majority of 109. The Lords met it with a hostility which seemed desperate—which resisted all argument—and was deaf to appeals of surpassing power. It was only upon the threat of a measure, which would have revolutionized the House of Peers itself, that the passage of the bill was permitted, and something like a popular representation became, in fact, though very imperfectly, the constitution of Great Britain.

Another reform of the same era was that which marshalled

the British power on the side of freedom against the negro slavery of the Western World. Such slavery had been declared illegal, in the last century, under the auspices of Clarkson and Sharp. The same philanthropic men pursued their labors against the African slave-trade, till, in 1806, it was condemned by Parliament, and in the succeeding year all legal tolerance of it was taken away.

The public mind of Great Britain had, however, become too much enlightened on this subject to rest there, and the agitation still went on. The slavery of the British West Indies appealed strongly to the humane spirit now thoroughly aroused in many a heart, that, amid the discussions of the former conflicts, had learned to cherish a deeper sympathy with the oppressed. Clarkson and Sharp supplied the materials which Wilberforce and Buxton used in Parliament. Through their writings the public mind was instructed, and through their public addresses it had already become excited; and the shameful persecution of the missionary, Smith, who was sentenced to death by the planters of Demerara for an alleged participation in an insurrection, greatly inflamed the popular hostility to slavery. The anti-slavery sentiment which had already found expression in a resolution by Mr. Canning, in 1823, declaring the expediency of preparing the blacks for freedom, rapidly settled now upon the doctrine of immediate emancipation. In 1824, O'Connell and Brougham powerfully enforced this view. The French Revolution of 1830 gave a new impetus to the progress of freedom, when the cause of emancipation was again powerfully aided by the extreme violence of the Jamaica planters, in suppressing an insurrection. Many hundreds of slaves were put to death, and the missionaries who were instructing them were driven to the mountains, their chapels torn down, and themselves hunted and banished. Their arrival in England greatly excited the public sentiment, and carried it forward to such a pitch, that, to avoid a decree of immediate emancipa tion, the ministry were obliged to propose a gradual one. The bill became a law Aug. 28, 1833, and proposed an apprenticeship which should last for six years; but this was ultimately found impracticable, and on the 1st of August, 1838, negro slavery finally ceased through the broad empire of Great Britain. This consummation has been happily effected without violence or blood,—has been followed by a general improvement in the character and condition of the negro population which it enfranchised,—and stands a lasting monument of honor to the men and the nation who consented to pay $100,000,000 for its peaceful accomplishment. Is it too much to say that it is for such purposes as these that so great a portion of the earth has been given into their hands?

Other reforms belong to this period, of no inferior interest, but our limits forbid more than the briefest allusion to them. In 1848, the Corn Laws were abolished, after a preliminary change some years before, which greatly reduced the duties on the importation of provisions. In 1849, a great measure for the relief of trade, was passed, in the Free Navigation Act. And still the public mind of Britain is agitated with the discussion of reforms of which it yet stands in urgent need. The history of the past fifty years is unparalleled. Never before have reforms so great been so peacefully effected. Never before have reforms so numerous been crowded into a period so brief. Never has the world so learned the value of the right of free discussion, and the power of peaceful agitation. Who can look back upon this period, without tears of joy for all the justice that society has rendered to the oppressed, and all the rights and privileges that humanity has won; or, without mighty and thrilling hopes for the achievements of future years.

Legal reform in America has been very constantly progressive. Many of our States have revised, since the present century began, their constitutions, and all have improved their laws. One half of our States have abolished negro slavery; and public sentiment is daily giving assurance of further progress. The great State of New York has been a pioneer in legal improvements. The severity of our system of imprisonment for debt had long been felt, and in 1831 it was abolished, and a certain amount of property declared exempt from execution. Contrary to the predictions of many strenuous opposers of the measure, it has approved itself to the public experience, and no one now advocates or desires a return to our former system. The abolition has been imitated in almost every one of our States.

The experience of the happy results of this change led to a farther enactment, in 1842, exempting an additional amount of property—in all $150—from execution. Advancing yet farther, the public mind is now deliberating on a homestead exemption law, which will permit a man to hold his residence free from legal process for debt. Such a law was passed in this State, in 1850, exempting property to the amount of $1,000; and several other States have adopted the same measure.

Perhaps the most important of these changes, however, is the adoption of the new constitution of the State of New York, in 1846. The common law system was dear to the people of this State, whom it had given an amount of freedom and security, such as no community on earth had ever surpassed. But the rapid growth of the State crowded its courts with more business than they could possibly adjudicate; and many applications called upon the Legislature for relief. A revision of the constitution was in consequence ordained, without which, a reorganization of the courts was not possible; and a convention was accordingly summoned for this purpose. They met in July, 1846, and prepared a draft of a constitution, with important provisions for legal reform, which was submitted to a popular vote, and adopted, in the November following.

The constitution provides for a revision and simplification of our whole law, both civil and criminal, in all its departments; and commissions were soon appointed to execute the provision.

The commission on the code of procedure has reported a system which is already in operation. It embraces two codes—one of civil, the other, of criminal procedure; and inaugurates methods which are believed to be a great and necessary reform. It abolishes all *forms* of declaration in commencing, and all forms of action in continuing, a suit; allows no more pleas of delay, and requires only a simple declaration by the plaintiff, of his cause of action, and of the remedy he seeks, which is met by the specific denial of the defendant—both verified by oath. It abolishes all mere forms of pleading, and blends legal and equitable jurisdiction in the same court,—all which are pronounced, even with all the difficulties of a new system, by high authority, desirable reforms. It provides, too, for an examination of parties themselves, in civil cases, and gives a summary remedy in cases of commercial paper. The court of chancery is abolished by the constitution itself.

Besides the requirement of a codification of the law, the constitution makes other changes of a most important character. It forbids the creation of any debt of magnitude without the consent of the people; appropriates certain branches of the public revenue, and establishes an elective judiciary,—changes which, however experience may decide upon them, must be recorded as forming an epoch in the history of constitutional law.

This code is the first in any common law country, and is substantially original and independent in its character. It adopts the principle of courts of arbitration, which are authorized by the constitution itself. It has already been adopted in Missouri, California, and Mississippi. A code conformed to it has been reported in Kentucky, Iowa, Michigan, and Massachusetts; and the new constitution of Ohio and Indiana modelled upon that of New York, tend strongly to a similar result. It will doubtless have an important effect in harmonizing, while it systematizes and improves, the legislation of the thirty-one sovereignties of our Union. It has attracted much attention among that portion of the British bar who are aiming at a reform in their own jurisprudence.

This brief review of legal history, shows an unwonted aspect of the subject. Law, formed more and more in the light of public discussion, rests now, as never before, upon justice and truth. How must it educate the conscience of the world for all acts of the public will, to disclaim any other foundation than that of absolute right! And what pledges of public morality and public humanity are not given in that fact, that henceforth the nations of the earth are aiming to enact and enthrone *Justice!*

SECTION II.

THE POST-OFFICE.

ANOTHER of the great elements and interests of civilization which has taken quite a new form within our period is the Post-office. Itself the product exclusively of the modern civilization, it assumed its character as a great public convenience, first in the time of Cromwell; under whose administration the regular conveyance of a public mail first became a function of government. It was not till the beginning of the present century that the magnitude and necessity of the institution became generally apparent. In 1728, the mail travelled once a fortnight from London to Edinburgh, occupying ten days in the journey, and bringing sometimes no letters but those which related to the business of the office. By the end of that century the mails departed daily, and the ten days' travel had diminished to three. The yearly revenue at the beginning of this century was about £85,000.

From this period it has grown in importance and in public estimation, till now no agency of government is more universally recognized as essential to the public welfare. The mail routes were extended to every village and hamlet, and the Post-office receipts formed an important part of the public revenue. The whole receipts were in 1839, £2,346,000; from which the government obtained, after deducting the expense of management, the sum of about £1,500,000 annually.

In the year 1837, an English gentleman, Mr. Rowland Hill, published a pamphlet on postage reform, in which the advantages of cheap postage were suggested. The author showed that the revenue of the Post-office no longer increased with the increase of the population and business of the country, and pointed out the necessity of some change.

It had been in 1815, £1,557,291; it was in 1835, £1,540,300. Mr. Hill showed that while the duty from stage-coaches had increased 128 per cent., that from letters had undergone no change in a prosperous period of twenty years. The contraband conveyance of letters was found to be from six to twenty fold that of the mail in many parts of the kingdom.

The suggestion thus made produced a strong impression on the public mind. In three months a petition in favor of it was presented to Parliament signed by a large number of the business men of London; and the Society for the Diffusion of Knowledge urged the reform upon the Lords of the Treasury. A committee was appointed by the House of Commons, which gave the subject a thorough examination in a laborious session of sixty-three days. Their report was published in 1838, and the number of petitioners soon rose to 262,000. The public mind of the nation set so high a value upon the proposed reform, that members of the government who deemed it impossible for the Post-office to support itself with the reduced rates, consented to the change as a matter of political necessity, and consented to forego a clear revenue of one million and a quarter in order to effect it. On the 10th of January, 1840, the new system went into operation. One of the most beneficent changes of modern times was successfully inaugurated in three years from the day of its first suggestion.

The system now introduced was distinguished by great simplicity and economy. As the average cost of transporting a letter was found to be only the ninth part of a farthing, the idea of graduating the price by the distance was abandoned; and the great principle substituted of a uniform rate of 1*d.* for all letters of a certain weight. Letters not prepaid were charged double; and facilities of prepayment are afforded by the sale of free stamps in the forms of labels, envelopes, and wrappers. All privileges of any particular classes of persons, in the mails, were abolished. To promote still farther the public convenience, the Post-office was authorized to sell money orders of a value not greater than £5, for which a small commission was charged. Nothing can exceed the public convenience of these simple provisions.

Under this system, the letters have risen in number almost incredibly. In the last year of the old system they were 80,000,000, the next year 170,000,000, and in 1848, they had risen to 350,000,000. The net income which in 1839 was £1,646,554, fell to £447,664 under the new law. It has steadily increased with the increase of the mails to about £750,000 in 1848. But though not pecuniarily useful to the government, the measure has been unspeakably advantageous to the people for every purpose of science, intercourse, business, and social improvement.

The success of this radical and beneficent change, which converts a public burden into a public privilege, early attracted attention in our own country. The difficulty of maintaining our post-office system by our postage receipts was constantly increasing with the rapid multiplication of distant routes through the newer portions of the country, which increased at an average rate of 450 miles per annum. At length it became apparent that something must be done, and several able and earnest writers urged the subject upon the government and the public. The routes which in 1832 amounted to 9,205,000 miles, had reached in ten years 13,778,000; and the expenses within the same period rose from $2,266,000 to $4,443,000, nearly double the former amount. The high rates of postage led to the establishment of many private mails between our principal cities; which, carrying at very low rates, and with great speed and certainty, absorbed a great portion of the revenue on what had been the most productive routes. In 1844, these circumstances compelled the attention of the government, and a highly useful though very imperfect measure of reform was carried through Congress. As first proposed, it established a uniform rate of five cents, without respect to distance; but this provision was altered in the House, and a double rate imposed on all letters carried more than 300 miles. It reduced, however, the average rate of postage from 15 cents to 7½; and established the capital principle of charging letters by weight, instead of by the number of pieces.

Unsatisfactory to all who valued the philosophical beauty and efficiency of the English system, our own could scarce be regarded otherwise than as an experiment in the right direction, which must after a short time give place to a system that affords the amplest facilities that government can yield to the intercourse of the people. When letters of affection and friendship—letters of business and science—letters of benevolent enterprise became multiplied four-fold through our extended borders, it was inevitable that yet another link should be added to the bonds which make us one people.

Accordingly, Congress went one step farther in its session of 1850–51, and decided that the prepaid postage on letters weighing not more than half an ounce, shall be, after July 1, 1851, three cents for any distance less than 3000 miles, and six cents to any place more distant; and that unprepaid postage shall be five cents for any distance within 3000 miles, and ten cents to places more remote.

SECTION III.

MECHANIC ARTS.

The general history of the industrial arts during this period is far too comprehensive to be compressed into the limits of such a sketch as this. We can only allude to a few of its more prominent characteristics.

Among these the wide introduction of machinery into industrial operations is a very conspicuous circumstance. In every department of labor, mechanical forces have been substituted for human hands; and machinery has been invented and adopted for the application of them.

The only agents yet extensively applied in this way are water power and steam. The application of these however has now become very general, and indeed for certain great purposes almost universal. Since the perfection of the steam-engine by Watt, it has been used more and more extensively—and for mechanical operations of the most diverse kinds; while in some parts of our country the cheaper power of running water has caused every little waterfall to be pressed into the service of human industry. At present the whole body of the textile fabrics, which employ so much labor in the manufacture of woollen and cotton goods are woven by such agencies—acting through the power loom, the spinning-jenny, and other similar inventions. The result is an immense production—an unlooked-for perfection, and a wonderful cheapness of such fabrics.

A similar change has come over the manufacture of many other products of industry. The ivory comb—the carpet tack—the metallic card for cotton and wool—the common nail—even the pin, so long proverbial for the illustration which it furnished of the nice division and adjustment of labor—are with the thousand other minute conveniences of social life and of industry manufactured in endless quantity by the turn of a wheel.

In every branch of labor similar expedients are employed to aid the operations of human hands. In every workshop machinery accomplishes some portion of the toil, from the ponderous trip-hammer which forges the massive shaft of a steamer, to the delicate arrangement which stamps and slits the pen with which we write. Even the primitive toil of agriculture takes a new efficiency, and a new interest, from the novel and numerous implements which now diversify its labors, and multiply its rewards. The invention of machinery is already one of the highest achievements of human ingenuity; and the manufacture of it one of the most extended branches of profitable industry.

What other motive powers another generation may discover—whether the lightning of heaven shall stoop to labor, and the ocean's swelling tides be subdued to the use of man, is beyond conjecture; but society is fast changing in both its spirit, and its form, under the influence of the mechanical agencies we already possess. The inventor takes higher rank in society since Watt, and Arkwright, and Fulton, and Whitney have lived. The wide extension of industry, and the vast accumulation of capital consequent upon their labors, have given us new views of the importance to society of stability, good government, and freedom. The vast and rich commerce of our age has taught men new lessons of the wastefulness and unprofitableness of war, and the incalculable advantages of peace. Labor itself, so long despised as the fit occupation only of slaves, has become honorable when vigorously and generously directed by intelligent minds to the great interests of society.

This great multiplication of manufactured products stands connected with an equal extension of industry in two other directions. On the one hand, commercial arrangements of great scope are required to diffuse, and dispose of them; on the other, agricultural labors of equal magnitude must provide both the raw material of the manufacture, and the food of the workman. It is in Great Britain and in our own country that these changes are most decided, and here accordingly we must look for their effects. It appears that in the last year the former nation employed in her traffic with the world 33,672 sailing vessels and 1,110 steam vessels, with an aggregate tonnage of 4,000,000. The number of seamen employed was 236,000. Calculating the value of each vessel as it was estimated before Parliament at £5,000, the capital thus invested amounts to £174,000,000. The quantity of cotton manufactured in 1800, was 56,000,000 lbs.; this has increased in 1850 to 775,000,000, more than 1200 per cent.

The other circumstance to which we referred—the stimulus of agriculture for the supply of the raw material, is chiefly exemplified in the cotton cultivation of the Southern States of our Union, which began to assume some importance about the commencement of this century. The sea island cotton was first brought to public notice about 1789.

Under the growing influence of this system of manufactures the crop has continually and steadily increased. The average of five years gives for this crop the following results:—

From	1825	to	1830	848,000	bales	per annum.
"	1830	"	1835	1,075,000	"	"
"	1835	"	1840	1,475,000	"	"
"	1840	"	1845	2,037,000	"	"
"	1845	"	1850	2,351,000	"	"

Of the crop of 1849, cotton was exported to the value of $66,000,000.

Out of this extension of manufacturing industry some of the highest social and moral questions of our day have arisen. Great marts spring up, of commerce, or of production; vast populations gather in a limited space; the moral influence in such communities is often far behind the wants of the population, especially if they have grown up with great rapidity; and public necessities arise, of educational and religious instruction—of social and domestic arrangements—which call into requisition all the knowledge, and skill, and benevolence of the age to supply them. The wide agricultural diffusion, too, of which we have spoken, brings up similar new and important aspects of social and religious questions. Thus the extension of the cotton cultivation has widely enlarged the area, and increased the influence, of the early slave system of our country; and given to that institution an industrial importance and a pecuniary value, which are at the bottom of all the painful dissensions which now agitate the country upon that subject. The slave population which is engaged in this wide cultivation has risen to 3,070,000; while the emigrant population of the northern states increases by fully 300,000 annually.

It is gratifying to know, that, rapid as is the growth of population, both in these crowded haunts and over these wide areas, the multiplication of the intellectual and religious agencies, which are to cultivate and sanctify men, is yet greater. In Great Britain, for instance, the population has increased within fifty years from 11,000,000 to 20,000,000,—almost double. The children in the schools of that country have increased from 500,000 to 2,000,000, four-fold, exclusive of 2,000,000 of scholars in their Sunday-schools. The number of stamped newspapers,—which affords a very fair test of the spread of popular intelligence,—has risen from 16,000,000, in 1801, to 72,000,000 in 1850,—more than four-fold. A yet greater ratio than this would be required to express the increase of institutions for the preservation and the improvement of the means, the morality, the health, the comfort, the instruction of the mass of society.

In the United States a similar state of things exists in a yet more marked degree. Education has become far more general, public morality has on the whole improved, public intelligence has increased the multiplication of religious and benevolent institutions has been unexampled. The Sunday School Union has spread elementary and religious instruction over the wide West, Home Missionaries—a thousand of whom have been sustained year after year by a single Society—have carried the Gospel through all the newer and more destitute portions of the country. Religious publications constitute now a far greater proportion of the annual issues of the press than ever before, while three million of members of evangelical churches,—forming a larger proportion of the population than at any previous period, —attest the inherent efficiency, and the Divine acceptance of these extended labors.

Two recent and remarkable structures will serve to illustrate the peculiar character, the degree of perfection, and the public estimation of the mechanic arts of our day. One of these is the Brittannia bridge, near the original iron structure over the Menai Straits. Like its predecessor, it is entirely of iron, but it differs from every other in the singular novelty of its form. It is a square tube, made of plates of wrought iron rivetted together, and has a double roof designed to resist the pressure by which the weight of such a structure, when supported only at the ends, tends to crush in its upper surface. It spans in one compact tube distances of 460 feet, and sustains the passage of a loaded train of cars, weighing 248 tons, without suffering a depression from the enormous weight of more than two thirds of an inch. Two such spans, together with a smaller one of half the length at each end and the approaches, make its total length 1841 feet. Portions of this immense tube, 472 feet long, were constructed on a scaffolding below, and, weighing 1600 tons, were raised 102 feet over a rapid stream, and united at that elevation.

The other great example of the mechanics of our own age is the Crystal Palace, the edifice designed to receive the products sent forward for exhibition at the World's Fair, which is to open in London, in May of the present year. It is constructed of two substances exclusively, neither of which, until within twenty years, had been used in the structure of any edifice,—iron and glass. Its length in feet indicates the year when it was proposed,—1848. A transept 108 feet high divides it into two equal parts, and encloses a row of large trees. Its width, 408 feet, gives it an area of eighteen acres, which marks it as the largest edifice ever constructed for any purpose. Its arrangements for drainage and ventilation are ample and admirable. In this extraordinary specimen of the modern architecture, the choicest products of the world's industry are to be exhibited to the world's inspection, and the four quarters of the globe are already sending forward their contributions. What prevalence of peace,—what perfection of arts,—what appreciation of industry,—what completeness of communications,—what universal confidence in the good faith of the suggestion, must concur to the accomplishment of a design like this!

Important improvements have been made in all that relates to that highest of all arts, the art of printing. The manufacture of paper has undergone essential changes. The enlarged production of cotton has supplied unlimited material, and the paper, instead of being laboriously formed by dipping frames for each sheet, streams from a vat in the fluid state, forms itself into an endless sheet, is dried upon steam-heated cylinders, and is at once ready for the press. The use of stereotype plates, introduced in 1795, has become exceedingly common. All standard works of literature, all approved school-books, and many other works, especially on the subject of religion, are immensely stereotyped.

The use of steam power for printing has greatly aided the multiplication of books. While the common hand press gives 250 impressions per hour, the London *Times* has been printed by steam, since 1814, at the rate of 4000 impressions per hour. More recently other inventors, among whom Mr. Hoe, of New York, is conspicuous, have greatly exceeded even this limit, and presses are now built that print from cylinders at the rate of 12,000,—and, even it is alleged, 20,000 per hour. Our great newspaper issues are brought out by these means.

What elements of power are here entrusted to us! These arts of printing that multiply the Word of God literally with every minute,—these accumulations of capital still active, still accumulating,—these means of communication over sea and land,—through the broad earth,—who does not hear the voice of God in all these? That voice which said, "Go teach all nations," and which furnished languages and gifts to the messengers it chose, is it not speaking to us in all the gifts with which we are endowed? And, as we are coming in contact with the broad tide of human life the world over, and must communicate, whether we will or not, of our civilization to their barbarism, is it not our duty thoughtfully to dedicate these vast endowments to the high claims of Heaven, and the spiritual interests of men, and sow broadcast the seed which shall spring up and bear its fruit to life eternal?

PART II.

CHAPTER I.

THE ENLARGEMENT OF CHRISTENDOM DURING THE FIRST HALF OF THE XIXTH CENTURY.

THE *growth* (if we may use the word) of Christendom, during any period in the History of the Christian Religion, is an interesting subject of inquiry and of study. But in no period has it been more so, since the earliest centuries of the Christian era, than during the half century which has just terminated. Let us look at it in detail, premising, however, that the growth of Christendom has respect not only to territorial enlargement, but also, and especially, to the increase of population, civilization, science, commerce, military power,—in a word, to everything that gives one portion of the world, or of the human race, influence over the rest.

SECTION I.

THE EASTERN HEMISPHERE.

Europe.—Of the three continents which belong to the Eastern Hemisphere, Europe is the most under the influence of Christianity.

The population of Europe cannot be less than two hundred and fifty millions. Of these, if we estimate the number of Mohammedans in Turkey (in Europe) and Russia to be 6,250,000, that of the Jews to be 3,000,000, and that of the Pagans* to be 750,000, we shall have two hundred and forty millions who profess the Christian religion, under one denomination or another.

There has been no territorial enlargement of Christendom in Europe during the last fifty years, but a decided increase of the population, and of all the resources which constitute power and confer influence. The great Christian nations—England and Prussia (Protestant), France and Austria (Roman Catholic), and Russia (Greek)—have wonderfully advanced in civilization and strength within this period; whilst Turkey, the only government not Christian, has remained stationary, if she has not retrograded. In most nations there has been a vast increase of population and material wealth; whilst in some,—such as Spain, Portugal, and Italy—this advance has not been so manifest. Upon the whole, the Europe of 1850 was greatly superior in all that constitutes progress to Europe of 1800. And this advance is steady as well as marked. The steamboat, the railroad, and the electric telegraph, are great exponents of that progress, and among the many fruits of it.

Asia.—Russia possesses and governs the northern end of Asia, or Siberia, (as it is more frequently called,) including more than a fourth part of that continent. And although heathenism and Mohammedanism prevail greatly among the inhabi-

* There is a considerable number of Pagans in the south-eastern parts of Russia in Europe. In the same category the *Nomadic* and very singular race called the *Gipsies*, must, for the most part, be placed. Their number is not known with certainty, but is supposed to exceed half a million. In some countries, a portion of them profess to be Christians, but the number of those who have much knowledge of the Gospel is very small.

tants, we apprehend that at least a nominal Christianity is gradually gaining ground, partly by immigration, partly by the natural increase of the Russian population in that vast, and for the most part, very inhospitable region.

And whilst Russia has extended her sway over the northern end of Asia, England has possession of the southern end, with one hundred and twenty millions of inhabitants, among whom Christianity, under her shield, is making sensible progress, and Hindoo forms of heathenism losing their hold upon the minds of the people, especially of the better educated classes.

And although England has not yet gained any territorial possessions on the eastern coast of Asia, she has compelled China to open to her commerce and to the commerce of the world, five important ports, through which European civilization and Christianity will find an entrance into that great but almost unknown empire.

Africa.—Christendom begins also to include portions of Africa.

England has possession of the Cape of Good Hope, as the southern end of that continent is called. She is planting colonies along the north-eastern coast, towards the Mozambique Channel. As has happened elsewhere, her colonies are coming into deadly conflict with Kaffirs and other indigenous tribes; nor can the issue be doubtful. Civilization will enable avarice to gain the ascendency over barbarous men. Alas! with the exception of a few cases, Christianity will follow after, instead of leading the way, and by her happy influences prevent extirpation. Just as certainly as that the Anglo-Saxon race has dispossessed the aboriginies of much of their Great Domain in the United States, and will take possession, by *extirpation* or *fusion*, of the remainder, will the same race take possession of all Southern Africa! The recent discoveries made by missionaries and others in that country, tend to demonstrate that it must be, in its interior, a very beautiful and fertile one—a country of hills and valleys, of mountains and plains, of extensive and charming lakes, of pleasant streamlets and majestic rivers.

Whilst England is extending her possessions in the south, France is desirous of gaining possession of some of the best portions of the north, and has already established herself between Mount Atlas and the sea. And although she is far from having yet colonized the entire of Algeria, who can tell how soon she may resolve to seize the whole Mediterranean coast, from the Nile to the Pillars of Hercules?

At the same time colonies of civilized negroes are planting under American and British auspices, from the Gaboon to Sierra Leone, on the western coast—the first of a line which will one day adorn that entire coast, with *flourishing cities, thriving villages, and cultivated fields.* In this way, Christianity will invade the western side of Africa, and bring it also within the pale of Christendom.

The Islands of the Eastern Hemisphere.—South-east of Asia lies an immense group of islands, many of them very small. England owns that which bears the name of Singapore, and several small ones which lie near by. But Holland owns,—at least to the exclusion of all other European claimants,—the magnificent islands of Sumatra and Java, together with half the great island of Borneo, and sundry small ones adjacent. These vast insular possessions bear the name of *Asiatic Archipelago,* and sometimes that of *Netherlands-India.* In these islands there is already a considerable European population—nominally Christian, for the most part Protestant, and constantly increasing. Thus the way is preparing for the entrance of the pure Gospel, and a great enlargement of Christendom is going forward in that direction.

Farther south, in the same vast oceanic domain, lie the islands of New Holland, Van Diemen's Land, New Guinea, New Zealand, and many others which constitute what is now commonly called *Australasia.* Of this vast Archipelago, New Holland is by far the largest, and has an extent almost equal to that of Europe. England claims this great island, and her colonies on the eastern and southern coasts, contain more than one hundred thousand inhabitants. Flourishing villages, towns and even cities are springing up, whose early population was chiefly composed of *convicts* banished from England. Extensive English colonies also exist in Van Diemen's Land, as well as in New Zealand. England, in fact, looks upon this whole archipelago as in some sense hers, and an Anglo-Saxon race, Christian, and in the main Protestant, will one day have the entire possession of it.

On the other hand, the almost innumerable, but, for the most part, small islands in the great Pacific Ocean between Asia and the two groups or archipelagos just named, on the one hand, and the continents of North and South America on the other, —which bear the euphonious name of POLYNESIA,—have been objects of great missionary interest during the last fifty years, and Christianity is gaining a foot-hold in them. This is particularly the case in the Sandwich Islands, the Society Islands, the Fegee Islands, and many others. In the extensive group called The Philippines,—for the most part belonging to Spain,—Christianity, not however of a high character, has a wide prevalence. But these islands are commonly reckoned to belong to the Asiatic archipelago.

It will be seen, from this statement, that the insular extension of Christendom has been great during the first half of the XIXth century, and the foundations have been laying for a wide spread of the Christian religion in that direction.

Thus much for the growth of Christianity in the Old World during the last fifty years: let us now turn our attention to the New.

SECTION II.

THE WESTERN HEMISPHERE.

In North America, Christianity has enlarged her domain greatly, within fifty years, by the colonization of the immense western districts of the United States, and the vast increase of the population of the country, which has augmented from less than 5,000,000 to 23,138,000.

The broad wave of population rolls steadily onward from the Atlantic States towards the West. At the epoch of the Revolution, (1775–83,) it had scarcely transcended the Alleghany range of mountains. It has since spread over the eastern side of the great Valley of the Mississippi, where it has already created fourteen States and two Territories, with a population of more than eight millions. It has been calculated that this grand movement of colonization and civilization makes the average rate of seventeen miles per annum! The immensely extended column is pursuing its westward way towards the Rocky Mountains. Even now there are not much less than two hundred thousand inhabitants, possessing the manners and the arts of civilized life, on the Pacific coast, in California and Oregon. The foundations of great States are now laying in these vast western districts of our immense country, where five years ago in the former, and ten in the latter there was scarcely an American to be found.

But these extreme western commonwealths, at whose feet the broad Pacific rolls and dashes, will contain a mixed race—Americans, emigrants from all parts of Europe, and natives of the islands in the Pacific Ocean. It is probable also,—or, rather, we should say, quite certain– that there will be a vast immigration to those shores from eastern and south-eastern Asia! And what a wide door will this open for the spread of the Gospel, and for the extension of Christendom in that direction! And who can predict the results which are to flow from all this?

A similar, but not equal increase, has taken place in the British Provinces, north of the United States, where the population has greatly augmented within fifty years, especially in Canada-West and New Brunswick.

There has been a decided increase in the population of Mexico, Central America, South America, and the West Indies. This increase has not been uniform. Whilst it has been steady and not very rapid in Mexico, it has been great in Brazil, and even remarkable in Chili and some of the other South American States. The domain of Heathenism in South America has, doubtless, decreased during the last fifty years. Nevertheless, the enlargement of Christendom in the Southern as well as the Northern Continent of this Western Hemisphere, during that period, has arisen mainly from the growth of the civilized nations of European origin.

With the exception of the extensive, but sparsely peopled regions north of the British Provinces and west of those Provinces and of the United States, still occupied by the Aborigines, the entire North American Continent may be said to be Christian, so far as the religion which is professed is in question.

And with the exception of the middle and extreme portions of South America, all that continent is to be considered as a portion of Christendom.

Including the Danish Provinces in the North-east, and the Russian in the North-west,—the former having, it is estimated, 6500 inhabitants, and the latter 6000,—the entire population of North America down to the Isthmus of Panama, of a European origin and professedly Christian, is 35,563,768.

That of South America, excepting the central and extreme southern portions—occupied by Pagan tribes—is 16,246,000. Whilst the population of the West India Islands is believed to be 3,549,512.

The entire nominally Christian population of the Western Hemisphere is, therefore, 55,359,280.

It would be far within the boundaries of strict accuracy to say, that this is twice as great as the nominally Christian population of this hemisphere was in the year 1800. We do not know the number of people of the American hemisphere that are Pagans, but it can hardly be five millions. That of the Jews may be one hundred thousand.

It appears from this statement, that Christendom now includes, with some exceptions of no great magnitude, three of the five great continents, the largest and most populous islands, and also some important portions and points of the other two continents. A great amount of this extension took place during the first half of the XIXth century; and the prospect of further extension during the remaining half, is certainly most encouraging, especially in North America, in the Insular world, and in Asia and Africa.

ANOTHER VIEW.

The population of the world is estimated by M. Balbi to be about *one thousand millions.* Until within a few years, it was not supposed to surpass eight or nine hundred millions. But let us suppose, that M. Balbi's estimate is as near the truth as it is possible for such a conjecture to be; and let us see how Christendom stands, in point of population, in comparison with the Unevangelized World,—as the non-Christian portion may be termed. The result will be as follows:—

The Protestants are more than eighty-two millions.*

* This will appear from the following estimate, which will hardly be questioned:—

England, Wales, Scotland, and Ireland, at least . . .	21,000,000
France, Switzerland, and Italy, at least	3,000,000
Germany, and Holland, and Belgium	22,500,000
Hungary and Poland, more than	3,000,000

The Roman Catholics, two hundred millions.*

The Christians of the Oriental Churches, at least, sixty millions.†

These numbers, when combined, give us 342,000,000, as the number of nominal Christians in the world. That is, rather more than *one third* part of the entire human race profess to be followers of our blessed Lord and Saviour, Jesus Christ. We are now speaking only of outward profession, or, of what they call themselves, in distinction from Jews, Mohammedans, and Heathen.

STILL ANOTHER VIEW.

Christendom now governs the world, directly or indirectly. Her military and naval strength is overwhelming. What are

The Scandinavian Countries	8,250,000
Russia (exclusive of Finland)	1,000,000
United States—North America, all of	20,500,000
Canada and other British Possessions in America (including the West Indies)	2,250,000
Australia, New Zealand, Van Diemen's Land, Cape of Good Hope, and other English Possessions in Asia, Africa, and Polynesia, at least	450,000
Converts in the Sandwich Islands, Society Islands, other islands, and among the Aborigines, at least	50,000
Making in all	82,000,000

* This is the estimate of his Holiness, Pius IX., who surely ought to know, inasmuch as he is the shepherd of this great flock! Nevertheless, it is very difficult to find more than one hundred and seventy or eighty millions of Roman Catholics in the world, even including several millions of people who are really *infidels*, in France, and other papal lands.

† The Oriental Churches are the Greek, Armenian, Nestorian, Syrian, Coptic, and Abyssinian. The number of their adherents cannot be put down at less than *sixty millions*, if the most authentic data which we have can be relied on.

the Heathen nations, in this respect, at present? The empire of the Great Mogul (with all the rest of India), once so formidable in Southern Asia, is in the possession of England. China may have three hundred millions of inhabitants,—it matters little whether she have more or less—but she has no military strength comparable to that of any one of the great Christian Powers. England, by sending a few ships of war, and an army of less than 15,000 men, compelled the Chinese Government, a short time since, to accept such a treaty as she chose to dictate! And what other pagan nation is there in the world that can be said to have any military power or influence?

And as to the Mohammedan world, the case is not widely different. The only Mohammedan country which has any power or influence, is the Turkish Empire. And yet, that empire, before which all Christendom trembled less than two centuries ago, has now scarcely the real strength of one of the third-rate Powers in Christendom. Holland, with little more than three millions of inhabitants, possesses more of the elements of national prosperity and strength, than the Turkish empire, with its twenty-six millions. Every one of the five great European Powers,—England, Prussia, France, Austria, Russia,—is incomparably stronger than Turkey. Such progress have they made, whilst she has remained in almost the same Asiatic barbarism that characterized her when the crescent first floated from the minarets of St. Sophia,—that even Russia, the least civilized of the five, could annihilate the Turkish empire in one campaign, and drive the followers of the Prophet of Mecca across the Bosphorus and the Dardanelles into Asia, whence they came.

Christendom has not only the military strength of the world, she has all the commerce worth speaking of. If she has not all the wealth,* she has a very large share of it. To her be-

* There is no doubt much wealth in China and in India, and some in Turkey and Persia—but what is there elsewhere out of Christendom?

long the Sciences, the Arts, the Literature, the Press, and all the high Civilization of the world. Her ships sail on every sea and every bay. Her steamboats are now found in all quarters of the globe, and will soon be seen on every navigable river of the whole earth, carrying the products of civilization, the fruits of Christianity, and the missionary of the cross, into all parts of the world. Her telegraphs will, before long, transmit intelligence with lightning speed, to all countries of the civilized world; and her railroads will soon cover, as with a network of iron, all the lands in which stable governments prevail. A great deal of this wonderful development has taken place within the last fifty years.

And what we must not fail to remark is, that those nations in Christendom in which the Papacy binds the minds of men most firmly in its chains of ignorance and superstition, are precisely those in which there has been least of progress; and this holds good in the exact ratio of the strength of that bondage. Mexico, Central America, South America, Spain, Portugal, Italy, and Ireland demonstrate this. Even Russia, with all the ignorance and superstition which the Greek Church embraces and cherishes, is advancing rapidly, and is extending its influence and its colonies far and wide. There is no papal nation that has any colonies, of much account, nor is there the least prospect of their having any. France, Spain, Italy, Austria, Portugal have few or no colonies, nor are they doing anything to extend Romanism in that way. But what is the case with Protestant Holland, England, and the United States? Their colonies are numerous and important. England and Holland have all the great islands in the Indian and Pacific oceans. England, especially, is extending her influence and her Protestantism immensely, by means of her vast Colonial Possessions in the Old and New Worlds. Whilst it will be the destiny of the United States to people almost the whole North American Continent with an Anglo-Saxon—an English-language speaking race. Nor is it by any means certain, that that race will not extend its dominion over South America, or very important portions of it.

It is remarkable, that those countries in Christendom, which are blessed with the Protestant religion—though far from being as pure and powerful in its influences as it ought—have the greatest prosperity, in every sense of the word. England, Holland, Prussia, and the Protestant States of Germany, the Protestant Cantons of Switzerland, and the Scandinavian Countries, in the Old World, and the United States and the British Possessions, in the New, establish the truth of this assertion.

England and the United States now have nearly the one fourth part of the habitable globe under their control! England sways a sceptre over one hundred and fifty-four millions of the human race; whilst the United States govern nearly twenty-four,—making a total of almost one hundred and seventy-eight millions; or, between a sixth and a fifth part of mankind! The population of Great Britain, and especially of her vast colonies, is increasing at a very rapid rate, and will long continue to do so. And, as to the United States, it is probable that by the end of the XIXth century, they will have a population of not less than ONE HUNDRED MILLIONS! And if the Protestants of this generation and the next do their duty, this hundred millions will be, by an overwhelming majority, PROTESTANT.

The same thing will be true of the great British Empire, if English Protestants do their duty to their divine Master, and His cause, as we firmly believe they will. What a glorious prospect! And does it foreshadow the DECLINE OF PROTESTANTISM? *Decline of Protestantism!* this is about the last proposition which we should like to be doomed to establish. From the influence of physical causes alone, it would seem that it must continue to increase, and to extend its influences in all directions. Protestantism has even now more of the elements of real strength, of an effective civilization, than all the rest of Christendom combined—certainly than all the Papal World, with its two hundred millions of inhabitants.

The first grand desideratum of this time is the revival of a pure faith and holy zeal amongst all Protestants. And the next, the resuscitation of primitive, apostolical doctrine throughout the Papal and Oriental churches. In other words, the great want of this age is the regeneration of Christendom! May it please the Saviour to implant deeply in the hearts of all His true followers this conviction; to excite them to put forth every exertion in behalf of this great object; and to smile upon and prosper the great *Home Missionary work of Christendom.* If there were but as much true Christianity throughout all the Christendom of the old world, as there is even in England or Scotland; if there was as much in Mexico, Central America, and South America, as there is in the United States,—what a mighty work the Church could do in the earth, and how soon the Gospel would be carried to every portion of the human race! It shall be our object to show in the succeeding chapters of this work, that there are many favorable omens, which should lead us to increased prayer, joyful expectation, and more vigorous exertion.

CHAPTER II.

PROGRESS OF RELIGIOUS LIBERTY.

Of all the advances made by mankind during the first half of the XIXth century, none has been so important as that which relates to Religious Freedom; for it lies at the foundation of all the great ameliorations which humanity can demand. It is conceded by all the ablest writers on the subject of Government and Jurisprudence, that the prevalence of sound Morality is essential to the sustentation of free governments. And that true Morality cannot prevail among any people unless it have the support of Religion, is a proposition which few will venture to deny. But how Religion is to flourish in any country without Religious Liberty, is what it is not easy to conceive of.

SECTION I.

WESTERN HEMISPHERE.

United States.—There has been little room for progress in regard to Religious Liberty, in this country, so far as *the preaching of the Gospel is concerned.* In no part of the United States is it forbidden by the government,—general, state, or municipal—to proclaim to men,—to all classes of men,—the glad tidings of Salvation. No prudent minister of the Gospel will experience any difficulty in his appropriate work, in any part of the country. Oral instruction may be imparted to people of all classes, and in all sections of the country. This is the greatest of all our spiritual blessings and privileges. We would rejoice to be able to say that it is permitted to teach all classes to read the Word of God;* but we would not lose sight of, nor undervalue, the inestimable right which all enjoy, of hearing the Gospel preached, if they live within its sound.

At all events,—and this constitutes what is more particularly embraced in the idea of Religious Liberty,—all religious sects and denominations of religionists are put on the same footing with us. Any man may hold, profess, and propagate such opinions as he prefers on the subject of religion, without hindrance from the government. The Protestant, the Romanist, the Jew, the Mohammedan, and the Pagan may all have their worship, and employ such efforts as they think proper to persuade others to attend it, if they choose. The government protects all,—equally, impartially, and effectively. Like the Carthaginian queen it says:

"*Tros Tyriusque mihi nullo discrimine agetur.*"

There are but two States we believe,—those of New Hampshire and North Carolina,—in which the Israelite may not enjoy all the political rights of citizenship; but there is not a State in the Union in which he may not profess and propagate his religious faith and practise its ceremonies.

In the United States there is now no union of Church and State. This cannot be said of any other portion of Christendom, we are sorry to say. In such of the Southern States as had, in the Colonial era, maintained this unhallowed alliance, it was dissolved either during the Revolution, or not long afterwards. Whilst in the Northern, it came to an end in Connec-

* In nine of the fifteen slave-holding States it is not allowed by law to teach those who are in bondage to read. Nevertheless, some are taught, if not publicly, at least privately, by masters or by fellow-servants.

ticut in 1816, and in Massachusetts in 1833,—the only portions of the United States in which it saw the beginning of this century. It is now almost twenty years since the last ligament that bound the Church to the State in any part of this country was severed, and it would be hard to find a man among us who regrets the fact. Indeed, we have not seen or heard of more than one native American who is now an advocate—and he a very uncertain one,—of the union of Church and State.

And yet it must not be inferred that the government with us, whether general or state, is indifferent,—much less hostile,—to the Church, or what concerns religion. This is not the position of things in the United States. "In your country," wrote one of the monarchs of Europe to the author of this volume, a few years ago, "if I understand the case, the State treats the Church as a stranger, and pushes her from it; but here [in Europe] the Church is the slave of the State." His majesty was speedily informed that his opinion respecting the state of things with us was wholly incorrect; alas, it was too true in relation to the Old World. No enlightened American could wish the government to do more for the Church than ours does,—protecting it in all its rights of property, defending it in all its modes and seasons of public worship, maintaining and enforcing the observance of the Sabbath, almost as far perhaps as it can well do without interfering with that degree of natural liberty which must be allowed in every well-ordered commonwealth. To do much more might provoke enmity, hostility, and reaction—results which would be greatly disastrous to the cause of truth and righteousness. Men cannot be made Christians by penal laws, or by police regulations. And it is the highest attainment of wisdom to ascertain and define the proper boundary of human legislation on this great subject.

We think that Christianity never had a fairer field than that which it possesses in the United States, on which to show what it can do, when relying on the Grace of its Divine Author—and its own native energies. And although we are far from believing that the Church with us is fully awake to her responsibilities and advantages, yet the experiment thus far has been anything else than a failure.

British Provinces.—There is toleration—we may even say, Religious Liberty—in these Provinces; but the great amount of real estate and other property secured to the Roman Catholic Church in Canada-East by the Treaty of Paris 1763, that transferred the Canadas to England, gives to that Church an overshadowing influence in that country. At the same time the Episcopal Church has claimed an undue pre-eminence in Canada-West. This state of things has led to many and very animated discussions in the newspapers, in the religious bodies, as well as in the Legislature of those portions of the British Provinces within the last few years. The ultimate influence of these discussions cannot fail to be good. The Presbyterians, Wesleyans, and other Protestant Churches in all these Provinces enjoy entire protection in their rights of worship and of property, and are steadily increasing in numbers and strength. Upon the whole the cause of Religious Liberty has advanced considerably in these Provinces of late years.

Mexico and Central America.—There is no Religious Liberty in Mexico and the States of Central America. We are not aware that the slightest advance has been made in this direction by these countries. It is said, however, that there is a small but effective and increasing party in Mexico, who are in favor of religious freedom, and disposed to make exertions to attain it. Nor will the subject be allowed to slumber in Central America.

South America.—The question of Religious Liberty has excited a good deal of attention in the Republics of New Grenada, Venezuela, Chili, Paraguay, and in the Empire of Brazil; and some progress has been made. Prudent efforts to distribute the Sacred Scriptures would meet with no insurmountable obstacles in those countries. In this respect all the Spanish and Portuguese portions of the American Continents are in a much more favorable condition than they were when colonies of the mother countries. In none of them, however, is there anything that approaches to complete Religious Liberty. Direct efforts to spread Protestantism in any part of South America, by way of forming churches composed of natives of those countries, would not be allowed. And yet the day when this will be practicable is much nearer than it was fifty years ago.

The West Indies.—There is now a great amount of Religious Liberty in the British portion of the West Indian Archipelago. In this respect the state of those islands is very different from what it was before the year 1838,—the epoch of the Emancipation of the slaves in those islands. As the Established Church of England is also the favored Church in the British West India Islands, as in all the other foreign possessions of the United Realm, it cannot be said, with the strictest propriety, that there is perfect religious liberty in any of them. Nevertheless all denominations of Christians are protected in their worship, and in their efforts to propagate their doctrines, and increase their adherents.

The Island of St. Domingo, or Hayti, has made great progress in respect to religious liberty. That important island is now remarkably open to judicious efforts to propagate the Truth. This is one of the fruits of the progress of civil and political freedom and republican institutions in that land. That progress has been real, notwithstanding the wild scenes of massacre and rapine through which it has been achieved. We cannot but believe that the way has been wonderfully prepared in that island for the introduction and spread of true Religion during the last fifty years. In the Danish and Dutch Islands there is a large amount of Religious Liberty; in the Swedish and French a little; and in the Spanish none at all.

SECTION II.

THE EASTERN HEMISPHERE.

Great Britain.—The question of Religious Liberty has not made as great progress in England and Ireland, during the last fifty years, as one might have reasonably expected. The Established Church of those portions of the British Realm, Episcopal in both, has exerted an injurious influence upon the Dissenting Communions. And although some forms of vexation and oppression have been abated, yet there is much still to be deplored. We should indeed be grateful that such a large amount of religious freedom is enjoyed in those countries, yet we cannot but pray that the day may speedily come when that entire liberty of conscience and worship shall be enjoyed, by all the inhabitants of those favored lands, which the principles of true Protestantism demand.

The "Disruption," as it has been called, which took place in the Established Church of Scotland, in the year 1843, was one of the most important events that characterized the first half of the XIXth century. That nearly 500 pastors, 200 licentiates, and 200 students—in all 900 men either in the ministry, or soon to be—followed by a million of the inhabitants, should abandon the Established Church in one day, as it were, and form a "Free Church," is one of the most striking evidences of the progress of Religious Liberty within that period of which it is possible to conceive.

France.—Religious Liberty has made great progress in France within the XIXth century. Great opposition has been encountered from the government at times, and from Rome always. And yet its sacred principles have been constantly gaining ground in the hearts of a large portion of the inhabitants, especially of all those who are the friends of civil and political liberty. Nor can we for a moment doubt what will be the issue of the struggle now going forward in that important country, however protracted or violent it may be.

Belgium.—In no country in Europe has there been more progress in regard to Religious Liberty than in Belgium. And this will appear the more extraordinary when we consider that Flanders, as that country was formerly called, was for a long period the most thoroughly papal country in the world. The Constitution of that country guarantees religious liberty to all,—although the Roman Catholic Church is still emphatically the Established Church of that country. This greatest of blessings has been secured by the Revolution of 1830, when Belgium dissolved the union with Holland.

Holland.—In the early part of this century Holland was under the government, direct or indirect, of France, for nearly fifteen years, and felt the influence of French laws and French opinions. During this period Religious Liberty may be said to have existed without restraint. Upon the overthrow of Napoleon and the succession of William I. to the throne, the four Protestant Communions (the Reformed Dutch Church, the Lutherans, the Mennonite Baptists, and the Remonstrants), as well as the Roman Catholics, were put on the same footing by the constitution and the laws. But no provision was made for those who might dissent from all these recognized religious bodies. The consequence has been that much oppression, and even disgraceful persecution, was suffered by thousands of excellent people who could not conscientiously remain in any of the Protestant bodies, from the year 1836 to 1848. Several thousands emigrated in the years 1845, '46, and '47 to the United States, and settled in Michigan, Iowa, Wisconsin, and New York. The great convulsions which occurred in so many nations in Europe, in 1848, so far affected Holland as to lead to some important modification of her laws, and now religious liberty is much more fully enjoyed, and tranquillity has been restored.

Germany.—It is no easy thing to give a clear and definite view of the state of things in Germany at this moment, either as respects the State or the Church. During the greater part of the first half of the XIXth century, there was nothing like real religious liberty in either the Papal or Protestant parts of that country, though there was more quiet and effective toleration in the latter than in the former. In neither was there entire freedom of religious worship and action. Men were persecuted in Silesia,—Protestants even,—in 1836, '37, and '38, and only because they would not conform to the Church of the State. Even in Hamburg, Baptists were persecuted in 1839 and '40. Whilst in Bavaria, and the Roman Catholic portions of the Austrian Empire, Protestants were oppressed, and their efforts to propagate the Truth hindered, and even prevented. Nearly 500 Tyrolese were expelled from Zillerthal, in 1837, for no other offence than the renunciation of the Papal superstitions for the Protestant Faith. The government of Prussia gave these exiles an asylum in Silesia,—in the country from which, at that very moment, it was compelling the "Old Lutherans" to emigrate to America!

The Revolution of 1848 has unquestionably done much to loosen the bonds which unite the Church to the State, in the Protestant countries of Germany, and to increase the toleration which, to some extent, existed previously. But in all the unholy alliance still remains, and so long as it continues entire, complete religious liberty will be impossible. That great progress has been made in the right direction in Germany, and even to some extent in the whole Austrian Empire, may be asserted without the fear of contradiction; but it is not easy to indicate it in detail, or to measure its influence.

Switzerland.—At the commencement of the XIXth century Religious Liberty was far from prevailing in the land of William Tell In all the Protestant Cantons there was a union of Church and State, without provision for Protestant dissent. Roman Catholics were tolerated in all of them. In the Roman Cotholic Cantons there were almost no Protestants at all, nor was Protestantism tolerated in most of them. The recent revolutions in that country have done much to weaken the union which subsists between the Church and the State in all parts of it. The monastic establishments have been, for the most part, broken up in the Papal Cantons. The disgraceful conduct of the government in the Protestant Canton of Vaud caused a secession to be made, by a large number of pastors, from the Established Church, in the years 1845, '46, and '47. Much suffering ensued. The seceding ministers were greatly persecuted and hindered in their efforts to promote the Gospel. This storm has now, we are happy to say, passed away in a good degree, and tranquillity is restored. Upon the whole, we are inclined to believe that the cause of Religious Liberty has begun to make real progress in Switzerland within the last few years.

Denmark.—The constitution of Denmark, given in 1848, guarantees Religious Liberty to a good degree, though there is much to be desired. Before that event, there was no toleration of any form of Protestantism save that of the Lutheran Church, whilst a few Roman Catholic Churches existed by special favor, or by sufferance, rather than by any other rule.

Norway.—Norway was detached from Denmark and united to Sweden in 1814. An equal degree of intolerance reigned in that country as in Denmark, Sweden, and Finland, the other portions of what is called Scandinavia. Nothing but the Lutheran Church was acknowledged. But the Storthing or Legislature, about the year 1845, made a law (which the King of Sweden approved) by which any Norwegian, who was nineteen years of age, may quit the Established Church, and have, in conjunction with others, such a religious worship as he may prefer, but for whose support the State will not be responsible. He must, however, continue to bear his share of the burden of sustaining the National Church. Imperfect and unjust as is this enactment, it is the commencement of what must one day end in entire religious freedom in Norway.

Sweden.—The question of Religious Liberty has been much discussed in Sweden, but to this day nothing of importance has been done. No form of Protestantism is tolerated but the Lutheran. If a Swede becomes a Roman Catholic, he is liable to 20 years' imprisonment, or to banishment! Indeed he will be liable to the same punishment if he become a Protestant of any other Communion than that connected with the State. A Mr. Nillson has lately been sentenced to banishment, because he has become a Baptist! This is disgraceful to the cause of Protestantism. The King feels it to be such, for he has hitherto refused to approve the decision of the court.

Russia.—We are not aware that the question of Religious Liberty has made any progress in Russia since the commencement of this century. The Established Church of that great Empire is the Greek, which embraces more than 47,000,000 of the 66,500,000 of the population. In that vast country all other forms of Christianity—Protestant, Armenian, and Roman Catholic—as well as Judaism, Mohammedanism, and Paganism, are tolerated. It is allowable to Protestants to convert Jews, Mohammedans, and Pagans, but the converts will be expected to join the great Russo-Greek Church, with all its errors and corruptions, which are almost as great as those of Rome itself. Nor is it permitted that any one quit that Church, for any other. The law is less rigidly enforced in Poland, the Baltic Provinces, and Finland, than in the rest of the Empire. And yet there is an open door in Russia for the circulation of Religious Tracts, and to some extent, for the diffusion of the Sacred Scriptures.

Spain and Portugal.—The constitution of neither Spain nor Portugal contains a word in favor of Religious Liberty. Nevertheless, the laws of Portugal are not so stringent as to prevent the existence of Protestant chapels at Lisbon and Oporto, for the benefit of foreigners. A converted priest has even preached the Gospel to as many of the native population as chose to come and hear him, at the former city, for the last five or six years. There is not a Protestant place of worship, so far as we are advised, in all Spain. At Gibraltar, beneath the British dominion, there are several Protestant churches and chapels. Much can be done in Portugal, and something in Spain, with prudence, to circulate the Word of God.

Italy.—In no part of the world has Religious Liberty been less known or enjoyed than in that which claims to be the centre of Christendom. The "Bishops of Rome" have ever been bold enough to demand, and ready enough to accept, liberty to propagate their system of religion, but never disposed to concede the same advantage to others. In this respect one is at a loss to determine which is the more astounding—their arrogance, or their utter want of all sense of justice.

No part of Italy has for fifteen centuries known the blessings of Religious Liberty, excepting the *Valleys of the Waldenses*, and that little district only at intervals, and as the purchase of much blood, and of the most dreadful sufferings. But even Italy is not to be despaired of. Light is breaking into that beautiful land,

"Where every prospect pleases."

The Revolutions of 1848 did not occur wholly in vain. Most important discussions took place in the newspapers of Sardinia, Tuscany, the Papal States, and even of Lombardy and Naples, during several months—discussions which related to the entire subject of liberty,—political, civil, and religious. These discussions have not been without good results. Although no governments in Italy are now Constitutional governments, excepting the Kingdom of Sardinia and the little Republic of San Marino, yet there is practically a far greater amount of religious liberty, or toleration rather, in the Kingdom of Sardinia than any part of Italy had ever before seen. This is the more remarkable, when we recall to mind the fact, that the Waldenses live in that Kingdom—that martyr-race who suffered so much for the cause of Truth, from the very ancestors of a monarch who now protects them. Let us be thankful that something like a beginning has been made in Italy, in regard to this most important subject. We ought to add, perhaps, as a sign of progress, that his Holiness has permitted an American Protestant Chapel to be opened in Rome itself—a privilege which was never granted before in Rome within—the—walls.

Greece.—There is, properly speaking, no religious liberty in the kingdom of Greece, but the subject has awakened the attention of not a few well-instructed minds, and the day is evidently drawing near, when governmental jealousy and priestly hostility will yield to the influences of truth and justice. Even now a great deal can be done—a great deal is doing by American and English and German missionaries to make known the pure Gospel in that small but interesting country—so dear to the classic scholar as well as to the sincere Christian. Had Greece been papal to the same extent that it is an adherent of the Greek church, we have reason to believe that nothing could be done to replace superstition and perverted doctrine by the glorious truth of God's Word. More than two hundred different religious tracts and books have been published through the exertions of the missionaries just referred to, in the Modern Greek, and have been widely circulated.

Turkey.—But in no part of Europe has there been so great a change, in this respect, as in the Empire of Turkey, within the last few years. The Sultan is determined to put Christians upon the same footing with the Mohammedans, as to the enjoyment of their religious, and probably, also, all their political rights. A recent act of his government has placed Protestants in as favorable circumstances as could be desired. This, under God, has been owing to the happy influence which our own American missionaries have exerted there, and also to the zealous but prudent efforts of Sir Stratford Canning, the English ambassador.

Other portions of the Old World.—It may not be amiss to remark, that in the English possessions throughout the Old World, as well as the New, there is now a very large amount of religious liberty. Nor has this been brought about without much effort. The time has been when those who carried on the government of the British Possessions and of British Colonies, were jealous of the efforts and influence of Protestant missionaries. A great contest on this subject was carried on in India in the early part of this century. In that important discussion, the Rev. Dr. Claudius Buchanan took a most important part, as did the American missionaries at Bombay at a later day. The result has been all that could be desired. Instead of being ordered out of them,—as were the first American missionaries who went to India,—Christian teachers are now freely admitted, and even welcomed, in all the possessions and colonies of England.

We are sorry not to be able to say as much of the colonial possessions of Protestant Holland and Papal Spain. Commercial jealousies in the former, and dread of the Protestant religion in the latter, concur to make them almost close up the avenues by which light and truth might penetrate into them.

The reader will gather from the foregoing survey of the state of things throughout the world, that Religious Liberty has made decided progress in both hemispheres since the commencement of the XIXth century. This is a fact of the utmost importance. There can be no view taken of Christendom more consolatory or encouraging than this. We see in this incipient and wide-spreading progress of religious freedom, that *preparation of the way of the Lord* which precedes and announces His speedy coming. Surely all this breaking down and removing of barriers which formerly, and for long ages, prevented the spread of the Truth, will soon be followed by a vast impulse of spiritual life and effort in all directions, which will not cease till Christendom shall be regenerated and the world subdued by the Gospel. In fact, we already see the commencement of this work—whose consummation is so devoutly to be desired—as we shall attempt to show in the next chapter.

CHAPTER III.

PROGRESS OF EVANGELICAL CHRISTIANITY DURING THE FIRST HALF OF THE XIXTH CENTURY.

We have spoken of the enlargement of Christendom and the Progress of Religious Liberty during the first half of the XIXth century. We come now to what is the most important of all:—The advance of Evangelical Religion in the Protestant Churches during the period under review. This is a subject of vital importance, compared with which all others diminish into comparative insignificance.

It must be admitted that the state of Religion in the Protestant Churches was far from being encouraging at the commencement of the present century. In the United States, a long period of spiritual death had oppressed the churches of almost every denomination. It is true that there had been seasons of cheering revival in some parts of the country, especially in New England and some of the Middle States. The visits of Whitefield and Wesley, the labors of the Tennents, of Edwards, and other faithful servants of Christ had done much to keep alive the piety of the churches during the middle portion of the last century. But as a general statement, it must be said that true Religion was in a very low condition in the churches in all parts of the country, and had long been so. The conflicts of the Colonies with the Aborigines; the "French War," as that between England and France (1756–63) which ended in the conquest of Canada by the former, was called; the exciting disputes with the mother country, from 1765 to 1775; the war of the Revolution (1775–83); the years of prostrated commerce and industry, of bankruptcy, and of disunion (1782–89) which preceded the formation of the Constitution and the organization of the present Government; the succeeding difficulties with England and France, leading to a temporary collision with the latter, (1792–99) together with several wars with the Indians:—all combined to injure and depress the interests of Evangelical Religion. To this must be added the unhappy effects of the union of Church and State which so long existed in the most important of the Colonies—now States—both North and South, developing themselves in the manifestation of most dangerous errors in the former, and in a chilling and worldly formality in the latter.

Blessed be God, in some parts of New England, especially in Connecticut, the horizon began to lighten up a little, during the last decade of the last century. Some precious revivals took place, and the spirit of Missions, especially in relation to the Home field, began to manifest itself. But it was not until the XIXth century had opened, and especially when the war with England, and some severe ones with the Aborigines (1812–15) had passed away, that the glorious era of our spiritual prosperity as a nation was fully ushered in.

In Great Britain very much the same thing occurred. The resuscitation of Religion, commenced by the labors of Wesley and Whitefield, and continued during the long life of the former, was strengthened and protracted by the labors of Romaine, Newton, Rowland Hill, Fuller, Cecil, Scott and others. As a fruit of this movement, the spirit of Missions, especially in reference to the Foreign field, sprang up among the Baptists and Independents first, and afterwards among the Evangelical portion of the Established Church, between the years 1790 and 1800, and led to the formation of the Baptist and London Missionary Societies. This glorious operation of the Spirit received a further development in the formation of the British and Foreign Bible Society in 1804, and of other kindred institutions which came into existence in the British Realm about that epoch.

Let us now trace the Progress of Evangelical Religion from this point, or rather from the commencement of the century, and notice some of the land-marks which may indicate both the extent and the rate of the movement, both in the Old and the New World.

SECTION I.

THE WESTERN HEMISPHERE.

The United States.—The blessed influences of the Holy Spirit, which began to be felt in great power in our Churches, as we have said, in the early years of this century, and especially after the restoration of peace and tranquillity in 1815, have ever since in a good degree pervaded almost all parts of the country, and produced the happiest effects. The piety, the knowledge, the zeal, and the devotedness of Christians were greatly augmented. The standard of duty and of personal holiness became more elevated. Christians began to feel more deeply that each had a work to do for Christ, and for humanity, as well as to secure the salvation of his own soul. The distribution of the Word of God, and of Religious Tracts, the instruction of the youth and uneducated adults in Sabbath-schools and Bible-classes, began to be appreciated and vigorously prosecuted. The outpouring of the Spirit from on high was seen to be the greatest of blessings, both for the individual and for the entire community. It was accordingly sought with heartfelt earnestness, and very richly and extensively enjoyed. "The churches then had rest" throughout all the land, "and were edified; and walking in the fear of the Lord, and in the comfort of the Holy Ghost, were multiplied."

This spiritual prosperity was confined to no section of our

country, although it was most marked, as may well be supposed, in those parts where the means of grace were the most abundant. Nor was it limited to any particular branch of the one true Church of God among us, although it was most visible in those portions of it in which the Gospel was preached with the most simplicity, discrimination, fervency, and faithfulness. Every evangelical branch of the Church felt the life-giving influence of the blessed movement. The number of individual churches rapidly increased. Societies were formed to assist those who emigrated to the new settlements in the West, to establish among them, even before they had felled the forests around them, the institutions of the Gospel. Whilst the rapidly-increasing population of our large cities began to call forth new and extraordinary efforts to multiply the number of places of worship, and secure the religious instruction of the people.

As might be expected, the visible Church in the United States received a great and rapid enlargement during the half-century which has just passed away, and especially during the last thirty-five years of it. A very brief notice of the several Evangelical Churches will prove this. It will be seen that some entire denominations have come into existence in this country within the last fifty years, and others have increased from small and insignificant beginnings until they have become powerful bodies. What, for instance, was the Methodist Episcopal Church in the United States, in the year 1800? We cannot speak with precision, but it probably did not have 40,000 members; now it has almost a million and a quarter! What were the Baptist Churches? What were the Presbyterian at the commencement of the XIXth century? They were small, feeble, and insignificant bodies in comparison with what they now are. The same thing may be asserted of the Protestant Episcopal Church, although it is the oldest of all the churches in this country. Even the Congregational body of churches, and the Reformed Dutch, which rank next in point of age, and which have increased less rapidly than many others, have, nevertheless, increased very greatly, and are several fold more numerous and powerful than they were in the year 1800.

The Cumberland Presbyterian Church did not exist until several years after the commencement of this century, and now it is a numerous and important body. The minor Presbyterian bodies* were extremely feeble at that epoch; but now, when taken as one body, they present a very highly respectable and commanding phalanx. The Lutheran and German Reformed Churches have received a greater increase in numbers by immigration from the Fatherland than almost any other; whilst several smaller bodies of Germanic origin have come into existence during the period of which we are speaking.

To make this subject more intelligible, we will present, under a general view, the several evangelical bodies as they were fifty years ago (if they then existed), as far as we can ascertain, and then state their present position as to number of members, ministers, and communicants.

THE PROTESTANT EPISCOPAL CHURCH.—This body had, in 1800, four bishops, and probably 250 ministers. In 1832, 15 bishops, and 583 ministers. In 1850, it had 27 dioceses, 26 bishops, and about 1500 other ministers, and nearly 72,000 communicants.

THE CONGREGATIONAL CHURCHES.—We have no definite knowledge of the number of these churches in 1800, but we suppose they did not exceed 400 or 500, having as many pastors, and probably 75,000 communicants. In 1850, there were 1971 churches, 1687 ministers, and 197,196 members.

THE REGULAR BAPTISTS.—We know not what their number was in 1800,† but their increase has been wonderful. In 1850,

* The Associate, Associate Reformed, and Reformed Presbyterian.

† In the year 1784, they had 471 churches, 424 ministers, and 35,101 members. In 1790–92, they had 1150 churches, 891 ministers, and 65,345 members. Even in 1810–12, they had only 2164 churches, 1605 ministers, and 172,972 members.

their churches were estimated at 8406, their preachers at 5142, and their communicants 680,807.

MINOR BAPTIST BODIES.—These were very insignificant in the year 1800. The last mentioned in the list but one did not exist. They are as follows:—*Freewill Baptists,* having, in 1850, 1252 churches, 1082 ministers, and 56,542 members. *Seventh Day Baptists.*—They had, in 1850, 63 churches, 58 ministers, and about 7000 communicants. In the year 1800, there were but few in the country. *The Disciples of Christ, Reformers, or Campbellites,* as they are interchangeably called, did not exist until the year 1816. Now they are reported to have 1898 churches, 848 ministers, and 118,618 members. *The Six-Principle-Baptists* have now about 3500 members. There are one or two other small Baptist bodies, whose statistics we have not been able to obtain; but they would not affect much the general estimate, which is all that we can aim at here. The *Mennonites* (German) have about 400 little congregations, 240 preachers, and the number of their members we do not know.

THE PRESBYTERIANS.—This body was an influential one, even in the time of the Revolution. In 1800 it had increased to about 300 ministers, 500 churches, and 40,000 members or communicants. In 1850, including the two bodies into which it was divided twelve years previously, it had 4093 churches, 3333 ministers, 863 licentiates, and 337,438 communicants.

MINOR PRESBYTERIAN CHURCHES.—The *Cumberland Presbyterians* commenced in 1812; they had in 1850, about 500 churches, nearly as many ministers, and not far from 75,000 members.—*Reformed Dutch Church.*—This body had, in 1784, only 82 congregations, and 30 ministers; in 1850 it had 282 churches, 299 ministers, and 33,780 members.—The *Scottish Presbyterian Churches* scarcely existed in 1800; now they have, in all, about 550 churches, 430 ministers, and 57,000 members.—The *German Reformed Church* has now about 600 churches, 260 ministers, and 70,000 communicants.—The *Lu-*

theran Church had, in 1850, 1,603 congregations, 663 ministers, and 163,000 members. Both these denominations were quite small in 1800, and almost confined to the State of Pennsylvania; they are now found in all the Middle States, and are numerous in the South and West.

THE METHODIST EPISCOPAL CHURCH had, in 1850, including both branches, 5,646 preachers, and 1,160,830 members. In the year 1784, this Church was organized, and had then 83 ministers, and 14,986 members!

THE MINOR METHODIST CHURCHES.—These have all originated, with one or two exceptions, since the year 1800.—The *Protestant Methodist Church* (organized in 1826) has 1,200 preachers, 500 places of worship, and about 62,000 members. —The *Wesleyan Methodist Church* (organized in 1842) had in 1850, twelve Conferences of ministers, and about 20,000 members.—The *United Brethren in Christ* (German) arose about 1790, held its first Conference in 1800, and had, in 1850, about 1,800 places of worship, 600 preachers, and 67,000 members. The *Evangelical Association* (German) founded in 1800, had, in 1850, 312 ministers, travelling and local, 900 places of preaching, and about 17,000 communicants.

THE MORAVIANS, or UNITED BRETHREN.—This body has increased less than any other in the United States during the last 50 years. They have about 23 churches, 27 ministers, and 3,000 communicants.

FRIENDS.—This body has not increased much. The orthodox portion is estimated to have about 300 congregations.

The preceding statements, though very general, will show that what are considered to be truly Protestant Churches, holding to the great doctrines of the Reformers, have rapidly increased in number since the year 1800. We think that it is easy to show that the number of evangelical churches, ministers, and members, was much greater in 1850, in proportion to the population, than it was in 1800: as to efficiency in all that relates to the work of extending the knowledge of the Gospel, the contrast between the churches of the two epochs is still more striking, as the succeeding chapters of this volume will show.

British Possessions in America.—We have not the means of measuring the progress of Evangelical Religion in the British Provinces north of us, and in the West India Islands; but we have no doubt about its reality. There is much more of vital piety and efficient action in the Protestant Churches in the Canadas, New Brunswick, Nova Scotia, Newfoundland, Prince Edward's Island, as well as in the English Possessions in the West India Archipelago, and in Guiana, than there was at the commencement of the present century,—unless we have been altogether misled by the documents before us.

SECTION II.

THE EASTERN HEMISPHERE.

Great Britain and Ireland.—That there has been a great increase of Evangelical Religion in England and Wales within the last 50 years, is the testimony of every well-informed Christian of those parts of the British Realm, with whom we have ever conversed, during the repeated visits which we have made to them. In the Established Church this increase of true piety and zeal has been very visible. The present alarming manifestation of a tendency Rome-ward in the unevangelical portion of that Church, does not disprove this assertion. The case is deplorable, but the Saviour will cause it, in some way or other, to work for the purification and strengthening of His true Church in that land. The formation of a pure, evangelical, and free Church must, sooner or later, be the result.

There has been a decided increase of enlightened piety, sound doctrine, and earnest zeal, among the various Dissenting Bodies. This is confessed on all hands, by well-informed men in England.

And what shall we say of Scotland? There has been unquestionably a great resuscitation of the Truth in the land of John Knox. How strikingly the wonderful movement which issued in the disruption in the National Church, and the formation of the Free Church, illustrates and establishes this fact! The interests of true Religion have made wonderful progress in North Britain since the year 1815. The Minor Presbyterian bodies there, and also the Independents, the Wesleyans, and other Dissenters, have felt the genial influence, and are manifesting effects in their increased exertions in behalf of the Kingdom of their Lord.

As to Ireland, true religion has decidedly increased among the Presbyterians in the North, as well as among the 1600 ministers and congregations of the Established Church. More is now doing by pious Protestants in that country for the diffusion of the Truth and the conversion of the adherents of Rome, than had been attempted for a long time. This is encouraging. Nor are their efforts without success.

The Continent of Europe.—If we cross over to the Continent, we shall find that the same blessed resuscitation is going on in every Protestant country—slowly, silently, but surely. There is evidence of this in Holland. The spirit of true piety and sound doctrine is gaining ground in the several Protestant Communions in that country, and especially in the Reformed Dutch Church, the most important of them all. Within a few years, much has been done to spread the sacred Scriptures and religious tracts in that country, by means of colportage. Two of the most active Christians in that land are Messrs. Da Costa and Coppadoce, converted Israelites. It is said that there are about 120 churches, mostly small, composed of those who have within a few years separated from the Established Church, because they could not find that spiritual instruction there which they needed.

The state of things is deplorable enough in Germany; but

that true religion is looking up in the "Land of the Reformation" is certainly undeniable. Error, as in England, becomes greater, —in its greater departure from the truth, and not really in the augmented number of its adherents—whilst truth becomes more developed. There is a far greater number of professors in the more than twenty universities of that country, who teach the doctrines of the Reformation; and there is a far greater number of students who receive them, and of pastors who preach them, than there was at the commencement of this century, or than there was even twenty years ago. What number, however, of the more than 16,000 Protestant ministers of that country hold and preach the primitive Gospel, God only can know. We have heard it estimated very variously—at from 1000 up to 2000. We do not believe that there were 200 at the beginning of this century.

The same thing may be asserted of the Scandinavian countries—Denmark, Norway, Sweden, and Finland. The last named is now a part of the Russian Empire, but enjoys in a great degree her own laws, and almost exclusively her own religion, which has been Protestant since the days of Gustavus Vasa, when Finland was united with Sweden.

In all those countries the Truth is gradually recovering the ground which it had lost. This has been brought about by the increased circulation of the Sacred Scriptures, and by the diffusion of religious tracts, through the agency of the Bible and Tract societies. The writer of these lines has been several times in all the Scandinavian countries since the year 1836, and can assure the reader that he but expresses the opinions of many of the best men in them all, whom it has fallen to his lot to meet with.

This same blessed work is silently going forward, slowly indeed, but steadily—among the Protestant churches in Poland, in Hungary, in the Germanic parts of Austria, and in the Baltic Provinces of Russia.

It has been more visible in the Protestant Cantons of Switzerland, among the Protestants of France, and amid the Waldenses in Italy.

These statements are general, but they are true, and should excite to grateful thanksgiving to God; to earnest prayer in behalf of the good work, that it may advance more rapidly; and to co-operation, in all practicable ways, whenever our aid can be made to advance the interests of truth in those countries. The conversion of the world demands the regeneration of Christendom, and the regeneration of Christendom will be effected through the recovery of the truth and power of the Gospel on the part of the Protestant churches.

In the chapters which follow, we shall show what have been the effects of this blessed resuscitation of true religion in the Protestant churches,—in both hemispheres—upon Christendom and the World.

CHAPTER IV.

SOCIETIES FOR THE DIFFUSION OF THE SCRIPTURES—EASTERN HEMISPHERE.

EFFORTS for the diffusion of the Holy Scriptures were coeval with the revival of pure Christianity in every part of the world where it occurred. But the organization of religious associations for this purpose is comparatively a modern enterprise. Several of the societies founded in Great Britain, during the eighteenth century, for the diffusion of Christian truth, contemplated as a part of their work the dissemination of the Scriptures. The Societies "for promoting Christian Knowledge" (founded 1696), "for the Propagation of the Gospel in Foreign Parts" (1701), "for promoting Religious Knowledge among the Poor" (1750), and the "Society in Scotland for promoting Christian Knowledge" (1709), were all of this character. There was also a Bible Society (founded 1780) for the supply of the Army and Navy of Great Britain, another (1792) for the Circulation of Bibles in France, and an association "for the Support and Encouragement of Sunday Schools" (1785). These, however, were efforts either limited to particular districts, or secondary to a distinct, though homogeneous enterprise.

SECTION I.

Great Britain.—The primary occasion of those measures out of which grew the BRITISH AND FOREIGN BIBLE SOCIETY was the scarcity of Bibles in the Principality of Wales. This scarcity had attracted some notice as early as the year 1787, and letters were written on the subject by several clergymen with a view to obtain a supply. "When I was in Wales last," says one of these writers, "I heard great complaining amongst the poor for want of Bibles, and that there were none to be had for money." The first attempts, however, to meet this exigency were unsuccessful. In 1799, the Society for promoting Christian Knowledge, issued an edition of the Welsh Bible to the amount of ten thousand copies, with two thousand extra Testaments. But thirty years had elapsed since the printing of the last edition, and this supply was altogether inadequate to the demand. The new edition was almost immediately bought up, and large districts were still unprovided for. If the joy of those who were successful in obtaining copies was excessive, the grief of the many who failed of it fell little short of anguish. "Their expressions of regret," stated a clergyman who had witnessed this disappointment, "were truly affecting."*

It was in this connection that occurred the touching incident which seems to have been the immediate occasion, under God, of the plan which resulted in the formation of this society. In the year 1802, the Rev. Thomas Charles, of Bala, in Wales, was walking in one of the streets of that town, when he met a child who attended his ministry. He inquired if she could repeat the text from which he had preached on the preceding Sunday. Instead of giving a prompt reply, as she had been accustomed to do, she remained silent. "Can you not tell me the text, my little girl?" repeated Mr. Charles. The child wept, but was still silent. At length she said, "The weather, sir, has been so bad that I could not get to read the Bible." This remark surprised the good man, and he exclaimed, "Could you not get to read the Bible! how was that?" The reason was

* Owen's History of the Origin and First Ten Years of the British and Foreign Bible Society, chap. I.

soon ascertained. There was no copy to which she could gain access, either at her own home or among her friends, and she was accustomed to travel every week seven miles over the hills to a place, where she could obtain a Welsh Bible, to read the chapter from which the minister took his text. But during that week the cold and stormy weather had prevented her usual journey. Surely "the Word of the Lord was precious in those days" to this lamb in the Saviour's fold.*

The proposition was first made in December, 1802, by Mr. Charles and Mr. Tarn, at a meeting of the Committee of the Religious Tract Society, to form a separate society, whose design should be, "to promote the circulation of the Holy Scriptures in foreign countries, and in those parts of the British dominions for which adequate provision is not yet made." Various measures succeeded this resolution, until, in January, 1804, the conductors of the enterprise, prominent among whom were the Rev. Messrs. Hughes and Steinkopff, and Mr. Joseph Tarn, convened a public meeting for the 7th of March, in that year. At this meeting, held at the "London Tavern," the British and Foreign Bible Society" was established, and a committee of thirty-six members elected. The Society received before long the approbation of many of the prelates of the English Established Church, and of several Synods of the Scottish Establishment, and secured the faithful co-operation of its first excellent president, Lord Teignmouth.

A correspondence was forthwith opened with leading men in various countries of the Continent, with a view to ascertain the want that might exist in those quarters, of such operations as the Society contemplated. As the first fruits of this correspondence, the Nuremburg Bible Society was founded. Among the replies elicited, was one of the most friendly nature from a

* Jubilee Memorial of the Religious Tract Society: London, 1850, p. 46.

Roman Catholic priest, in Suabia. A Roman Catholic Bible Society was shortly after established at Ratisbon. The Berlin Society (1806), the Russian Society (1813), and the Danish Society (1814), followed.

The British and Foreign Bible Society has encountered at different periods, but especially within the first few years of its existence, no small amount of opposition. The source of this opposition has been almost wholly among the less evangelical portion of the clergy and members of the Church of England. The ground of it lay chiefly in the fact, that the Society was not a "Church" institution, and that Dissenters were associated in it with the members of the Established Communion. It may be added, that although the Bible Society has never been without its warm supporters among the clergy of the Church of England, the larger number of its prelates have stood aloof from the enterprise. Of this party the "Society for Promoting Christian Knowledge" is understood to be the organ.

A more reasonable motive for disagreement, was to be found in the early position of the Society relative to the uncanonical books of Scripture. Previous to the year 1826, it had aided in circulating (more particularly in Roman Catholic countries, and with a view to facilitate the dissemination of the Scriptures under Roman Catholic auspices) editions of the Bible containing the Apocrypha. This course could not but be distasteful to many of the friends of the institution at home; and the agitation of the subject resulted finally in the adoption of three resolutions, which confined the Society, for the future, to the circulation of the canonical books.

We cannot enter at any length into the history of the operations of the British and Foreign Bible Society. Their extent and importance would claim too large a space in this sketch. We must be satisfied with a brief view of the results of this great and blessed institution, as they may be gathered from the following statistics.

The number of *languages* and *dialects*, in which the British and Foreign Bible Society has promoted, in whole or in part, the distribution, printing or translation of the Scriptures, is one hundred and forty-four. This has been done: directly, in eighty-five languages or dialects; and indirectly, in fifty-nine. The whole number of versions made (omitting those which are printed in different characters only) is one hundred and sixty-six. Of these, one hundred and fourteen are translations never before printed.

The number of *copies of the Scriptures* issued by the Society, from the beginning, has been twenty-three million one hundred and ten thousand and fifty. Of this amount, over eight million eight hundred and forty thousand were copies of the Bible; and the remaining number of the New Testament only. The issue for the last year alone, was one million one hundred and thirty-six thousand six hundred and ninety-five.

The *expenditures* of the Society, from the beginning, amount to no less than three million six hundred and forty-eight thousand pounds sterling, or $17,800,000. Its annual expenditures have risen as high as one hundred and thirty-three thousand pounds; for the last year, however, they were ninety-seven thousand two hundred and forty-six pounds ($464,560).*

Connected with the British and Foreign Bible Society, there are three thousand six hundred and seventy-eight auxiliaries, branches, and associations, in Great Britain and the colonies. This number does not include the auxiliaries of the Hibernian Bible Society, which has four hundred and ninety-nine; nor the various independent societies that have arisen under its fostering care, on the continent of Europe, and in India and America. These societies, sixty-two in number, have sprung up for the most part in the German States. We shall speak of them with greater detail in another chapter.

The Edinburgh Bible Society was originally an auxiliary of the

* Forty-sixth Report of the B. and F. Bible Society, 1850.

British and Foreign; having been organized in the year 1809; but in 1830, the controversy respecting the Apocrypha occasioned its separation, and since that time it has been entirely independent. It has a number of auxiliaries, and has been very successful in promoting the circulation of the word of God.

Besides its operations through the medium of these corresponding bodies, the Bible Society employs, in various countries, its agents and colporteurs for the more immediate dissemination of the Holy Scriptures. Its foreign agents, having the superintendence of Bible depôts, are stationed at Paris, Brussels, Amsterdam, Breda, Frankfort, Cologne, Stockholm, Christiania, and other towns in Norway, and at St. Petersburg. There are also depôts at Odessa, Constantinople, Smyrna, Athens, Corfu, Malta, Gibraltar, and other places. The agents are, for the most part, men of great activity and zeal, whose names are well known among us, such as M. Pressensé, at Paris, M. Tiddy, in Belgium, Dr. Pinkerton, in Germany, Mr. Lowndes, at Malta, and others. The celebrated George Borrow was for some years an agent of the Society, in Spain and elsewhere. Its colporteurs are generally men of humble circumstances, but of good character, who spend their whole time in visiting families and places of resort, to offer the Scriptures for sale at reduced prices. Eighty-one of these laborers are employed in France alone; twenty in Germany; and several in Belgium, Holland, Switzerland, Sweden, Italy, and Hungary;—in all, about one hundred and thirty. Of the fruits of this system of Bible dissemination, we cannot speak at large. They are already visible to a most encouraging extent, in France and Italy more particularly, in the increase of interest in religious matters, and of readiness to receive and embrace the Gospel, which is evinced so generally throughout the population.

The British and Foreign Bible Society is at present under the presidency of Lord Bexley; its first efficient president having died in 1834. In the course of that year and the preceding one, this institution also lost three of its most devoted friends: Joseph Hughes, its first Secretary; William Wilberforce, one of its Vice-Presidents; and Hannah More. It now numbers among its officers nineteen prelates of the Church of England; the excellent Archbishop of Canterbury being one of them. The names of the Treasurer, and Secretary—John Thornton, Esq., and Rev. Mr. Brandram—are also widely known.

The interests of this noble association are dear to every Christian heart. If there be one organization whose history is peculiarly identified with the commencement and progress of the century in which we live, and whose prosperity we regard as intimately connected with the increase of pure religion in the present age, it is certainly the British and Foreign Bible Society. Long may it continue, with its kindred societies, to carry forward the standard of our Reformed Faith, in the spirit of its ancient motto: "THE BIBLE is the Religion of Protestants."

SECTION II.

Other countries of Europe.—On the continent of Europe there have been formed at various periods since the origin of the British and Foreign Bible Society, a number of independent societies of a nature similar to it; nearly all of which have borne more or less intimate relations with that body. We have mentioned several of these associations in a preceding connection; and at the conclusion of this chapter will be found a list of the Bible Societies extant, with the date of their formation and the amount of their issues.

Of the more important of these Bible Societies on the continent, we will here mention only the French and Foreign Bible Society, instituted at Paris in 1833. The comparatively feeble churches of France have nobly engaged in almost every branch of Christian benevolence; and although their efforts cannot be measured by those of British and American Christians, they are more than proportionate to their resources. At the time of the foundation of this Society, there already existed in France a "Protestant Bible Society," instituted in 1818, and which still continues. But by a singular provision in its constitution, that association is restricted to the circulating of Bibles among professed Protestants. The evangelizing of the Roman Catholic population formed no part of the plan adopted by those who founded the Protestant Bible Society; and indeed it has been supported mainly by that portion of the French Protestants who are not regarded as evangelical in their religious principles.

The French and Foreign Bible Society has been considerably assisted in its operations by the British and American Societies. The former, in addition to its liberal grants to the French Bible Society, supports at Paris an agency, which during the year 1849–50 put into circulation over one hundred and eight thousand copies of the Scriptures; and has circulated in all nearly two millions of copies within the last seventeen years. The latter has from time to time made large donations to the French Society; in the year 1848–9 it voted a grant of ten thousand dollars; and has promised another similar grant.

The number of copies of the Scriptures issued by the French and Foreign Bible Society during the year 1849–50 was eighty-seven thousand eight hundred and forty-nine; making the total amount of its issues from the beginning nine hundred and five thousand eight hundred and thirty-nine.

The income of this Society for the last year was one hundred and eleven thousand four hundred and seventy-three francs ($20,622). In the circulation of the Scriptures it employs a number of colporteurs; an instrumentality which has been remarkably successful in France, where more than one hundred and fifty of these laborers are at present supported by the Bible Societies, and the Evangelical Society of Geneva.

The president of this Society is the talented and pious Count de Gasparin; among its secretaries and directors, are Count de Laborde, Rev. Mr. Burnier, and Rev. Drs. Monod and Grand pierre.

SECTION III.

Asia.—In the several "presidencies" of British India, there have been formed, from time to time, associations corresponding with the British and Foreign Bible Society, for the dissemination of the Scriptures in that country. The first of these, in order of date, was the Calcutta Bible Society, instituted in 1811. This society, with its various branches, has distributed more than six hundred thousand copies of the word of God. The Bombay Society, established in 1813, has distributed about one hundred and eighty-two thousand copies; the Madras Society, established in 1820, five hundred and seventy-four thousand; and the North India Society, instituted at Agra in 1845, nearly thirty-four thousand copies.

In the island of Ceylon, there are two Bible Societies—at Colombo and Jaffna—the former of which, instituted in 1812, has a number of branches. The amount of their issues is about one hundred and thirty thousand copies.

A correspondence with these bodies has lately been entered into by the committee of the parent society, on the subject of a proposition made by the Rev. W. Arthur, to give to every family in India a portion of the word of God. Communications of much interest have been received in reply; but the prevailing sentiment seems to be, that the measure is not at present practicable in its full extent; whilst the earnest desire exists to carry it out as far as circumstances may allow.

In nearly every other country occupied by the various missionary societies of Europe and America, as a field of labor, there have been extensive efforts for the distribution of the Scriptures; and in many of them, associations auxiliary to the

British and other Bible Societies, have been formed and successfully carried on. Thus in New South Wales, Australia, New Zealand, and the South Sea islands, there are flourishing auxiliaries; as also in British North America. It is unnecessary, however, to enter into detail respecting their operations, as they are included in the general statements already made respecting the British and Foreign Bible Society.

SECTION IV.

WESTERN HEMISPHERE.

United States.—The earliest movement of any importance in the United States, for supplying the people with copies of the Holy Scriptures, was made by the Congress of 1777. In answer to a memorial on the scarcity of Bibles throughout the country, that body proceeded to appoint a committee to advise as to the expediency of printing an edition of thirty thousand copies. It was thought best, instead of printing, to import a sufficient supply; which was accordingly ordered. Again, in 1781, the subject was brought before Congress; and a resolution was adopted, approving and recommending to the people an edition of the Bible then just published at Philadelphia.

These interesting historical facts show, that there was no want of attention, even at this early period, to the importance of disseminating the word of God in this country.

Prior to the formation of the AMERICAN BIBLE SOCIETY, there existed various local associations of a similar nature. The example of English Christians, and the loud call for a more extensive plan of operations, had also enforced upon many minds the necessity of forming a general, national organization for the systematic distribution of the Holy Scriptures. The subject was agitated for several years; until in 1815, a project to this effect was drawn up by the New Jersey Bible Society, and was sent to the sister societies for concurrence. A general meeting was finally appointed, to be held at New York, in May, 1816.

Of the causes which prepared the way for the establishment of the American Bible Society, the Rev. Dr. Beecher, one of its earliest friends, says :—" The first, no doubt, was the existence and prosperous operations of the British and Foreign Bible Society. The second was the foreign missionary spirit that was awakened a few years anterior; and the organization of the Foreign Missionary Society. The primary agent in this movement, I am well assured, was the Rev. Samuel J. Mills; in whose heart the fire of foreign missions first burned for several years. In his travels West and South, he had the organization of an American Bible Society at heart. It was by personal conversation, I doubt not, with thousands of the most influential men all over our nation, and addressing, when he had opportunity, ecclesiastical bodies, that he prepared the way for a harmonious concurrence in favor of the organization when the convention met."*

At this convention, on the 11th of May, 1816, the American Bible Society was organized. "It was a sublime spectacle," says the writer from whom we have just quoted. "Each one had his own mind prepared by an agency which he had scarcely recognized, and of whose ubiquitous influence he had no knowledge. We came to the meeting in great weakness, humility, and prayer; feeling the difficulties in combining all denominations; and feeling every one the necessity of keeping his heart and tongue, and walking very softly, lest a spark of unhallowed fire falling on a train, it should explode. We felt that the place was holy where we stood, and that God was there; and our fears were not realized, and our hopes were surpassed exceedingly abundantly, so cordial was our unity."

* History of the Am. Bible Society; by W. P. Strickland; p. 26.

The first president of the Society was the Hon. Elias Boudinot. Among the vice-presidents were some of the most eminent statesmen of the day. The secretaries were the Rev. Drs. Mason and Romeyn.

The local societies which were in existence at the date of the formation of the national society, speedily connected themselves with it as auxiliaries. During the first year of its existence, eighty-four associations were thus annexed.

The operations of the American Bible Society at home have been mainly carried on through the auxiliary associations connected with it. One of its regulations has been, to distribute no Bibles gratuitously, except through the auxiliaries, as the proper media of its benefactions. The number of these associations has increased yearly at a rapid rate, and now amounts to more than twelve hundred, with about twenty-five hundred branches, located in all the States and territories of the Union. Among the more important of them we may mention the New York, New York Female, Pennsylvania, Virginia, Cincinnati, and Louisville Bible Societies. To organize such associations, explore unoccupied fields, and collect funds, agents are employed, of whom there are at present twenty-seven. Much of the prosperity of the institution has been owing, under the Divine blessing, to the faithful labors of these agents. No colporteurs or distributors of Bibles are employed directly by the Society; but under the direction of the auxiliaries, a number of such laborers are at work.

Through instrumentalities of this nature, the Scriptures have also been widely circulated among *special classes* of our population,—in the prisons and hospitals,—among seamen and boatmen,—in the army and navy,—among the colored people in the South,—and the Indians in the West. Through the various missionary organizations, too, the American Bible Society has contributed largely to the distribution of the Scriptures in the Roman Catholic countries of Europe, South America, and

Mexico, and in China, India, Ceylon, Africa, the Levant, &c. This has been done partly by grants of books, and partly by appropriations in money, for the specific purpose of Bible distribution. The total amount of remittances made, in money, has been about $330,000, which must have put into circulation some 700,000 Bibles, or portions of the Bible, in about sixty different languages.

Of the versions of the Bible issued by the British and Foreign Bible Society, the American Bible Society has aided in publishing, or has purchased and circulated copies of several. It has also been at the sole expense of publishing the Armeno-Turkish Bible and the Modern Syriac, the Hebrew-Spanish Old Testament and the Modern Armenian Bible. It has, moreover, published the entire Hawaiian Bible at the Sandwich Islands, the Modern Greek New Testament, the Ojibwa Testament, and the Choctaw Testament, two of the Gospels in the Sioux Dingon tongue, the books of Genesis and Isaiah in Mohawk, one of the Gospels in Seneca, two in Cherokee, one in the Grebo, and the book of Acts in the Arrowacb.*

The number of copies of the Scripture issued by this Society, from the beginning, has been six million nine hundred and eighty thousand five hundred and thirty-five. Of these more than two million seven hundred and fifteen thousand were Bibles, and the remaining number Testaments. For the last year alone the Society issued six hundred and thirty-three thousand three hundred and ninety-five copies.

The receipts of the Society for the last year amount to two hundred and eighty-four thousand six hundred and fourteen dollars. This sum shows an increase of thirty-two thousand seven hundred and forty-four dollars over the receipts of the preceding year (1848–9). It is also considerably larger than the income of any previous year. The total amount of the So-

* Thirty-Fourth Report of the Am. Bible Society, 1850.

ciety's receipts, from the beginning, is three million eight hundred and forty-four thousand four hundred and eighty-six dollars.

Nearly all of the officers appointed at the organization of the American Bible Society have been removed by death. The present president is the Hon. Theodore Frelinghuysen, LL.D. Amongst the vice-presidents are several distinguished jurists and statesmen. The secretaries are the Rev. Drs. Brigham and Holdich.

This institution is at present in a highly-flourishing condition. The ability and efficiency of its conductors, and the liberality of its friends, have been already blessed of God in its great prosperity and usefulness. Its operations and influence are still on the increase, and the firm hold which it has secured upon the general confidence of the churches, encourages us to hope that a wide and glorious career is yet opening before it.

American and Foreign Bible Society.—The American and Foreign Bible Society was formed by the secession of members of the Baptist denomination from the American Bible Society. This secession occurred in the year 1836, and under the following circumstances. A letter was received from Mr. Pearce, a Baptist missionary at Calcutta, inquiring whether aid could be obtained in printing the Bengalee Scriptures, translated on the principle adopted by the American Baptist missionaries in Burmah. This proposition was submitted in August, 1835, to the Board of Managers, and was by them referred to a committee; who reported that it would be inexpedient to recommend appropriations, until the Board should settle a principle in relation to the translation of the word *baptizo.* This report was concurred in; and another committee was appointed, who reported that it was inexpedient to appropriate the funds of the Society in aid of translating or distributing the Bengalee New Testament or any other version containing translations of the Greek word *baptizo* and its cognates. The reasons given for this decision were chiefly that such a translation would necessarily impede the operations of missionaries of other denominations in India; and that it was not competent for the American Bible Society to assume a sectarian attitude by favoring the denominational views of any particular church, whether at home or abroad. A protest against this decision was presented by the dissenting members of the Board; and it was forthwith resolved by them to call a convention of the Baptist denomination for the purpose of forming a distinct Bible Society. Accordingly, such a meeting took place at New York on the 12th of May, 1836, and the American and Foreign Bible Society was organized.*

Much of the labor of this Society has been expended upon foreign fields, in connection with the missions of the Baptist denomination. Thus its appropriations for the last year, to the American Baptist Missionary Union, for the issue of the Karen, Assamese, Siamese, Chinese and Teloogoo Scriptures, and for Bible distribution in Germany and France, amounted to nearly seventeen thousand dollars. The largest grant was to Mr. Oncken, in Germany, where the operations of the Society are the most extensive.

Besides direct appropriations to missionary fields, the American and Foreign Bible Society acts through the medium of auxiliary associations, of which there are three hundred and sixteen in connection with it. By this instrumentality also the funds of the institution are to a great extent collected.

The receipts of this Society for the year 1849–50 amounted to forty-one thousand six hundred and twenty-five dollars; being an advance of more than three thousand dollars over the income of the preceding year, which was itself larger than that of any previous one. The number of copies of the Scriptures issued by it, from the beginning, is seven hundred and ninety-four thousand three hundred and ninety-eight.

* Proceedings of the Bible Convention in 1837.

A controversy has lately arisen in the American and Foreign Bible Society, the result of which has been the formation of another association, by some of its leading members. This secession was occasioned by the refusal of the Society to publish a new translation of the Scriptures in the English language, with a view to a more correct rendering of the original. Such a translation, it was contended by the advocates of the measure, was required in consideration of the defects of the authorized version, and from the fundamental principle of the Society, to diffuse the Scriptures in the most faithful and accurate translations. To carry out this purpose, the "American Bible Union" was organized at New York on the 10th of June, 1850, under the presidency of the Rev. Dr. Cone, former president of the American and Foreign Bible Society. The new institution held its first annual meeting in October of the same year; at which date its subscriptions &c., amounted to thirteen thousand three hundred dollars. Of its operations little can be said as yet; so short a time having elapsed since its foundation. The avowed object of the Union is sufficiently expansive—"to procure and circulate the most faithful versions of the Sacred Scriptures in all languages throughout the world."

SECTION V.

LIST OF BIBLE SOCIETIES, WITH THE AMOUNT OF THEIR ISSUES.

	Bibles and Tests.
1. British and Foreign Bible Society, instituted 1804	23,110,050
2. American Bible Society, instituted 1816 . .	6,980,535
3. American and Foreign Bible Society, instituted 1837	794,398
WESTERN EUROPE.	
4. Protestant Bible Society at Paris, instituted 1818, with 132 Auxiliaries	254,673

	Bibles and Tests.
5. French and Foreign Bible Society at Paris, instituted 1833, with Auxiliaries	905,839
6. Strasburg Bible Society, instituted 1815—(chiefly German Bibles and Testaments) .	71,503

NORTHERN EUROPE.

7. Icelandic Bible Society, instituted 1815 . .	10,445
8. Swedish Bible Society, instituted 1809, with Auxiliaries	638,427
9. Norwegian Bible Society, instituted 1816 .	32,189
10. Stavanger Bible Society, instituted 1828 . .	7,017
11. Finnish Bible Society, instituted 1812, at Abo, with many Branches	110,561
12. Danish Bible Society, instituted 1814, with Auxiliaries	193,692

CENTRAL EUROPE.

13. Netherlands Bible Society, with Auxiliaries .	403,448
14. Belgium and Foreign Bible Society, at Brussels, instituted 1834	7,623
15. Belgian Bible Associations, instituted 1839 .	14,909
16. Antwerp Bible Society, instituted 1834 . .	439
17. Ghent Bible Society, instituted 1834 . . .	8,980
18. Sleswick-Holstein Bible Society, instituted 1815, with Auxiliaries	125,826
19. Eutin Bible Society, instituted 1817, for Principality of Lübeck	5,296
20. Lübeck Bible Society, instituted 1814 . . .	11,972
21. Hamburg-Altona Bible Society, instituted 1814, with Branches	93,792
22. Bremen Bible Society, instituted 1815, with an Auxiliary	26,913
23. Lauenburgh-Ratzeburgh Bible Society, instituted 1816	10,675

	Bibles and Tests.
24. Rostock Bible Society, instituted 1816 . .	19,154
25. Hanover Bible Society, instituted 1814, with Auxiliaries	125,539
26. Lippe-Detmold Bible Society, instituted 1816	3,569
27. Waldeck and Pyrmont Bible Society, instituted 1817	2,800
28. Hesse-Cassel Bible Society, instituted 1818 .	30,000
29. Hanau Bible Society, instituted 1818 . . .	3,316
30. Marburg Bible Society, instituted 1825 . .	7,832
31. Frankfort Bible Society, instituted 1816 . .	73,565
32. Hesse-Darmstadt Bible Society, instituted 1817, with Auxiliaries	31,484
33. Duchy of Baden Bible Society, instituted 1820, with Auxiliaries	18,585
34. Würtemberg Bible Society, instituted 1812, with Auxiliaries	552,627
35. Bavarian Protestant Bible Institution at Nuremberg, instituted 1821, with Auxiliaries	155,989
36. Saxon Bible Society, instituted 1814, with Auxiliaries	173,302
37. Anhalt-Bernberg Bible Society, instituted 1821.	4,786
38. Anhalt-Dessau Bible Society	3,310
39. Weimar Bible Society, instituted 1821 . .	3,773
40. Eisenach Bible Society, instituted 1818 . .	4,938
41. Brunswick Bible Society, instituted 1815 . .	700
42. Prussian Bible Society at Berlin, instituted 1805, with Auxiliaries	1,566,660
Issued to the Prussian troops, since 1830 .	327,000

SWITZERLAND AND ITALY.

43. Bâsle Bible Society, instituted 1804 . . .	418,855
44. Schaffhausen Bible Society, instituted 1813 .	13,179

	Bibles and Tests.
45. Zurich Bible Society, instituted 1812, with Auxiliary at Winterthur	15,163
46. St. Gall Bible Society, instituted 1813 . .	37,436
47. Aargovian Bible Society, instituted 1815 . .	19,454
48. Berne Bible Society	44,646
49. Neufchatel Bible Society, instituted 1816 .	6,430
50. Lausanne Bible Society, instituted 1814 . .	32,000
51. Geneva Bible Society, instituted 1814 . . .	36,651
52. Glarus Bible Society, instituted 1819 . . .	5,000
53. Coire or Chur Bible Society, instituted 1813 .	12,267
54. Waldenses Bible Society at La Tour, instituted 1816	4,238
GREECE AND TURKEY.	
55. Ionian Bible Society, instituted 1819 at Corfu, with three Auxiliaries	7,377
RUSSIA.	
56. Russian Bible Society, Petersburg, previous to its suspension by an imperial Ukase, in 1826, had 289 Auxiliaries, and had printed the Scriptures in various languages; the circulation of which is still allowed . . .	861,105
57. Russian Protestant Bible Society at St. Petersburg, instituted 1826, with numerous Auxiliaries	250,325
INDIA.	
58. Calcutta Bible Society, instituted 1811, with various Branches	602,266
Serampore Missionaries	200,000
59. North India Bible Society, at Agra, instituted 1845	33,900
60. Madras Bible Society, instituted 1820 . . .	574,154

	Bibles and Tests.
61. Bombay Bible Society, instituted 1813 . .	182,115
62. Colombo Bible Society, instituted 1812, with various Branches in Ceylon	36,114
63. Jaffna Bible Society	94,091
Total of copies of Scriptures . .	40,414,879

CHAPTER V.

SOCIETIES FOR THE CIRCULATION OF RELIGIOUS BOOKS.

SECTION I.

EASTERN HEMISPHERE.

Great Britain.—The Rev. George Burder, minister of a congregation at Coventry, was, under the providence of God, the originator of the London Religious Tract Society. Having felt the need of popular tracts of a more decided religious character than those of Mrs. More, which were then in circulation, he prepared six essays of this nature, under the title of "Village Tracts;" which were committed for publication to a bookseller in London. The failure of this publisher interfered with the circulation of the tracts, but led its author and his friends to consider the importance of forming a society, which should attend to the preparation and publication, at a cheap rate, of such productions as those which had been attempted. Accordingly, on the 10th of May, 1799, the Religious Tract Society was organized, at a meeting of gentlemen held at the St. Paul coffee-house, London. The committee elected on that occasion embraced among others the celebrated Rowland Hill, together with Alexander Waugh, Matthew Wilks and Joseph Hughes.

The early friends of the institution took a decided position in reference to its catholicity. Nothing was to be published that in any way reflected upon a particular denomination of evangelical Christians. The great object which it contemplated from the outset, was "to hold forth to view those grand doctrinal and practical truths which have in every age been mighty through God in converting, sanctifying and comforting souls."* This catholic spirit has been maintained in all the subsequent proceedings of the Society. The union which has prevailed in its councils has been a pleasing evidence of the Divine blessing upon the labors of its conductors.

The Religious Tract Society has numbered among its friends and officers many of the most eminent Christians of our times. The excellent Legh Richmond became, in 1813, one of its Secretaries. Several of his invaluable tracts were written for publication by the Society; and the others were reprinted by it.

So intimately has the Tract cause been connected with that of the Bible, that nearly all of the more prominent advocates of the latter were members of this institution. Hughes, Steinkopff, Bogue, Henderson, Pinkerton, Bickersteth, were earnest friends to both of these enterprises.

It is not practicable, and would be unnecessary, to enter into much detail respecting the internal history of the Religious Tract Society. Its course has been quiet and unobtrusive, but steady and prosperous. The opposition it has encountered from time to time, has been upon grounds of too little importance to require specification here. The progress of the cause, and its fruits thus far, can be better displayed by a brief statistical statement, than in any other way.

At the semi-centennial celebration or Jubilee of the Society, which occurred in 1849, upon the completion of its fiftieth year, the results of the enterprise were given as follows:†

The total amount of receipts for the first fifty years of the Society's existence, was one million two hundred and two thousand two hundred and forty-two pounds sterling ($5,860,000).

* Dr. Bogue; in his first Sermons for the Society.

† Jubilee Memorial of the Religious Tract Society; London, 1850.

The total amount of issues of publications, within the same term of years, was five hundred millions. These publications are in one hundred and ten different languages and dialects; and have been distributed in all parts of Europe, in Persia, India, Ceylon, China, Polynesia, Africa, North and South America, &c. The total amount of grants to these various countries is one hundred and fifty-five thousand three hundred and seventy-two pounds sterling.

The number of the separate publications of the Society, is five thousand one hundred and forty-eight. At its anniversary in 1848, the Report strongly urged generous offerings to the institution on the completion of its fiftieth year, to be devoted to the issue of publications calculated, by the divine blessing, to counteract the unchristian and demoralizing tendency of a vast portion of the cheap literature of the day, and to the promotion of an enlarged distribution of the Society's works in Ireland, and in the countries opening to its labors on the continent of Europe. The result of this special appeal has been the liberal contribution of eight thousand six hundred and fifty-nine pounds sterling.

From the *fifty-first* annual Report of the Religious Tract Society, we learn that its receipts for the last year—1849–50—amounted to sixty-one thousand three hundred and twenty-seven pounds sterling ($299,270). The issues of its publications during the year were nineteen millions two hundred and forty-five thousand four hundred and forty-one; making the total circulation of the Society's tracts and books, in one hundred and ten languages, including the issues of affiliated societies in foreign lands, about five hundred and twenty-four millions.

With regard to the mode of this Society's operations, in the distribution of its publications, the following statement is made in its last report. "In applying the funds contributed to the Society, care is taken to secure as wide and as promising a field of operation as can be attained. By the aid of missionaries abroad, and disinterested friends at home, the gratuitous circulation is carried forward without any charge or expense for agents. By a carefully arranged system, in the concerns of the Depository, the sale of the publications is made to cover all the expenses of producing them, and of the necessary establishment of the Society. Thus the whole amount of subscriptions, donations, and contributions is applied to the gratuitous circulation of its publications, without any deduction or charge whatever; and the favor with which the works have been received by the Christian public, has enabled the Committee, of late years, to distribute to a larger extent than the sums received; so that the Society has rendered back to the public an amount exceeding in value what has been thus contributed. In this course, the Committee trust the Society will be enabled to proceed, without risking its important and fundamental object, of presenting a large and varied list of works, at such prices as the religious public have a right to expect."*

As early as the year 1806, the Religious Tract Society, having issued three or four millions of tracts, including a cheap narrative series with cuts, adapted to counteract the influence which a flood of infidel and other vile publications was exerting upon the lower classes, gave attention to the formation of Tract Societies in foreign countries. In the preceding year, the Rev. Drs. Patterson and Henderson, forbidden by the East India Company to go to India, went to Denmark to seek liberty to station themselves at Serampore. This being denied, they obtained the translation of "The Great Question Answered" into Danish; which led to the extensive Tract and Bible operations in the north of Europe, under the labors chiefly of the Rev. Drs. Pinkerton and Steinkopff.†

"There is one view of the Society's foreign labors," says the

* Fifty-first annual Report of the Religious Tract Society: 1850.

† Quarter-Century Reminiscences; American Tract Society.

author of the *Jubilee Memorial*, already quoted, "which it would be improper here to overlook; namely, the manner in which they have extended the influence of Christian writers through the world. Authors who only contemplated the improvement of their own countrymen when they composed their works, have had their thoughts conveyed into languages, the very names of which were unknown in their days. Little did John Bunyan foresee that in future times missionaries would go forth to the heathen, and by twenty-eight different translations of his enchanting volume interest the people of many nations, the civilized and the rude, so that the learned and polished inhabitant of France and Greece, the tawny wanderer of Arabia, the persecuted believer in Madagascar, the sunburnt Kaffir, and the degraded Hottentot, should read with avidity the book which is the delight of the lowly cottagers of our own land.

"The pious writer of the touching narrative, 'Poor Joseph,' in all probability only contemplated its usefulness within the limits of his own country: how surprised he would have been if one endowed with prophetic vision had told him that his 'half-witted man' would speak in seventeen languages, and be the means of teaching the knowledge of Christ to the Chinese in the east, the Greek in the west, the Esquimaux in the north, and the African in the south. Neither did the amiable and devoted Legh Richmond, when employing his persuasive advocacy and active labors for the Society, imagine that he was sustaining an agency which would convey his 'short and simple Annals of the Poor,' through twenty-one languages, to the Russian, the Armenian, the Arab, the Icelander, and the Turk. Nor did the esteemed writer of the 'Anxious Inquirer Directed and Encouraged' suppose, when he sent out that useful production, that his affectionate appeals would find an utterance in five continental tongues, in one of the most difficult dialects of India, and in the words of the islanders of the Pacific Ocean. In a similar manner, also, other Christian authors, as Baxter, Doddridge,

Pike, Stokes, Keith, and Barth, have had their influence extended and perpetuated to an extent they could never have anticipated."

SECTION II.

From England the beneficent influence of a religious literature has extended over nearly all parts of the continent; and the example of the Religious Tract Society has given rise, in several of the countries where Protestant institutions exist, to similar enterprises of benevolence. Some of these we proceed to mention, giving, however, only a brief statement of their statistics.

France.—The Paris Religious Tract Society has circulated during the last year about six hundred and five thousand tracts, besides one hundred and thirty thousand copies of the "Almanac of good Counsels." The receipts have amounted to 45,842 francs, and the expenses to 42,593 francs.

The Toulouse Religious Book Society has issued during the past two years, eighty-nine thousand five hundred books. In the same period, about sixty-four new libraries have been either formed or assisted. This aid has not been confined to France, but has been extended to other lands, including Africa, Greece, Canada, and Russia. During the past year various new works have been issued.

Holland.—Rotterdam Tract Society. The colporteurs meet with much acceptance among the people, and are greatly encouraged by finding that sinners have been led to God through the tracts distributed. The Society has translated twenty-eight of the handbills of the Parent Society, and in a few months upwards of 22,000 were sold. The total issues in the year were 127,800 tracts and children's books.

Germany.—The Lower Saxony Tract Society, at Hamburg, has printed 638,000 tracts: out of which 524,853 have been distributed. The total circulation in twenty-nine years has been 7,054,792. Several new tracts were printed in the year, and among them one addressed to soldiers on Mr. Gossner's recommendation.

In addition to the extensive labors of the Lower Saxony Committee, there have been large appropriations of tracts to numerous emigrants; and pious colporteurs have conveyed them to thousands who are living in awful ignorance of the way of salvation. The receipts of the society for the year have been £563, which include the grants received from the Religious Tract Society.

The Hamburg Tract Society. The issues in the year "have reached 500,000 copies of different tracts, and these have led to the circulation of upwards of 22,000 copies of the Scriptures, the employment of forty missionaries and colporteurs, and the issue of several thousand copies of larger publications." In Hamburg, nearly forty brethren are regularly engaged as loan-tract distributors, and others visit neighboring districts.

The Berlin Tract Society is now employing colporteurs for the circulation of the Scriptures and religious tracts. Mr. Elsner, the secretary, writes:—"The revolution of last year has roused in many places the hearts of men for a more willing reception of the word of God, and we have never distributed so many copies of the Scriptures as in the present year; and we are enabled to report the same of our tracts." The Rev. G. W. Lehmann, of Berlin, has given an encouraging report of the circulation of the Society's works voted to him.

Russia.—The friends at St. Petersburg have not been able to circulate their tracts and books to the same extent as in former years. Although a somewhat smaller number of publications has been sent from the depôt, yet the sales have considerably increased. The tracts received in the year amount to 180,335, in Russ, Finnish, German, English, French, Swedish, Dutch, and Danish, about 147,800 having been printed at St. Petersburg. These, added to the stock on hand in 1849, made the supplies for the year to be 464,210. The issues have been 186,730; of these, 100,493 were sold at the depository. The total issues, in various languages, amount to 3,822,830.

SECTION III.

THE UNITED STATES.

American Tract Society.—The cause of Tract distribution belongs, in this country, to the present century exclusively. As early as 1803, the Massachusetts Society for promoting Christian Knowledge entered upon the systematic publication of tracts and books; and in succeeding years various associations with the same design, sprung up in Boston, New York, Philadelphia, Baltimore, and other chief cities of the Union. All these societies had, in 1824, printed about ten millions copies of religious publications; of which the greater portion were issued by the Tract Society at Boston, founded in 1814.

In the autumn of the year 1824, a correspondence was commenced between the New York Religious Tract Society and the American Tract Society at Boston, which resulted in a public meeting held in New York, at which the plan of an American Tract Society, to be submitted to the principal Tract Societies in the country, was adopted; and subscriptions were raised to the amount of $25,000 for erecting a Tract House.

May 10th, 1825, a convention of Delegates from Tract Societies throughout the country was convened in New York, the Rev. Dr. Milnor being chairman, at which a constitution was recommended for adoption; and on the following day the Society was solemnly organized, with public religious exercises, and proceeded to lay the corner-stone of its present edifice. S. V. S. Wilder, Esq., was elected President; Rev. William A.

Hallock, (then Assistant Secretary of the Society at Boston,) corresponding Secretary; and Moses Allen, Treasurer.

The last words which the lamented SUMMERFIELD spoke in public, were uttered in an enrapturing address near the close of the meeting for organizing the Society. "In all the anniversaries," said he, "which I have ever attended in Europe or America, I have never been so conscious of the presence of the Holy Spirit, and Christian love pervading every heart. Again and again I could not refrain from weeping. The very atmosphere we breathe is the atmosphere of heaven; one which angels come down to inhale, and in which God himself delights to dwell."

Previous to commencing their operations, the Executive Committee issued an address to the Christian public, constituting Tract No. 1, in which they specify the following great doctrines of the Gospel as those in which they all harmonize, and which "constitute the basis of their union:" viz. "Man's native sinfulness; the purity and obligation of the law of God; the true and proper divinity of our Lord Jesus Christ; the necessity and reality of his Atonement and Sacrifice; the efficiency of the Holy Spirit in the work of renovation; the free and full offers of the Gospel, and the duty of men to accept it; the necessity of personal holiness; and an everlasting state of rewards and punishments beyond the grave."

The American Tract Society at Boston, at its annual meeting during the same month, resolved to become a branch, and transferred its stereotype plates to the new institution; to which, like all the other Tract institutions in the country founded on kindred principles, it has since given its cordial and efficient co-operation.

The Society's operations were commenced by issuing a series of Tracts and Children's Tracts; but attention had already been directed both to the issuing of volumes like those of Baxter and Doddridge, and to operations in foreign lands. The question occurred whether its title should not be the American Tract and Book Society, or the American and Foreign Tract Society; but the institution formed in London in 1799, had simply the title, "Religious Tract Society;" the term TRACT, Latin *tractum*, a TREATISE, or thread of discourse drawn out, was equally applicable to a larger or smaller publication; and it was conceived that the term AMERICAN might imply exertion wherever American benevolence should reach. The same views governed the Board in applying for the act of incorporation.

The Society's first Report recognizes the imperative claims of *pagan lands*, and the second contains the principles on which foreign pecuniary grants should be applied. Those principles were drawn up and presented to the Society by one of its earliest and most steady friends, the lamented JEREMIAH EVARTS, Esq., then Secretary of the American Board of Commissioners for Foreign Missions. Appeals from some foreign stations had already been received, and in the two following years the Society's first foreign pecuniary grants were made to the missions of the Board of Commissioners in Malta and Ceylon, the mission of the Protestant Episcopal church in Greece, and the mission of the American Baptist Board in Burmah.

In its third year it entered on the volume circulation, by stereotyping Doddridge's Rise and Progress, which was ere long followed by issuing the Saint's Rest, Call to the Unconverted, Pilgrim's Progress, and kindred works.

In the fourth year, attention was drawn to *systematic Tract distribution*. A deep interest had been awakened in behalf of the destitute of our country, especially in the Western States, and a meeting of gentlemen convened to raise funds, when one of them, previous to subscribing $1,000, said he wished to give at least *two Tracts to every family* at the West; and as the effort to obtain means was prosecuted by the Secretary, the question occurred, why not supply the accessible population of the East as well as the West. The work was soon entered upon by the

New York City Tract Society, and in various places throughout the country.

After two years the thoughts of some of the laborers, and especially the late HARLAN PAGE, were turned to the necessity of connecting with the distribution *faithful personal efforts for the souls of men;* which greatly increased the interest and efficiency of these endeavors, and were prosecuted to some extent in most of our principal towns and villages, and in numerous congregations. The Society's energies were directed to the extension of these means of grace throughout the country generally. The branch societies in New York city, Philadelphia, and other important cities, towns and villages, have persevered; the former having now more than 1,000 visitors, and having reported an average for the last ten years of about three hundred hopeful conversions, besides abundant incidental good.*

Of late years the American Tract Society has adopted another instrumentality for the dissemination of its excellent publications; one which had long been in use abroad, particularly in France, where it has been attended with great success; we allude to the system of *colportage.* By employing men of ordinary education but well-attested piety, in visiting families and conversing with individuals on the subject of religion, and introducing to their attention the religious volumes or tracts which they carry with them, an influence has been exerted throughout the country, but especially in the remote and sparsely-settled parts of it, which perhaps could be obtained by no other agency. In 1841 the Society's annual report directed attention to the religious destitution in portions of the South and West, and urged the importance of extending the circulation of its publications in those quarters. An appeal having been made, for well-qualified laborers to go to such destitute places, several young men responded; and in the course of the year eleven colporteurs

* Instructions for Agents. American Tract Society.

were commissioned. This number has rapidly increased. During the year 1849–50, the Society employed no fewer than five hundred and eight colporteurs, for the whole or a part of the year. The aggregate number of families visited by these agents within that period, was 428,300. Of these 44,800 were Roman Catholic families.

The American Tract Society extends its influence to foreign countries, through the missionary and other associations who occupy foreign fields, as well as through committees at various missionary stations. Its appropriations in this way, for the year 1849–50, amounted to fifteen thousand dollars. The Society, and the institutions which it aids, have issued publications in one hundred and ten languages and dialects. The total amount of sums appropriated for foreign distribution, since the formation of the Society, is $239,626.

The whole number of the Society's publications has been 1,528; of which 284 are volumes. The whole number of pages printed and circulated, from the beginning, has been 2,483,793,562. The receipts of the Society, for the year 1849–50, were $308,266; the whole receipts from the beginning amount to $2,771,038.

CHAPTER VI.

SOCIETIES FOR HOME EVANGELIZATION.

SECTION I.

WESTERN HEMISPHERE.

The necessity for Home Missions is, of course, most obvious and urgent in a newly settled country; and hence, in this department of our statement, we shall give prominence to those movements which have taken place in the United States, instead of commencing with the European institutions, as we have done in previous chapters.

American Home Missionary Society.—Various Domestic Missionary Societies had sprung up in the United States before the formation of a national association; among which was the United Domestic Missionary Society, out of which the American Home Missionary Society was formed, in the year 1826. During its first year, it supported one hundred and sixty-nine missionaries; its receipts being about twenty thousand dollars. The president of the Society at its institution was the Hon. Stephen Van Rensselaer; among its vice-presidents and directors were many of the most distinguished clergymen of the day.

It was not designed that the American Home Missionary Society should supersede the local associations already existing, but draw them into affiliation with it, as it did in a short time. There are at present connected with it fourteen important and flourishing state auxiliary societies and agencies, by which funds are collected and missionaries supported, in connection with the parent society.

The progress of this institution, during the twenty-four years, is well illustrated by the following facts:

"Beginning with 169 missionaries, in ten years it increased the number to 755; and in twenty-four years to 1,032. It sought to "lead out the enterprise of the churches in pursuit of our emigrant population; and has kept pace, in a good degree, with the crowds of pioneers who have pressed on, year by year, further towards the setting sun. For some twenty years, the progress of the line of settlements was at the average of seventeen hundred miles from north to south, and two thousand from east to west."*

In a field so extensive, and so promising, we are naturally led to inquire, what efforts have been and are now put forth for its entire evangelization, how many laborers are now engaged in this work, and what have been the results of their exertions. The number of ministers of the Gospel, as well those who have been engaged in superintending the missionary work, and those who are connected with the auxiliary boards and agencies, as those who are personally occupied in discharging the peculiar duties of home missionaries, amount, as we have already seen, to upwards of a thousand. So large a body of ministers, whose support is either wholly or in part furnished by this Society, must exert a powerful influence in their respective fields of labor. Of these brethren, 677 have been during the past year the pastors or stated supplies of single congregations; 229 have ministered to two or three congregations each; and 126 have extended their labors over still wider fields—the destitute localities of a county, or of several contiguous counties, or those within the limits of an ecclesiastical body. In this way not less than 1,575 congregations and missionary districts have been

* Home Missionary, Feb., 1851.

supplied either in whole or in part, at stated intervals; and many others have, at the same time, enjoyed the occasional preaching of the word of life.

The labors of the Home Missionary Society have not been restricted to the mass of our population who speak the English language, or to the white inhabitants only. Five missionaries have been commissioned as pastors or stated supplies of churches of colored people; ten have preached to Welsh, and twenty-eight to German congregations; one to a congregation of Norwegians; and one to a congregation of Swedes.

Nor have the missionaries neglected the establishment of Sabbath-schools, and the imparting of religious instruction to the rising generation, who are soon to hold in their own hands the destiny of their country. At least 75,000 children and youth have been connected with the Sabbath-schools, under the care of the missionaries of this Society, during the last year. The missionaries have likewise paid much attention to the progress of temperance in those communities among which they have resided; and the number of those who have pledged themselves to temperance may be estimated at 93,000. They have been careful, however, to base all their efforts on moral principle, witnessing as they frequently do the inefficacy, if not the injurious tendency, of all other motives. Their efforts have not been fruitless. In Wisconsin, where the Society has for years been laboring with much encouragement, a law has been enacted by the legislature, making the vender of intoxicating drink responsible for all the injury which his iniquitous traffic inflicts upon the persons, the property, and the peace of the community. But though this law has met with much opposition, it has been made still more effective by an amendment recently passed, which renders it obligatory on the town supervisors to prosecute all cases of its violation. Its happy effects have already become visible in the increase of sobriety and good order throughout the state.

The contributions of many of the churches, assisted by the Society, to benevolent objects, have not been inconsiderable; in 512 congregations, they amounted to $21,756, or more than one third of the amount expended during the past year to aid these congregations in sustaining the ministry.

Yet the number of hopeful conversions and additions to the Church, as it is so closely connected with the missionary work, is also the most interesting sign of the effectiveness of the operation of this Society. During the year 1849-50, the additions to the churches, as far as they were ascertained, amounted to 6,682; of whom 3,815 were admitted upon profession of their faith, and 2,867 upon letters of recommendation from other churches. This is a larger number than has been reported in any one year since 1844, and has been exceeded only in three years since the formation of the Society. The missionary stations seem to have been remarkably blessed by the influences of the Spirit of God; and revivals are reported to have occurred, by no less than seventy missionaries. Less than one third of the missionaries report 3,108 cases of hopeful conversion.

The external prospects of the churches are likewise cheering. Numerous church edifices are every year raised, and not less than forty congregations, which have hitherto depended, in part at least, upon the Society for the support of their pastors, have become independent, and are now enabled to sustain them by their own contributions.

The receipts of the Home Missionary Society for the year 1849–50, were $157,160 78 cts.; and for the twenty-four years which have elapsed since its formation, $2,054,417 91 cts.

SECTION II.

We proceed to mention some of the operations of denominational societies and boards in our own country, in the field of domestic missions.

Presbyterian Board of Domestic Missions.—The Presbyterian church (old-school organization) sustains, through its Board of Domestic Missions, an important part in this great enterprise. During the last year, the number of ministers supported in whole or in part by this body was five hundred and seventy; and the number of feeble congregations aided, and missionary stations supplied, so far as reported, was 1461. These operations extend over twenty-five States of the Union. The additions to the church within the year amount to about five thousand; the sum contributed by the mission churches to foreign and domestic missions, was about ten thousand dollars. The receipts of this Board for the year were $79,049.

Protestant Episcopal Board of Domestic Missions.—The number of laborers at present supported or assisted by the Domestic Board of the Protestant Episcopal Church, is ninety-six; of whom three are bishops, ninety presbyters and deacons, and three laymen. About the same number of stations are occupied by these missionaries; extending through twenty States and Territories. The receipts for the last year were $30,657.

Domestic Missions of the Methodist Episcopal Church.—Under the separation between the Northern and Southern portions of the Methodist Episcopal Church, the Home Missionary work, as well as the Foreign, has been divided. The Missionary Society of the Church, North, sustains, in the sphere of domestic operations, missions among the German and Swedish immigrants, the Indian tribes, and our own population. Among the Germans, it supports one hundred and eight missionaries, at ninety stations, principally in the West, comprising one hundred and fifteen churches, with 7128 members. The Indian Mission, likewise located in the West, consists of twelve stations, occupied by seventeen missionaries, and containing 1075 church members. Among the Swedes, a missionary is supported at New York, and another in Illinois. In the destitute portions of the various districts of the church, this Society employs 337 missionaries, at 320 stations, containing 30,438 church-members. Total number of missionaries, 464; and of church-members, 38,882. Appropriations for the past year (to Home Missions), $58,070.

The Missionary Society of the Church, South, restricts its operations to the home field almost exclusively, having but two missionaries abroad. Its missions are distributed among the destitute fields at home, the colored population, the Germans, and the Indians. In the first of these departments it supports 117 missionaries, at 124 stations, in which are included 20,921 church-members. Among the colored population are employed 104 missionaries, at 116 stations, containing 34,459 members. Among the Germans eight missionaries are at work, chiefly in Louisiana, and among the Indian tribes there are thirty-nine missionaries. Total number of laborers, 273; and of church-members, 59,707. Receipts for the last year, $60,871.

Baptist Home Mission Society.—This Society employs, in fifteen States and territories, and in Canada, one hundred and eighteen laborers. Of these, twenty-two are stationed in Illinois, eighteen in Michigan, and sixteen in Canada. Since the formation of the Society, 1432 ministers have received its commission. Its receipts for the last year were $30,369.

The Southern Baptist denomination sustains, in connection with its Convention, a Board of Domestic Missions, which employed, during the last year, fifty missionaries. Many of these are laboring among the colored population. Receipts for the year, $10,692.

Evangelical Lutheran Home Missionary Society.—Under the direction of the General Synod of the Evangelical Lutheran Church in the United States, this Society was organized in 1845, and now supports twenty-two missionaries in the States of Maryland, Illinois, Indiana, Pennsylvania, Kentucky, and Ohio. The receipts for the three years (in the interim of the Synod's convention), ending April, 1850, amounted to $2,081.

Free-Will Baptist Home Mission Society.—Ten churches have received aid from this small, but growing association, during the last year. The amount of its income was $5,525.

The Seventh-Day Baptists, and some other denominations of Christians in this country, have their own organizations for the extension of religion in their peculiar spheres; but it is needless to go into further detail.

SECTION III.

EASTERN HEMISPHERE.

England and Ireland.—There are in Great Britain several religious associations in operation, whose design is the evangelizing of the native population, whether in Great Britain or in the colonies. Three of these societies are comprehended under the title of "The British Missions;" namely, the Home, Colonial, and Irish Evangelical Societies.

The *Home Missionary Society*, which was founded in 1819, employs, at present, in whole, or in part, one hundred and sixteen missionaries or agents, and nearly one hundred lay-preachers, who have, as their weekly coadjutors, 1652 Sunday-school teachers, and whose ministrations are attended by upwards of forty-one thousand hearers, and about twelve thousand five hundred Sunday-school scholars. The chapels, or preaching-rooms of the Society's laborers, number nearly four hundred and fifty, and are scattered among four hundred and forty towns, villages, and hamlets. The entire receipts of the Home Missionary Society for the year 1849–50, amounted to £6,159, or $29,810. Its expenditures exceeded this sum by £200.

The *Irish Evangelical Society*, founded in 1814, employs in Ireland twenty-four pastors and missionaries, and twenty-six Scripture readers and teachers. Its receipts last year were

£2,791, or $13,508; but this sum being inadequate to meet the engagements of the Society, it is obliged to diminish the extent of its operations.

The *Colonial Society* was founded in 1836. The sphere of its labors is in New Brunswick, Nova Scotia, the Canadas, New South Wales, Australia, and Van Dieman's Land. For the last year, the number of its agents in these colonies was thirty-seven, the number of its stations being the same. Its receipts were £2,765, or $13,382.

Kindred to these bodies is the *Christian Instruction Society*, instituted in 1835, whose operations for the year 1849–50 are thus specified in its last annual report. "One hundred and five churches are united as associations with the parent society, and two thousand one hundred and fifty Christian men and women are visiting fifty-two thousand one hundred and five families, for the purpose of Christian instruction by book or word. By the personal efforts of the visitors, two thousand and sixty-three children have been reclaimed from the streets, and are found in Sabbath-schools, 1655 adults have felt the force of Christian persuasion, so as to go from the once Sabbath-neglecting homes to the house of prayer, 2782 of the distressed, among whom are many of 'Christ's brethren,' have had their temporal necessities relieved, and 442 copies of the Scriptures have been distributed. Religious services are conducted on Sabbath and week evenings in ninety rooms and cottages in the various districts of the associations. In the Tabernacle district alone, 300 services have been held at such meetings. The tents have been much in requisition during the year, and much good has been the result of the services held in them; 150 sermons and addresses have been delivered during the season in them. In the open air, too, attempts have been made to call on men to repent and believe the Gospel. One of the most interesting and successful undertakings has been the delivering of lectures to the working classes, in various halls and schools, in different parts of the metropolis. Fifty-two thousand religious books have been circulated among as many families at the stations; thirty thousand tracts were distributed during the visitation of the cholera." Receipts for the last year £784, or $3,795.

The *London City Mission*, with the same general object, was established in 1835. Its statistics for the last year are given as follows: Number of Missionaries employed, 242; number of visits made, 1,018,436; of tracts distributed, 1,197,953; of meetings for prayer and familiar exposition, 19,931; of adults prevailed on to attend public worship regularly, 2,803: of children sent to school, 5,168; of individuals admitted through the instrumentality of the missionaries, to the Lord's Supper, 554. The receipts of this association were £20,320, or $98,350.

The *Baptist Home Mission* sustains, in whole or part, one hundred and seven missionaries; it numbers three hundred stations; in connection with which there are 23,000 hearers, 113 Sabbath-schools, and 7,600 scholars. During the year, 639 persons were baptized and added to the mission churches. The receipts were £4,521, or $21,890.

The *Irish Church Mission* employs, in Ireland, fifteen missionaries, and eighty-one agents. Within the year 1849–50, four hundred and one persons were converted from Romanism in Galway alone; and in Dublin, Dungarvon, and other districts, equally gratifying results have attended the labors of the Society's agents and missionaries. Its receipts were £5,798 or $28,070.

The *Church Pastoral-Aid Society*, founded 1836, is an institution for the support and assistance of clergymen in destitute parishes, and the establishment of churches and chapels in such localities. Since its formation, it has sustained 798 clergymen and lay-assistants, and has led to the erection, or use as places of worship, of 298 churches, chapels, and public halls. It now aids in supporting 581 clergymen, besides 91 lay-assistants. Receipts for the last year, £35,660, or $172,635.

SECTION IV.

Scotland.—The home missions of the Established Church of Scotland are chiefly directed towards the aiding of unendowed churches, and the employing of missionaries. Something, however, is also done towards church extension, and the assisting of young men to prepare for the ministry. Last year there were under the charge of the committee 124 places of worship deriving assistance from them; of which 64 were churches, and about 60 missionary stations. The expenditures were £4,995, or $23,176.

The Free Church of Scotland is prosecuting, with the energy and earnestness that characterize its foreign operations, the important work of evangelizing those parts of the home population which are destitute of adequate means of grace. Its Home-Mission, Church-Extension and Sustentation schemes, are faithfully advocated and supported. Up to the year 1848, the number of new churches built, since the disruption, under the Church-Extension scheme, was seven hundred and one; and the receipts for that purpose during the year, amounted to £1,125.

The following are the statistics of these departments of the Free Church domestic missions at the present date: The expenditure of the Home Mission and Church-Extension scheme for the year 1850–51, is estimated at £2,500, or $12,000. The receipts of the Sustentation fund for the seven months ending December, 1850, amounted to £49,925 19*s.*; and may be estimated for the year, at £85,600.

SECTION V.

On the Continent.—The evangelical Christians of France and French Switzerland sustain several institutions, whose object is the promotion of pure religion among the Roman Catholic population, the principal of which are the Evangelical Societies of France and Geneva. But as these efforts belong more particularly to another head of our subject, we will speak here only of a society which is designed for the evangelizing of the Protestant population. This is the *Central Protestant Society*, the aim of which is to increase the means of instruction and preaching for dispersed Protestants. The committee employ special agents, who go from place to place to seek out isolated members of the Reformed communion, and bring to them the good tidings of salvation. They also sustain a preparatory school for the training of young men who are looking forward to the ministry.

In Germany, various associations have been formed for home evangelization in different regions of that country. Among them is the *Gustavus Adolphus* Society, established in 1841, at the instigation, and under the patronage of the King of Prussia. Its object was mainly a home missionary one; and it soon extended its labors in various directions, accomplishing a great amount of good. It did much for the dispersed Protestants in the Papal portions of Germany, particularly in Austria and Bavaria. It also extended its efforts abroad,—to some degree in Australia, and in a few instances, in this country. It was unfortunate, however, that in the formation of this society, men of heterodox, as well as orthodox sentiments, were associated in its direction; and consequently its action did not give entire satisfaction to either party.

At the Wittemberg Conference, in 1848,—a convention of evangelical ministers and laymen, for consultation on the interests of religion—a Committee for Home Missions was formed, with a view to uniting and superintending these several enterprises. This measure was warmly sustained by a number of excellent men—particularly by a Mr. Wichern, with whom the design originated. An auxiliary association was forthwith formed at Hamburg, and several individuals came forward to offer themselves as laborers in this important work. In the programme of the Central Committee of the "German Home Mission," published, in the early part of 1849, the objects of the society were stated as being, 1st, The combining and organizing into one harmonious whole, the hitherto isolated, and consequently, ineffective efforts of a home missionary nature throughout Germany; and 2dly, the formation of new spheres of operation, in places hitherto unoccupied.

One of the fields towards which the new society first directed its attention, was the German population in some of the foreign cities, particularly London and Paris. Another, and to us, most important one, was among the many thousands of German emigrants, who yearly leave the seaports of that country for our own, and for other lands. A third, and very interesting enterprise upon which the society has entered, is the evangelizing of the district of the Schwarzwald, particularly in the neighborhood of Neukirch, where the labors of the missionary, Wilhelmi, have already produced happy results.

At the Conference of 1850, which met in September at Stuttgart, the Committee of Home Missions made its report for the year. We learn that the number of its laborers at present is one hundred and fifty; scattered over the various states of Germany, and actively engaged in the home missionary work. Sixty-one associations are connected with the Central Committee as auxiliaries. But in addition to these important instrumentalities, the Committee operates in other ways for the evangelization of the country; such as the publication of religious books, the dissemination of the Scriptures, colportage, itinerancy of preachers, chapels established for the benefit of workmen on the railroads, the foundation of asylums and schools for orphans, &c. Respecting the last of these departments it is stated, that within the past year alone, forty houses of refuge for neglected children were established, in eighteen different states of Germany.

This home missionary enterprise is of a most hopeful and

encouraging nature. We trust we shall soon hear of its firm establishment and rapid development, as a successful instrumentality in the spread of the Gospel throughout the destitute portions of that country.

We here terminate our statements respecting the work of domestic evangelization in Protestant lands. It will be seen, how small and insignificant are these efforts, compared with the extent of the wants that exist for them. Yet there is much to excite high expectation and earnest prayer, that the next fifty years may witness a great improvement in these respects.

CHAPTER VII.

SUNDAY-SCHOOL SOCIETIES.

SECTION I.

England.—We shall not enter at any length upon the history of the Sabbath-school enterprise, in its commencement and early history in England. The labors of Robert Raikes of Gloucester, and William Fox of London, are well known. It was in 1785 that the "*Sunday-school Society*" was established, for the purpose of organizing and sustaining Sunday-schools throughout Great Britain. This society still exists and prospers; though its operations are not so extensive as those of some other bodies. Its expenditures for the last year amounted to £112 10*s.* 5*d.*; the number of schools assisted was one hundred and three. The total number of books granted to schools, from the commencement of the institution, has been 52,297 Bibles, 217,684 Testaments, and 1,610,551 class-books.

The *Sunday-school Union*, in England, is a much larger and more efficient association. It was established in the year 1803. Its expenditure for the last year amounted to £1,251 9*s.* 6*d.*; sales £6,595 15*s.* 8*d.* The number of schools in connection with the Union is six hundred and twenty-three; of which five hundred are in London. The total number of scholars is 123,949. The Committee opened, some years ago, a reading-room and library for the use of Sunday-school teachers; an excellent plan, which we should be glad to see adopted in our cities and large towns. The number of subscribers to this reading-room is more than one thousand.

The *Church of England Sunday-school Institute* was established in 1844. Its income for the last year was £907 8*s*. The number of its schools is 191, most of which are located in London and suburbs. The number of scholars in London is 12,640.

Ireland.—The *Sunday-school Society for Ireland* was formed in 1819, and is one of the most flourishing and successful in existence. Many thousands of ignorant, neglected children has it been instrumental in bringing to a knowledge of religious truth. We are not informed as to the present number of its schools and scholars. Its income for the last year amounted to £2,394.

The Continent.—On the Continent of Europe, very little has been done for this enterprise. Some interest in it has been awakened in France, Switzerland and Germany; but we believe there are but few Sunday-schools in either country.

SECTION II.

The United States.—In our own country, the Sunday-school cause has received its most extensive development. The first permanent organization of which mention is made was the "First-day or Sunday-school Society," established in Philadelphia in the year 1791. Various denominations of Christians united in its support, and its first president was the late Bishop White. The New York Sunday-school Union was instituted in 1816. It continues to the present day, as an auxiliary body, and is one of the most active and efficient organizations of the kind. The "Philadelphia Sunday and Adult School Union" was formed in 1817.

These societies, in 1824, were merged into the *American*

Sunday-school Union, established at Philadelphia, a society whose object and plan have been to unite Christians of the several evangelical denominations in the work of establishing, sustaining and supplying Sunday-schools throughout the country, particularly in destitute portions of it. The affairs and funds of the Union are intrusted to a Board of laymen, consisting of officers elected by the managers, and Managers elected by the Society. One of the instrumentalities of this Society's operations has been the employing of agents, to visit remote settlements where no Sunday-schools exist, and by personal labor to organize such schools. Another is, the furnishing of these schools with the requisite books. The publication of religious books for the young, both for instruction in the school and for reading in the family, has been an important department of the Sunday-school enterprise. The number of library books thus issued is more than seven hundred; and the total number of the Society's publications nearly two thousand. During the last year alone fifty-five volumes were issued. The number of agents employed was one hundred and three; they established during the year 1,238 new schools, and visited and re-organized 2,345 others; embracing altogether, in round numbers, 20,000 teachers and 157,000 scholars. The receipts of the Union for the last year were, from donations $52,151: from sales &c., $207,764.

Although the Sunday-school Union is supported by Christians of all the principal religious denominations, two of them have separate societies, which are of a denominational character. The Methodist Episcopal Church sustains a Sunday-school Union, with which are connected 7,334 schools, and nearly 400,000 scholars. The library published by this Society numbers 860 volumes; the total number of its publications being 1,885. Receipts for the year 1849–50, $5,150; the amount of sales is not given.

The Sunday-school Union of the Protestant Episcopal Church, was formed in 1826. The number of its publications is about three hundred. This Society is sustained by many of the members of the Episcopal Church; a large portion of them, however, adhere to the Union at Philadelphia.

The Massachusetts Sabbath-school Society is another very important organization, for the establishment of Sunday-schools and the publication of suitable books and other requisites. The total number of its publications is over three thousand. The business of the depository for last year amounted to $21,056, being an increase of $2,000 over the preceding year. Donations, $4,676.

CHAPTER VIII.

EDUCATION SOCIETIES.

SECTION I.

The Education Society is an institution of comparatively recent date, whose design is to assist pious young men of good qualifications, but having small means, in preparing for the ministry of the Gospel. Of such institutions there are but few abroad; of which we shall speak at the close of this chapter. The principal societies of the kind are to be found in the United States; we will briefly notice them.

United States.—The *American Education Society* was formed at Boston, in 1816. It was not of a denominational character, but had for its object the assistance of pious students for the ministry in any of the evangelical churches; imposing upon the recipients of its bounty no conditions save an engagement to go through a full course of collegiate and theological education in some approved college and seminary, and to refund the sum advanced to aid them, should they acquire the means to do so. It has accordingly rendered help to young men belonging to eight different denominations; and the number of its beneficiaries at one time amounted to eleven hundred. The sums granted by this Society to those assisted by it, vary from forty-eight to seventy-five dollars a year. Its funds have from time to time been liberally augmented by bequests from its friends; the late Dr. Porter, among others, bequeathed to it the sum of fifteen thousand dollars. Many of our most eminent ministers of the Gospel have received assistance from it; and a large proportion of the missionaries of the American Board obtained their preparatory education under its patronage. Of late years, however, the number of young men supported by the American Education Society has very much diminished; a fact which is to be accounted for partly by the establishment of separate educational societies by several of the denominations who formerly united in it. Its expenditure for the last year was $30,181 53. This Society has permanent funds of a considerable amount under its control. The number of young men aided during the last year was 436; of whom 207 were receiving a classical, and 229 a theological education.

The *Society for the Promotion of Collegiate and Theological Education at the West*, has been in existence seven years. Its object is "to afford assistance to collegiate and theological institutions at the West, in such a manner and so long only as, in the judgment of the Directors of the Society, the exigencies of the institutions may demand." The main ground of this Society's claim upon the support of the religious community is in the fact that the colleges which it aids are almost exclusively the fruits of home missionary labors; that they were founded mainly with the view of raising up a ministry for the West; and that all efforts made for the founding of such institutions go upon the supposition that an educated and evangelical ministry constitutes, under God, the great central instrumentality for the evangelization of the West. The field of the Society at present embraces the four states of Ohio, Indiana, Illinois, and Wisconsin. Six colleges have been aided during the year 1849–50; and the receipts for the same year amounted to $44,623 31.

The *Board of Education of the Presbyterian Church* (Old School), is another very efficient and successful organization for the education of young men for the ministry. The whole number of students whom it has carried through a preparatory course, from its foundation in 1819, is 1,876. During the past year it has assisted 373 young men. This Board has also the charge of the Assembly's schemes for parochial schools, presbyterial academies, and colleges. The number of parochial schools already established is 100; of academies, under the superintendence of different Presbyteries, 32; and of colleges, strictly under the supervision of the Church, 11. Of the colleges, seven have received aid from the Board. The seminaries at Alleghany and New Albany have also been aided. Receipts, &c., for the year 1849–50, $35,975 81.

Other religious denominations, as we have already intimated, sustain their own educational enterprises; of which, however, we have not space to speak in detail.

SECTION II.

Europe.—There is but little for us to say of Education Societies abroad; for there is not much doing in this way either in Great Britain or on the Continent. There are, indeed, in England several societies for the education of children and youth, such as the Home and Colonial School Society, and the Ragged School Union, as it is called, and in Ireland the Church Education Society. But our subject refers more particularly to the education of young men for the ministry. In the English Establishment, there are, as is well known, scholarships in the Universities for the support of young men, who have not the means of obtaining an education, and provision is also made in some of the Dissenting Colleges and Seminaries for the same purpose. The Church Missionary Society has, at Islington, an institution, which would come under this designation, for the training of young men for the missionary work. This institution numbers at present nineteen students.

The Established Church of Scotland has, among its benevolent enterprises, an Education Scheme, whose income for the last year amounted to £6,453 9*s.*, or $31,234 52. Its operations, however, are mainly directed to the education of the young.

The number of its schools is 214, with an attendance of sixteen to seventeen thousand pupils. Its Normal Schools for the training of teachers, contain 207 young men and women. The Free Church has a similar scheme, the operations of which we are not able to state in particular. Its income last year was £12,196 15*s.* 5*d.*, or $59,032.

CHAPTER IX.

THE TEMPERANCE REFORMATION.

Among the fruits, as well as the exponents of the Progress of Evangelical Religion during the first half of the XIXth century, we must place what has been called The Temperance Reformation. This movement should be ranked with those moral reforms which have exerted the most benign influence upon mankind in our times.

SECTION I.

THE WESTERN HEMISPHERE.

The United States.—The steady and dreadful increase of intemperance in the United States, during the early part of the present century, excited great solicitude in the minds of many good men of that day. As early as 1804, Dr. Benjamin Rush, of Philadelphia, published a tract, entitled: "An Inquiry into the Effects of Ardent Spirits upon the Human Body and Mind," which called the attention of the public, especially the religious portion of it, to this fearful subject. Ecclesiastical bodies passed resolutions, discouraging the habitual use of ardent spirits, at different times after that epoch. The "Massachusetts Society for the Suppression of Intemperance," was formed in 1813. Discourses by the Rev. Dr. Lyman Beecher, Dr. Humphrey, and others, about this period, created a deep impression in regard to the evils of intemperance.

On the 10th of January, 1826, the first Temperance Society was formed at Boston, the members of which pledged themselves to abstain entirely from the use of distilled liquors, except when prescribed by a physician. This was called "The American Temperance Society." From this event we may date the great Temperance movement in the United States, and in the world entire. The Rev. Drs. Hewitt and Edwards were among its earliest advocates. By means of the pulpit, the public meeting, and the press, this noble cause was ably and zealously advanced. Temperance Societies were soon formed in many places throughout the country. State Temperance Societies, County Temperance Societies, City Temperance Societies, were speedily organized. The number of the members of these societies increased rapidly, until it was estimated that in less than ten years it had reached two millions! In 1840, successsful efforts began to be made to reform inebriates. The first society composed of such persons was formed in Baltimore. Mr. John Hawkins, who was a member of that Society, travelled extensively in the United States, and was eminently useful in forming what are called "Washingtonian Societies," composed of those who had once been drunkards. Great success attended, for several years, this movement. Many intemperate people were saved.

The American Temperance Union was formed in 1837, and soon became the leading society of the land. Its agents, and its monthly periodical and other publications, have done a vast amount of good.

Among those whose writings have contributed much to advance this blessed work, we may mention those of Drs. Beecher, Humphrey, Edwards, Cheever, and Marsh, among the clergy; Drs. Rush and Kittredge, and L. M. Sargent, Esq., among the laity. Among the eloquent and effective public speakers, who have advocated it, we may name Messrs. Hewitt, Kirk, Gough, Marsh, Hunt, and Jewett.

Almost all the Presidents of the United States, a great number of Members of Congress, Governors of States, Judges, Clergymen, Physicians, and other persons of influence have enrolled themselves under the banners of these societies. Thousands of distilleries have ceased. The consumption of intoxicating liquors has greatly diminished. Hundreds of thousands of men have been rescued from the drunkard's end. Crime and pauperism have been wonderfully restrained. The best interests of mankind for this life and that to come have been signally advanced. And yet, such is the depravity of human nature, that this work must be constantly performing! It is like weaving Penelope's web. But so it is with every other species of moral reformation. It is to be always done till the close of the career of the human race on this globe of ours.

British Possessions in America.—The Temperance movement soon reached the British Provinces, and numerous societies sprang up in the Canadas, New Brunswick, Nova Scotia, Prince Edward's Island, Newfoundland, as well as in the remote settlements in the northern part of the continent of North America.

Everywhere the Temperance Reformation has been most salutary in preparing the way for the reception of the Gospel.

SECTION II.

THE EASTERN HEMISPHERE.

Great Britain and Ireland.—The Temperance movement soon extended to Great Britain and Ireland, and Temperance Societies sprang up in all parts of the "three Kingdoms." But for a long time their progress was not rapid. The usages of society, the power of fashion, and the inveteracy of habit were great obstacles. To this perhaps, ought to be added the unfavorable influence which the characters of some of the prominent advocates of the cause in England, in later times, have exerted upon it.

In Ireland the labors of such men as the Rev. Dr. Edgar, were not without happy effects. But those of Theobald Mathew, a benevolent and zealous Roman Catholic priest, have been attended with wonderful success. Several millions have taken the pledge from his hand to abstain from all intoxicating drinks, and whilst many have fallen again, vast numbers have adhered faithfully to it.

The Continent of Europe.—A little was done in Sweden at an early day, in the way of establishing Temperance societies on the plan of the Massachusetts Society for the suppression of Intemperance; but they accomplished little good. It was not until the year 1836 that the Temperance cause was placed on a proper basis, and began to make substantial progress, under the auspices of the late King, and his son the present monarch. In 1840 and '46, the author of this volume visited Sweden a second and third time. During the latter visit, he attended a grand Temperance Convention at Stockholm which lasted three days, and which was attended by the King and Queen, the Heir-apparent, and many of the most distinguished persons connected with the Court. At that Convention, it was reported that there were nearly one hundred thousand members of the Temperance Societies in Sweden, many thousands in Norway, Denmark and Holland, and more than a million in Germany! The number in the last named country has since increased to more than a million and a half!

A little progress has been made in Russia, Poland, Switzerland, and France; but it is not worthy of special notice.

Other portions of the Old World.—Temperance Societies have sprung up also in the British Possessions in India, at the Cape of Good Hope, in the Colonies on the coast of Africa, as well in Australia and other islands in the possession of the English. They have also been formed in the Sandwich Islands, whose monarch, like the King of Sweden, has taken a deep interest in the good work, and attends in person the public meetings of the National Society. It is to be deplored that Louis Philippe did not feel a like interest in this blessed cause; for had he done so, French brandy would not have been forced at the point of the bayonet, upon the poor people of these islands, recently converted to Christianity.

CHAPTER X.

AMERICAN COLONIZATION SOCIETY.

In this chapter it is our intention to speak of the colonizing of the colored race on the Western Coast of Africa only in its relations to the great work of extending the kingdom of God in this world; the planting of Christianity on the Western side of that vast but benighted Continent, whence their ancestors were carried away by violence to the Western Hemisphere.

Of the influence of the American Colonization Society upon the great and very difficult question of Slavery in the United States it is not our intention to say anything. Its friends maintain that it opens the way for the discussion of the subject of Slavery and all its evils, even in those portions of the country where there is the greatest reluctance, or rather an utter impossibility at present, to discuss the subject in a direct and abstract manner at all; that it enables those slaveholders who desire to liberate their slaves to send them to a country where there is more prospect of their doing well than in the Northern States; and that it opens a surer pathway for the elevation of the black man than can be found in this the land of his servitude and degradation, where an overwhelming immigration of the poorest classes of Europe threatens to crowd him out of employment, and to keep him in a state of perpetual depression and poverty.

On the other hand, the enemies of the Society and of the cause which it advocates, deny the impossibility of liberating the slaves and letting them remain in this country consistently with their own advantage, and ultimate rescue from their present degradation; that the Colonization scheme tends to perpetuate the prejudice which exists among the white population against the color of the black race, etc. etc.

"*Non nostrum inter vos tantas componere lites.*"—Without, therefore, undertaking to discuss the bearing of the Colonization Society upon the question of Slavery, we shall do what falls rather within the scope and design of this volume,—speak of its probable, or rather certain, influence upon the work of civilizing and Christianizing Africa. Should it turn out in the progress of this world's history that the Almighty Ruler of the Universe has ordained that the carrying of the negro race from the coasts of Africa, though most cruel on the part of those who did the deed, and their enslavement in America for centuries, should be so overruled as to lead to the return of many of them to the land of their ancestors, not a Heathen and savage people, but Christian and civilized, and charged with the mission of diffusing the blessings of Christianity and civilization in that dark and degraded continent, who will not admire the wisdom, and goodness of that God who "maketh the wrath of man to praise him, and restraineth the remainder thereof?"

The project of colonizing the free people of color of the United States on the Western Coast of Africa was first suggested by the late Rev. Dr. Finley, of the State of New Jersey, and was at once received with much favor by many of the most distinguished men of the country, both in the Church and the State. In the year 1817, the American Colonization Society was formed, with the Honorable Bushrod Washington, a nephew of the illustrious "Father of his country," at its head.

Its objects, as set forth in its constitution, were—

"1st. To rescue the free colored people of the United States from their political and social disadvantages.

"2d. To place them in a country where they may enjoy the

benefits of free government, with all the blessings which it brings in its train.

"3d. To spread civilization, sound morals, and true religion throughout the continent of Africa.

"4th. To arrest and destroy the slave-trade.

"5th. To afford slave-owners, who wish, or are willing, to liberate their slaves, an asylum for their reception."

In the year 1822, the first permanent settlement was formed, at Cape Messurado, and called Monrovia. The name given to the territory on which this colonization is going forward is LIBERIA. The extent of country which has been bought by the American Colonization Society from the native chieftains is now about 400 miles in length, stretching along the coast—between 4 deg. 21 min. and 7 deg. north latitude. Its eastern or interior boundary is not well defined; it is probably upon an average about 20 miles distant from the coast.

In the northern end of the territory, the greater part of the population is to be found. There is Monrovia, the Capital of the New Republic, and within the circuit of fifteen or twenty miles are quite a number of well-built and growing towns and villages. In the southern part of the country is the Maryland Colony, at Cape Palmas, with several flourishing villages. The number of colored persons who have been sent to Liberia proper, or the northern end of the territory, is 7,160; to Cape Palmas, 800; total 7,960,—from the commencement of the enterprise.

At first the government was administered by an agent, or governor, appointed by the Society. As the population increased and the way was prepared for it, the people were gradually put in possession of the law-making and law-executing power. In 1847, a regular republican and independent government was formed, having a *President*, (J. J. Roberts, Esq.,) a *Vice President*, (S. A. Benson, Esq.,) a *Secretary of State*, a *Treasurer*, a *Senate*, and a *House of Representatives*. England, France, and Prussia have acknowledged the independence of the

Liberian Republic, and the first named has made a treaty of commerce with it. Upwards of 80,000 of the natives have become partially civilized, and have enrolled themselves as citizens of the Republic. The colonists have a flourishing commerce. They have not only succeeded in suppressing the slave-trade along their own coast, but have also made treaties with several tribes, numbering more than 200,000 souls, for the discontinuance of that traffic.

The country is watered by many streams, some of them navigable for thirty or forty miles. Though low along the coast, it gradually becomes undulating and even hilly. At the distance of less than 100 miles, there are high mountains, which defend the colonies from the burning winds of the Sahara towards the north-east.

The productions are numerous, among which we may name rice, corn, coffee, all tropical fruits, cotton, etc. Camwood and other dye-woods, ivory, shells, palm oil, and many other things are articles of export, and the commerce of the country is now estimated to be worth $500,000 annually.

The progress of this colony has been, indeed, wonderful in all that concerns its material interests. And it will not be long till the 400 miles of its coast will be adorned with settlements of civilized men, nor will it be many years till these colonies will penetrate into the interior, and open roads up to the mountains, whilst its steamboats will be seen ploughing its rivers and their estuaries, as well as pursuing their way along its coasts.

But what shall we say of the progress of these colonies in all that relates to their moral and religious interests? Impartial visitors represent this progress to have been still more remarkable. The same unvarying testimony is borne by the ministers and missionaries, who labor among them, of every denomination.

There are now more than thirty schools, and among them several, such as the *Alexander High School*, at Monrovia, the

Episcopal Mission School, at Cape Palmas, the *White Plains Methodist School*, on the St. Paul's River, hold quite an elevated rank.

Faithful ministers of the Gospel, of the Methodist, Presbyterian, Baptist, and Episcopal Churches, are laboring with success in these colonies. We very much doubt if the glorious Gospel of our Lord has had greater success in any part of the New World in proportion to the number of the people than among these colonies. The Methodist Mission has had sixteen missionaries, thirteen principal stations, and between 1,100 and 1,200 communicants, of whom from 100 to 200 are native converts.

The Presbyterian Board of Missions has three missions in Liberia, and one among the natives, at *Settee*, near Cape Palmas.

The American Baptist Union has had a mission, for several years, among the *Bassas*, comprising one station, several outposts, and five or six native helpers.

The Board of Missions of the Protestant Episcopal Church has had a mission at Cape Palmas and its vicinity for fifteen years. This mission now includes four ordained missionaries, a physician, a teacher, and several native assistant teachers.

The reports of all these missionaries (of whom only two are white men) display a remarkable spirit of devotion to the work, and strong confidence in its importance and success. They rightly judge that these colonies furnish admirable points of irradiation from which the Truth may be made to shine far into Africa, and ultimately enlighten it, even in its most interior portions,—now so filled with ignorance and degradation.

Northward of Liberia is the English possession of *Sierra Leone*, with its 43,000 inhabitants, its printing presses, its prosperous missions, its schools, its many churches and chapels,—from which the Gospel is destined to penetrate far into Africa.

CHAPTER XI.

EVANGELIZATION OF PAPAL COUNTRIES.

It was one of the characteristics of the first half of the XIXth century, as well as one of the fruits of that resuscitation of true religion which commenced about the beginning of it, that the duty and importance of imparting the Gospel in its purity—as contained in the sacred Scriptures—to Papal nations began to be felt by a goodly number of devout and zealous Protestants, especially in England. In the XVIth century, and especially during what may be called the "Reformation Era," which, alas, was of short duration, the work of converting the many millions who still adhere to Rome, was rightly appreciated, and with a good degree of vigor prosecuted. But after Protestant nations had been formed, and under the influence of a worldly and ambitious policy began to be arrayed against Papal ones, the wars which ensued had the deplorable effect of making Protestants hate Romanists, and regard them as being beyond the pale of hope. The bloody persecutions which the Protestants suffered at the hands of the Roman Catholics in France and Flanders; in Bohemia, Moravia, and Hungary; in Poland, in Spain, and in Italy, as well as the massacres which they suffered in Ireland, greatly contributed to produce the same result. The consequence was, that Papal countries became closed to all Protestant effort for a long time, and the Reformation entirely ceased to advance.

Let us bless God that this long night of unbelief and unkindness has passed away in a good degree. The progress of civil and political liberty has opened, within a comparatively short period, and is steadily opening still more widely the door for the entrance of the Truth into some of the most important portions of the Papal world. This is seen in the case of France and Belgium, in most of the Papal countries of Germany, in the kingdom of Sardinia, and to some extent in South America. Conquest has opened Poland somewhat, and the Canadas completely.

As might be expected, the infinite God, who by His providence was beginning to open Papal lands to the Gospel, also by His Spirit began to put it into the hearts of some of His dear children to attempt the work. One of the first movements of this sort manifested itself in England in the formation of the "Continental Society," which, in a silent and cautious manner, —publishing no reports,—employed the best men it could find to distribute the Scriptures in France, Belgium, and various other countries on the Continent of Europe. And although its operations were never conducted on a large scale, yet this Association did much, in this quiet way, during the reigns of Louis XVIII. and his brother Charles X. It was truly the "day of small things," but it was important as a beginning.

The Revolutions of 1830, in France and Belgium, greatly opened the way in both those countries for the spread of the Gospel. This gave a decided impulse to the Protestant Societies for doing good, which had existed for a few years, and led to the formation of others, among which were the "French and Foreign Bible Society" (1831), and the "Evangelical Society of France" (1833), both of which have steadily and zealously pursued their work to this day. The aid of the British and Foreign Bible Society has been most important. It is supposed that more than three millions of copies of the Scriptures, in whole or in part, have been put into circulation in France since the year 1819. More than 150,000 copies are now distributed annually, and some 800,000 religious tracts and books. On the other hand, the Evangelical Society of France, together with the local ones at Lyons, Lille, and Bordeaux have employed many ministers, evangelists, colporteurs, and pious school-teachers for the promotion of the truth, with most encouraging success, notwithstanding the violent opposition of the Romish priests, and often of the Government, in the very face of the *Charte* of 1830, and that of 1848.

The Evangelical Society of Geneva, in Switzerland, formed in 1831, has done much in the eastern and southern parts of France. Its receipts have, of late years, exceeded 100,000 francs, nearly $20,000; whilst those of the Evangelical Society of France have sometimes reached 150,000 francs, or nearly $30,000. The Wesleyan Missionary Society of England has long taken an interest in the work in France, and had last year forty-eight chapels, seventy-six preaching places, and twenty-four missionaries, 115 Sabbath-school teachers, 1,099 Sabbath-school scholars, thirty-nine local preachers, 950 church members, and 6,160 attendants on public worship.

The American Baptist Missionary Society has two missionaries in France, eighteen stations and out-stations, twenty native ministers and assistants, fifteen little churches, and 200 or 300 members.

Much has been done also in Belgium, where a quarter of a million of the Scriptures have been circulated since 1830, and where there are now between twenty and thirty Protestant ministers and evangelists, ten or twelve colporteurs, and several pious teachers. Great success has attended the preaching of the Gospel in a considerable number of villages and cities of Belgium, and that country is now one of the most promising fields in the whole papal world.

The resuscitation of the true Protestant Faith in France and French Switzerland, has led to a similar movement in Canada. In the year 1835 or '36, the Rev. Mr. Olivier and his wife, the

Rev. Mr. Roussy and Madame Feller, came over to Canada to commence a mission at Montreal. The first-named two soon were compelled, by the rigors of the climate, to return to Europe; but the labors of Mr. Roussy and Madame Feller led to the founding of the "Grande Ligne Mission," with its several stations, its schools, and its hundreds of converts from Rome, in the southern border of Canada-East.

Not long afterwards the French Canadian Missionary Society was organized, which has several missionaries, evangelists, colporteurs, and school-teachers, and a College for young men at Pointe aux Trembles, ten miles below Montreal, and another for young women and girls at the same place,—institutions which are admirably calculated to promote the work of evangelization among the French Romanists in Canada.

In the year 1834, a few gentlemen in New York and other cities in the United States formed an association, and sent the writer of these lines with his family to Paris, to learn what the American Churches could do for the work of evangelization in France, and other papal countries, in Europe. This led to the organization of the "Foreign Evangelical Society," in May, 1839, in whose service he afterwards visited Europe four times, and resided there a second time with his family, from the Autumn of 1839 to that of 1843.

This Society existed ten years, and extended effective help to the work in France and Belgium, employed one missionary in Sweden, one in Russia, one or two in Germany for a while, aided for years the "Grande Ligne Mission," and afterwards the "French Canadian Missionary Society" in Canada, had a missionary at Valparaiso, in South America, another in Hayti, and had a French missionary in New Orleans, and another in New York.

In 1849, the Foreign Evangelical Society was united with the "American Protestant Society,"—which had been organized for the benefit of the increasing hundreds of thousands of

Romanists of foreign origin in this land,—and the "Christian Alliance," a society which had silently been operating in Italy for two or three years. The new society took the name of the "American and Foreign Christian Union," and has been in existence two years. Its number of laborers at home and abroad, last year, exceeded eighty. It has but just commenced its career, and after some struggles its prospects begin to brighten. France, Belgium, Northern Italy, Ireland, Canada, Hayti, South America, are inviting fields abroad; whilst the Germans, the Irish, the French and Canadians, the Spaniards and Mexicans, the Italian, and the Portuguese, who have come among us, are very accessible by proper efforts.

We are fully persuaded that the times demand of the American and British Protestants the most vigorous efforts, not only to repel the invasions which Rome would make, but to carry the banners of the Truth into her own domains, and even to the walls of the "City on seven Hills."

We must now turn to the work outside of Christendom.

CHAPTER XII.

MISSIONARY EFFORTS PREVIOUS TO THE XIXTH CENTURY.

To obtain a correct estimate of the development assumed by the enterprise of Christian Missions within the present century, it may be of service to consider, at the outset, how much had been accomplished in previous centuries, since the Protestant Reformation. We shall do this briefly, that we may give the wider space to a review of the period more immediately under our contemplation.

To CALVIN, the Reformer of Geneva, belongs the credit of having first attempted, in the Protestant Churches, to excite interest in behalf of a heathen nation. An expedition was fitted out, in the year 1555, by Villegagnon, a knight of Malta, under the patronage of Henry II. of France, with the view to establish a French colony in the New World. The approbation of the monarch was secured through the medium of the excellent Admiral de Coligny; whose favor Villegagnon propitiated, by the secret understanding that the projected colony should protect the Reformed religion. Accordingly, Calvin was applied to, in order to obtain ministers to embark with the expedition. After consultation with the other pastors of Geneva, he sent two,—Guillaume Chartier, and Pierre Richier,—who were afterwards joined by several others. Their object was, at once, to labor among the colonists and to evangelize the heathen aborigines. The expedition reached fort Coligny, as it was named, on the Rio de Janeiro, Brazil, in March, 1556. On their arrival, the Genevan ministers proceeded to constitute a church, according to the forms and rites of the Reformed Churches, and celebrated the Lord's Supper. But Villegagnon soon betrayed his true character and disposition; and after cruelly maltreating the missionaries, forced them to re-embark and return to France.*

The next attempt to send the Gospel to heathen countries, was made by the celebrated Reformer and King of Sweden, Gustavus Vasa. About the year 1559, a missionary was sent by that monarch into Lapland, for the purpose of teaching them the principles of Christianity. The natives were at the same time commanded to congregate at a certain season of the year, to pay their tribute, and receive religious instruction from this missionary.

In the early part of the 17th century, efforts were made by the Dutch to convert to Christianity the natives of the island of Ceylon, which they had taken from the Portuguese. One of the measures which they adopted for this end, was the passage of a law to the effect that none could inherit property or obtain office, who had not been baptized and registered. The consequence of such a regulation may be imagined; in 1663, the number of persons professing Christianity, in the single district of Jaffnapatam, had risen to about sixty-three thousand. At the present day, there are many Cinghalese who call themselves Christians, but are in reality worshippers of Boodha.†

In 1634 the Dutch also obtained possession of the island of Formosa; and soon after, Robert Junius and others labored there with great success for the conversion of the natives. In a few years, however, the Dutch were expelled from Formosa, and Christianity was extirpated.

It was towards the middle of this century that the Puritan

* De Thou, *Histoire Universelle,* Liv. xvi. tom. ii. p. 381—4. De Thou mentions that a full and faithful narrative of the expedition, with a description of the country, was published by Lery, one of the party.

† Selkirk's *Recollections of Ceylon.*

colonists of New England commenced their noble labors for the propagation of the Gospel among the Indians. In 1646, the legislature of Massachusetts passed an act to encourage this enterprise; and the celebrated Eliot began his missionary career at Nonantum. This devoted servant of God, with his fellow-laborers and successors, the Mayhews, Bowen, Cotton and others, achieved a great and thorough work in the field of their exertions. In 1675, there had been formed fourteen settlements of Christianized Indians, with a population of thirty-six hundred souls. Twenty-four congregations had been organized, with six constituted churches, and twenty-four Indian preachers.*

Two missionary societies were founded in the course of the XVIIth century. The "Society for Propagating the Gospel in New England," was incorporated in 1649; a consequence of the interest excited by the labors and success of Eliot and his associates. And in 1698, the "Society for Promoting Christian Knowledge" was formed by members of the Church of England.

The XVIIIth century witnessed, at its very dawn, a large increase of Christian zeal in behalf of missions among the heathen. In 1701, the "Society for Propagating the Gospel in Foreign Parts," was instituted in England. Of this organization we shall speak more fully in the next chapter. In 1705, the Danes undertook a mission in Southern India; and in 1708 another in Greenland. The former mission was located in Tranquebar, on the Coromandel coast. Two Danish missionaries, with several assistants, labored here for several years, and with considerable success. In 1710, they came under the patronage of the Society for Promoting Christian Knowledge; by whose encouragement the operations of the mission were soon extended to Madras and Ceylon; and in 1775, it consisted of five principal branches, the stations of which were occupied by thirteen missionaries and over fifty native assistants. The schools at that period con-

* Tracy's History of the Am. Board, p. 14.

tained 633 children; and in the space of a single year, 909 new members were added to the different churches. The labors of the Danish and Moravian missionaries in Greenland, are too well-known to require notice here. Their persevering and self-denying career, like that of the venerable Swartz in India, form a rich portion of the memoirs of Christian heroism.

The "Society in Scotland for Propagating Christian Knowledge," was formed at Edinburgh in the year 1709. It employed schoolmasters, catechists, and missionaries, and distributed the Scriptures and other religious books, in the Highlands of Scotland, the neighboring islands, and to some extent in North America. It was under the care of this association and its committee in America, that several laborers were supported among the American Indians; and in particular the celebrated Brainerd. But the earlier missions among this interesting people, though successful and promising at the outset, were doomed to interruption by the frequent removal and dispersion of the tribes among whom they were situated. Yet they are not to be regarded as failures. "Among no other heathen in modern times has the Gospel had such early and decided success. No other savages have so readily thrown off their barbarism, and become civilized men. And of all the tribes which once inhabited the older parts of the United States, scarce a fragment can now be found, but such as Christian missions have preserved."*

The first missions of the United Brethren, or Moravians, were undertaken in the year 1732. Their designation was to the West Indies and Greenland. Of the history and present extent of the operations of the Moravian Brethren, we shall treat under the appropriate head.

It was towards the close of the XVIIIth century that several of the more important missionary organizations of the present day were founded. In 1792, the Baptist Foreign Missionary

* Hist. of the Am. Board, p. 26.

Society was formed in England; in 1795, the London Missionary Society; in 1796, the Edinburgh Missionary Society; and in 1800, the Church Missionary Society. These associations engaged extensively in the work of missions to the East Indies, the Islands of the Pacific, and Africa. But the time had not yet arrived, when India, Burmah, China, South Africa, and Turkey were to be thrown open to the efforts of the Christian churches. Hindrances of every kind—from heathen rulers or from the civilized conquerors—were raised up in their way. It was in consequence of this, that so much of the efficiency of these societies was expended, in their first years, upon small and comparatively unimportant fields. It pleased God in his wise providence, as it were, to obstruct the passage of the stream of benevolence in his Church, until it should have gathered sufficient strength to sweep with wide and permanent force over the more distant and powerful nations of the heathen world.

CHAPTER XIII.

SOCIETY FOR THE PROPAGATION OF THE GOSPEL IN FOREIGN PARTS.

THE Gospel Propagation Society is not the oldest of existing institutions in Great Britain, whose object at the outset was the extension of the Gospel in foreign parts. But the "Society for Promoting Christian Knowledge," organized three years previous to it, relinquished, about twenty-five years ago, the missions which it had established in Southern India, which were transferred to the care of the more recent Society; and though still extant, confines its labors to the publishing and circulating of Bibles and other religious books. The receipts of that institution for the year 1849–50, including those from the sale of its books, amounted to £86,408.

The Gospel Propagation Society, as we have already seen, was founded in 1701: and was chartered by William III., as a "corporation with a perpetual succession." The object of its institution was "the receiving, managing, and disposing of such funds as might be contributed for the religious instruction of British subjects beyond the seas; for the maintenance of clergymen in the plantations, colonies, and factories of Great Britain, and for the propagation of the Gospel in those parts." It is an interesting fact, that the celebrated John Wesley was a missionary of this Society; and in that character proceeded to America in 1735, and returned to England in 1738.

"The Society," says its last annual report, "has now been permitted to attain the one hundred and fiftieth year of its labors. For nearly a century it was the only society which gave witness to the missionary character of the Church of England. Latterly that privilege has been shared with others. Whatever has been effected through the instrumentality of the Society for the glory of God and the salvation of men, must be humbly ascribed to his undeserved goodness." The progress of the Society will be best seen by the following table of income received and missionaries employed at successive periods:—

	Income.	Missionaries.
1725	£1,550	31
1775	2,294	86
1825	8,350	103
1835	15,435	200
1849	54,000*	355

During the last year the Society has undertaken several new missions: two in Labrador, one in the island of Tristan d'Acunha, and another in British Caffraria. Its other missions are as follows: In the Western Hemisphere—In Nova Scotia, Cape Breton, and Prince Edward's Island; in New Brunswick, East and West Canada, and Newfoundland; in the Bermudas, Jamaica, the Bahamas, Barbadoes, Antigua, and Guiana. In the Eastern Hemisphere, the missions of the Society are in India, Ceylon, Australia, New South Wales, Van Dieman's Land, and New Zealand.

The total number of missionaries supported by the Gospel Propagation Society is, as we have seen, three hundred and fifty-five, all of whom are ordained clergymen. Their labors, however, are in many localities restricted to the British population in the colonies, particularly in the British possessions of North America. It may, therefore, be questioned whether the operations of this Society should be included in a view of foreign

* This amount includes only general donations and subscriptions; the whole income, as will be seen, is much larger

missions. But such being the method of most of the writers on the subject, we have thought best to conform to it here.

It must also be stated, that many of the laborers employed by the Gospel Propagation Society at the present day, are sadly deficient in the true missionary spirit, and in the reception of the pure doctrines of Christianity. It is generally understood, we believe, that the sympathies of the High Church party in the English Establishment, are with this institution, while the more evangelical portion of its members attach themselves to the Church Missionary Society. It is painful to hear such complaints as not unfrequently reach us, from India and New Zealand more especially, of the pernicious influence of Tractarian tenets preached to the half-converted natives of those lands.

The receipts of the Gospel Propagation Society, for the year ending May, 1850, amounted to £91,874 8*s.* 8*d.*, or $444,700. This sum includes several sources of revenue not mentioned in the comparative view given above, among which is a "Queen's Letter," or royal circular, requiring collections for the Society's missions in all the churches of the Establishment.

CHAPTER XIV.

ENGLISH BAPTIST MISSIONARY SOCIETY.

The circumstances under which the Baptist denomination in Great Britain entered upon the work of carrying the Gospel to the heathen, are briefly as follows. On the 2d of October, 1792, a yearly meeting of the Baptist ministers, in the county of Northampton, was held at Kettering. After public worship, the members met separately for the purpose of taking into consideration the moral condition of the world, and deciding their own personal obligations in reference to it. It was their solemn and unanimous resolution "to act together in society for the purpose of propagating the Gospel among the heathen." They further resolved, that, "as in the present divided state of Christendom, it seems that each denomination, by exerting itself separately, is most likely to accomplish the great ends of a mission, it is agreed that this Society be called, The particular Baptist Society for propagating the Gospel among the heathen." This title is still retained, but the institution is more generally known by the designation of "The Baptist Missionary Society." The term "*particular*" is simply a doctrinal distinction, applied to those who receive the dogma of election; general redemption being the theory of those who are denominated General Baptists.

The committee originally appointed, was composed of the Rev. Messrs. John Ryland, Reynold Hogg, William Carey, John Sutcliff, and Andrew Fuller; Reynold Hogg being appointed treasurer, and Andrew Fuller, secretary.

The first publication of the Society commences with the following words, written by Mr. Fuller. "The origin of the Society will be found in the workings of our brother Carey's mind, which, for the last nine or ten years, has been directed to this object with little intermission. His heart seems to have been set upon the conversion of the heathen, before he came to reside at Moulton, in 1786." William Carey was, at this period, the pastor of a small village church at Moulton. Having been at first a journeyman shoemaker, and then a village schoolmaster, he had improved his leisure moments under the pressure of poverty in acquiring several modern languages. But since his settlement at Moulton, in the 25th year of his age, his attention had been more and more drawn to the claims of the heathen; which he was not slow in enforcing upon his brethren. At first he had been opposed with all those objections which are so readily adduced against every foreign missionary enterprise at its commencement: the amount of destitution at home, the obstacles to the propagation of the Gospel abroad, and the prophecies of Scripture which many interpreted as foretelling the present unpropitious condition of the heathen world. But Carey was instant in season and out of season, and though he was considered by some at that period importunate in his urgency, the churches soon came up in some degree to the measure of zeal which actuated him.

Mr. Thomas, formerly a surgeon in Bengal, and who had returned to England with the view to awaken interest in the establishment of a mission in that country, was appointed in connection with Mr. Carey to proceed to India; and on the 13th of June, 1793, these brethren embarked in a Danish vessel for Calcutta.

The first station occupied permanently by these missionaries in India was Serampore, which has ever since been retained by the Society, as a missionary post. Mr. Carey, after sojourning at several localities, arrived at Serampore on the 10th of January,

1800. Reinforcements soon after reached the mission, and the various branches of the enterprise were prosecuted with vigor. These departments were the Bengalese school, the printing and circulating of the Scriptures and Tracts, and the preaching of the Gospel. On the 22d of December, four native converts came forward as candidates for church-membership. Among these was Krishno, one of the most eminent of the early converts. In the subsequent year, the printing of the Bengalee Testament was concluded.

A mission undertaken in 1795 under the auspices of the Society at Sierra Leone, on the Western coast of Africa, had a less fortunate result. The health of one of the missionaries sent out to that colony became so poor, as to oblige him to return to Europe soon after the commencement of the enterprise; and the misconduct of the other compelled him to return likewise, when the Society dismissed him from its employ.

Calcutta, Agra, Cutwa, and other stations in India were successively occupied by the missionaries of the Society. In 1827, certain difficulties between the parent institution and the Serampore mission resulted in a separation, and for several years that mission remained independent, sustaining itself by means of funds which had accumulated there. A reunion was effected in the year 1837. Without entering further into the detail of the Society's operations in India, we refer the reader for an interesting account of them to Dr. F. A. Cox's valuable history of the Baptist Missions.

The Baptist Mission in Jamaica was undertaken in the year 1813. Previous to this there had, however, been a private effort made by Mr. Liele, a colored man from the United States; who had labored with much encouragement among the native negroes, until compelled to desist from any further endeavors by the opposition of the colonial government of Kingston. Mr. John Rowe was the first English missionary sent to the island, where he arrived in February, 1814, and labored with great efficiency during the short period to which his career was limited—scarcely more than two years. His place was soon filled by other missionaries sent from Great Britain, under whose care a number of flourishing stations were established, and chapels erected where the Gospel was regularly taught to the crowds of natives who assembled both on the Sabbath and on week-days. At the same time efforts were made for the religious instruction of the inhabitants both Indians and Negroes of the British settlement of Belize on the coast of Honduras, whither missionaries were sent in 1822.

At the time of the negro insurrection at Jamaica, in 1831, there existed in that island under the charge of the Baptist Missionary Society, twenty-four churches having fourteen pastors, and containing nearly eleven thousand members. Unfortunately, the missionaries of the Society became implicated in that insurrection, and although the trial to which they were subjected terminated in their acquittal from the charges preferred against them, the mission was to a great extent broken up, and Messrs. Knibb, and Burchell, returned to England. They resumed their work, however, after laboring at home to interest the churches in it, in the autumn of 1834. New churches were gathered; and in 1837, the number of members amounted to nearly nineteen thousand.*

Respecting the present condition of the operations of the Baptist Missionary Society, the following statements are furnished by its last annual report (1850).

The missionaries sustained by the Society labor in Asia, on the Western coast of Africa, in France, and in the islands of the Western Sea. At about one hundred and ninety-four stations and sub-stations, the Gospel of Jesus Christ is regularly preached to many thousands by the missionary brethren from week to week, while their itinerant labors extend to many hundreds of

* Cox's History of the Baptist Mission, *passim.*

villages and towns, and the message of God is daily proclaimed to thousands more at fairs and at markets, by the road-side and at the nightly resting places.

The service of Christ is carried on in this extensive field by fifty-four missionaries with their wives, and nine females engaged in the special department of education. It has been, however, one of the blessed results of their toil, that from the midst of the converts there have been raised up by the grace of God, not less than one hundred and twenty-one natives of the different lands where the Gospel has been proclaimed by the brethren, to aid them in the further extension of the Redeemer's kingdom. The total number of laborers supported by the Society in foreign lands, therefore, including missionaries, catechists, preachers and assistant teachers, is three hundred and seventy-eight. These laborers are located as follows:—In India, 36 missionaries, 72 preachers and catechists, 19 teachers; in the Asiatic Islands, 5 missionaries and 14 preachers, &c.; in the West Indies and Central America, 7 missionaries, 23 preachers, &c., 183 assistant teachers; in Africa, 5 missionaries, 9 preachers, &c., 1 teacher; in France, 1 missionary, and 3 preachers and catechists. This however is not the whole of the means that have been brought into operation; about two hundred other Christian brethren gratuitously devote more or less of their time to making known the unsearchable riches of Christ. To these must be added thirty or more schoolmasters, in order to embrace in a brief view the whole of the Christian agency employed or set in motion by the Society.

There are at present in fellowship in India and Ceylon, 1,971 persons; in Africa and the West Indies, 3,037; making in all more than five thousand professed disciples of Christ, and about three hundred and eighty seeking admission into the fold. This does not include the members of churches in Jamaica, which have become independent of the Society. The clear increase during the last year was one hundred and ninety. The most flourishing of the mission churches are to be found in Bengal and the Bahama islands. In these places the largest additions have been made, and the prospects are most promising and hopeful. The number of mission churches is one hundred and eight.

At nearly all the stations of the Society, day and Sunday-schools are established. The returns of these schools are not sufficiently precise to enable us to specify their exact number, or to give the sum total of the children attending them ; but, as far as the accounts have been supplied, there are at the various stations of the Society one hundred and five day schools, in which are taught four thousand two hundred and seventy-six children ; and fifty-eight Sunday schools, with two thousand six hundred and eighty children. Many schools are supported by Sunday-school scholars at home ; those in the West Indies in great part by grants liberally bestowed by the Society of Friends, and many more, especially in India, by contributions on the spot.

In addition to these educational instrumentalities, the Society has hitherto engaged to some extent in the training of young natives for the ministry. The College at Montreal, formerly under its care, has, however, been closed. At Calabar, Jamaica, one young man has completed his studies, and has been settled as pastor of the church at Moneague. Several other young men, negroes by birth, are preparing for the ministry at the same place.

The subject of Bible translation has always engaged much of the attention of the Society. The number of versions in which the Scriptures were printed by its missionaries, from 1801 to 1850, was forty-four. The total number of copies printed was 961,622. During the last year no new language was undertaken, although much progress was made in several versions. In the Hindi, for the use of the population on the Ganges, between Monghir and Benares, 4,500 copies of the Gospels and Acts have been printed ; in Hindustani, Persian, and Bengali, 62,500 ; and in Sanscrit, 7,500. The total number of copies printed during the last year was, therefore, 74,500 ; the number distributed about 35,000.

Translations are also in course of preparation in the Isubu and Dualla, for Western Africa, the Maya for Central America, and the Breton in France.

Although the condition and prospects of the various fields of the Society's labors present so many encouragements, it is to be regretted that the strength of the institution at home is not proportionately increasing. "In no case are the laborers equal to the toil demanded of them. Western Africa has lost one after another of its most energetic evangelists. They are reduced to the lowest possible number to hold the ground that had been occupied. In Ceylon, where three missionaries were not enough for the service of thirty-five stations, and the oversight of four hundred and fifty members of churches, one only is left,—and, must we not say, to *sink* under the accumulated responsibility and toil? In India, with one or two exceptions, every station needs additional aid. Some places have already been abandoned for want of it. Large tracts of country are unoccupied where it would appear the fields are white unto the harvest. Many of our brethren are aged. Should they be taken to their rest, as in the course of nature they must speedily be, the Committee are unable to supply their places. And others are overwhelmed with care and anxiety, induced by the scarcity of help."*

The total receipts of the English Missionary Society, for the year 1849–50, including donations for general and special purposes, amounted to £19,776 13*s.* 1*d.*, or $95,719.†

General Baptist Missionary Society.—As already mentioned, the designation adopted by this Society indicates the doctrinal peculiarities of its supporters. It was not until several years after the establishment of the institution above described that

* Report for 1850.

† The computations of English into American coin, throughout this work, are made at the *real* value of $4 84 to the pound sterling, not at the *nominal* value of $4 44.

the smaller denomination of the General Baptists entered upon the work of foreign missions; and in 1816, at the association of its ministers, held at Boston, it was resolved, after much discussion, that a society for the prosecution of this object should be formed. The first missionaries appointed, Messrs. Bampton and Peggs, reached Serampore in 1821, and after much deliberation and prayer, decided upon the province of Orissa as the scene of their future labors. In 1825, the Rev. Mr. Sutton arrived, a missionary of much activity and zeal, whose visits to the United States have greatly contributed to awaken a missionary spirit in the churches of his own denomination here. Since that period a number of laborers have been sent out to India by this Society. The stations occupied are Khundita, Coga, Cuttack, Pooree, Ganjam, and Burrampore. At Cuttack, there is a native church with one hundred and thirty-five members, with two schools containing one hundred and six scholars. The mission press has issued 1,516,000 pages of the Scriptures, and 2,050,000 pages of tracts and other books. This mission is occupied by six ordained missionaries, one printer, and nine native preachers.

The Society has also established a mission in China, at Canton, where Messrs. Hudson and Jarrom were stationed in 1845.

The receipts of the General Baptist Missionary Society, for the year 1849–50, amounted to £1,887 8*s.* 4*d.*, or $9,135.

CHAPTER XV.

LONDON MISSIONARY SOCIETY.

THE *London Missionary Society* was formed with the design of uniting Christians of all evangelical denominations in one great enterprise for the diffusion of religious truth among heathen nations. An appeal made by the Rev. David Bogue, in 1794, was the immediate occasion of its formation. In the month of September of the following year, a succession of public meetings was held in London, the result of which was the organization of the Society, and the election of thirty-two directors.

The resolution adopted by the London Missionary Society, from its very commencement, to secure agreement and harmony in all its operations, deserves special mention as an evidence of the catholicity of its founders. It was framed by the late Dr. Waugh, one of the most zealous and useful of the Society's directors. "As the union of GOD's people of various denominations, in carrying on this great work, is a most desirable object, so to prevent, if possible, any cause of future dissension, it is declared to be a fundamental principle of the London Missionary Society, that our design is not to send Presbyterianism, Independency, Episcopacy, or any other form of church order and government (about which there may be a difference of opinion among serious persons), but the glorious Gospel of the blessed GOD to the heathen; and it shall be left (as it ought to be left) to the minds of the persons whom GOD shall call into the fellowship of his Son from among them, to assume for themselves such form of church government as to them shall appear most agreeable to the word of GOD."*

The first mission of the Society had been determined upon previous to the dissolution of its first general meeting; and it was resolved to direct its efforts to the islands of Polynesia, at that time newly discovered. Subscriptions to a considerable amount were accordingly raised, and a number of persons who had expressed their willingness to devote themselves to the work of preaching the Gospel to the heathen, were examined by a committee appointed for that purpose. At length, on the 10th of August, 1796, there embarked in the Duff, a vessel purchased by the Society, thirty missionaries, with their wives and children, under the care of Captain Wilson, a retired seaman, who voluntarily undertook the command of the vessel.

Upon the arrival of the missionaries at Tahiti, one of the Georgian Islands, an interview was obtained with the king, and the object of their visit was represented to him by means of an interpreter. The entire district of Matavai was ceded to them, and they prepared to commence their labors in the island. Discouragements, however, soon fell upon the work, and, after a few years of great insecurity, a rebellion broke out which compelled the missionaries to leave Tahiti, whence some repaired to Eimeo, and others to Huahine, both lying a short distance westward of Tahiti. The new king, who bore the name of Pomare, had been likewise obliged to escape to Eimeo, where he first renounced idolatry, and embraced the Gospel. Upon his restoration to the sovereignty of his island, which occurred soon after, he became the steady friend and protector of the missionaries. Until their arrival he himself exerted all his influence in persuading his people to abandon the degrading superstitions of their fathers, and his labors were not in vain. In 1819, a vast chapel was erected, where the Gospel might be

* Memoirs of the late Rev. Dr. Waugh. New York: R. Carter.

preached simultaneously by three ministers to several thousand hearers; and the zeal of the converts, which had already given rise to a "Tahitian Auxiliary Missionary Society," inclined them to use all instrumentalities to spread the same benefits they had received, to the unenlightened about them.

Such was the early history of the Tahitian mission, one of the most interesting and remarkable in the annals of Christianity. The progress of religion in these islands continued uninterrupted until the aggressions of the French government, by whom every effort has been made to hinder and counteract the labors of the English missionaries. Of the opposition at present encountered, the report of the Society for the last year speaks as follows: "The directors very deeply regret that their missionaries in Tahiti, contrary to former hopes, have suffered considerable obstruction and embarrassment in their labors, from the interference of the French Governor, Captain Lavaud. He has employed his authority to prevent the people from repairing the Missionary buildings, unless his permission were first obtained; and he has employed his influence, also, to prevent them from making their accustomed contributions for the diffusion of the Gospel in the yet unenlightened islands of the Pacific. When certain of the stations and districts have become vacant, he has not allowed our Missionaries to remove thither, unless his permission were previously granted. And from one particular locality, where two Catholic priests were endeavoring to instil their principles into the minds of the young, our brethren were strictly prohibited, lest, as the Governor pleaded, there should be any controversy about religion." It is, however, gratifying to find, notwithstanding these adverse circumstances, that the Tahitian churches are receiving numerous accessions, and exhibiting much improvement in Christian character. The total number of church-members at present in connection with this mission, is about six hundred; the number of children in the schools, one thousand. In Eimeo there are two hundred and five communicants, with a considerable number of children in the schools. At Huahine, Raiatea, Tahaa, and Borabora, in the Society group, the number of church-members is between six and seven hundred, and of scholars, about six hundred.

The other missions of the Society in the South Seas have been located among the Hervey, Samoan, and New Hebrides groups. With the former of these is associated the hallowed memory of Williams, "the martyr of Erromanga," whose unwearied exertions for the diffusion of Christianity among those islands, laid the foundation of its present success. In the Hervey Islands, there are about one thousand communicants in the mission churches; in the Samoan Islands, the war that broke out in 1847, has greatly impeded the prosperity of the churches; there are, however, upwards of a thousand church members at the various stations.

In the year 1806, the London Missionary Society determined to commence a mission to China. The hostility of the Chinese Government, however, being a great impediment to Missionary operations, the object at which the founders of the Protestant Mission to China aimed, was the preparation of works that should facilitate the future cultivation of Chinese philology by Europeans, and secure a standard of appeal on theology for Chinese in their own language. In the beginning of the year 1807, the Rev. Robert Morrison sailed from England for China, with a particular view to the translation of the Holy Scriptures into the Chinese language; in acquiring a knowledge of which, he had to make it as much a matter of secrecy as if he had been plotting the overthrow of the Government of the empire, and the persons who assisted him trembled for their own safety. Soon after his arrival in China, Mr. Morrison was appointed Chinese Interpreter to the East India Company; which office secured at the same time his residence at Macao, and contributed to his acquisition of the language.

The printing of the New Testament in the Chinese language

was completed in January, 1814. The four Gospels, the closing Epistles and the Book of Revelations, were translated by Mr. Morrison; the Acts of the Apostles and the Epistles of St. Paul were copied for the most part from a Chinese manuscript in the British Museum, with such alterations as Mr. Morrison judged advisable. The next five years were employed by him in translating the Old Testament, which was printed in 1823, the British and Foreign Bible Society granting £6,000 towards the expense. Thus there have been published in the Chinese language, a Dictionary, a Grammar and other minor works, to assist Europeans in acquiring it; and above all the Scriptures have been translated, printed, and published in a language spoken by four hundred millions of the human race, in addition to numerous excellent tracts, chiefly on theology.

After a long season of diligent preparation and patient waiting, China has at length been opened to the Christian Missionary. Dr. Morrison was prevented from preaching publicly, either in Canton or Macao, by the jealousy entertained by the government against foreigners, and especially against foreign religions. But toleration was extended, early in the year 1845, to all professing the Christian religion throughout the empire. In consequence of this long-hoped-for but almost unexpected boon, the Chinese missions have received a great extension; new laborers have been sent from Europe to assist in preaching the Gospel to this interesting people, and the minds of Christians at home are awakening to their claims upon their Christian benevolence.

The missions of the London Missionary Society in China are located at Hong-Kong, Canton, Shanghai and Amoy. At Hong-Kong, where are stationed an ordained missionary and a physician, there have been two chapels opened, at each of which the average attendance is about one hundred persons. A native preacher Tsun-Sheen preaches in one of the chapels and teaches a flourishing Bible-class. There is, likewise, a school for boys, at which thirty-eight scholars are now regularly taught.

There have been six members added to the church at this place, during the past year. There is also here a Theological Seminary, as yet, however, but feeble. At Canton are stationed three missionaries. At Shanghai there are four missionaries, together with a physician and a superintendent of the Press. There is a Mission Chapel in the city; and the missionaries labors extend to the surrounding villages. The press which is here, is in active operation, and during the past year (1849–50) issued twenty thousand tracts. At Amoy there are residing three missionaries and a physician, assisted by Tan Li-ch'un, a native colporteur. At each of these stations there is an hospital, where not only are the efforts of the physicians exerted in behalf of the sick, but the Gospel is regularly preached to them. At Hong-Kong there about forty or fifty patients in regular attendance; and nine hundred have sought relief since the opening of the establishment. At Canton the usual attendance is about two hundred. At Shanghai five hundred and fifty-seven patients were admitted during the past year.

The London Missionary Society commenced its operations in the East Indies in 1798, by the appointment of Rev. Mr. Forsyth to undertake a mission at Calcutta. Subsequently and in succession were commenced the stations of Berhampore, of Benares, of Surat, and of Madras. Finally, in 1817, the Society extended its operations to Travancore, the southern extremity of India, where they first established a permanent mission. The principal stations of the Society in Northern India, are located at Calcutta, Berhampore, Benares, Mirzapore, and Guzerat; in Peninsular India, at Madras, Vizagapatam, Chicacole, Cuddapah, Belgaum, Bellary, Bengalore, Mysore, Salem, Combaconum, and Coimbatoor; and in South Travancore, at Nagercoil, Neyoor, Quilon and Trevandrum. Churches and schools have been established at each of these stations, but the returns given in the reports of the Society, are too incomplete to enable us to obtain their statistics. There are fifty-one missionaries now laboring in this field under the patronage of the Society, including two native and three or four assistant missionaries.

"The actual increase of our mission churches," says the last report, "during the year has been, especially in Southern India, unusually encouraging, demanding peculiar thankfulness to God, who has vouchsafed His Spirit to the labors of his servants. Among the converts received into Christian fellowship, there are many striking illustrations of the power and grace of the Redeemer."

One of the most formidable barriers to the progress of Christianity in India, has been the operation of the Hindoo law, involving the forfeiture of property by every native who renounces Caste and embraces the Gospel. It will, therefore, be learned with great pleasure, by all Christians, that the Government of Calcutta have determined upon repealing every law or usage which inflicts forfeiture of rights or property on any person, by reason of his renouncing, or being excluded from, the communion of any religion.

Encouraged by the success which had attended its missions to the islands of the Pacific, the Society commenced an African mission, in the same year with that in India. Dr. Vanderkemp and Messrs. Kircherer, Edmonds, and Edwards, were accordingly sent out to the Cape of Good Hope; where they separated, and whilst two of them repaired to Caffraria, the others commenced preaching the Gospel to the Bushmen. In 1812, Mr. Thorne was settled as a missionary at Cape Town, and was succeeded in 1818 by the Rev. Dr. Philip, who was appointed superintendent of the Society's operations in Africa. This mission now comprises thirty-one stations within and beyond the limits of the colony, and is carried on by thirty-four ordained missionaries and five lay assistants. During the last year, the Rev. J. J. Freeman has continued his missionary visitation of the Society's stations in South Africa, the state and prospects of which are thus described by him:—"The Society has been honored to accomplish a great work in Africa. There is revision and supervision wanted, most certainly; but as a whole, I am convinced that, if our Directors could personally inspect all that I have seen, they would say not half had been told them; they would enter on their work with a vastly augmented amount of delight, confidence, and gratitude; they would see that the hand of God has been with their missions, and that they have but to continue steadfast and unmovable, abounding in work and faith, and the result is certain. The great ends of our labor are being gained; the people, taken as a whole, are industrious; multitudes of them are highly improved, sober, moral, and correct in all their deportment; very many are truly pious, and walk in all godliness as well as honesty. I have been much delighted with the spirit and character of many: they adorn their profession, and are blessings in the midst of their communities. Besides the various mission churches *within* the Colony, containing an aggregate of upwards of two thousand communicants, we have one thousand eight hundred members in church-fellowship on this north side of the Orange River, that is, among the native tribes lying beyond the boundaries of the Colonial Government, Bechuanas, Griquas, and Corannas. I exclude Caffreland, as that is now more properly within the Colony called British Caffraria, and is altogether distinct from these missions. Their auxiliaries raise about £500 per annum, which is one fifth of the expense they incur; and thus it will be seen that even these missions, which embrace so largely the poor of Africa, raise their proportion equally with others."

In the island of Madagascar, a mission was undertaken in 1818, by Messrs. Bevan and Jones. It was interrupted for some years by the death of these missionaries, but was resumed in 1822 by Mr. Jeffreys. Such was the success of this mission, that in 1828 there were ninety-three schools and four thousand scholars under its care; but upon the death of the king, who was favorable to Christianity, the queen, his successor, manifested the most bitter hostility to Christianity, and has succeeded in a great measure in suppressing it by persecution and exile. There are, however, a considerable number of the Malagasy converts at the neighboring island of Mauritius, among whom the Rev. Mr. Le Brun is now laboring.

In the West Indies and Guiana, the London Missionary Society have missions at Demerara, Berbice, and Jamaica. The Demerara mission includes seven stations, which are occupied by five missionaries and five teachers. The day-schools of the mission contain about nine hundred scholars; and there are several hundred communicants in the various churches. The Berbice mission comprises eight stations, occupied by six missionaries and two assistants. The Jamaica mission contains twelve stations and eight missionaries; with about eight hundred communicants.

The present operations of this Society, as we have just surveyed them, consist of twelve missions, with one hundred and three stations, occupied by one hundred and seventy-one missionaries, and above seven hundred native assistants.

Two important branches of its labors have not been noticed hitherto: the translation of the sacred Scriptures, and the training of a native ministry. During the last year (1849–50) the translation of the Old Testament has been prosecuted in Rarotongan, Samoan, and Sechuana; and the New Testament in Chinese, Canarese, and Teloogoo has been revised. These learned labors are in different stages of progress; but the entire Scriptures in Rarotongan, and the New Testament in Chinese and Canarese, approach completion. To secure the earliest practicable attainment of an object of so much importance, it has been deemed a sacred duty to make use of the valuable acquirements of missionary brethren whose vigor may soon fail. Dr. Medhurst, whose knowledge of Chinese is unequalled, is yet engaged, together with his well-qualified coadjutors, in the important work of revising the Chinese Old Testament.

Scarcely inferior in importance is the preparation of a native ministry, by a suitable course of mental and theological training; and it is an encouraging fact, that native Christians, of tried character and promising qualifications, are enjoying these preparatory advantages; at Tahiti, Rarotonga, and the Navigator's islands, in Polynesia; and at Nagercoil, Bangalore, and Calcutta, in India. At Hankey, in South Africa, the Society has also an institution for the ministerial education of young men born in the Colony; and it is hoped that the same desirable object will soon be accomplished in the West Indies. In connection with this subject, it will be gratifying to learn, that, during the tour of Mr. Freeman, he took part in the ordination of Mr. Arie Van Ruyer, as pastor of a native church at Tidmanton, a station of the Kat River settlement; and also that two native pastors, Enoch Paul and N. Shadrach, were recently ordained in India over the Tamil churches at Bellary and Bangalore.

The receipts of the London Missionary Society, for the year 1849–50, were as follows:—

	£	*s.*	*d.*
Received in Great Britain and Ireland, . .	50,778	5	9
Do. at missionary stations and from auxiliaries abroad, ...	11,766	15	2
Total receipts,	62,545	0	11

or $302,637.

The total expenditure was £64,489 9*s.* 5*d.*

CHAPTER XVI.

CHURCH MISSIONARY SOCIETY.

THE Church Missionary Society had its origin in the revival of evangelical religion among members of the Church of England in the latter part of the last century, and numbers among its earliest friends the excellent Simeon, the Venns, and Cecil. In the year 1801, this Society was founded with the specific purpose of evangelizing Africa and the East. Some time elapsed before suitable persons could be obtained to send forth as missionaries. The first who embarked were two young Lutheran ministers,—Melchior Renner and Peter Hartwig. Their destination was to the colony of Sierra Leone, which they reached in 1804, their intention being to plant a mission among the Susoos, in the vicinity. A reinforcement of three other clergymen was sent to join them after two years, and several more in 1809. With these auxiliaries, the brethren began their operations at the two stations, at the Rio Pongas river and Fantimania. The natives, and especially the slave-traders, having become exasperated by efforts made in 1811, to break up the slave-trade at Rio Pongas, and suspecting the missionaries of instigating them, conceived great animosity against them, and burnt several of their buildings. At length, in 1818, the opposition of the traders continuing unabated, the mission was removed from the Susoos to the colony of Sierra Leone itself. After the slave-trade was abolished by the British Government, a wider and more promising field of usefulness was opened among the rescued negroes who were brought—often in numbers—to the colony, and supported for a time by the government. Land was given to the missionaries at Leicester Mountain, for the erection of an institution for the instruction of the rescued slaves; whence they subsequently removed to Regent's Town, where they established a College.

The labors of the Society in the colony of Sierra Leone have not only been directed to the instruction and pastoral oversight of the Africans who inhabit the colony, but also to the evangelizing of the heathen tribes of Western Africa, "that from Sierra Leone as a centre the light of Christianity may issue forth to illuminate and bless distant kingdoms." The missionary corps employed consists of fourteen European and three native missionaries, fifty-one teachers, nine catechists, and a surgeon. The mission comprises fifteen stations. The number of communicants is 2061, of scholars in the various schools 6184, and of students in the grammar-school and Christian Institution sixty-six. During the past year there have been large additions to the church by the baptism of adults who had long been under instruction, and gave good evidence of their sincere and intelligent profession of faith in Christ.

The Society has extended its operations in West Africa to the kingdom of Ashantee, where the Yoruba mission was established in 1845–6 at Abbeokuta and Badagry. At these stations it has six ordained missionaries, with nine native teachers, a catechist, and two European assistants.

On the Eastern coast of Africa, the Church Missionary Society has undertaken a mission at Rabbai Mpia, south of Abyssinia, among the Gallas and other tribes. The Rev. Dr. Krapf has been laboring there since 1844, chiefly in exploring the field. After a short return to England, he has gone forth again, accompanied by the Rev. Messrs. Diehlmann and Pfefferle.

In Australasia the first mission of the Society was commenced in August, 1809, by Messrs. William Hall and John King, who sailed to Port Jackson, in New South Wales, where, on account of unfavorable intelligence, they were detained until 1814, when they repaired to New Zealand, and commenced their efforts at Rangheehoo, on land formerly granted to the Church Missionary Society. A reinforcement arrived in 1819, at which time the missionaries purchased a tract of land upon which they commenced a settlement to counteract the roving habits of the natives, and place them more under the influence of the mission. Notwithstanding the discouragements which the missionaries encountered from the savage habits and wars of the native tribes, they formed several new settlements from time to time, and extended their labors to the instruction of the youth, and to the printing and circulation in the islands of such portions of Scripture as they had translated into the vernacular language.

At present the New Zealand Mission is prosecuted by twenty ordained missionaries, ten European, and four hundred and sixty-one native catechists and teachers. The number of stations is twenty-three, in connection with which there are 5213 communicants. Schools have been established, but the number of scholars is not specified.

In Northern India, the operations of the Church Missionary Society were commenced in the year 1816, by the sending of the Rev. Mr. Greenwood, his wife, and Mr. Schroeter to Calcutta. They decided to reside at Garden Reach, within a few miles of that city, and to open schools at the neighboring village of Kidderpore. The mission gradually extended, and reinforcements were from time to time sent to its assistance, until, in 1823, it embraced twelve European clergymen within its limits. It was in this year that Bishop Heber reached India, and, through his untiring exertions in its behalf, the Society's affairs were much improved. An auxiliary society was formed under his superintendence to assist the parent institution in its operations in Northern India. A great loss was sustained by the mission upon the death of Bishop Heber, which occurred in the early part of the year 1826. Several other valuable laborers in the mission have been removed from their earthly toils, among whom are mentioned the names of Bowley, Corrie, Robinson, and Abdool-Messeeh, the last of whom was converted under the preaching of Henry Martyn, and whose labors at Agra were productive of saving benefits to many of the heathen.

The stations of this mission are twenty-one in number, the principal of which are Calcutta, Krishnaghur, Benares, Agra, etc. The Corresponding Committee, in their report to the Society, estimate the whole number of native Christians in connection with the Society Mission in North India at 6164, of whom 1134 are communicants. The number of new converts during the year has been seventy-one, exclusive of children. In the Society's schools in North India are 5161 pupils, of whom 1092 are native Christian boys and girls, and the remainder heathen and Mussulman. The schools of various sorts are ninety-eight in number. The Himalaya mission is restricted to one station at Kotghur, that of Simla having been abandoned. Two boarding-schools have been established, in which, within the last year, two interesting conversions have occurred.

The Bombay and Western India Misson was founded in 1820. It has been prosecuted on a less extensive scale than the other missions in India. The stations are five in number, at which seven missionaries, and forty native and other teachers and catechists are engaged. The number of communicants is forty-three; of scholars 1373.

The Madras and South India Mission was commenced in 1814, when the Rev. Messrs. Schnarre and Rhenius reached Madras, who, after studying the language at Tranquebar, located themselves at Blacktown, where great interest was manifested by the Hindoos, as well as the Moslems and Roman Catholics, in the new doctrines preached to them. Soon after their arrival the missionaries established schools, and, notwithstanding the prejudices of the people, had soon gathered about two hundred scholars. In succeeding years reinforcements were sent to the mission. The New Testament was translated into the Tamul language; and, in the year 1823, when the version was nearly completed, more than thirty-five thousand five hundred copies had been printed. There were at that time five hundred and eight children in the schools. The mission establishment at present consists of thirty-four ordained missionaries, eight native catechists, four European and six East Indian catechists, 417 native teachers and schoolmasters, seventy native, five European, and two East Indian female teachers, and one printer. The stations are nineteen, the communicants 3733, which, however, does not include the whole number of baptized converts. The Tinevelly Mission is one of the most interesting under the care of the Society. The whole number of converts on the 1st of January, 1850, was 23,994, above one half of that number consisting of baptized converts. A very small portion of these, however, are communicants. It is gratifying to find established among these converts various religious and benevolent societies, such as the Bible, the Book and Tract, the Church-Building, and the Friend-in-Need societies, and various associations for mutual support in sickness. These enterprises have been carried on with increasing spirit and success during the past year, and a new association has been added to the number of a peculiarly interesting character, termed the "Heathen's Friend Society." It was commenced in the early part of 1849 by a few poor native Christians, being entirely a scheme of their own. They propose it as their object to open day-schools in the surrounding heathen villages, where the light of the Gospel has not yet shined, and where the glad tidings of salvation have not yet been proclaimed, to educate heathen children in the Christian religion. In this work they intend to employ native Christians as teachers and tract distributors. Six months after its establishment, this Society had obtained the cordial support of the native and European Christians, and was in active operation, sustaining two catechists, three schoolmasters, one tract distributor, and three schools containing 140 pupils.

The Ceylon mission was commenced in 1818 by four missionaries sent from Europe, the Rev. Messrs. Lambrich, Mayor, Ward and Knight, who were stationed at Kandy, Calpentym, Galle, and Jaffnapatam. The field was an inviting one, although much injury had been done to the cause of Christianity by the measures of the Dutch government who disqualified all from inheriting property who had not been baptized. The operations of the mission were increased and extended in 1820, by the association of two more missionaries with those who already occupied the field. They undertook, in 1822, in addition to their other duties, the superintendence of about forty government schools in the district of Galleana Matura. Through this agency they expected to have a control over the whole of the religious instruction of the youth, and so to exert a very wide-spread influence in favor of Christianity. The Ceylon mission at present comprises thirteen ordained missionaries, including three natives of the island; fourteen native catechists; eighty-five native teachers and schoolmasters, and nineteen native schoolmistresses. There are six stations connected with the mission, with 296 communicants, and 2,808 attendants on public worship. There are three seminaries which contain forty-eight pupils, and seventy-seven schools with 2,788 scholars. Besides the churches established at the stations, the missionaries report the formation of twenty-five village congregations at which there is a considerable attendance, notwithstanding the efforts of the Buddhist priests and their abettors. No obstacle to the spread of the Gospel is found to be so great in the island, as the incorrect notions which the natives have conceived of the nature of Christianity. Almost the whole adult population, even the priests, have been baptized; and crowds of these *nominal Christians* may be seen flocking to the heathen temples, from distances often of from seventy to one hundred and fifty miles, and worshipping false gods. Many of these nominal Christians are rigid Buddhists.

The Society commenced a mission to China in the year 1844. There are now stationed there seven ordained missionaries, who are distributed at the stations of Shanghai, Ning-po and Hong-Kong.

On the Mediterranean, three missions have been established; at Syra, Smyrna and Cairo. At Syra the mission establishment consists of one ordained missionary, with ten assistant teachers. The missionary Mr. Hildner, has been engaged chiefly in instructing youth, of whom there are now 462 in his schools. At Smyrna the Society has one missionary with two assistants, who labor principally among the nominal Christians at that port; and at Cairo it supports two missionaries with five assistant teachers. The number of communicants at the last station is eighteen; of scholars 178. Abyssinia, once a promising field of the Society's labors, is at present abandoned in consequence of the expulsion of missionaries by instigation of the Romanist emissaries. It is reported, however, that the Romanists, in turn, have been expelled; and the king seems disposed to invite back the Society's laborers. He has lately proposed to the excellent bishop Gobat, to undertake the superintendence of the Abyssinian convent at Jerusalem; which will afford him a favorable opportunity for imparting religious instruction to the many natives, who visit that city.

In the Western Hemisphere, this Society has established missions in some of the British colonies, commenced in 1823. The North West American mission is near the lakes Winnipeg and Manitoba. It consists of six stations under the charge of five missionaries, and nine schoolmasters and catechists. The converts, chiefly from among the Indians, number 489; the schools contain about seven hundred scholars. In British Guiana, two missionaries and five teachers are employed, among the Arrowaks and Carribeese. The communicants number seventy, and the scholars about the same. This mission was established 1827. In Jamaica, the operations of the Society have been reduced to a single station occupied by a catechist; the stations previously formed having been added to the colonial Church Establishment. Communicants, 358; scholars, 286.

In reviewing these various missionary operations, the Committee of the Church Missionary Society, in their last report, dwell on the evidences of the divine favor resting upon their work; in proof of which they appeal "to the increase of converts, to the grace manifested by many of them, and to the evident establishing, strengthening, and settling of their principal missions. They appeal, also, to the favor given to their missionaries in sight of the Heathen; such as the support afforded by the heathen chiefs of Abbeokuta, the protection of our missionaries by the heathen tribes of East Africa, the welcome given by the heathen population of Travancore to a zealous missionary returning to his work; and the toleration now granted in Turkey and China. They appeal, also, to the open doors which the Providence of God is setting before the Society; such as, the invitation given to it by a zealous naval officer to follow up the benevolent enterprise at the Gallinas, which he had achieved by naval force, the voice from Scinde, and the special call to the Punjab. In one and the same letter, lately received from Calcutta, applications for help were conveyed from the widely-separated localities of Bhagulpur, Delhi, Deyrah, Assam, Penang, and the Punjab."

To sum up; the missions of the Society are twelve in number, comprehending one hundred and six stations, and prosecuted by 1,726 laborers, of whom one hundred and forty-seven are ordained ministers, and 1,339 native male assistants. The total number of communicants in connection with the missions, (not including all baptized converts,) is 13,551. The total number of scholars in the mission schools is not specified, but must be in the neighborhood of thirty thousand.

The income of the Church Missionary Society, for the year 1849–50, amounted to £104,273 6*s.* 10*d.*, or $504,685.

At the semi-centennial celebration of the Society's formation, a "Jubilee fund" was raised, for the purpose of providing for the relief of disabled missionaries, the endowment of native churches, and the erection of missionary buildings. In the first of these purposes was included the establishment of a "Home," for the children of missionaries. This interesting establishment has been recently opened, and affords accommodation for forty children. The "Jubilee fund" amounts already to £56,822 3*s.* 7*d.*, or $275,040.

CHAPTER XVII.

ENGLISH WESLEYAN-METHODIST MISSIONARY SOCIETY.

THE Wesleyan enterprise, from its very outset, assumed a missionary character; and such in its development, both in Great Britain and in the United States, it has continued to be. But without entering into the history of the labors of its earliest missionaries in our own country, we shall glance only at those efforts which have been made by English Wesleyans, to propagate the Gospel in heathen and Roman Catholic countries.

In the West Indies, under the direction of the celebrated Dr. Coke and others, missions were commenced by members of the Wesleyan connection, as early as the year 1778; and in the island of Antigua alone, there were, five years after, more than one thousand members of that denomination. The first missionaries in this island were Messrs. Baxter and Warrener, whose labors were attended with great success. Subsequent missionary operations were extended to the islands of St. Vincent, St. Christopher, Barbadoes, Dominica, Jamaica, Bermuda, and St. Domingo, and also to Demerara in British Guiana.

In British North America, missions were commenced in the year 1779, by Mr. Black, in Nova Scotia, including Cape Breton and Prince Edward's Island, and subsequently in New Brunswick, Newfoundland, Canada, and Honduras.

Through the assiduous efforts of Dr. Coke, the Wesleyan Conference determined to send the Gospel to the East Indies; and in 1813 commissioned a corps of missionaries to Ceylon, where they had resolved to commence their efforts. These brethren were, besides Dr. Coke, Messrs. Harvard, Clough, Ault, Erskine, Squance, and Lynch. But the principal mover of the enterprise, was not spared to behold the shores of the island for whose evangelization he had put forth such efforts. Upon their arrival at Ceylon, the missionaries were distributed at the stations of Jaffna, Batticaloa, Galle, and Matura; where they prosecuted their study of the Tamul and Cingalese, and began their labors.

The rapidly increasing claims of these missions induced in 1817 the formation of the General Wesleyan Missionary Society, in which the affairs of the missions are conducted by a joint committee of ministers and laymen, under the direction and final decision of the annual conference. "The object of this Society," says one of the fundamental regulations, "is to excite and combine, on a plan more systematic and efficient than has heretofore been accomplished, the exertions of the societies and congregations of the Wesleyan-Methodists (and of others who are friends to the conversion of the heathen world, and to the preaching of the Gospel generally, in foreign lands), in the support and enlargement of the foreign missions which were first established by the Rev. John Wesley, M. A., the Rev. Thomas Coke, LL.D., and others; and which are now, or shall be, from year to year, carried on under the sanction and direction of the Conference of the people called Methodists."

The present missions of the Wesleyan Missionary Society are located in Ireland, Germany, France, Switzerland, and Spain; in India and Ceylon; in Australasia and Polynesia; in South and West Africa; and in the West Indies and British North America.

"The Society's missions in Ireland are eighteen in number. They embrace many counties, and are scattered throughout the kingdom. The reports furnished by the missionaries abundantly prove that these operations are instrumentally productive of a large amount of benefit." There are at present attached to the mission two hundred and seventy chapels and other preaching places, with twenty-four missionaries and fifty-six other paid agents. There are thirty-five local preachers, and 2,485 church members; and 3,677 scholars attend the day and Sunday-schools.

"The operations of the Society in Wirtemberg are still prosecuted by Mr. Müller and his assistants, in the midst of many difficulties. Weekly religious services are held at about sixty places, at which upwards of one thousand individuals are now united together in church-fellowship. Mr. Müller has sixteen fellow-laborers associated with him, who read and expound the Scriptures, and conduct public worship in the several congregations."

In several of the principal towns of France and French Switzerland, the Society has flourishing missions; as also among the Waldenses of the French and Italian Alps. The number of its stations in this portion of the field, is eight; preaching places and chapels one hundred and nine; missionaries and assistants nineteen. At Gibraltar, are stationed two missionaries, with two teachers, under whose care are 131 scholars.

The missions in Ceylon are divided into the Cingalese and Tamul districts; in the former of which, including the southern portion of the island, are eleven stations, with twelve missionaries and ninety-one catechists and teachers. The value of the native agency, which has been so largely raised up in South Ceylon, is made the more apparent by the increased amount of labor and responsibility devolved upon it. The members have increased to twelve hundred and fourteen, chiefly native converts; and the schools have received considerable additions. Four new chapels have been built during the year, and four more are in course of erection.

In the Tamul district, which includes the northern district of Ceylon, there are five stations and twenty-eight chapels and preaching places, with seven missionaries and assistants. There are fifty-seven day and Sunday-schools attended by 1,365 scholars. The labors of the missionaries in this district during the last year have met with considerable encouragement.

In continental India, the missions of the Society are comprised within the Madras and Mysore districts; the former among the Tamul and the latter among the Canarese natives. The number of missionaries and assistants is fifteen; of catechists and teachers fifty-seven; and of scholars, 1,960. The printing establishment has issued more than 1,200,000 pages.

In Australasia, the Society's missionaries are located in New South Wales, Australia Felix, South Australia, Western Australia, and Van Dieman's Land, or Tasmania. The local reports recently received from the stations in Australia, communicate very encouraging information with regard to the advancement of the cause in many districts. In several places the chapels already erected are found too small to accommodate the increasing numbers who are desirous of attending upon the preaching of the Gospel. At other localities places of worship are in process of erection; while in many where no missionary has yet been stationed, a great desire is expressed that one may be procured. In South Australia, the Society's mission is rising in importance, and extending its beneficial influence throughout the colony. The financial affairs of this colony are prosperous; the expenses for the support of missionaries are met by the voluntary contributions of the people; and two more laborers, it is expected, will be sustained in like manner. The schools are rapidly increasing in efficiency and number. In Van Dieman's Land, the missions are in a flourishing condition, and large additions have been made to the churches. In the Australian and Van Dieman's Land mission, there are twenty-seven stations and two hundred and forty-one places of worship; with thirty missionaries and assistants, and fifty-seven teachers and catechists. Church members, 4,210; schools, 127, with 6,585 scholars.

A mission was commenced in New Zealand, by Rev. Mr.

Leigh, in 1822. The prospects of this enterprise were at first such as to warrant sanguine expectations of its success; but the natural ferocity of the inhabitants, and their treachery were soon evinced in the plundering of the missionary establishment by a furious band of warriors, and compelled the missionaries who had reinforced Mr. Leigh, to escape from the island. After a suspension of a few years, this mission was recommenced in 1840. At present its condition is encouraging, although the hindrances to the spread of the Gospel among the islands are not few. Great attention is paid to the education of the youth, and at Three Kings there is a native Institution to assist those who desire to pursue the more advanced branches of learning. The fruits of the efforts of the missionaries cannot better be represented than in the words of the Governor of New Zealand, in a despatch to the British Government:—"This short review of the present state of the principal settlements in New Zealand, will, I think, satisfy your Lordship of the general state of prosperity of this colony. It only remains for me to add that the exertions of our most excellent bishop and his clergy, together with those of the numerous, and I may say, admirable body of missionaries of different denominations, have secured to this colony a greater amount of religious supervision and of religious instruction than any other young country has probably ever enjoyed; and this circumstance cannot fail ultimately to produce a very powerful effect upon the future population of this country; while at the present day it secures to New Zealand advantages which may be readily imagined, but which it would be difficult to describe in detail, as they enter into all the ramifications of the society of the country, and of the domestic life both of the natives and Europeans. However, there can be no doubt that the present state of tranquillity and prosperity of this country, and the rapid advances which the native population are making, are in a very great degree to be attributed to the exertions of the various religious bodies in New Zealand."

In the Friendly Islands, at the stations of Tongatabu, Habai, Vavau, Niua Tobutabu, etc., there are located ten missionaries, with nine catechists; the number of communicants being 7,202, and the number of scholars 7,426. In the Feejee district, which has been in a great degree reclaimed from heathenism under the efforts of the Society, there are stationed five missionaries, and thirty-eight catechists. Communicants 1,713; scholars 1,960.

The operations of the Society in Southern Africa are on a large scale; they are divided into the districts of the Cape of Good Hope, Albany and Caffraria, and Bechuana. The total number of stations is forty-two; of missionaries, forty; and of catechists and teachers one hundred and five; of communicants there are 4,365; and of scholars, 4,580. The labors of the missionaries are among the colonists, as well as the Caffres, the Bechuanas, and other natives. In Caffraria, the benefits of the mission-schools and Institution are now becoming strikingly manifest. An improved class of native teachers is rising up, and the whole country, embraced within the district, presents a more hopeful and inviting prospect than was ever before witnessed. The mission press is in active operation, and among its most recent issues is a new and improved grammar of the Caffre language.

In the colony of Sierra Leone is situated one of the most prosperous of the Wesleyan Missionary Society's fields of labor. There is an evident improvement in the tone of personal piety among the people, and there has been a net increase of three hundred and fifty-eight in the number of full and accredited church-members during the past year. There are three stations in this district; under the charge of seven missionaries, and forty-three teachers and catechists. The number of church members is 4,712, and of scholars 2,958. There are also eight missionaries stationed at the Gambia and on Cape Coast, at nine different stations; and churches have been organized with 1,285 members. The schools contain 1,765 scholars.

The Society's missions in the British West Indies present in some respects an unfavorable aspect. The alteration in the duties on sugar has so far affected the worldly condition of the people, as greatly to diminish their contributions towards the support of religious ordinances, and withdraw their attention from the subject of religion. In many places, however, there have been encouraging indications of the success of missionary efforts during the past year. The field is divided into the districts of Antigua, St. Vincent and Demerara, Jamaica, Bahama, and Hayti, and includes forty stations with seventy-four missionaries and 128 catechists. The number of members is 50,567, and of scholars 8,090.

The missions in British North America comprise the United province of Canada, the provinces of Nova Scotia, New Brunswick, the territories of the Hudson's Bay Company, and the islands of Prince Edward, Cape Breton, and Newfoundland. The missions in Western Canada are divided into two classes— Domestic, embracing the new settlements; and Indian, established for the benefit of the aboriginal tribes. The domestic missions are twenty-seven in number, the Indian stations twelve. The total number of stations in British North America is 117; the number of missionaries 131.

To sum up the operations of the Wesleyan Methodist Missionary Society: the total number of its stations in various parts of the world, is three hundred and twenty-four; and of chapels and other preaching places, in connection with these stations, 2,992. Its missionaries and assistant-missionaries, including fourteen supernumeraries, are four hundred and twenty-seven, and its other paid agents, as catechists, interpreters, day-school teachers, etc., 781. Its unpaid agents, as Sunday-school teachers, etc., amount to 8,087. The full and accredited church-members, in connection with these missions, number 105,394, and there are on trial for church membership 4,830 persons. In attendance upon the schools there are 78,548 scholars. Eight printing establishments are in operation.

The total income of this Society, for the year ending April, 1850, amounted to £111,685 13*s.* 6*d.*, or $540,560, and the expenditure for the same term to £109,168 10*s.* 7*d.* The receipts exhibit a large increase over those of the previous year.

CHAPTER XVIII.

MISSIONS OF THE SCOTTISH PRESBYTERIAN CHURCHES.

In Scotland, as in all other thoroughly Protestant lands, the revival of evangelical religion after a long period of formalism and inaction, was closely followed by a manifestation of the missionary spirit. The epoch of this manifestation was coeval with the foundation of the great benevolent enterprises in other parts of Great Britain. It was in the year 1796, and under the presidency of the venerable Dr. Erskine, that missionary societies were first instituted in Glasgow and Edinburgh. An overture was forthwith transmitted to the General Assembly, praying that body to take into consideration "by what means the Church of Scotland might most effectually contribute to the diffusion of the Gospel over the world;" and soliciting the recommendation of a "general collection throughout the Church, to aid the several societies for propagating the Gospel among the heathen nations." It is difficult to believe that a proposition so natural and so entirely in accordance with the spirit of the Gospel, should have been received in the high ecclesiastical court of Scotland with the most bitter opposition, from the prevailing Moderate party; and that after much abuse of the cause which it advocated, the motion met with a complete defeat.

Thirty years elapsed before another effort was made. Meanwhile the societies instituted at Glasgow and Edinburgh continued in existence; but their means were comparatively small and their energies contracted. The Rev. Dr. Inglis was the distinguished and successful advocate of the missionary cause in the Church of Scotland. His eminent position secured for the subject a respectful consideration. "A Committee was appointed," says Hetherington, "to consider and report on the subject; and in 1826 a Pastoral Address to the people of Scotland, from the pen of Dr. Inglis, appeared, and tended powerfully to direct the attention of the Kingdom to the sacred duty of propagating the Gospel among the heathen, and especially in India. Collections were made, and subscriptions obtained, till a sufficient fund was raised to enable the Committee to proceed with their holy enterprise; and at length in 1829, Dr. Duff, the first missionary ever sent forth by any national Protestant Church in its corporate character, left his native land, commissioned by the Presbyterian Church of Scotland to convey to India the light of Gospel truth, and to offer for her acceptance the simple, pure, efficient, and most truly apostolic form of Christianity, which is the glory and strength of the Presbyterian Church."

The succeeding twelve years manifested a great and encouraging progress in the missionary activity of the Scottish Church. In 1833, it supported only two departments or "schemes" of evangelical labor, those of Education in the Highlands, and Foreign Missions; and the amount collected for these objects was about £3,500. Other departments were gradually added for Home Missions, and missions in the colonies and among the Jews; and in 1841, the total sum contributed to these several purposes was more than £22,000.

It is an interesting fact, that the Free Church of Scotland, in separating from the Establishment, carried with her almost all the missionaries, and most of the missionary spirit, of Scotland. The veteran soldiers of the Cross who had labored for many years in heathen lands, clung to the cause of pure and independent religion at home, with all the ardor of a holy patriotism. Wilson, Duff, and others whose names are well known and honored in the field have adhered to the Free Church of Scotland.

We proceed to specify some of the missionary organizations which are now in operation in Scotland.

1. The *Glasgow Missionary Society* commenced soon after the London Missionary Society, in 1795, with which it held early connection in a mission to the Foulah tribe on the western coast of Africa. For a number of years it was unable to effect anything further than aiding the funds of other societies—until an opening occurred in 1821, in Southern Africa, where the colonial government had made peace with the Caffre tribes that lie without the boundaries of the Cape Colony, and the chief Gaika had shown a desire of obtaining missionaries for his people. Rev. H. Thompson, of the Glasgow University, and his associate Mr. Bennie, therefore proceeded to Southern Africa to act with Mr. Brownlee, of the London Missionary Society, who had lately been appointed by the colonial government as a missionary to the Caffres; the Gaika having made it one of the conditions of peace that missionaries should reside in his country. This Society soon established a printing press, and furnished themselves and the London missionaries with several books in the Caffre language. In 1831, they had 75 scholars from among the natives, all dressed in European style; and the missionaries had translated the Gospel of St. John. Their system of education was the same as that employed by the "Society for teaching the native Irish to read their own language," that is all who can read are employed to teach their neighbor at so much per head, and without any apparatus beyond books. Besides this system, the Glasgow Society has ten schools, four of which, in 1841, were taught by natives. Its receipts, for the year 1846, were £1,671 19*s.* 9*d.*, or $8,095.

2. The *Edinburgh Missionary Society* was established in 1796. Its first mission was in Jamaica; but the largest, and for a time the most successful of its undertakings, was among the

Tartar tribes on the borders of the Black and Caspian Seas. In 1825, however, by the jealousy of the Russian government, the missionaries were driven from these territories, and the mission has been given up.

This Society has since been known as the *Scottish Missionary Society.* It has relinquished to the Established and Secession Churches, its missions in India and Jamaica; and it is, we believe, no longer in active operation.

3. *Established Church of Scotland.*—In India, the missions of the Established Church are at Calcutta, Bombay, Madras, and Ghospara. These missions are principally directed, like those of the Free Church, to the education of the young, as a work preparatory to the great object of the preaching of the Gospel. At Calcutta, the mission institution has at present an average attendance of 1,021 pupils. The Bengali chapel is open three days every week; the Sunday evening service is attended by thirty to fifty Hindus. The missionaries of this station are three —Messrs. Anderson, Ogilvie and Hurdman. At Madras, five missionaries are stationed; the institution contains about 690 scholars. The Bombay mission, founded in 1828 by the Scottish Missionary Society, was transferred in 1835 to the care of the General Assembly. It is now occupied by two missionaries; with two female assistants, who are supported by a Ladies' Association. The number of pupils in the schools is 370. At the station of Ghospara, occupied by two native assistants, there is a flourishing school of fifty pupils. The Indian missions of the Established Church, therefore, are prosecuted by ten missionaries and four assistants; and the number of pupils in the institutions is 2,131. Under the Colonial Scheme of the Assembly are included missions in British North America, Grenada, Mauritius, Australia, and New Zealand; and among the Jews, in London, Carlsruhe, Gibraltar and Cochin, the Church employs four missionaries, and three female assistants.

The expenditures of the last year, for these three departments of foreign labor, amounted to £10,591 or $51,260.

4. The *Free Church of Scotland*, likewise, devotes most of its energies in the foreign work to its missions in India, and particularly to the education of the young. Its missions are at Calcutta, with the out-stations of Culna, Baranagar, and Bransberia; at Bombay; at Madras, with the out-stations of Conjeveram, Triplicane, and Chingleput; at Puna, with the out-stations, of Indapur and Kotrur; and at Nagpore and Kampti. The Calcutta mission is occupied by five missionaries, with four native catechists, and a large number of assistants. At the head of the mission institution is the venerable and excellent Dr. Duff; the number of pupils in the several educational establishments is about two thousand. At the Bombay mission, three missionaries, among whom is Dr. Wilson, with two native missionaries, are laboring. About twelve hundred children are receiving instruction. The Madras mission employs five missionaries and several native assistants; ten schools are educating about fourteen hundred youth. At Puna, with its stations, there are three missionaries, with one European and nine native assistants; the number of communicants is twenty-eight; and of pupils about six hundred. At Nagpore and Kampti, one missionary, two teachers, and four native assistants are laboring; about six hundred pupils attend the schools. In South Africa, the Free Church has missions at Cape Town, Lovedale, Burnshill and Pirie. At Cape Town are two missionaries and one assistant; at Lovedale, three missionaries and two native assistants; at Burnshill, one missionary and two assistants; and at Pirie, one missionary, one female teacher, and one assistant: making on the whole seven missionaries and seven assistants. In Caffreland no fewer than sixty-three of the natives applied to the missionaries for baptism at one time. At the Cape of Good Hope the average attendance upon Christian instruction is five hundred, and the number on the roll is about nine hundred.

Among the Jews, the Free Church has missions at Constantinople, Pesth, Berlin, and Lemburg. The total number of missionaries supported by the Free Church of Scotland at its various stations, is thirty-seven ; with fifty-seven native ministers and preachers. About six thousand youth are receiving Christian instruction in connection with its mission institutions. The total expenditure for the last year, including the aid afforded to colonial churches, amounted to £20,802 2*s.* 2*d.*, or $100,681.

5. The *United Secession Church*, composed of the Secession and Relief Churches, which united some years ago, has missions in Canada, Jamaica, Trinidad, Western and South Africa, Persia, and Australia. The mission in Canada was commenced in 1832. Twenty-eight missionaries, under whose care are about four thousand church members, are connected with it. The Jamaica Mission was lately transferred to the Secession Church by the Scottish Missionary Society. In 1847, there were thirteen stations, with more than a thousand members, and fifteen young natives preparing for missionary labor. The stations in West Africa are two, in Calabar. The mission was undertaken in 1846 by three missionaries. In South Africa, three stations and two out-stations are occupied by two missionaries, with one female teacher, and eight native assistants. The income of the Missions of the United Secession Church was, in 1847, £9,322 13*s.* 7*d.*, or $45,125.

The Presbyterian Church of Ireland sustains a mission in India, founded in 1841, at the stations of Rajkot, Gogo, and Surat, occupied by six missionaries and two native assistants. We have no further particulars respecting its operations.

The Presbyterians of England, also, have been doing something in the way of sustaining foreign missions. At Canton, China, the Rev. Mr. Burns, sent out by them, has entered upon the occupancy of the premises vacated by the London Missionary Society, and carries on the Chinese services, with the aid of several native preachers.

CHAPTER XIX.

FRENCH, RHENISH, AND BASLE MISSIONARY SOCIETIES.

The *French Evangelical Missionary Society* was formed in the year 1822, by members of the Reformed and Lutheran Churches in France, together with several excellent English and American Christians, among whom were Daniel Wilson, now Bishop of Calcutta, and Jonas King, the missionary at Athens. The object of the new organization, whose title was the "Society of Evangelical Missions among non-Christian nations," was two-fold: the establishment of an institution for the education of young men as missionaries of the Gospel, and the support of these and other laborers in heathen lands. It began by sustaining Mr. King as its missionary in Jerusalem, but that gentleman soon connected himself with the American Board. The educational institution, founded by the Society, was placed under the care of M. Gallaud and subsequently of the Rev. Dr. Grandpierre. From among the students educated in it, the Society selected, in 1829, its first missionaries to the heathen,—Prosper Lemue, Isaac Bisseux, and Samuel Rollaud. They were ordained on the 2d of May, and shortly after left for their sphere of labor. The field chosen by the Society was South Africa; and, in a speech at the second anniversary of the Society, the following statement was made by its president, respecting this selection. "It is worthy of observation, that, in the part of Africa whither our young brethren are proceeding, there are, at some distance from Cape Town, a number of families descended from former French refugees, who quitted their country and home for the preservation of their faith. The Dutch East India Company granted them a considerable portion of land, where they formed for themselves a new country. Our young brethren will be received by them with kindred affection."

In this connection, a statement made in the last annual report of this Society, is of peculiar interest. During the pecuniary difficulties of the mission, at the time of the recent revolution in France, when the resources of the Society were in a great measure cut off, the Dutch Reformed Synod of the Cape of Good Hope determined to render it assistance, and sent a deputation to visit the stations of the mission. One of the deputies was the descendant of a family of French refugees, who had emigrated to the Cape in the time of Louis XIV. They reported to the Synod in the following favorable terms:—"The undersigned have not only attended public services at many of the stations, but besides, they have visited the native Christians in their houses, and have examined a considerable number of pupils in one of the schools, all without the possibility of any of them having learned beforehand of this visit. Consequently they have received the most favorable impression from what they have seen in this very important and interesting mission, and they would regard it as a deplorable calamity that the country of the Bassutos should ever, in any manner, be deprived of the labors of these excellent and truly devoted men." To this honorable testimony we add that of the Secretary of the London Missionary Society:—"Amongst all the men that have labored in South Africa, the French Protestant ministers have toiled with singular consistency, and have been honored by God with most abundant success."

The first president of the French Missionary Society was the distinguished Count Ver-Huell, admiral and peer of France, who continued in this office deeply interested and actively engaged in its service until his death, about eight years since. Among the first students who were graduated at the missionary institution, was Mr. Gobat, for many years a missionary of the Church Missionary Society, and now Bishop of Jerusalem.

The missions of the Society in South Africa are chiefly among the Bechuana and Bassuto tribes. The stations are those of Carmel, Bethulia, Beersheba, Bethesda, Moriah, Berea, Thaba-Bossiou, Wellington, Motito, and Mekuatling. The number of communicants is 1,185, of scholars 350, of attendants upon public worship 2,240. The number of missionaries is ten, with four assistants. The receipts of the Society for the year 1849–50 amounted to 136,173fr., or $25,600. It was indebted at that period to the amount of 88,868fr.

The *Rhenish Missionary Society* in Germany, was formed in 1828 by a union of three smaller associations. One of these, the Barmen Missionary Society, had published a missionary gazette, of which 20,000 copies were in circulation; and had for three years maintained a missionary seminary. These came under the charge of the united society. The other societies were those of Cologne and Wesel. Different local associations have united with it, to the number of fifty, who meet by their delegates annually, and intrust the management to a committee of twelve, meeting once a month or oftener; while the executive power is vested almost exclusively in a single officer known as the inspector of the Mission-house.

The first missionaries were sent to South Africa, in 1829. There were four of them, one a physician, and they founded three stations. One of these combines instruction in the arts of civilization as well as in Christianity, a company of German mechanics having been introduced to aid in diffusing various sorts of handicraft among the people. In this way the station was made self-supporting, but some of these colonists have set bad examples to the natives, and the Society has felt obliged to desist from further colonization of this kind. In 1830 two other stations were founded. Each station is regularly organized with a complete system of ecclesiastical government modelled after the Presbyterian discipline, schools are maintained, and missionary associations formed to lead the people to contribute according to their ability.

In 1840 the Society extended its operations to the northern limits of Cape Colony, where three stations were established, and seven stations have been formed still further northward in the interior of the country. The missionaries have found extreme difficulty in acquiring the native languages, and in contending with the wandering habits of the people; while the tyranny of the Dutch Boors follows the natives, threatening to deprive them of their land as fast as they bring it into cultivation.

They had succeeded in forming several prosperous communities; but in the autumn of last year—1850—the hostilities of the neighboring tribe of Namaquas being provoked, a dreadful massacre took place. The Rev. Mr. Hahn, missionary of this society at New Barmen, wrote on the 6th of September: "The whole country is in ferment, and the excitement has risen to a higher pitch than ever. Our mission among the Ovaherero is on the brink of destruction. The 23d of last month, Jonker Afrikander fell upon the Kahitjane (Weerligt) who lived on Mr. Kolbe's station, Schuslen's Ewartung. Numbers were killed, and cold-hearted cruelties committed to which you will find scarcely any parallel in the history of the most barbarous nations." By the latest intelligence, we hear that the whole colony is in a state of disturbance, and the British government will probably be compelled to increase the military forces already there, before quiet can be restored. Of course, nothing could be more unpropitious to missionary labors.

In 1834, a mission was established on the island of Borneo, to which, in all, eleven missionaries have been sent. Some have died, and others compelled by the unhealthiness of the climate have withdrawn, leaving only five in the field. They have translated the New Testament, and collected 500 pupils in the mission schools. In 1835–39 ineffectual attempts were made to establish a mission among the Oregon Indians, and on their failure the persons who were sent out settled in this country as pastors, in communities of German emigrants. In 1847 a mission was established in China, to which three missionaries have been sent.

The London *Evangelical Christendom* furnishes this summary of the Society's operations:—It supports twenty-five stations, with several out-stations, in South-eastern Africa, Borneo and China. It has sent out fifty missionaries, mostly married, of whom seven have died. It has a mission-house, where missionary candidates are educated, ten at a time. Annual missionary meetings are held in all the congregations connected with the Society, and missionary prayer-meetings monthly. Periodical reports are published once in two weeks, besides the Annual Report. In Borneo and China, the work of their missionaries is of a preparatory kind, from which no important results, as yet, have been obtained; in Africa there are over 4,000 nominal Christians, and about 1,400 communicants, connected with their churches.*

The income of the Rhenish Missionary Society, for the year 1848–9, was about $25,630.

Missionary Institute and Society of Basle.—The origin of this institution and society possesses unusual historical interest. In the year 1815, after the escape of Bonaparte from Elba, a large army of Russians and Austrians, under the allied powers, having crossed Germany, arrived on the banks of the Rhine near Basle. A powerful, but inferior, French force occupied the strong fortress of Hüningen, on the frontier of France, at the distance of but little more than a mile and a half from that city. The archduke John, who commanded the combined forces, having taken possession of the portion of the city north of the Rhine, prepared to cross the bridge which unites it to the southern and larger part. The French commandant was fully aware of the advantage which the possession of that point would give the in-

* Baptist Missionary Magazine.

vaders, and prepared to prevent it by a heavy cannonade. At that critical and awful moment, when the inhabitants of Basle beheld themselves about to be placed between two fires, and in danger of becoming a prey to both, the magistrates hastened to implore the Austrian general to desist from his undertaking, and represented to him the certain ruin of their city (which was entirely neutral) should the battle proceed. To his everlasting honor, the archduke ordered the incipient firing to cease, marched his forces up the Rhine, crossed that river a few miles above, and came down upon the French from the south. This movement led the French general to change his position also; and so Basle escaped destruction.

The good people of the city, who now flocked to the churches to express their gratitude to Almighty God for their preservation, were naturally led to inquire, in what manner they might testify their gratitude for this signal interposition in their behalf. It was finally resolved to found a school at which missionaries might be trained, who might go into Russia to instruct the poor ignorant Cossacks, of whom many thousands had just passed by their city. In a few months a seminary was opened, and several pious young men were engaged in the prosecution of their studies for the ministry. Contemporaneous with the rise of the Basle Institution was the origin of the Basle Missionary Society, to employ those who had been trained for the enterprise of carrying the Gospel to the destitute.

The first young men who left the Institute finished their studies in the summer of 1818. Since that time, that is to say, within the last thirty-two years, more than two hundred ministers of the Gospel have left its sacred walls to carry the glorious tidings of salvation to the four corners of the globe; of whom about one hundred and sixty are yet alive, and about one hundred and thirty are laboring in foreign lands; the rest are preaching Christ within the pale of Christendom. And whilst many of these heralds of salvation are supported on the field by the Basle Missionary Society, a greater number have been employed by other societies. At our latest accounts, fifty-two were in the employ of the English Church Missionary Society, and twenty-nine under the Basle Society itself.*

The missions of the Basle Society, so far as we are able to indicate them, are located in India, Western Africa, China, and Assam. In India, its stations are fifteen in number, with several out-stations. The principal of these are Mangalore, Calicut, and Dacca. The first was commenced in 1834 ; the other stations are of more recent date. The number of missionaries in this field is thirty-four, with several assistants and native catechists. In nearly all the stations there are flourishing schools, the total number of whose scholars is upwards of seventeen hundred. In China, a mission was begun under the Society in 1847, in the province of Quangtung, by two missionaries, besides several native preachers. They are laboring in connection with the Chinese Missionary Association, under the direction of Mr. Gutzlaff. In Assam, a mission was commenced at Tezpoor, in 1848, by two missionaries. In Western Africa, three stations—at Akropong, Danish Accra, and Abude—are occupied by seven missionaries with assistants. The schools contain 267 pupils.

Two of the missionaries of this Society deserve particular mention. The distinguished Gobat, whom we have named as among the first graduates of the Paris Institute, is a native of the canton of Berne, and studied for some time at the Institute of Basle. The other is Lacroix, who has been laboring more than thirty years in India, in the employ of the London Missionary Society. He is a man of admirable talents and spirit. Few men in India are his equals. We had the pleasure of seeing much of him, in the summer and autumn of 1842, during a visit which he made to his native Switzerland.

The income of the Basle Missionary Society, for the year 1848–9, was about $54,000.

* The Missionary Memorial: in an article by the author of this work

CHAPTER XX.

MISSIONS OF THE UNITED BRETHREN AND THE SMALLER GERMAN SOCIETIES.

THE United Brethren seem early to have been actuated by a desire to spread the knowledge of the Gospel among the heathen. It was in 1732 that it was first resolved in the small colony of Herrnhut, to send missionaries abroad; and three of the brethren, Christian David, Matthew Stach, and Christian Stach, offered themselves for the work. Having obtained the approval of the community, they repaired in 1733 to Copenhagen, and there received permission from the Danish government to undertake a mission in Greenland; where, however, some Danish missionaries had previously been laboring. The expenses of their voyage were generously defrayed by some friends, and they reached the field of their labors after a prosperous trip. The success of the mission, however, during the first few years, did not realize the anticipations they had formed: not only were the laborers exposed to much physical suffering and to many privations, but they encountered more obstinate obstacles in the prejudices and malevolence of the natives, from whom they were sometimes even in danger of assassination. It was five years, therefore, before the missionaries had occasion to rejoice over Kayarnak, the first native convert. The cause of the Gospel began to advance gradually in Greenland, especially through the efforts of the native community of New Herrnhut; and presently a spirit of inquiry was diffused even into distant places. The baptized Greenlanders on their excursions in quest of food, were met by their anxious countrymen, who entreated them to instruct them in the things of God; and constrained them to delay their journey that they might hear the glad tidings more fully announced and explained. In 1747, the first Moravian church was erected at New Herrnhut; and this colony contained about two hundred and thirty Greenlanders, of whom thirty-five had been baptized in the course of that year. In 1752, during an extremely severe winter, beside the miseries of a famine, a dreadful disease cut off thirty-five of the new converts.

Another mission was established in 1758, by Matthew Stach and two new laborers from Europe, in a more southern latitude than New Herrnhut; and received the appellation of Lichtenfels. Here they subsequently erected a mission-house and chapel. From this time the Moravian missions commenced to flourish, and there were annually added to the church about thirty or forty persons by baptism; and in 1768 a revival occurred in which about two hundred persons were added to the church. In 1774, a new and most important station was established at Lichtenau, about four hundred miles south of Lichtenfels, in the midst of a numerous population. About this time, too, additional attention began to be paid to the translation of the Scriptures and other works. The progress of the mission in Greenland was greatly hindered during a number of years following, both from the severity of the seasons and from the embarrassments arising from the war between Great Britain and Denmark.

The missions of the United Brethren in the West Indies were commenced in 1732, by Leonard Dober, at St. Thomas. The first years of the mission were not prosperous, the laborers who had been sent to reinforce the station, being cut off by the unhealthiness of the climate. They were succeeded, however, by others, in 1736, who soon had occasion to rejoice over "the first-fruits of the slaves" in the island. The next year they purchased a small plantation, to which they gave the name of New Herrnhut.

In 1739, Count Zinzendorf visited the island, accompanied by two missionaries. He found the Brethren in prison, upon unfounded charges advanced by the enemies of religion; but he soon succeeded in securing their liberation. The religious interest among the negroes, at this period, greatly increased. Another plantation was purchased in 1753, which was called Niesley, and at this place also the Gospel was preached with great success.

To the island of St. Croix a number of missionaries were sent in 1734; but the climate proved so unfavorable that several died, and the mission was given up. A second attempt, in 1740, likewise failed. But in 1753, George Ohneberg, with two others, resumed the work with great success. Two estates were purchased, and, with the exception of the ill effects of the climate, the subsequent condition of the mission was highly favorable. Missionaries were stationed at the island of St. Jan but a few years after the establishment of the St. Croix mission, having been invited over from St. Thomas by an overseer on one of the plantations, who was solicitous for the welfare of the negroes.

At Jamaica the first missionaries arrived in 1754, in compliance with a request from several of the proprietors, who became responsible for their support, and furnished them with a house and land. The early history was prosperous, but was clouded for a time by differences between some of the missionaries. In 1804, at the end of fifty years, 938 negroes had been baptized. In Antigua, a mission was commenced two years after that at Jamaica, but was, for several years, quite unsuccesssful. In 1769, however, the labors of the missionary, Brown, resulted in a revival of zeal and piety, and in the following years a number of conversions took place. The first efforts made in the island of Barbadoes were also unfavorable, and did not reach any high degree of prosperity until the commencement of this century. In 1777, a mission was undertaken at St. Christopher's.

The labors of the Brethren in North America among the Indian tribes have been less fortunate. They were commenced in 1735, in Georgia. Nearly every station, however, has been disturbed and broken up.

In South America, the missions in Surinam, Dutch Guiana, were undertaken about the year 1738. During the first ten years, but thirty-nine were admitted to the Church. The missionaries prosecuted their work with great diligence, but were compelled at last to abandon their first stations; and, in 1777, founded the stations at Paramaribo and the vicinity. The progress of the work, though not rapid, appears to have been steady, and the converts manifested much sincerity and firmness in their attachment to the truth. This mission, as we shall see, is now one of the most flourishing under the care of the United Brethren.

The first attempts to establish a mission in Labrador were made in 1752, but nothing permanent appears to have been effected until 1770, when the grant of a tract of land was made to the United Brethren for the purpose of establishing a mission among the Esquimaux. Messrs. Haven, Drachart, and Jensen sailed from London in that year, and were soon after followed by fourteen other missionaries. To the station which they formed, these laborers gave the name of Nain, and here they quickly erected a church. Two other settlements were successively undertaken at Okkah and Hopedale. The history of the Labrador Mission abounds in thrilling incidents of perils and deliverances, and in instances of the unaffected piety of the converts. On the 9th of August, 1820, a semi-centennial jubilee was held by the Brethren at the expiration of the fiftieth year, since the foundation of the mission.

In South Africa, a mission was begun, in 1737, by George Schmidt, among the Hottentots, near Serjeant's River, where he labored with much success, and established a school. Having visited Europe a few years subsequent, the jealousy of the Dutch East India Company prohibited his return. The station was broken up, and the few converts dispersed. At length, in 1792, the mission was renewed by permission of the Company, and three laborers were sent out who established themselves at Bavian's Kloof, the very spot where Schmidt had preached forty years before. On the conclusion of peace between Great Britain and Holland, the colony was restored to the latter, and the name of the settlement changed to Gnadenthal. When the colony, in 1806, was transferred to Great Britain, the mission remained undisturbed, and stations were successively planted at Gruenckloof, on the Witte River, at Enon, and on the Klipplaats River.

We will not speak in detail of the Sarepta Mission among the Calmucks, or of others, which, proving unsuccessful, have been abandoned. We proceed to speak of the present condition of the mission under the care of the United Brethren.

The long-established stations in the south of Africa continue to present a most encouraging aspect. Upon the express invitation of the Governor of the Cape Colony, a new station has been founded on the Beka, among a tribe of Caffres recently subjected to the British rule. One hundred Christian colonists from Gnadenthal have removed thither to form this new settlement. The Fingoes and Tambukkies, at the station Shiloh, have made great progress. They are assiduous in their attendance upon religious worship. Gnadenthal, however, continues to be the most prosperous of the stations. It now contains over two thousand five hundred Hottentot converts, who, though doubtless not free from defects, afford great encouragement to their spiritual leaders. An examination entered into by the Government, in consequence of calumnious reports circulated by enemies of the mission, resulted in its complete vindication. The number of stations in the South Africa mission is nine, occupied by twenty-seven missionaries and four assistants.

In Surinam, the total number of negroes who are under the instruction of the Brethren, is seventeen thousand. At each of the stations numerous conversions have taken place, and a general desire is manifested for religious knowledge. The Indians in the neighborhood are also more accessible than they have ever before been. The Government of the colony has shown great favor to the missionaries, and several of the planters have permitted them to establish schools on their lands. It is to be regretted that the number of laborers is inadequate to the extent of the work, and frequently reduced by the unhealthiness of the climate. The stations are nine in number, and the missionaries nineteen, besides seven assistants, and five laborers who are on their way thither.

The missions in the West Indies have suffered considerably from the commercial crisis of the country and the gradual impoverishment of the inhabitants. It had been hoped at one time that the churches of free negroes would soon become able to sustain themselves; but that expectation must, for the present, be given up. Their zeal has even, for a time, appeared to grow languid; but it begins to be reanimated, and to manifest itself in a renewed assiduity of attendance upon Divine worship. The negroes of one station of Jamaica gave, during the last year, a proof of disinterestedness which does honor to their faith. In order to assist in the erection of a new chapel, they of their own accord agreed to furnish among themselves, without any remuneration, a thousand days of labor, and of labor as difficult as it was fatiguing. The number of stations in the Danish islands is eight, and of missionaries twenty-six; in Jamaica, thirteen stations and twenty-nine missionaries; in Antigua, seven stations and twenty-one missionaries; in St. Kitts, seven stations and ten missionaries; in Barbadoes, four stations and nine missionaries; in Tobago, two stations and five missionaries; and on the Mosquito Coast one station with four missionaries.

There is little to be said of the Brethren's missions among the North American Indians. The only stations occupied are those of Fairfield and Westfield among the Delawares; New Springplace and Canaan among the Cherokees; and Woodstock Mills in Florida. Thirteen laborers are engaged at these stations.

In Labrador and Greenland, the work is prosecuted silently but successively. A heathen tribe, formerly residing at Sœglek, has removed to Hebron for the sole purpose of placing itself under Christian influence. Twenty-three missionaries are laboring in Greenland at four stations; in Labrador, thirty at the same number of stations.

At Port Philip, in New Holland, two missionaries have located themselves recently to labor among the natives. This mission, and that on the Mosquito Coast, were founded in the course of 1849.

The total number of missionaries now in the employ of the United Brethren's Missions, is two hundred and eighty-two; the number of district missions is thirteen, and of principal stations sixty-nine. The reports do not give the number of communicants in connection with the various missions. In 1848, the number of persons under the spiritual care of the missionaries amounted to nearly seventy thousand souls. The receipts of the Missions, for the year 1849, amounted to $53,540.

We shall now glance at the smaller Missionary Societies which have been organized in Germany and the neighboring countries.

1. The *Berlin Missionary Institute and Society* were founded in the year 1800 by members of the Lutheran Church. The number of students who, up to 1825, had been educated at the Institute, under the care of its director M. Jaenické, was forty. Many active and excellent missionaries from this institution have

been employed at different times by various associations; as the Rotterdam and London Jews' Societies. The missions of the Berlin Society are: In South Africa, where it has six stations, with nine missionaries; and in India, at Ghazeepoor, where two missionaries are laboring. Receipts, about $17,000.

2. *Gosner's Missionary Society at Berlin*, was established by a pious pastor whose name it bears. It supports missions in Australia, at Moreton Bay, where there are fourteen missionaries; and in New Zealand, at Chatham Island, where there are five missionaries. Its receipts are $3,630.

3. The *Dresden Lutheran Missionary Society*, has two stations in New Holland, with four missionaries. We have no account of its other missions. Receipts, $9,200.

4. The *Leipsic Lutheran Missionary Society*, has missions in India, at Tranquebar, Mayaveram and Poreiar; with six missionaries. There have been baptized 137 Hindoos; and the schools contain one thousand scholars. Receipts, about $8,000.

5. The *Hamburg North-German Missionary Society* supports, in Western Africa, one missionary at Cape Coast; in India, three missionaries, at Rajamundry; and in New Zealand, two missionaries with two assistants, at three stations. Mr. Schmid, at Ootacamuud, in Southern India, was formerly connected with this Society, but is now laboring on his own resources. Receipts of the Hamburg Society, about $5,000.

In *Sweden*, there is a Missionary Society at Stockholm, whose receipts for the year 1848–9 amounted to $4,555; and another at Stavanger, whose receipts were $3,365. We have no details respecting their operations.

In *Norway*, a Missionary Society is mentioned by Hoole, as having sent out, in 1842, two missionaries with the intention of establishing a mission among the Zulus in South Africa. They were however unable to locate themselves there, and were seeking another sphere of labor.

Netherlands Missionary Society.—This association was organized in 1797, having owed its origin to an address from the London Missionary Society, translated and circulated by Dr. Vanderkemp, a zealous laborer under that Society in South Africa. The disturbed condition of the continent at the time repressed the newly-excited missionary spirit; and it was not until 1818 that the Netherlands Society sent forth missionaries. The Indian Archipelago has been the chief and appropriate sphere of its operations; since those islands are under the rule of the Dutch government, which, in its strange course of opposition to Christian missions, has made exception in favor of those under Dutch superintendence. We have no very full accounts of the present condition of these missions; what we have, however, is of no little interest. Mr. Schuh, a graduate of the Paris Institute, has recently gone out to Java, under this Society, and is now actively engaged in missionary labor. He states that at Samarang, in that island, there are several missionaries, besides Mr. Bruckner, of the Baptist Society, who came thither in 1811, when the English invaded Java, and is living privately; and in the island of Timor, there are two more. To the latter station, Mr. Schuh with his companions, making three missionaries, were appointed. Mr. Schuh states, that at the time of Mr. Bruckner's arrival, with his fellow-laborers, they translated the New Testament and several tracts into the Javanese; but were not allowed to circulate them after the island became again subject to the Dutch. A pious old German watchmaker, however, concealed some of the books among the sacred trees of the people, where they were found and read. Many of the natives became converted; and there is now, at Soudakari, a Christian village containing 130 communicants, with a large number in the vicinity; who are under the instruction of four native evangelists. At the time Mr. Schuh wrote, there were as many as one hundred applicants for baptism.

The receipts of the Netherlands Missionary Society, for 1848–9, amounted to about $27,000.

CHAPTER XXI.

AMERICAN BOARD OF COMMISSIONERS FOR FOREIGN MISSIONS.

The origin and history of the American Board are so well known, as to preclude the necessity of our devoting much space to their narration. With the exception of the missions of the United Brethren, the American Board is the oldest society for foreign missions in the United States. It was in the year 1809 that several of the students at the Theological Seminary at Andover agreed to unite their efforts in establishing a mission among the heathen in some foreign land. In this resolution they were encouraged by the Faculty of the Seminary, and they determined to lay the matter before the General Association of Massachusetts. Messrs. Mills, Judson, Newell, and Nott, accordingly presented to that body, at its meeting in June, 1810, a paper in which they made a statement of their desire to preach the Gospel to the heathen, and proposed some inquiries respecting the proper method of putting their plans into execution. This gave rise to the appointment by the Association of a board of commissioners for foreign missions, who at their first meeting in September of the same year adopted the name of the American Board of Commissioners for Foreign Missions; thus recognizing their high calling to act for all in every part of the nation who might choose to employ their agency in the work of missions among the heathen. The transaction of ordinary business, however, was delegated to an executive committee called the Prudential Committee, the members of which reside at or near Boston, which is the centre of the Society's operations.

It is among the remarkable facts in the history of this institution, and in the ecclesiastical history of the country, that, at the outset, neither the Board, nor its Prudential Committee, nor, indeed, any of the leading minds in the American Churches at that time, conceived the possibility of raising sufficient funds to support the four young men who were then waiting to be sent forth to the heathen world. One of them was accordingly sent to England, mainly to see whether an arrangement might not be made with the London Missionary Society, by which a part of their support might be received from that Society, and they yet remain under the direction of the Board. The London Society wisely declined such an arrangement, and encouraged their American brethren to hope for ample contributions from their own churches so soon as the facts should be generally known. From this time no further thought was entertained of help from abroad. On the 6th of February, 1812, the Rev. Messrs. Samuel Newell, Adoniram Judson, Gordon Hall, Samuel Nott, and Luther Rice, the first American missionaries, were ordained at Salem, Mass., and they forthwith proceeded to Calcutta, in the East Indies, but without being designated to any specific field. The Prudential Committee appear to have been unable to decide upon any particular country as preferable to any others; so little knowledge was there in Europe and America of the precise condition of heathendom.

Messrs. Judson and Rice had not been long with the Baptist missionaries at Serampore, near Calcutta, before they embraced the peculiar views of those brethren in relation to baptism; and having consequently dissolved their connection with the Society which sent them forth, a new institution was formed for their support—the Baptist Board for Foreign Missions. The remaining missionaries, after many vexations and much painful travelling from place to place, arising from the intolerance of the East

India Company towards missionaries of any nation, and especially from their jealousy of Americans, at length commenced in 1813 a mission at Bombay among the Mahrattas of Western India. In this field of labor as yet untouched by missionary agency, they encountered all the obstacles incident to the commencement of so important an enterprise. The manifest superiority of the Mahrattas over many, if not most, of the remaining races of India, however, induced the missionaries not to despair of success.

Some preparatory work had been performed among the Tamul people, of the northern district of Ceylon and Southern India, when a mission was commenced among them in 1816: in Ceylon through the Portuguese and Dutch; and on the continent by means of the celebrated missionary Swartz and his associates. Here the systematic measures which the mission speedily adopted for the training of a native agency, and the success attending them, did much to give an early maturity to the plans of the Board for raising up a native ministry in connection with all its other missions. The most efficient seminary of such a nature is believed to be the one connected with the mission in Ceylon. In 1834, a branch of this mission was formed at Madura, on the continent; and in 1836, another at Madras, with the special object of printing books in the Tamul language on a large scale.

The first mission sent by the Board to Eastern Asia was to China in 1830. A pious merchant of New York city furnished many of the facts and arguments which justified its commencement, and gave two missionaries their passage to China and their support for one year. One of these missionaries subsequently visited Siam and opened the way for a mission there; as he did also in Borneo. The missions in Siam and Borneo, however, have not been successful, and are for the present discontinued.

Of the missions in Western Asia and on the Mediterranean,

that at Athens was commenced in 1829 by Dr. King. It had its origin in the deep interest which America, in common with the most of civilized Europe, entertained for the cause of Greek emancipation and renovation. Dr. King, who commenced it, had previously been connected with the Palestine Mission. It was to the Holy Land, in fact, that the first American mission in this quarter of the globe was sent, in the year 1821. Messrs. Fisher and Parsons were pioneers in the enterprise. In 1828, after their decease, war and the hostility of the Maronites towards the mission, compelled the surviving laborers to retire for a time from Syria. To this circumstance, in the developments of Providence, we trace the establishment of the mission among the Armenians of Constantinople and Asia Minor, which has since been so signally blessed to that people. In 1830, Messrs. Dwight and Smith were sent on an exploring tour into Armenia, and were instructed to visit the Nestorians in the province of Aderbaijan, in Persia. This visit brought to light that remnant of the most noted missionary Church of ancient times, and induced the Board to send a mission to restore the blessings of the Gospel to that people. The mission was commenced at Oroomiah, and has been extended to the independent Nestorian tribes in the Kurdish Mountains. The leading object of the mission has been to educate the clergy, and by reviving, through the blessing of God, the spirit of the Gospel, to induce them to resume its faithful preaching. The Nestorian Mission has during the last few years assumed a new importance and interest. The Syrian Mission of the Board is located among the Druzes of Mt. Lebanon, where a seminary has been undertaken. The Armenian mission is an equally interesting field of labor with the Nestorian, and proposes to itself the same end of renovating the spirit of that nominal Christian Church. But the attempt to do this under connection with the old ecclesiastical body has failed, and the formation of a separate evangelical Protestant community is now the object of missionary labor among the Armenians. Since the late outpourings of the Holy Spirit at this mission, and the violent persecution (now happily ceased,) which it has undergone, it has become one of the most interesting and promising under the care of the Board.

The mission of the American Board in South Africa was commenced in 1836; and is located among the Zulus. The cause has here been gradually advancing, notwithstanding the obstacles from the wars of the natives and their prejudice against the pure morality of the Gospel. The mission to Western Africa was commenced in 1834, and is situated along the coast near the Gaboon River.

The results of the mission of the Board to the Sandwich Islands in the North Pacific Ocean, the most important group of Polynesia, constitute one of the great moral wonders of the age. The first missionaries landed on these islands in the year 1820. At that time the natives were savage and pagan, without letters, without a ray of Gospel light, though they had just before strangely burned their idols—a fact unknown in the United States when the missionaries embarked on their errand of mercy. For a number of years this same people has properly claimed the title of a Christian people. Though destitute, in some measure, by reason of their poverty, of the more imposing insignia of civilization, they have the elements and basis of it in Christian institutions, schools, a written language, the press, books, newspapers, and commerce, and in the extensive prevalence of pious dispositions and habits. Their language has been reduced to writing, and about one hundred and eighty millions of pages have been printed by the mission in the native language. As the alphabet contains but twelve letters, and each letter has but a single sound, it is easy to learn to read it. A large proportion of the population can read. The common schools, supported now by the Hawaiian Government, contain about eleven thousand pupils, who are instructed in the elementary branches of education. The higher schools contain upwards of two hundred more scholars. The number of church members, at the last accounts, was 23,102. The Hawaiian churches are not inactive. Gradually they are becoming able to do more and more in support of the preaching of the Gospel among themselves, and are contributing not only to the spread of true religion among the surrounding heathen, but even to the assistance of Christian missionaries from France,—the land from which they have received so many insults and injuries.

The Board has spent a portion of its funds in missions among the Cherokees and Choctaws, and other influential Indian tribes. Their missions to the former commenced in 1816 and 1818, and were prosecuted with great success, until the time of the removal of those tribes beyond the Mississippi River, whither the missionaries followed them. There were also founded missions among the Creeks and Chickasaws (now abandoned); among the Ojibways, Sioux, and Pawnees; and among the tribes in the Oregon territory, and in the State of New York.

Of the missionaries in the employ of the American Board, twelve are located among the Zulus in South Africa, five are attached to the Gaboon mission in West Africa, one to the Greek mission, three to the mission to the Jews at Salonica and Constantinople, eighteen to the Armenian mission, ten to the Syrian mission. Among the Nestorians there are six missionaries, at the Bombay mission four, at the Ahmednuggur mission seven, at the Madras mission four, at the Madura mission eleven, at the Ceylon mission eleven, at the Canton mission three, at the Amoy mission two, at the Fuh-Chau mission six. At the Sandwich Islands are stationed twenty-five missionaries, among the Oregon tribes three, among the Choctaws five, among the Cherokees five, at the Dakota mission six, among the Ojibways two, and among the New York Indians five.

The following summary of the operations of this Society is given in the last annual report. The Board has twenty-four missions under its care, embracing one hundred and six stations, and twenty-eight out-stations. In these missions are one hundred and fifty-seven ordained missionaries, and two licensed preachers. Of teachers, printers, etc., there are twenty-five, and of female assistant missionaries two hundred and four. The whole number of laborers, male and female, sent from this country and now living, is three hundred and ninety-five. The number sent out from the beginning is nine hundred and sixty. Six native pastors, and twenty-two other native preachers, and ninety-four native helpers, make the whole number of native assistants, not including schoolmasters, and comparatively uneducated helpers, one hundred and twenty-two. The whole number of laborers, foreign and native, now connected with the mission, who depend for the means of living and usefulness on the treasury of the Board, is five hundred and seventeen.

The number of churches formed in the missions is eighty-five. These contain twenty-five thousand eight hundred and seventy-five members in regular standing. The admissions to the churches by a profession of faith, during the year, were one thousand nine hundred and sixty-seven. The contributions received by the Board from foreign lands, the amount of which is steadily increasing from year to year, were $8,249 04, and a considerable portion of this came from these native mission churches.

The seminaries for training native preachers and teachers are seven in number, and contain three hundred and thirty-nine pupils; and there are seven hundred and fifty-five pupils, male and female, in other boarding-schools. The number of children in free schools is twenty-one thousand seven hundred and thirty, about half of whom are at the Sandwich Islands, and supported by the Hawaiian Government. Altogether, therefore, there are in the schools under the care of this Society, twenty-two thousand eight hundred and twenty-four scholars.

Twelve printing establishments are in operation, in as many of the missions, with seven type and stereotype foundries, and type for printing in nearly thirty languages. During the past year 37,644,828 pages are reported to have been printed. This swells the amount of printing from the beginning, in all the missions, to 819,706,481 pages.

The receipts of the American Board of Commissioners for Foreign Missions, for the year ending 31st July, 1850, were $251,862 28. The expenditures for the same period were $254,329 35. The debt of the Society was $34,071 05.

CHAPTER XXII.

AMERICAN BAPTIST MISSIONARY UNION.

THE first movements among the Baptist churches of America, in behalf of evangelical missions, were made like those of other denominations, in favor of the new settlements on our own frontiers. For this object the Massachusetts Baptist Missionary Society was organized, in 1802. The labors of the men employed by this Society, together with the intelligence arriving from time to time from the English Baptist missionaries at Serampore, excited and fostered the interest of the churches in the work; and in 1811, the Boston Association of Baptist ministers recommended a general collection in behalf of the East India mission.

The immediate occasion, however, of the formation of an independent missionary organization by the Baptists in America, was the conversion of two American missionaries, Messrs. Judson and Rice, to the views entertained by that denomination on the subject of baptism. These missionaries, who had been sent out originally by the American Board of Commissioners, proceeded to Rangoon, and undertook the acquisition of the Burman language. Meanwhile, the change in their denominational connection becoming known at home, it was determined to proceed immediately to the formation of a society for their support; and accordingly, a meeting of twenty-six clergymen and seven laymen, from various parts of the Union, assembled at Philadelphia, and was organized, on the 18th of May, 1814, as the General Missionary Convention of the Baptist denomination in the

United States. This body continued to exist until 1846, when it was merged in the American Baptist Missionary Union.

The Burman Mission founded at Rangoon by Dr. Judson, was recruited in 1816 by the arrival of Mr. and Mrs. Hough. The necessity of preparing and printing religious books, and especially of translating the Scriptures, immediately presented itself to the missionaries; and their first efforts were directed to these objects. Two years after, Messrs. Wheelock and Coleman arrived; and in 1819, the first place of worship was opened, and the first convert baptized. The number of inquirers and converts soon increased rapidly, until the war between Great Britain and the Burmese, when the mission was broken up and removed, after many vicissitudes and afflictions, to Maulmain, which had become the chief city of the English provinces. The next year, Mr. and Mrs. Boardman, who had recently arrived at Burmah, were stationed at the city of Tavoy, 150 miles south of Maulmain. Here was commenced an important department of labor in the Burmese missions, among the race of Karens—a people scattered over the forests and mountains of Burmah, and Siam, but living entirely distinct from the Burmans, by whom they are despised as inferiors or slaves. At the death of Mr. Boardman, in 1830, thirty-five of these interesting people had been baptized as hopeful converts under his labors; and in a few months after, thirty-nine more were received into the church. "Beyond all precedent," says the last report of the Union, "the Karens are a people for whom the Lord has prepared his way. Were the instrumentality adequate, the millions of Karens of even the present generation would receive the Gospel of the Son of God; a nation would be born in a day."

The present operations of the Missionary Union in Burmah, comprehend five missions; none of which, however, are in Burmah Proper, but in the provinces ceded by the Burmese to the British East India Company. Attempts are now making which, it is to be hoped, will prove successful, to resume the occupation of Rangoon and Ava. Of the five missions alluded to, three are among the Karens—at Maulmain, Tavoy and Sandoway: the others are the Arracan and Maulmain Burman missions.

The Burman mission at Maulmain consists of two stations, at which are laboring seven* missionaries, and eight female assistants. The recent removal of Dr. Judson is, of course severely felt by this mission. Two of the laborers, Mr. and Mrs. Howard, have temporarily withdrawn, and are now in this country in quest of health. The Burmese church at Maulmain consists of 141 members; the average attendance on public worship is about 350. The sabbath-schools at the two stations (Amherst being the other) number 130 pupils; the other schools, about 300 pupils. Of publications, the whole number of pages printed from the beginning, is 92,590,237.

The Maulmain Karen mission, with one station and seven out-stations, has four missionaries, six female assistants, five ordained native preachers, three teachers, and twenty-six other native assistants. The number of churches organized among the Karens is nine; the number of members 1,708. The Theological Seminary contains twenty-seven native students preparing for the ministry; the other schools have 174 scholars.

The Tavoy Karen mission, consisting of two stations and fourteen out-stations, with five missionaries, five female assistants, and nineteen native assistants, contains thirteen churches, with 933 members; and has in its schools 377 pupils. The whole amount of printing executed has been 2,096,960 pages. This mission has been reinforced by the appointment of Mr. and Mrs. Thomas, recently embarked.

The Arracan mission comprises two stations and an out-station, at which four missionaries, two female assistants, and six native assistants are laboring. Its schools have under instruction 59 children.

* Dr. Judson having died since the publication of the Annual Report.

The Sandoway Karen mission has 36 out-stations, with three missionaries, two female assistants, and 44 native preachers and assistants. The estimated number of church-members in connection with the churches, of which there are thirty-six, is 4,500; the whole number of baptized persons, since the beginning, has been over 5,500; there are also 5,124 unbaptized persons, whose life is not less exemplary in all respects than that of the baptized members. The schools contain 495 pupils.

The mission in Siam, is designed in part for the Chinese, who are very numerous in that country. It was commenced in March, in 1833, at Bangkok, the capital of the kingdom. The Siamese department consists at present of three missionaries and three female assistants. There are two out-stations. Fifty-six persons in all have been baptized, "There never was a time, perhaps," says the last Report, "when the people of Siam were so accessible to missionary efforts as now. Missionaries are free to travel throughout the country, and books are taken and read, it is believed, by all classes." The total number of pages printed at this station is 2,214,167.

The China mission has two stations,—at Hong Kong and at Ningpo,—with four out-stations; it is occupied by five missionaries, three female assistants, and seven native assistants. There are 27 church members in connection with it, and 60 children under instruction at the schools.

The mission to Assam, undertaken in 1836, comprehends three stations; five missionaries are employed with six female assistants, and four native assistants. The number of church-members is 57; of scholars in the various schools, 700.

The mission to the Teloogoos is prosecuted by two missionaries, with their wives; it has 250 pupils under instruction.

The mission to the Bassas in West Africa, consists of one station and two out-stations; it has 5 native laborers. The schools number 39 scholars.

On the continent of Europe, besides a mission in France, and one in Germany, the Missionary Union sustains a third in Greece; its stations are at Corfu and Piræus; it has two missionaries and three native assistants.

The labors of this Society, in behalf of the Indians in our own country, comprise missions among the Ojibways, Ottawas, Tuscaroras, Shawanees, and Cherokees. These missions are conducted by nine missionaries, with ten female assistants, and ten native assistants. They contain twelve churches, numbering 1,382 members; the schools contain 195 pupils.

We close with a brief summary of the operations of the American Baptist Missionary Union. Its receipts for the past year were $87,537 20: its expenditures, $84,147 23. The number of its missions is 17; the stations and out-stations are 155, besides more than 150 places of stated preaching. Its missionaries are 56; female assistants, 55; native assistants, 195; whole number of laborers, 306. The number of churches is 141, with more than 12,500 members; of schools, 106, with 2,772 pupils. The number of pages printed during the past year, is 17,814,411.

CHAPTER XXIII.

BOARD OF FOREIGN MISSIONS OF THE PRESBYTERIAN CHURCH.

PRIOR to the formation of this Society, some efforts had been made by the Presbyterian Church for the propagation of the Gospel among Indians and settlers on our frontiers; and for this purpose the Western Missionary Society had been formed in 1802 by the Synod of Pittsburg. The missions of this Society were however transferred in 1825 to the United Foreign Missionary Society; and again with it to the American Board of Commissioners soon after. A new organization, under the name of the Western Foreign Missionary Society, was attempted in 1831, with some success, and several missions were undertaken. But until the formation of the Board of Foreign Missions, in 1837, many of the churches continued to co-operate with the American Board; and this, indeed, is done to some extent even now. The present institution, however, arose out of the prevalent conviction among the Presbyterian churches of the "Old School" connection, that it is the duty of the Church, as a separate body, to labor for the promotion of Christ's kingdom, under the direction of its own supreme ecclesiastical court. In this opinion and its consequent course of action, it harmonizes with the Church of Scotland; whose benevolent operations are conducted entirely under the superintendence and control of the officers of the General Assembly.

The number and wealth of the churches under whose patronage the Presbyterian Board is laboring, has naturally secured for it an efficient and increasing support. The receipts of the Western Society transferred to it upon its formation, already amounted (for the year 1836–37)—to more than $40,000. In 1839, the income of the Board was nearly $63,000; and at the last annual meeting, May, 1850, it had risen to $126,075. So rapid a growth indicates of course a corresponding extension of missionary spirit in the church, and promises a still more active efficiency for the future.

The Missions of the Board are chiefly located in Northern India, China, West Africa, and among the Indian tribes of our Western territories. The Northern India mission was commenced in 1833, by Rev. Mr. Lowrie, at present one of the Secretaries of the Board. The north-western provinces of India were then, and continue, in a great measure, to be unoccupied by another missionary body, as a field of labor. Besides this advantage, the vicinity of other countries where no effort had been made to extend the knowledge of the Gospel, was a feature which strongly recommended this region to the Board. Lodiana, Furrukhabad and Allahabad, are the localities in which its missions are now centred. The Lodiana mission includes six stations, at five of which, Lodiana, Saharunpur, Sabathu, Jalandar, and Ambala, churches have been organized, numbering at present fifty-three members in all. Eleven ordained missionaries, most of whom are married, are laboring at these stations; with ten assistants, catechists, readers, &c. The religious services at the stations are well attended; frequent tours are also made through the towns and villages of the country. The whole number of children under education is 433. The whole number of pages of religious publications printed since the beginning has been 4,014,186. The important city of Lahore, capital of the Punjaub, has within the past year been occupied for the first time as a missionary station.

The Furrukhabad mission, including the stations of Futtehgurh, Mynpurie and Agra, has seven ordained missionaries, with their wives, three catechists and a teacher. At the first of these churches, there is a flourishing church of seventy-two members; at Agra, the church contains thirty-five members. The schools connected with this mission have 398 pupils. The Allahabad mission, with five ordained missionaries, and a native preacher, and five assistants, has a native church of thirty-four communicants; its schools contain 399 children; the whole number of pages of religious publications issued from its presses has been 2,310,319.

The whole number of missionaries, male and female, sent out by the Board to labor in Northern India, has been *seventy;* including nine who have gone forth within the present year.

In SIAM, the Presbyterian Board sustains a mission, consisting of two ordained laborers with their wives, a physician, and a Chinese native assistant. The only station is at Bangkok where some converts have been made. The principal agency of the mission is in the distribution of religious books: a work of the highest importance in a country where a majority of the male adults are able to read.

In CHINA, the missions at Canton and Ningpo have been for some time in existence; a new mission is to be established also at Shanghai. Three missionaries are laboring at Canton; a chapel has, after some opposition, been opened, and a school of eighteen boys is in operation. At Ningpo, eight ordained and two lay laborers are stationed; of whom eight are married. The mission church has eight native members; public services are generally well attended; the schools contain 70 pupils, and the press has issued 2,123,258 pages of religious publications.

In WEST AFRICA, the Liberia mission is in a prosperous condition. It occupies three stations, in each of which there is a church. The day school at Monrovia numbers fifty-two scholars. The mission at Settra Kroo is occupied at present by one missionary only. About two hundred boys and a few girls have been taught to read the Bible; a school of fifteen scholars is now sustained. The mission near the Equator is a new one, but already holds out strong encouragements.

The missions of the Board among the INDIAN TRIBES, in and upon our own borders, constitute an important part of its operations. They are seven in number, embracing the Choctaw, Chickasaw, Creek, Seminole, Iowa, Sac, Otoe, Omaha, Chippewa, and Ottawa tribes. Ten ordained missionaries, with their wives, and sixteen assistants, are now laboring among these tribes in connection with this Society. In the Choctaw mission, they have under instruction more than one hundred youth. Among the Chickasaws, a female boarding-school, designed to educate at least 80 girls, has recently been founded. Among the Creeks, a day-school of 30 scholars, and a boarding-school of as many more, is sustained, at Tallahassee; and at Kowetah, with a church of 17 native members, there is a boarding-school of 33 pupils. The Seminole mission has a school of 11; the Iowa and Sac mission, of 35; the Otoe and Omaha, the same number. In the Chippewa and Ottawa mission, there is a boys' school of 47, and a girls' school of 28; the church numbers 29 native members, and the services on the Sabbath are well attended.

In addition to these labors among heathen nations, the Board has of late years undertaken to aid in the great enterprise of evangelizing the Papal population of Europe. It is to be hoped that in future it will occupy a larger portion of this important field. Hitherto the appropriations of the Board for this object have been comparatively small; amounting for the year ending in May last, to $3,658 only.

Finally, the Presbyterian Board supports in New York and Philadelphia, three ordained missionaries among the Jewish population. We do not learn that these missionaries have met with much success in this difficult field of labor, which requires the most persevering and untiring exertion.

The missions of the Presbyterian Board, therefore, exclusive of its operations in Papal Europe, are eighteen in number. Its ordained missionaries are fifty-five—many of them married men; assistant laborers, forty-three.

CHAPTER XXIV.

BOARD OF FOREIGN MISSIONS OF THE PROTESTANT EPISCOPAL CHURCH.

A FOREIGN and Domestic Missionary Society was organized by the General Convention of the Protestant Episcopal Church, in the year 1820. Its constitution was amended in 1829; it prescribed that the meetings of the Society should be held triennially, at the time and place appointed for the meeting of the Convention. It also provided that the Society should be composed of the bishops, and of all annual subscribers to the amount of $3. It was, therefore, from the outset, an ecclesiastical enterprise; but without that official character which it assumed, when merged into the "Board of Missions of the Protestant Episcopal Church;" a change which took place in 1835. At that period, "the organization was entirely altered, and the Church undertook and agreed, in her character as a Church, to carry on the work of Christian missions." "The General Convention, as the constituted representative body of the whole Protestant Episcopal Church in the United States," now became the agent for prosecuting this work; entrusting its superintendence to a Board of Missions, in the recess of its triennial sessions; and to two separate committees appointed by that Board.

Attempts were made, at an early period in the history of the Society, to found missions on the western coast of AFRICA; but it was not until 1836, that a missionary teacher was appointed, and a small school begun, at the town of Harper, in Liberia.

The next year, three missionaries were sent out, and in 1839, a fourth. Their success in forming schools and in preaching to the natives, was very encouraging. At present, the African mission includes five stations: at Cavalla, River Cavalla, Fishtown, (or Fair Haven,) Rocktown, and Cape Palmas. Besides these stations, there are towns and villages, with an aggregate population of twelve thousand souls, which are visited weekly by the missionaries.

The station of Cavalla is in a highly flourishing condition. The number of communicants is forty; of whom eleven were added within the year 1849. The boarding-schools number 63 pupils; the congregations on the Lord's-day average 200; and a Christian village, consisting of persons who have been trained up at the schools, has been recently formed; it now contains ten families. The Sunday-school is attended by 80 to 100 children. Seven villages are regularly visited by the missionaries connected with this station.

At the River Cavalla station, a small school is kept up, containing eight pupils. This post is a sort of appendage to the station previously spoken of.

The station of Fishtown, or Fair Haven, has a school of 29 pupils; there are fourteen native and five colonist communicants in connection with it. Seven villages are visited by the missionaries here. The station of Rocktown is to be occupied on the arrival of Mr. and Mrs. Herring.

The central station at Cape Palmas, is called the "Church in the Colony." Its prospects are most encouraging. The school has in the male department fifteen, and in the female forty-five pupils. The congregations are large; the present number of communicants in good standing is twenty-seven.

There are now laboring at these several stations of the West Africa mission, five ordained missionaries, one teacher, five female assistants employed in the mission-schools, and several native teachers. The boarding and day-schools contain 160 scholars; besides those receiving instruction in the evening-schools. The whole number of communicants connected with the mission, is eighty. The Rev. John Payne, one of the missionaries, has been elected by the General Convention as Missionary Bishop in Africa; and has been recalled for the purpose of consecration.

CHINA, as a field of labor, engaged the attention of the Episcopal Missionary Society, as early as the year 1834; when the Rev. Mr. Lockwood was appointed missionary to that country. The early history of this mission was not fortunate; several of the laborers were compelled from ill-health to return; and finally, in 1840, the difficulties between Great Britain and China occasioned its abandonment for a time. Dr. Boone, one of the first missionaries sent forth, came home and spent some time in laboring to interest the churches in the work to which he had devoted himself; and in 1844, having been consecrated bishop, he went out again, accompanied by two missionaries and five female assistants. Mr. Syle embarked for the same field a few months afterwards. The station fixed upon for this mission, was the port of Shanghai, where it continues at present. It is to be regretted, however, that notwithstanding the great encouragements met with in this mission, and the readiness of the Church at home to sustain it, it is languishing for the want of laborers. Bishop Boone and Mr. Syle, with two female assistants, are the only persons now occupying the field. The chapel of the mission, within the walls of the city, built at the expense of an American layman, has been completed, and is now used for public worship in the Chinese language. The earliest convert under the labors of the missionaries, has been recently ordained to the ministry; his name is Chai. The mission-school continues in successful operation, with forty-six pupils. The whole number of natives baptized is sixteen; of communicants ten; and of catechumens under religious instruction, ten.

The mission at Athens is the oldest of the foreign enterprises of the Board. Upon the inquiries and observations of the Rev. Mr. Robertson, in 1830, it was concluded to commission that gentleman, with the Rev. Mr. Hill, and their wives, as missionaries to Greece. Schools were established at Athens and Syra; and a mission press at Syra issued up to the year 1841, 8,826,900 pages of religious publications. The latter station was, however, abandoned, in the retrenchments which became necessary. The schools at Athens continue, under the care of Mr. Hill, in a prosperous state; and contain at present between four and five hundred children, who are receiving not only the ordinary branches of education, but also a thorough training in the principles of religion, and especially in the study of the word of God. "A large class of Bible Christians," says Mr. Hill, "has been formed in these schools, consisting of some thousands; who are now dispersed over every part of Greece."

A mission was commenced in 1837, at Canea in the island of Crete. In seven months, the schools numbered 239 pupils, and in 1840 had reached 460. But in 1843, this mission was discontinued.

The mission at Constantinople was projected in 1838. Previous missions had been attempted, but without success, in Persia. In 1840, Mr. Southgate, afterwards elected bishop, was sent to Constantinople, where he spent some time. But the experience of this mission, in its relation with the Syriac and Armenian churches, goes only to corroborate that of the Church of England Missionary Society, given in the words of its secretary: "Its attempts to establish missions among the ancient but lapsed Christian churches of the East have been failures." The mission in Turkey has been finally closed, by the return of Bishop Southgate to this country.

Missions to the Indians have been at various times undertaken by the Missionary Society, and the Board of Missions of the Protestant Episcopal Church. As early as 1825, a station was formed among the Indians at Green Bay, in the north-eastern part of Wisconsin. Extensive buildings were erected, and a large school founded, which in 1836 contained seventy Indian children. But the rapid diminution of the tribes, and their removal to their new locations west of the Mississippi, compelled the abandonment of this promising station. The Board of Domestic Missions has now in charge a mission among the Oneidas at Duck Creek, Wisconsin, where are stationed a missionary, an interpreter, and a teacher.

The Board of Domestic Missions also support a missionary in New York, who is laboring among the Jewish population of that city. He reports a few converts.

In conclusion, the present operations of the Board of Foreign Missions of the Protestant Episcopal Church, comprehend five missions.* It sustains ten missionaries, nine female missionaries, and a number of native assistants. Its mission schools contain 656 scholars, and its mission churches number ninety-six communicants. The receipts of the Board for the year ending in June last, were $36,114. Its expenditures, $32,404.

* That of Constantinople is nominally sustained for the time being, Bishop Southgate being still in connection with the Board.

CHAPTER XXV.

METHODIST EPISCOPAL MISSIONARY SOCIETY.

THE energy with which the Methodist Episcopal Church, from its earliest planting in this country, has undertaken and prosecuted the work of Domestic Missions, will in some measure account for the lateness of its efforts toward the propagation of the Gospel in heathen countries. Emphatically may that church be called a missionary church, in its character and its operations. But the necessity of a separate organization, to carry out and develop the missionary spirit, became apparent. At a meeting of the preachers stationed in the city of New York, in 1819, the subject of forming a missionary society was agitated: and a meeting of the friends and members of the Methodist Episcopal Church was called for this purpose. The first organization was under the title of "Missionary and Bible Society;" and, in fact, it continued its operations in this two-fold capacity—establishing and supporting missions, and printing, publishing, and circulating Bibles—until the year 1828; when the latter department was separated from it, and a Bible Society organized, which was finally merged into the American Bible Society, in 1836.

The first mission undertaken by the Methodist Missionary Society, was among the Indian tribes of our own territories, and of Canada. Five years prior to its formation, a colored preacher of the church went forth of his own accord, and commenced to labor among the Wyandott Indians. In 1817, an interesting revival took place through his labors, and many of the tribe were converted. This mission was maintained with great success by the Society, until the division of the church in 1844, when it fell within the jurisdiction, and is now under the management of the Methodist Church South. The membership of this mission consists of 189 persons, of whom three are local preachers. A mission among the Creek Indians, established in 1822, prospered greatly for several years, during which many were added to the church; but in 1830, the evil influence of dissipated white men, and other influences, compelled its abandonment. Missions were successively undertaken among the Mohawks, Mississangas, Cherokees, Choctaws, and Potowatamies. Some of these are still flourishing under the auspices of the Church South.

The Indian Missions at present sustained by the Methodist Missionary Society, are twelve in number: the Brothertown, Oneida, Sault St. Marie, Kewawenon, Fond du Lac, Sandy Lake, Flint (two), Nottaway, Oneida and Onondaga, St. Regis, and Wyandott Missions. They are carried on by seventeen missionaries, and the total number of church members in connection with them is 1,079.

The Liberia Mission was undertaken in 1832, by the excellent Melville Cox, who soon fell a victim to the climate, exclaiming with his dying breath, "Africa must not be given up." It consists at present of fifteen missionaries, besides a number of local preachers, who occupy eighteen stations, and visit the native towns in the vicinity, which are accessible. The churches connected with the mission number 1,117 members; the schools, of which there are twenty, contain 810 scholars, among whom within the first year there have been seventy-five conversions.

The Oregon Mission, begun in 1833, resulted in the formation of the "Oregon and California Mission Conference," in September, 1849. This Conference is now composed of seven missionaries, and there are fourteen local preachers in the Mission, which consists of eight stations in Oregon, and six in California. The three mission churches in Oregon contain 404 members; the schools number 261 scholars.

The Mission to South America is chiefly designed for the benefit of British and American residents. In 1836, a missionary was sent to Buenos Ayres, and another to Rio de Janeiro. The latter, Rev. D. P. Kidder, has published, in an interesting work, the results of his experience and investigations in Brazil. A third mission to Montevideo was begun in 1838. Two of these efforts have proved unsuccessful; the mission to Buenos Ayres is alone continued at present. The church connected with it contains fifty-one members, and the Sunday-school has an average attendance of one hundred.

The Mission to China is the most recent of the enterprises of this Society. It was commenced in 1847, by sending forth two young ministers; and in the course of a few months, two more were commissioned. One of the latter number, Mr. Hickok, has since been compelled, by reason of ill-health, to return. The missionaries are engaged in daily preaching in the streets, in the distribution of tracts, and in the care of the sick. Each of them has under his supervision a day-school taught by a Chinese master. The three schools contain sixty-four scholars, with an average attendance of fifty a day. This mission is strictly in its infancy, but its laborers are not without encouragement already, in the yielding of prejudices, and the willingness to listen to the preaching of the Gospel.

The Society has recently sent one missionary, and has since appointed another, to labor in Germany. They have been quite successful in this enterprise, of which, however, it does not enter into our design to treat more fully here.

The Methodist Episcopal Missionary Society, during the year ending in May last, expended for its various missions the sum of $100,989 63; its receipts having amounted to $107,835 73. At the meeting of the General Missionary Committee and Board of Managers, it was decided, in view of the wants of the missionary world, to increase this sum, by a special effort for the succeeding year, to $150,000. It is to be hoped that a hearty response will be given to this call for renewed exertion and sacrifice.

The present operations of this Society may be briefly summed up as follows. The number of its missionaries in the foreign department, exclusive of printers, teachers, mechanics, &c., is thirty-four; in the home department, including the Indian, German, and Swedish missions, 464. The number of church members connected with the foreign missions is 1,611; connected with the home missions, 38,882; total, 40,493.

CHAPTER XXVI.

SMALLER AMERICAN MISSIONARY SOCIETIES.

WE proceed to mention briefly some of the missionary organizations in this country, which have not yet attained equal size with those we have already noticed.

The *American Missionary Association* was constituted in 1846, at a convention held at Albany. It was formed by the union of three similar associations which had existed for a few years. It is well known that this Society is supported mainly by individuals of the abolitionist party, who are unwilling to unite with the American Board, from the alleged countenance it has given to slavery in some of its missions among the Indians. The first mission undertaken by the association, was that to the Mendi country, in West Africa. The liberation of the captives of the Amistad, and their return to Africa, were the occasion of this enterprise. It was planted at Kaw-Mendi, where there are now laboring three missionaries, six assistants and three native assistants. The mission school is in a prosperous state, and numbers eighty scholars. Since the arrival of Mr. Thompson, thirty individuals have been hopefully converted. The Siam Mission, for some time interrupted by the removal of its laborers, has been re-occupied by three missionaries, who arrived at Bangkok in the spring of 1850. The state of things at that station is represented as more favorable than previously to the success of the mission. In the Island of Jamaica, four stations and two out-stations are occupied under this Society, by five missionaries and five teachers. The congregations are large; and the schools contain about 200 scholars. Among the Ojibways in the Minesota Territory, six missionaries with five assistants are laboring at three stations. In the Sandwich Islands, one mission at Makawao, East Maui, is still connected with the Association, but supports itself; and at Mount Hope in Canada, a school with two hundred scholars is sustained by it. The number of this Society's missions is five, with ten stations; it supports twelve missionaries, and eleven male and twenty female assistants. There are also four native assistants, and seven laborers under appointment. Receipts for the last year, $26,849 66.

The *Foreign Missionary Society of the Lutheran Church* was founded in 1837, in response to an appeal from Mr. Rhenius and his associates the German missionaries in India. The only mission as yet under its direction is situated in the district of Guntoor, in the Madras presidency, India. Three missionaries are now laboring in this field: Mr. Martz at Guntoor, and Messrs. Heyer and Gunn at Guyal. The former station has five schools containing 160 scholars; several persons have offered themselves for baptism. Mr. Heyer has met with great success at Guyal. In eight villages of the Palvaud he has baptized 32 adults, and 24 children. He has 27 candidates for baptism, and 103 children under instruction. Besides these laborers, two missionaries and their wives have recently sailed to reinforce the mission. The receipts of the Society, for the last year, were $4,230 42.

The General Synod of the *Associate Reformed Presbyterian Church* established in 1844 a mission at Damascus, composed of two missionaries, Dr. Paulding and the Rev. James Barnett. In the autumn of 1850, two more missionaries, the Rev. Messrs. Frazier and Lansing, were sent out—the latter by the Associate Reformed Synod of New York. The first-fruits of this mission were gathered a few months since, in the conversion of two adults. But one other mission is sustained by this Church—in Oregon, where the Rev. Mr. Blair has been laboring for two years. Receipts for the last year, $3,182 32.

The *Methodist Episcopal Church South* has a missionary society, whose operations as yet are almost wholly of a domestic character. It supports, however, a mission at Shanghai, in China, where two missionaries, Messrs. Taylor and Jenkins, have been laboring for a short time. In California, also, it sustains three missionaries, who have but recently arrived there.

The *Southern Baptist Convention* sustains through its Board of Foreign Missions, twelve laborers in heathen lands, besides twenty-four assistants. Its stations in China are at Shanghai, where there are three missionaries, who preach to large congregations in two chapels, and at Canton, where two missionaries are stationed. At the former place, three Chinese were baptized within the last year; a school of twenty scholars has been established at a short distance from the city. In Africa, ten stations are occupied, in the colony of Liberia; there are several flourishing schools with upwards of three hundred scholars. The churches at these stations have received large accessions during the last year. A mission is contemplated, also, in Central Africa, and three missionaries are now engaged in exploring the country. This Society has projected a great extension of its foreign work, and we trust will rapidly increase in strength and activity. Its receipts for the past year were $28,697 70.

The *Baptist Free Mission Society* was formed in 1843, by a convention of Baptists at Boston. It is supported by those who refuse to unite with the main society of the denomination from a determination to "separate from all connection with the known avails of slavery, in the support of" Missionary operations. The only foreign mission of this Society is one at the island of Hayti, in the West Indies. It consists of two stations: Port-au-Prince, and Port-de-paix; with two missionaries and five female assistants. Its receipts for the last year, were $6,571 81.

The *Free Will Baptist Foreign Mission Society* was organized in 1833, in connection with the English General Baptist Society, of which we have given some notice. In 1837, however, it undertook a separate enterprise. Its missions are two: at Balasore and Jellasore, in the province of Orissa, Bengal. Three missionaries with four assistants and three native preachers occupy this field. About one hundred and thirty youth are receiving instruction at the school. The receipts for the last year, were $4,433 05.

The *Seventh Day Baptists* sustain a mission at Shanghai in China, where two missionaries are now laboring. A chapel has been opened, and one convert baptized. Receipts for the last year, about $1,200.

CHAPTER XXVII.

SOCIETIES FOR EVANGELIZING THE JEWS.

SEVERAL of the missionary bodies we have already noticed are engaged to some extent in the work of evangelizing the Jewish population, in various parts of the world. Among these we have specified the labors of the Free and Established Churches of Scotland, the American Board, and the Presbyterian Board. There are, however, several institutions whose peculiar sphere of labor is among the Jews.

The *London Society for promoting Christianity among the Jews* has reached its forty-second year. It employs at present sixty-five laborers, chiefly in Great Britain, and operates through other instrumentalities, as a Temporal-Relief Fund, a Hebrew College, and two schools. It has, also, issued during the last year 20,000 tracts, principally in Hebrew, and about 5,700 Bibles and Testaments. The number of converts from Judaism during the last year was one hundred, besides about thirty who are only prevented by civil authorities from uniting with the Church. The receipts of this Society for the last year amounted to £28,278 4*s*. 10*d*., or $136,867.

The *British Society for the Propagation of the Gospel among the Jews* was formed six years ago. During the last year it supported some ten missionaries, in England, Germany, and Holland. It has a mission college with about twelve pupils who are preparing for the missionary work. During the year, five converts have been baptized in England, and five at Frankfort in Germany. Its receipts were £3,829 3*s*. 4*d*., or $18,540.

The *American Society for meliorating the Condition of the Jews* has been in existence twenty-seven years. It now sustains eight missionaries among the Jews, who are laboring at Charleston, New York, and other stations with some success. It is only eight years since this Society has directly sustained any laborers, and the converts from Judaism during that time have been twenty-seven. The receipts for the last year were $5,641 76. We are happy to add that the increase for the present year (1850–51) promises to be considerable; the receipts will probably amount to $11,000.

It would be difficult to make any precise estimate of the number of Jews who have been brought into the Christian Church of late years by various instrumentalities. Da Costa, the author of a valuable work recently published, observes that the number of Jews baptized in Germany during the last twenty years, is estimated at 5,000; and mentions 3,000 as the number of those baptized in Russia within the last few years.

CHAPTER XXVIII.

CONCLUSION AND SUMMARY.

We have now reached the end of our undertaking. How we have executed it, we must leave to others to decide. It has not been an easy one, and the time which was allowed us for its execution has been very short. We have endeavored to do what we proposed as the object to be accomplished with a heartfelt conscientiousness. Wherein we have, in the estimation of our readers, come short of making such a work as they had expected to find this, we beg them to forgive us. We cannot be surprised if others should not judge this book to be what it ought, for we are far from being satisfied with it in all respects, ourselves, notwithstanding the partiality of authors for the productions of their pens.

But whatever may be desired in this volume, written in the course of a few weeks, we think that it demonstrates that Mankind have made great advances in all that concerns their temporal well-being during the Half Century of which it treats. No one will undertake to maintain that, in all that relates to their Material Interests, our race has not made great progress since the commencement of the XIXth century. The great expansion of Commerce; the vast augmentation of Wealth; the rapid growth of Manufactures; the increased application of Science to the arts of production; the multiplication of the facilities of intercommunication, as seen in thousands of Steamboats and in the many Railroads made or making; the remarkable attention given to institutions for the reformation of delinquents and criminals, restoration of the sick to health, and the insane to the possession of reason; the instruction of the deaf and dumb, of the blind and of the idiotic; the successful efforts to promote the education of the masses; the enlarged freedom of the press; the widening diffusion of the principles of constitutional liberty, and their manifestation in more popular forms of government—all proves that there has been an astonishing movement in this direction since the year A. D. eighteen hundred. History records, in our opinion, no similar progress during any fifty years of the long period of 5854 which has elapsed since the creation of man. That the latter half of the century will show still greater progress, we are far from being disposed either to deny, or to doubt. That there has also been a great progress in all that has a bearing on the MORAL AND RELIGIOUS INTERESTS of Humanity, during the same era, is a position which none can question. This is especially true of the Protestant World. The increased spirit of prayer, and the effort to which it has prompted, in behalf of both Home and Foreign Missions; the greatly augmented attention to the religious instruction of the youth in Sunday Schools and Bible-classes; the wonderful exertions made to translate, print and diffuse the Sacred Scriptures, and Religious Tracts; the enlarged liberty to preach Christ's Gospel; the opening up of the way to carry Christianity into nations which have never known it, and to restore it to those which have corrupted it; the more frequent visitations of the Holy Spirit, by which many have been made to submit to the Saviour in a short period—all this demonstrates that there has been a glorious advance in whatever concerns the best, (because spiritual,) interests of mankind.

We are pained to be compelled to admit, however, that the progress in the Moral and Religious Interests of our race, during the period under review, has not equalled that of their Material Interests. Great as has been the resuscitation of a true Christianity, and numerous and happy as have been its fruits,—for which we cannot be too thankful,—still it is deplorable to think that a few merchants in New York can raise with almost no effort at all, more than twice as much money to build four splendid Ocean Steamers as all the receipts of all the Religious Societies in the United States to send the Gospel to millions of men who have never heard it. But what is the building of four Steamships, gigantic and splendid as they may be, to the vast outlay for many lines of Steamers, for numerous and costly Railroads, as well as for other enterprises by which the wealth of the contributors may be augmented?

We are far from regretting the prosperity in material interests of which we have just spoken; we only mourn over the fact that there is not an equal prosperity in spiritual affairs. We are far from being disposed to estimate for nothing the fact that, in the year 1850, $1,750,000 were raised in the United States, $3,500,000 in Great Britain, and $750,000 on the Continent of Europe and other parts of the world,* for the promotion of Christianity at home and abroad; but we cannot but deplore that it was not far greater, when we think of the infinite importance of the blessings which it brings to men, and of their hopeless condition without it. We bless God for the success of the Gospel in turning men unto God, wherever it has been preached during the last fifty years; still we cannot but ask, with the deepest sorrow, why has it not had greater success? Why are so few interested, awakened, convinced, converted, and saved by all the efforts which the churches are making? Oh, what malignant influence, what dreadful obstacle, what Heaven-provoking offence prevents the Divine blessing from coming down upon God's own word and ordinances, in all that abundance which He himself has encouraged us to look for? Is it because of too great a reliance upon our own wisdom,—upon our organizations, which are so characteristic of the age? Where is the

* Total, $6,000,000.

evil? Whose is the fault? Reader, these are serious inquiries for us, and for all who profess to be the followers of Christ. Can it be that we are faithfully acting the part of the LORD'S REMEMBRANCERS?* Can it be that the people of God are fully awake, or anything like it, to their great privileges, their momentous duties, and their solemn responsibilities?

But we must here bring this volume to a close. May our blessed Lord deign to make it the means of contributing, in some degree, to the advancement of His glorious kingdom in this world; and to Him alone be the glory,—to us, the joy.

N.B.—After the portion of this work relating to the British and Foreign Bible Society had been printed, we received intelligence of the death of those excellent men, Lord Bexley and the Rev. A. Brandram, the former President, and the latter Secretary, of that institution.

* Is. chap. lxii. 6, (Marginal reading).

APPENDIX.

TABULAR VIEW OF MISSIONS:

I.—BY MISSIONARY SOCIETIES.

*** THE total number of missionaries, assistants, and stations, as given below, may be taken as nearly complete. The amount of receipts is likewise exact. But the number of communicants is necessarily quite incomplete; it may, however, be stated in round numbers at 300,000 at the lowest estimate.

Societies.	Missionaries.	Ass'ts.	Stations.	Communicants.	Scholars.	Receipts.
Gos. Propagation	355					$444,700.00
Eng. Baptist Miss.	54	324	194	5,008	4,276	95,719.00
Gen. Bapt. Miss.	8	10	7	135	106	9,135.00
London Miss.	171	700	103	9,808*	17,000*	302,637.00
Church Miss.	147	1579	106	13,551	32,268*	504,685.00
Eng. Wesl. Miss.	427	781	324	105,394	78,548	540,560.00
Glasgow Miss.						8,095.00
Scottish Ch. Miss.	14	7	8		2,131	51,260.00
Scot. Free Church	37	57	22		6,000	100,681.00
Scot. Secess. Ch.	33	9				45,125.00
Irish Presb. Ch.	6*	2*	3*			
Eng. Presb. Ch.	1*	*sev.*	1*			
French Miss.	10	4	10	1,340	350	25,600.00
Rhenish Miss.	43		25	1,400*	500*	25,630.00

* Returns incomplete.

Societies.	Mission-aries.	Ass'ts.	Stations.	Communi-cants.	Scholars.	Receipts.
Basle Missionary	29		20		1,967*	54,000.00
Unit. Breth. Miss.	282		69	70,000†		53,540.00
Berlin Missionary	11*		7			17,000.00
Gosner's Miss.	19		2			3,630.00
Dresden Miss.	4*		2			9,200.00
Leipsic Miss.	6*		3	137*	1,000	8,000.00
Hamburg Miss.	6	2	5			5,000.00
Stockholm Miss.						4,555.00
Stavanger Miss.	4*					3,365.00
Norway Miss.						
Netherlands Miss.	8*	4*	3*	130*		27,000.00
Am. Board	157	360	134	25,875	22,824	251,339.35
Am. Bapt. Union	56	250	155	12,500	2,772	87,537.20
Presb. Board Miss.	55	43	28	282	1,709	126,075.40
Epis. Board Miss.	10	9*	8	96	656	36,114.11
Methodist Miss.	34	*sev.*	8	1,611		38,193.14
Am. Miss. Assoc.	12	31	10	380		26,849.66
Lutheran Miss.	5		2		263	4,230.42
Assoc. Pres. Church	5		2			3,182.32
M. E. Ch., South	5		2			6,000.00
Baptist Ch., South	12	24	12		320	28,697.70
Bapt. Free Miss.	2	5	2			6,571.81
Free-Will Bapt.	3	7	2		130	4.433.05
Seventh-Day Bapt.	2		1			1,200.00
38	2033	4208	1280	247,867*	172,720	$2,959,541.16

II.—BY COUNTRIES AND STATIONS.

I. WESTERN AFRICA.

Stations.	Mission-aries.	Ass'ts.	Nat. Ass'ts.	Commu-nic'ts.	Schools.	Scho-lars.
CHURCH MISSIONARY SOCIETY,						
Freetown,	5	2	8	213	9	1727
River district,	2	1	25	839	14	2126
Mountain district,	3	1	12	722	10	1501

* Returns incomplete. † Including all under religious instruction.

Stations.	Mission-aries.	Ass'ts.	Nat. Ass'ts.	Commu-nic'ts.	Schools.	Scho-lars.
Sea district,	1	1	9	280	13	854
Timneh mission,	1		2	7	2	42
Abbeokuta,	4		7	102	4	324
Badagry,	2	2	3	20	2	94
At home,	5					
WESLEYAN MISSIONARY SOCIETY,						
Sierra Leone district,	7	43		4712	16	2958
Gambia district,	3	8		476	3	751
Cape Coast district,	5	66		809	23	1014
BAPTIST MISSIONARY SOCIETY,						
Fernando Po,	2			113		
Clarence, &c.,	1	4				
Bimbia, &c.,	3	4			1	100
Cameroons,	1			5	6	350
BASLE MISSIONARY SOCIETY,						
Akropong,	4		1		2	70
Danish Accra,	3	1			2	128
HAMBURG MISSIONARY SOCIETY,						
Cape Coast, &c.,	1					
AMERICAN BOARD OF MISSIONS,						
Gaboon River,	5	3		22	4	67
AM. BAPTIST MISSIONARY UNION,						
Bassa tribe,		2	5	20	3	60
AMERICAN PRESBYTERIAN BOARD,						
Liberia,	2	2		62	3	72
Settra Kroo,	1	3			1	15
Near the Equator,	2	2				
AM. PROTESTANT EPISCOPAL BOARD,						
Liberia,	5	6	*sev.*	80	6	160
AM. M. E. MISSIONARY SOCIETY,						
Liberia,	15	*sev.*		1117	20	810
AMERICAN MISSIONARY ASSOCIATION,						
Mendi country,	3	6	3	26	1	80
AM. SOUTHERN BAPTIST BOARD,						
Liberia,	5	12		*many*	7	328
Boporah,	2	1				

II. SOUTHERN AFRICA.

Stations.	Mission-aries.	Ass'ts.	Nat. Ass'ts.	Commu-nic'ts.	Schools.	Scho-lars.
MISSIONS OF UNITED BRETHREN,*						
Gnadenthal,	15			890		†2795
Groenekloof,	8			344		1347
Robben Island,	2			15		43
Elim,	8			298		1186
Enon,	4			92		392
Clarkson,	4					320
Shiloh,	7			74		691
Mamre,	4					100
Goshen,	8					
LONDON MISSIONARY SOCIETY,						
Cape Town,	2			23	2	491
Paarl,	1			100	3	184
Tulbagh,	1			73	4	284
Caledon Institution,	1			262		160
Pacaltsdorp,	2			70	2	160
Dysalsdorp,	1			110		75
Hankey,	1	1		186		300
Bethelsdorp,		1		98	2	72
Port Elizabeth,	1	1		230		200
Uitenhage,	1			220		90
Graham's Town,	2			231		104
Graaff Reinet,		1		64		100
Theopolis,	1			59		54
Colesburg,	1			40		90
Somerset,	1			123		36
Kat River,	2			41		
Tidmanton,	1					
Cradock,	1			32		106
Long Kloof,	1			70		110
Fort Beaufort,				105	5	237
Buffalo River,	1			67		52
Knapp's Hope,	1			16		30
King William's Town,	1			40		50

* The United Brethren include among their missionaries the wives of such as are married.

† Including all who are under religious instruction.

Stations.	Mission-aries.	Ass'ts.	Nat. Ass'ts.	Commu-nic'ts.	Schools.	Scho-lars.
Griqua Town,	2			540	7	435
Lekatlong,	1			300		100
Philippolis,	1			353		110
Kuruman,	3			400		158
Mamusa,	1			115		40
Mabotsa,		1		7		20
Kolobeng,	1					
Matebe,	1					20
WESLEYAN MISSIONARY SOCIETY,						
Cape of Good Hope district —9 stations,	10	24		1439	17	2961
Bechuana district—7 stations,	7	11		597	9	925
Albany and Kaffraria district—26 stations,	23	70		2329		4396
FREE CHURCH OF SCOTLAND,						
Cape Town,	1	1				
Lovedale,	3	3		45	1	28
Burnshill,	1	3				70
Pirie,	1	2				
UNITED SCOTTISH PRESB. CHURCH,						
Chumie, &c.,	2	1	8			
FRENCH MISSIONARY SOCIETY,						
Carmel,	1	1		35		20
Bethulia,	1			200		6
Beersheba,	1			391		80
Bethesda,	1	1		23		8
Moriah,	1	1		326		46
Berea,	1			27		
Thaba Bossiou,	1	1		114		9
Mekuatling,	1			73		50
Wellington,	1			41		70
Motito,	1			100		
RHENISH MISSIONARY SOCIETY,						
Whale Bay,	1					
New Barmen,	2					
Rehoboth,	1	1		100		
Nama Bethania,	2	1				
Steinkopff,	1	2		36		

Stations.	Missionaries.	Ass'ts.	Nat. Ass'ts.	Communic'ts.	Schools.	Scholars.
Ebenezer,	2					
Wupperthal,	4			61		
Amandelboom,	2					90
Tulbagh-Steinthal,	2	2		44		180
Worcester,	2			140		206
Stellenbosch and Sarepta,	3	4		229		
Berlin Missionary Society,						
Zoar,	1					
Platberg,	1					30
Pniel,	2					
Hebron,	2					
Sharon,	1					
Port Natal,	2					
Stavanger Missionary Society,						
Port Natal,	4					
Gospel Propagation Society,						
Cape Town,	3	1				
Stellenbosch, &c.,	12					
American Board of Missions,						
Umvati (12 stations,) .	12	20		78	8	185

III. EASTERN AFRICA.

Stations.	Missionaries.	Ass'ts.	Nat. Ass'ts.	Communic'ts.	Schools.	Scholars.
Church Missionary Society,						
Rabbai Mpia,	5					
London Missionary Society,						
Port Louis (Mauritius,)	1			*sev.*	1	

IV. THE EAST.

Stations.	Missionaries.	Ass'ts.	Nat. Ass'ts.	Communic'ts.	Schools.	Scholars.
Church Missionary Society,						
Greece—Syra,	1	1	9	14	5	462
Asia Minor—Smyrna,	1	1	1			
Egypt—Cairo,	2	1	4	18	2	178
Jews' Society,						
Smyrna,		1				
Salonica,	1	1				
Bucharest,	1	1				
Jerusalem,	4	6				

Stations.	Missionaries.	Ass'ts.	Nat. Ass'ts.	Communic'ts.	Schools.	Scholars.
Safet,		1				
Cairo,	1	1				
Bagdad, &c.,	2					
AMERICAN BOARD OF MISSIONS,						
Armenians:						
Constantinople,	4	5	6	105		
Bebek,	2	2	2			
Broosa,	2	2	1			
Smyrna,	3	3	4			
Trebizond,	2	2	3	132	9	159
Erzeroom,	2	2	1			
Aintab,	2	2				
Nicomedia, &c.,			9			
Syria:						
Beyroot,	2	6	3	16	3	83
Abeih,	3	3	1	3	6	111
Tripoli,	2	2		1	1	15
Aleppo,	2	2			2	12
Mosul,	2	1				
Hasbeiya, &c.				7	2	50
Nestorians:						
Oroomiah,	3	7	9	*sev.*	33	633
Seir,	2	2	4	*hundreds.*	1	44
At home,	2	2				
AM. PROTESTANT EPISCOPAL BOARD,						
Athens,	1	2	*sev.*			450
AM. BAPTIST MISSIONARY UNION,						
Greece—Piræus,	1	1		10	1	60
Corfu,	1	2				
AM. ASSOC. REFORMED CHURCH,						
Damascus,	3	4			2	

V. INDIA.

Stations.	Missionaries.	Ass'ts.	Nat. Ass'ts.	Communic'ts.	Schools.	Scholars.
GOSPEL PROPAGATION SOCIETY,						
Calcutta,	1					
" (Bishop's College,)	1	2				
Howrah,	2					
Tallygunge,	2		28			

Stations.	Mission-aries.	Ass'ts.	Nat. Ass'ts.	Commu-nic'ts.	Schools.	Scho-lars.
Barripore,	2					
Nerbudda,	1					
Cawnpore,	1					
Tamlook,	1					
Ahmedabad,	1					
Madras Mission,	23	14	205	15,642	169	4912
CHURCH MISSIONARY SOCIETY,						
Bombay,	4	3	23	14	16	883
Nassuck, Astagaum, and Malligaum,	2		10	29	7	340
Junir,	1		4		3	150
Calcutta,	4	2	39	136	14	1169
Burdwan,	2	1	11	54	9	624
Krishnaghur,	9	4	106	548	38	1525
Bhagulpur,	1					
Benares,	4	6	31	74	6	456
Chunar,	1		7	46	6	336
Jaunpore,		2	16	19	4	409
Gorruckpore,	1	1	6	70	3	167
Agra,	3		12	153	10	333
Meerut,	1		4	30	2	75
Kotghur,	1		7	4	6	67
Madras,	4		19	145	9	362
Tinnevelly districts,	14		425	2680	239	6245
Travancore districts,	17		109	889	63	2059
Telugu,	3		18	19	3	127
At home,	4					
BAPTIST MISSIONARY SOCIETY,						
Calcutta—Circ. Road,	1			96		
" Lal Bazar,	2		1	140	2	120
" Kolinga,	3			54		
Intally,	2		2	49		
Haura and Salkiya,	1		3	26	3	180
Nursikdachoke,	2		3	52	1	25
Lakhyantipur,	2		3	67	4	100
Khari,	2		1	48	1	40
Malayapur,	1		1	7	1	45
Dum Dum,	1		1	25		
Serampore,	3		5	127	8	750

Stations.	Mission-aries.	Ass'ts.	Nat. Ass'ts.	Commu-nic'ts.	Schools.	Scho-lars.
Cutwa,	1		4	31	1	10
Suri, Birbhum,	1		3	36	2	100
Dinajpur,	1		1	18	2	86
Jessore,	1		10	206	4	150
Burisal,	2		10	177	8	150
Dacca,	1		4	21		
Chittagong,	1		7	39	2	42
Monghir,	2		7	49	2	90
Benares,	3		13	20	5	270
Agra,	1		1	119		
Saugor,	1		1	21		
Chitaura,	1		4	23	2	60
Muttra,	1		2	9	1	60
Delhi,	1		2	15		
Madras,	1		2	41	3	
General Baptist Miss. Society,						
Cuttack,	2		1	141	2	120
Choga,			1	50		
Khundita,			2			
Piplee,	2		2			
Berhampore,	2		4	44	2	58
London Missionary Society,						
Calcutta,	8		8	255	12	1148
Berhampore,	2		1		3	115
Benares,	4	1				380
Mirzapore,	2	2		18	5	192
Guzerat,	2					
Madras,	2			108	17	224
Vizagapatam,	3			40	2	150
Chicacole,	1		3	15	2	58
Cuddapah,	1		6	32	7	272
Belgaum,	2		3	20	12	445
Bellary,	3		4	86	12	417
Bangalore,	4		7	56	12	445
Mysore,	1			12	4	77
Salem,	1		9	38	6	141
Combacorum,	1				9	327
Coimbatoor,	1		28	30	14	938

Stations.	Mission-aries.	Ass'ts.	Nat. Ass'ts.	Commu-nic'ts.	Schools.	Scho-lars.
Nagercoil,	4				19	760
Neyoor,	2	1	66	65	42	1444
Quilon,	1		9		13	321
Trevandrum,	1		11	13	8	171
WESLEYAN MISSIONARY SOCIETY,						
Madras,	3		6	161	4	275
Negapatam,	3		18	20	9	267
Manaargoody,	2		10	22	10	454
Bangalore (Tamul,)	1		5	148	4	140
" (Canarese,)	2		5	27	5	202
Mysore,	2		3	1	3	116
Goobbee, &c.,	1		5	8	5	157
Coonghul,	1		5	1	5	169
CHURCH OF SCOTLAND,						
Calcutta,	8					1021
Madras,	5					300
Bombay,	2	2				395
Ghospara,			2			50
FREE CHURCH OF SCOTLAND,						
Calcutta,	5	*sev.*	*sev.*		4	2000
Bombay,	3		2		1	1200
Madras,	3		*sev.*		10	1400
Poonah,	3	1	9	28	10	600
Nagpur and Kampti,	2	2	4			600
IRISH PRESBYTERIAN MISSION,						
Katiawar,	6		2			
BASLE MISSIONARY SOCIETY,						
Mangalore,	6		5	250	2	
Moolky,	1			40		
Dharwar,	2		6	49		412
Hoobly,	2		7	5	7	330
Bettigherry,	2			3	5	204
Malasamoodra,	2			7	2	25
Catery and Catagherry,	3		1	19		70
Cannanore,	1		10	130	4	130
Tellicherry,	4	1	14	161	12	355
Calicut,	2		13	45	7	271
Dacca,	4					

Stations.	Missionaries.	Ass'ts.	Nat. Ass'ts.	Communic'ts.	Schools.	Scholars.
Dayapoor,	2		1	50		
Comilla,	2		1			
BERLIN MISSIONARY SOCIETY,						
Ghazeepoor,	2					50
LEIPSIC MISSIONARY SOCIETY,						
Tranquebar,	2					
Mayaveram,	2		19	137	28	1070
Poreiar,	2					
HAMBURG MISSIONARY SOCIETY,						
Rajamundry,	3					19
Ootacamuud (independent miss.,)	1		*sev.*		3	76
AMERICAN BOARD OF MISSIONS,						
Bombay,	4	3	2		11	404
Ahmednuggur,	7	7	10	112	24	900
Madras,	4	5	7	30	13	400
Madura,	11	13	53	202	21	1540
AMERICAN PRESBYTERIAN BOARD,						
Lodiana,	11	8	10	53	10	433
Furrukhabad,	8	5	4	107	7	398
Allahabad,	5	3	6	42	6	399
AMERICAN BAPTIST MISS. UNION,						
Nellore,	3	3			10	250
AMERICAN LUTHERAN MISSIONS,						
Guntoor	3	1			5	160
Guyal,	1		6			103
AMERICAN FREE-WILL BAPTISTS,						
Balasore,	1	1	2	13	3	66
Jellasore,	2	3		16	1	17

VI. CEYLON.

Stations.	Missionaries.	Ass'ts.	Nat. Ass'ts.	Communic'ts.	Schools.	Scholars.
GOSPEL PROPAGATION SOCIETY,						
Putlam,	1					
Matura,	1					
Neura Ellia,	1				30	1500
Colombo,	2					
Kandy,	1		30			
CHURCH MISSIONARY SOCIETY,						
Cotta,	6		62	104	40	1216

Stations.	Mission-aries.	Ass'ts.	Nat. Ass'ts.	Commu-nic'ts.	Schools.	Scho-lars.
Kandy,	2		11	28	5	132
Baddagame,	2		6	32	6	182
Nellore,	1		13	44	12	540
Copay,	1		7	8	6	287
Chundicully,	1		19	80	11	479
Baptist Missionary Society,						
Colombo,	1		1	85	4	131
Byamville,			1	107	5	163
Kottigahawatta,			1	68	6	172
Toomboville,			1	17		
Weilgama,			1	28	1	25
Hendella,			1	26		
Gonawella,			1	35	3	80
Hanwella,			1	29		
Matura,	1		2	20	7	121
Kandy,	1			25	2	43
Gahalaya, &c.,			3			
Matella,			1	15	2	45
Wesleyan Missionary Society,						
Singhalese, or South Ceylon district,	12		91	1214	74	2760
Tamul, or North Ceylon district,	7		51	341	29	1365
American Board of Missions,						
Ceylon Mission—Batticotta, Oodooville, &c.	11	16	22	345	102	4373

VII. CHINA, SIAM, BURMAH, ETC.

Stations.	Mission-aries.	Ass'ts.	Nat. Ass'ts.	Commu-nic'ts.	Schools.	Scho-lars.
Church Missionary Society,						
China: Shanghai,	3					
" Ningpo,	2					
" Hongkong,	1					
" On their way,	2					
London Missionary Society,						
China: Hongkong,	1	1		6	1	38
" Canton,	3	1	1			
" Shanghai,	4	2				
" Amoy,	3	1		3	2	27

Stations.	Mission-aries.	Ass'ts.	Nat. Ass'ts.	Commu-nic'ts.	Schools.	Scho-lars.
GENERAL BAPTIST MISSIONS,						
China: Ningpo,	1	1	1	1	1	24
BASLE MISSIONARY SOCIETY,						
China: Hongkong,	2			7		
AMERICAN BOARD OF MISSIONS,						
China: Canton,	3	5	2		1	14
" Amoy,	2	2	1	3	1	25
" Fuh-Chau,	6	5			2	18
AMERICAN PRESBYTERIAN BOARD,						
China: Canton,	3	1			1	18
" Ningpo,	8	10		8	3	75
Siam: Bangkok,	2	3	1	1		
AM. PROT. EPISCOPAL BOARD,						
China: Shanghai,	2	2		7	1	46
M. E. MISSIONARY SOCIETY,						
China: Fuh-Chau,	3				3	64
M. E. CHURCH SOUTH,						
China: Shanghai,	2					
AM. BAPTIST MISSIONARY UNION,						
Burmah: Maulmain,	3	8	13	212	8	345
Karen: "	4	6	34	1708	9	201
" Tavoy	5	5	19	933	20	377
" Sandoway,	3	2	44	4500	21	495
Arracan:	4	2	6	55		
Assam:	5	6	4	57	22	700
Siam: Bangkok,	3	3	4	29	2	25
China: Hongkong,	2		6 }	27	3	60
" Ningpo,	3	3	1 }			
SOUTH BAPTIST BOARD,						
China: Shanghai,	3	3		3	1	20
" Canton,	2	2	6	1		
SEVENTH-DAY BAPTISTS,						
China: Shanghai,	2	2		1		
AM. MISSIONARY ASSOCIATION,						
Siam: Bangkok,	3	3				

VIII. INDIAN ARCHIPELAGO, AUSTRALASIA, AND POLYNESIA.

Stations.	Mission-aries.	Ass'ts.	Nat. Ass'ts.	Commu-nic'ts.	Schools.	Scho-lars.
CHURCH MISSIONARY SOCIETY,						
New Zealand: northern district,	3	4	99	871		

Stations.	Missionaries.	Ass'ts.	Nat. Ass'ts.	Communic'ts.	Schools.	Scholars.
New Zealand: middle district,	8	4	74	1224		
" eastern district,	4	1	132	2054	80	3500
" western district,	4	1	156	1064	28	2322
at home,	1					
London Missionary Society,						
South Seas: Tahiti,	6	1		600		1000
" Eimeo,	1			205		
" Huahine,	1			380		270
" Raiatea,	2					200
" Tahaa,						
" Borabora,				235		257
" Rarotonga,	1			29		
" Avarua,	1			170		300
" Arorangi,	1			150		300
" Aitutaki,	1					
" Mangaia,	1			518		
" Savaii,	3			413		387
" Upolu,	8	2				
" Tutuila,	1			531		833
" Anatom,	2	1				
Wesleyan Missionary Society,						
New South Wales,	14		37			
Australia Felix,	3		12			
South Australia,	5		6	4210	31	1899
Western Australia,	1		2			
Van Dieman's Land,	7					
New Zealand,	20		17	4328	75	2973
Friendly Islands,	10		9	7202		
Feejee,	5		38	1713	49	1960
Baptist Missionary Society,						
Sumatra,	1					
Java,	1					
Rhenish Missionary Society,						
Borneo: Banjarmassing,	1		1		1	20
" Palingkau,	1		1	12	1	120
" Bethabara,	1		1	6	1	120
" Bintang,	1		2	6		130
Gosner's Missionary Society,						

Stations.	Missionaries.	Ass'ts.	Nat. Ass'ts.	Communic'ts.	Schools.	Scholars.
Australia: Zion Hill,	14					
DRESDEN MISSIONARY SOCIETY,						
New Holland: Adelaide,	2					
" Encounter Bay,	2					
UNITED BRETHREN'S MISSIONS,						
New Holland: Port Philip,	2					
AMERICAN BOARD OF MISSIONS,						
Sandwich Islands: Hawaii,	8	10		23,102 (Hawaii, Maui, Molokai, Oahu, Kauai)	393 (Hawaii, Maui, Molokai, Oahu, Kauai)	12,012 (Hawaii, Maui, Molokai, Oahu, Kauai)
" Maui,	4	4	2			
" Molokai,	2	2	1			
" Oahu,	4	14	2			
" Kauai,	2	7				
at home,	2	1				
Corresponding members, 10.						
AMERICAN MISSIONARY ASSOCIATION,						
Sandwich Islands: Makawao,	1	1				

IX. NORTH AMERICA.

(Chiefly among the Indians.)

Stations.	Missionaries.	Ass'ts.	Nat. Ass'ts.	Communic'ts.	Schools.	Scholars.
CHURCH MISSIONARY SOCIETY,						
N. W. America:						
Red River,	1	2	3	331	5	321
Indian settlement,	1		1	91	2	104
Cumberland,	2		2	61	4	152
Manitoba,	1		1	6	2	46
WESLEYAN MISSIONARY SOCIETY,						
West Canada,	50		24	6129	12	
East Canada,	20		3	3849		
New Brunswick,	24		2	3725		
Newfoundland,	13		8	2193	8	466
Hudson's Bay,	2		4	119	2	54
UNITED BRETHREN'S MISSIONS,						
Delaware Indians,	5					
Cherokee Indians,	5					
Florida,	2					
AMERICAN BOARD OF MISSIONS,						
Oregon,	3	3				
Choctaw,	5	28	1	1100	6	215

Stations.	Mission-aries.	Ass'ts.	Nat. Ass'ts.	Commu-nic'ts.	Schools.	Scho-lars.
Cherokee,	5	11	5	209	4	120
Dakota,	6	14		63	3	144
Ojibwa,	2	4	1	25	1	37
New York,	5	13	1	227	8	201
Abenaquis,			1	56		
AMERICAN PRESBYTERIAN BOARD,						
Choctaw,	3	5	1			
Chickasaw,		2				
Creek,	3	7		21	4	93
Seminole,		3			1	11
Iowa and Sac,	2	2			1	35
Otoe and Omaha,	1	2			1	35
Chippewa and Ottawa,	1	2		29	2	75
AM. PROTESTANT EPISCOPAL BOARD,						
Oneida, Duck Creek, Wis.	1	1	1			
California,	2					
M. E. MISSIONARY SOCIETY,						
Brotherton,	1			75		
Oneida,	1			97		
Sault St. Marie,	3			46	1	52
Kewawenon,	2			56	1	
Fond du Lac,	1			8		
Sandy Lake,	1			15	1	42
Flint,	3			400	4	99
Nottoway,	1			75	1	18
Oneida and Onondaga,	1			90	1	
St. Regis,	1			24		
Wyandott,	2			189		
M. E. CHURCH SOUTH,						
Kansas, Cherokees, Choctaws, Creeks,	39			4042	8	380
AM. BAPTIST MISSIONARY UNION,						
Ojibwas,	2	1	1	45	2	57
Ottawas,	1	1		18	1	30
Shawanoes, &c.,	3	5	3	119	2	43

Stations.	Missionaries.	Ass'ts.	Nat. Ass'ts.	Communic'ts.	Schools.	Scholars.
Cherokees,	3	3	6	1200	1	65
AM. MISSIONARY ASSOCIATION,						
Chippeways,	6	10	1			

X. GREENLAND AND LABRADOR.

Stations.	Missionaries.	Ass'ts.	Nat. Ass'ts.	Communic'ts.	Schools.	Scholars.
UNITED BRETHREN'S MISSIONS,						
Greenland: New Herrnhut,	4			202		408
" Lichtenfels,	5			161		350
" Lichtenau,	5			259		637
" Friedrichsthal,	5			199		436
" On their way,	4					
Labrador: Nain,	7			81		277
" Hoffenthal,	7			57		216
" Okkak,	7			167		397
" Hebron,	5			56		336
" On their way,	4					

XI. WEST INDIES AND GUIANA.

Stations.	Missionaries.	Ass'ts.	Nat. Ass'ts.	Communic'ts.	Schools.	Scholars.
CHURCH MISSIONARY SOCIETY,						
British Guiana: Barticagrove,	2	1	4	70	2	66
Jamaica:		1		358	2	286
LONDON MISSIONARY SOCIETY,						
Demerara: Georgetown,	2	4		33	3	405
" Canal, No. 1,	1			351	2	137
" Montrose,	1			335	2	155
" Lusignan,	1			221	2	145
" Leguan,	1			70	1	45
Berbice: New Amsterdam,	1					
" Lonsdale,		1			1	120
" Ithaca, &c.,	1					
" Rodborough,	1			50	1	80
" Fearn,	1			341	1	
" Blyendaal,	1					
" Brunswick,			1			
" Albion Chapel,	1					
Jamaica: First hill,	1			48		
" Dry harbor,				118		
" Ridgemount,	1			159	1	90

Stations.	Missionaries.	Ass'ts.	Nat. Ass'ts.	Communic'ts.	Schools.	Scholars.
Jamaica: Davytown,	1			117	1	78
" Whitefield,	1			166	1	59
" Four Paths,	1					
" Chapelton,	1			128	1	98
" Mount Zion,	1			60		
" Kingston,	1			14		
" Shortwood,				6		
" Morant Bay,	1					90
" Prospect Penn,					1	80
WESLEYAN MISSIONARY SOCIETY,						
Antigua, &c.,	20		36	12,589	32	2341
St. Vincent's and Demerara,	20		50	13,542	49	2961
Jamaica,	28		33	20,717	28	2072
Bahamas,	11			3352	1	50
Hayti,	6		14	387	7	666
BAPTIST MISSIONARY SOCIETY,						
Trinidad,	5		8	80	6	181
Bahamas,	5		203	2810	8	511
Hayti,	1	3		17	1	76
Central America,	1	1				
UNITED BRETHREN'S MISSIONS,						
St. Thomas, St. Croix, St. John,	26			3078		
Jamaica, Antigua, St. Kitts, Barbadoes, Tobago,	29, 21, 10, 9, 6			12,437		
Musquito Coast,	4					
Surinam,	52			1756		
M. E. MISSIONARY SOCIETY,						
Buenos Ayres,	1			51		
AM. BAPTIST FREE MISSION,						
Hayti,	2	5		42	2	50
AM. MISSIONARY ASSOCIATION,						
Jamaica,	5	10			4	200

INDEX.

CATALOGUE
OF
VALUABLE PUBLICATIONS
ISSUED BY M. W. DODD,
PUBLISHER AND BOOKSELLER,
Cor. City Hall Square and Spruce St.
(OPPOSITE CITY HALL, NEW YORK.)

CHARLOTTE ELIZABETH'S WORKS,
WITH AN INTRODUCTION
BY MRS. HARRIET BEECHER STOWE.
2 Volumes, Octavo.
CONTAINING PORTRAIT OF THE AUTHOR ON STEEL,
WITH SEVERAL OTHER ILLUSTRATIONS,
ENGRAVED EXPRESSLY FOR THE WORK.

The Publisher invites the attention of the public to this new Edition of one of the most popular and useful writers of the present age.

It contains, in the compass of nearly 1700 large octavo pages, all the productions, in Prose and Poetry, of this admirable authoress, suited to a Standard Edition of her Works. Several of these were furnished in *manuscript* for this edition by Mrs. Tonna, which has her express endorsement, and is the only one in this country from which she has derived any pecuniary benefit.

To give additional value to the work by illustrating and embellishing it, we have, at considerable expense, added to it several Engravings from Steele, got up expressly for this purpose. It is believed few works can be found surpassing these in value for family reading. They combine, to an unusual degree, an elevated moral tone, with reading attractive to both old and young. And for the requisites of *beauty*, *cheapness*, and *legibility* combined, this edition of Charlotte Elizabeth's works is not excelled by anything in the market.

The last edition contains her Memoir by her husband, designed to be a Supplement to Personal Recollections, and embracing the period from the close of her Personal Recollections to her death. Also, "War with the Saints; or, Count Raymond of Toulouse,"—the work she finished almost simultaneously with her earthly career.

A NEW MEMOIR OF HANNAH MORE;

OR, LIFE IN HALL AND COTTAGE. BY MRS. HELEN C. KNIGHT. 12mo. Illustrated with an accurate Portrait of Mrs. More, and a beautiful View of Barley Wood, her residence, from fine steel Engravings.

"This is a volume of rare attractiveness. It is not burthened, as others are, with dry details and with correspondence heaped together without discrimination, and it will introduce to the young female society of this country and this generation the genius of Barley Wood, in a most winning garb, as a companion, an instructor, and a guide."—*Ind.*

"It is a very beautiful and instructive picture of the excellent Hannah More that Mrs. Knight has here eliminated from the biographies, correspondence and works, to which her genius and her goodness gave being. The spirit of her life as well as the peculiarities of her genius, are finely appreciated, and the history is narrated with remarkable animation and interest. We hardly know of a more attractive and suggestive history than Hannah More's; and the presentation of it in a form, so well adapted to bring out its features, and to commend its lessons to the sex of which she was an ornament, is a great public good, as well as a great matter of literary attraction."—*Evangelist.*

"It is seldom a book issues from the American press with so many attractive points as this new life of Hannah More. Familiar as most persons are with the character and writings of this celebrated woman, in Mrs. Knight's hands the subject glows and fascinates as though it were a freshest novelty. The style is sparkling and graphic; the arrangement and order of the topics judicious and striking; the introduction of contemporary persons and incidents, is skilfully done, so as neither to crowd the canvass, or convert a Memoir of Miss More into a general history of her times. We have Burke, and Johnson, and Garrick, we have Montagu, Boscawen, and Carter, and other eminent friends of Hannah More; but they all contribute light and shade to her character and principles without distracting our attention."—*New York Organ.*

"This Memoir is not a mere arrangement of old materials for the sake of making a book; but a fresh life-like picture of an old scene, in which we discover points of beauty that never struck us before. She does not present her subject as an isolated statue to be examined and admired; but with a vividness only attainable by true genius, she reproduces to our gaze the circle in which that woman moved and acted, the home influence which laid the foundation of her character, and the associations which gave her the means and opportunities of such great and varied usefulness. It is in reality the *life* of Hannah More. She lives it over again under our eyes, and as it were, for our pleasure and profit."—*Christian Intelligencer.*

"A book which has the charm of enthusiasm and a sincere devotion to its subject; circling, too, about that delightful society of which Dr. Johnson was the grand centre."—*Literary World.*

"Mrs. Knight here presents, in a concise and vigorous outline, her own ideal of Hannah More, and we may say, that a more beautiful and attractive portrait is rarely to be found. We could wish it were to form the study for every young lady, for the elements of woman's highest excellence, as well as broadest usefulness and moral power, are here revealed."—*Parlor Magazine.*

"We hesitate not to say that whoever may be attracted to this book, may yield to the impulse without the fear of disappointment."—*Christian Secretary.*

"It is a work full of interest and instruction. We hope it will be found in every family."—*Genesee Evangelist.*

"A contribution to biographical literature of rare interest and excellence. The style may be called *pictorial*, the author presenting before the reader a panorama of Hannah More's pure and useful life; her own task performed with superior tact and judgment—being limited to directing the attention of the spectators to each scene as it appears, in vivid but not over-wrought colors, upon the canvass."—*Com. Adv.*

"Those who have read the former Memoirs of Mrs. More, will not find this a whit the less interesting on that account, and those who have not read them, have a rich treat before them in the work of Mrs. Knight."—*New York Observer.*

"There was room for this New Memoir of one of the choicest Christians any age has produced. Mrs. Knight, than whom the country could hardly produce a more suitable person for this work, has sketched the traits of character and events of the life of her subject with great judiciousness, skill, and Christian earnestness, and has produced a volume that her countrywomen especially will be grateful for in generations to come."—*Religious Recorder.*

"The subject of the work is happily presented in all her positions in life. We see the playful child at Stapleton; the industrious student at Bristol; the admired one in the circles of London; the thoughtful and serene Christian at Cowslip Green; the central figure among the benevolent sisterhood at Barley Wood, and the dying Christian, radiant with celestial hope, at Clifton."—*Western Literary Messenger.*

"We hesitate not to say that in Mrs. Knight, she has a biographer of kindred spirit, competent to do justice to her subject, one who has admirably executed her task, and in a continuous narrative, of increasingly absorbing interest from the commencement to the close, has given a portrait, which leaves its strong impression on the reader; showing, too, what a feeble mortal sustained by faith, and aided by help from above, can accomplish.

"The book can be usefully read by persons of any age, but for young ladies it is invaluable."—*Daily Courant.*

"Precisely such a Memoir of Hannah More as was needed has not been written *until now.* Of the two English sketches of her life and character, one is cumbered with useless correspondence, and the other is sadly deficient in attractiveness of style. Yet no modern life needs to be written for all Christendom more than hers. Mrs. Knight has accomplished her task in the happiest manner. On the whole, we regard the book as one of the very best and most useful books of the season, and shall be much disappointed if it does not win an extensive circulation, and an established place among the choice literature of the day."—*Christian Register.*

"The work we cordially recommend, especially to our young friends, not only on account of the correct moral picture it gives of the life of Mrs. More, but as affording much valuable information concerning the literary history of her times, and the distinguished authors with whom she was associated."—*Portsmouth Journal.*

"It is written in a graphic style, and forms the best Memoir we have seen of one whose life was an admirable example of healthy, vigorous piety."—*Albany State Register.*

"It is according to our taste a *model* biography—a truthful, graphic, eloquent portraiture of the main features in the life and character of this transcendant woman. Instead of tiring as we are wont to do over the heavy and almost endless pages of modern biography, we follow her with eagerness to the conclusion, and regret she has not given us more."—*Bib. Repository.*

FIRST THINGS.

A Series of Lectures on the Great Facts and Moral Principles First Revealed to Mankind. In Two Vols.

By Gardiner Spring, D.D.

CONTENTS.

In the chapter on the Unity of the Human Race the theories of Agassiz and others are thoroughly refuted. That on Woman is regarded as one of the most popular discourses ever delivered in New York, and one of the finest presentations of her character and relations there is in the language. The one entitled First Rebellion is, in substance, the celebrate Discourse delivered by Dr. Spring, on Thanksgiving Day, December 12, 1850, in the course of which are extended observations on the Fugitive Slave Law and Slavery.

Of the many highly popular productions of the author, now one of the oldest and most accomplished ministers in the country, none will add more to his reputation than this.

"It is impossible but that the work should attract great attention, and be very widely circulated. If this should be his last offering through the press, the Author might very well afford to leave it as the crown of his reputation and usefulness."—*N. Y. Observer.*

"These lectures have excited the greatest interest in the delivery, and they will excite no less in the perusal. They are full of strong thought and exquisite beauty, quite out of the beaten track, and yet eminently plain and practical. It is, altogether, a production of rare attractiveness."—*Journal of Commerce.*

"This is a work of rather singular, though not inappropriate title, which, we venture to predict, will have a very extensive circulation."—*Presbyterian of the West.*

"These Lectures are the ripe fruits of a golden age. * * * We are made to feel the importance of *first things* in man's history as we go on with these Lectures from the *first* man to the *first* rebellion in the Hebrew Commonwealth (which concludes the series)."—*National Intelligencer.*

"The venerable author has seized hold of them with his accustomed clearness of perception and good judgment; and in deducing the important truths they contain, has invested them with surpassing interest. Elegant in style, thorough in discussion, sound in sentiment, and replete with the spirit of reverence and piety, the lectures are among the most attractive religious essays that we have ever met."—*N. Y. Evangelist.*

"In the variety and importance of the truths inculcated, in richness of illustration, in vivacity of style, no preceding work of Dr. Spring excels this. There is much able discussion; there are some passages of striking beauty and eloquence; while the Author never loses sight of his great aim, the enforcement of the fundamental principles of morality and religion."—*Newark Daily Advertiser.*

"As against infidelity and science, 'falsely so called,' the work is one of much power; while to the meditative Christian it is rich in those unfoldings of divine truth, providence, and grace, that 'justify God's ways to men.'"—*Independent*

"On perusing them, we are at a loss to say whether the truly Christian spirit which pervades them, or sound morality and elevated views of the duties of citizens which they inculcate, are most to be admired."—*Washington Union.*

"The lectures in these volumes are more learned, elaborate, and inviting than any the Author has yet produced, and will be read profitably by all who appreciate important thoughts in elegant forms. They combine stately eloquence, beautiful, and even imaginative description, and weighty and sound discussion."—*Central Christian Herald.*

"Anything from the pen of this learned and eloquent divine must be of interest, but these lectures are so well conceived and gracefully executed as to attract more than usual admiration. * * * * The interesting discussion of the disputed Unity of the human race, in the fourth chapter, is an excellent specimen of close reasoning, and utterly refutes, as we think, the theories of some of our Modern Philosophers. * * * * The chapter on the 'First Woman' contains an elegant and discriminating analysis of the Female Mind, and the most touching and beautiful eulogy on the female character that we remember to have read."—*Commercial Advertizer.*

"There is, perhaps, nothing from the pen of Dr. Spring, who has long been known as a distinguished writer, that will be read with more avidity and interest, than his mature, lucid, and discriminating views on 'First Things.' The themes here discussed form the base of the spiritual edifice, which reflects the glory of God. They embrace questions concerning which there has been great diversity of opinion among philosophical and theological writers."—*Christian Observer.*

"The book will be an invaluable treasure in every Christian family, and may be profitably consulted as a clear and faithful exposition of the first pages of the word of God, by all who delight to 'search the Scriptures;' while, at the same time, such are its treasures of truth drawn from all parts of the Bible, and from every department of science, and such the beauty of its style, that no one of cultivated intellect and refined taste can fail to peruse it with pleasure."—*Buffalo Morning Express.*

THE MERCY SEAT;

THOUGHTS SUGGESTED BY THE LORD'S PRAYER. BY GARDINER SPRING, D.D.

"In this volume intrinsic excellence and mechanical beauty are well combined. Richness and maturity of evangelical thought and sentiment are its characteristics; the ripe experience of a devout Christian clusters on every page; it is full of 'marrow and fatness, of wine on the lees well refined,' and contains food for both heart and intellect. 'The Mercy Seat' will be—cannot but be—highly prized by Christians of all denominations."—*Commercial Advertiser.*

"We regard it as the most valuable of all the distinguished author's valuable works. It is a book for the family and the closet, and is equally well adapted to profit the plainest Christian, and the most cultivated man of letters."—*N. Y. Observer.*

"The present work is among the author's happiest productions. We think it surpasses them all in richness of instruction, tenderness of spirit, earnestness and fidelity of appeal, and power to awaken and sway the best feelings of the sanctified heart. His general observations on prayer, and his remarks on the matter and manner of prayer, are most excellent, and worthy of careful and thorough study."—*Bib. Rep.*

"The volume contains some of his best and most interesting discourse, and cannot fail to be most heartily welcomed by the religious public. The style in which it is published is exceedingly neat and attractive."—*N. Y. Courier and Inquirer.*

"It is a delightful work, and replete with noble Christian views, which ought to obtain in all spheres, and to exert an influence upon all minds."—*N. Y. Evangelist.*

"This volume will not please because it contains ingenious speculations or startling novelties; but because it presents the old, rich themes of Gospel truth in a clear and chaste style. The doctrinal and the practical are happily blended in its discussions—not a page is dull or dry. The author's judicious remarks on 'Forms of Prayer' are commended to all who would like to see this subject kindly exhibited in its true light—the Bible and the History of the Church. We say to all, get 'The Mercy Seat' by Dr. Spring."—*Newark Daily Advertiser.*

"It is certainly one of the most favorable exhibitions of Dr. Spring's powers in illustrating and enforcing truths of the highest moment. His theme is a delightful one, and the method of treating it is all that could be desired. The publisher has presented it in a very attractive dress."—*Phil. Presbyterian.*

"This work is in Dr. Spring's best style,—vigorous, perspicuous, and breathing the true Christian spirit. It is not a book intended simply for the closet. It seizes upon man in his daily walks—amidst the cares of his business—at his desk or in his workshop, and recalls him to a sense of his divine relations—and is worthy of a place in the choicest niche of the library."—*Journal of Commerce.*

"We give a cordial welcome to this new work of Dr. Spring. It is refreshing to meet with a book like this, so clear and chaste in style, so fraught with important instruction, and above all, so eminently spiritual in its tone, and so well fitted to promote devotional feeling."—*N. Y. Presbyterian.*

"A rich and valuable work, replete with the distinguished author's best thoughts on a great subject, of universal interest—the communion of man, weak, sinful and mortal, with the Infinite Jehovah, his God and Saviour."—*Christian Observer.*

THE ATTRACTION OF THE CROSS.

The Attraction of the Cross, designed to illustrate the leading Truths, Obligations and Hopes of Christianity By *Gardiner Spring*, D.D. 12mo. Fourth edition.

" We are not surprised to hear that Mr. Dodd, the publisher, has already issued the third edition of the Attraction of the Cross, by the Rev Dr. Spring. It is the ablest and most finished production of its author, and will undoubtedly take its place in that most enviable position in the family, as a volume of standard reading, to be the comfort of the aged and the guide of the young. We commend it as one of the most valuable issues of the press."—*N. Y. Observer.*

" This is no ordinary, every-day volume of sermons, but the rich, ripe harvest of a cultivated mind—the result of long and systematic devotion to the proper work of the Christian ministry. We regard Dr. Spring as one of the most accomplished preachers of the country. We never heard him preach a weak discourse; and whenever he appears from the press, it is with words of wisdom and power. A careful perusal of this admirable book has afforded us great pleasure. We do not wonder to find it so soon in a third edition. It will have a lasting reputation."—*Baptist Memorial.*

" This volume, which we announced two weeks ago, and which we then predicted would prove to be the most excellent and valuable work yet written by Dr. Spring, has more than equalled our expectations...... We trust that every family in our land will read this precious work, which illustrates so beautifully and attractively the leading truths, obligations and hopes of Christianity, as reflected from the Cross of Christ."—*Albany Spectator.*

" We mistake if this neatly-printed volume does not prove one of the most attractive religious works of the day. It presents the practical truths of religion, which all ought to know, free from the spirit of sectarianism or controversy. The book is prepared for permanent use, and bids as fair, perhaps, as any book of the kind in our times, to live and speak long after the author shall have gone to test the realities he has so eloquently described."—*Journal of Commerce.*

" Dr. Spring's new work, which we had occasion recently to announce, is very highly commended elsewhere. A New-York letter in the Boston Traveller thus introduces it to notice:—'A new work of Dr. Spring, " The Attraction of the Cross," has been published by M. W. Dodd, of this city.... " The Attraction of the Cross" is destined to live among the very best productions of the church with which its respected author is connected. The style is remarkably pure, the arrangements of the topics lucid and methodical, and the arguments addressed with great force to the reason and conscience. It will stand by the side of " Doddridge's Rise and Progress," " Wilberforce's View," or the " Way of Life," in the libraries of future generations.' "—*Newark Daily Adv.*

" None will wonder at the rare success which this volume has won, who have read it. For comprehensiveness of views, beauty of style and excellence and fervor of devotional feeling, few works have lately appeared that surpass it '—*New-York Evangelist.*

" The grand relations of the Cross, its holy influences, its comforts and its triumphs, are here exhibited in a manner cheering to the heart of the Christian. And the perusal of this book will, we venture to say, greatly assist and comfort the children of God...."—*Presbyterian.*

A PASTOR'S SKETCHES:

OR, CONVERSATIONS WITH ANXIOUS INQUIRERS RESPECTING THE WAY OF SALVATION. BY ICHABOD S. SPENCER, D.D., PASTOR OF SECOND PRESBYTERIAN CHURCH, BROOKLYN, N. Y.

This work has had an almost unequalled sale, for one of its kind, being now in its FIFTH EDITION in little more than three months.

For individuality and graphic delineation of character, and for absorbing interest to the reader, it is hardly surpassed by anything in the language.

A few of the opinions of the press are here subjoined:—

"This is a book of remarkable interest. It is one of pastoral *experience;* and the thrilling interest that gathers about many of the scenes and incidents which it describes, justifies the comparison which has been made of it in this respect to the well-known 'Diary of a Physician.'"—*Independent.*

"It is a work of intense interest, and is destined to a wide circulation and great usefulness."—*Albany Argus.*

"We leave this book with reluctance. It has all the interest of Warren's Sketches, entitled 'Diary of a Physician,' and it is an interest of a much higher order. It is a book, too, of pointed and solemn instruction, on the gravest of all themes. Nothing like it exists."—*American Biblical Repository.*

"This is a remarkable book. The work is written in a bold, clear, straightforward style, that carries the idea direct to the heart."—*N. Y. Recorder.*

"We have rarely read a book of a religiously didactic character that has abounded with so much strong practical good sense, or so much interest to us, as this volume.

"We warmly commend it to Christian pastors of every denomination. After reading it, they will, we are sure, recommend it with equal fervor to those in their congregations who need its counsels."—*Com. Adv.*

"We can convey no idea of the exceedingly happy and triumphant logic often displayed in this volume. As an intellectual work, it is of surpassing interest. But in a spiritual point of view, the earnest, absorbing desire to open plainly the way to Christ, and the tender religious feeling pervading all these discussions, give the work an interest and value which we feel in no danger of exaggerating."—*N. Y. Evan.*

"The pictures are true to life, and are sketched with such graphic skill as to forbid the possibility of their having been the product of mere fancy. We earnestly hope that the work will have a very wide circulation."—*N. Y. Observer.*

"These Sketches are forty in number. The few that we have as yet been able to read are *intensely* interesting, especially that of the 'Dying Universalist.' To those who are fond of *lending* good books, we would vehemently commend this as one which will be very sure to be read." —*Puritan Recorder.*

"The Book is in the dramatic form, and so vividly drawn that the reader becomes not merely a spectator, or a listener, but an actor in all that is described. Few will be able to leave it until they have read its last page."—*Literary Messenger.*

"The rapid appearance of successive editions of these Sketches is proof that the public has put as high an estimate upon the work as we expressed on its first appearance in October. It is indeed a book of remarkable interest and power of instruction."—*Biblical Repository.*

JOURNAL AND LETTERS OF THE REV. HENRY MARTYN, B.D.

EDITED BY THE REV. S. WILBERFORCE, M.A., RECTOR OF BRIGHTSTONE. FIRST AMERICAN EDITION.

"The name of Henry Martyn is a sweet savor to the church. His memory is embalmed in the depth and intensity of his piety and the extent of his usefulness. There breathes a refreshing fragrance through every page of his JOURNAL AND LETTERS."—*Southern Meth. Quarterly.*

"To American readers, this will be an entirely new book, and is perhaps one of the richest combinations of religious experience and epistolary counsels ever given to the world. There have been few men like Henry Martyn. The Christian church of all denominations, and especially the Young Men of the church, are greatly indebted to the American publisher for this reprint."—*Commercial Advertiser.*

"It is a book to make one sad, on very many accounts, but it is such a sadness as will tend to make the heart better."—*Watchman and Observer.*

"It is remarkable that this most interesting and valuable work has not been previously given to the American public. The numerous admirers of Martyn will rejoice to possess a volume containing the records of his heart. We have here spread out before us, a picture of his progress in Divine life. As a book for the closet, it is even more valuable than the Memoirs which have been so widely and profitably read. It shows us in what way his eminent spiritual attainments were made, and stimulates us to follow his example. Let those who are seeking to become holy, avail themselves of the aid which the perusal of this volume will furnish, and let those who would promote the spiritual growth of others, place it within their reach."—*N. Y. Observer.*

"The reader of this volume will be admitted to a still nearer view of Martyn's character, than is given in his Memoir. He will become familiar with the processes by which Martyn's eminent attainments in piety were made."—*Rochester Democrat.*

"Those who have read the Memoir of the pious and talented missionary to the Mohammedans of Persia will need nothing but the announcement of this volume of his 'remains' to lead them to possess and read it. The letters are admirable specimens of the epistolary style, and cannot be read without benefit."—*Syracuse Religious Recorder.*

"Though short was his career, and though he fell in the midst of his labors in India, he has left a name which will never perish. The JOURNAL AND LETTERS now presented to the public commence in 1802, and continue through the space of ten years, till his death in 1812. While we commend this volume to all Christian readers, we would especially invite to it the attention of young men in our various institutions of learning."—*Western Christian Advocate.*

"This book leads us into a knowledge of his inner life. 'No portion of the matter contained in it has been previously given to the American public.' It is filled with those 'distracting riches of his journals,' spoken of by his biographer—those 'masses of ore' left by him unused, when he made the extracts which are woven into his narrative."—*Chris. Mirror.*

"The reader is brought into contact with the warm heart of this devout Christian and eminent scholar; can see its movements and feel its throbbings without the presence of a third person, as is necessary in reading a memoir prepared by another. Here we have Martyn's own description of his inner and higher life."—*Western Christian Advocate.*

VINET'S MISCELLANIES.

THE ENDLESS STUDY, AND OTHER MISCELLANIES. BY ALEXANDER VINET. TRANSLATED, WITH AN INTRODUCTION AND NOTES, BY ROBERT TURNBULL. 12mo., pp. 430.

"Vinet was one of the most distinguished divines and preachers in Switzerland, and, unlike most in that country, thoroughly evangelical in sentiment. The just appreciation of his character and writings, given in another column, renders it needless here to do more than give the subjects of the principal essays in this volume:—Montaigne on Morality—The Endless Study—Man Created for God—Centre of Moral Gravitation—Mysteries of Christianity—Natural Faith—Christian Faith—Practical Atheism—Foundation of Christian Morality—Claims of Heaven and Earth Adjusted—Grace and Law—Man Deprived of all Glory before God—Pursuit of Human Glory incompatible with Faith." —*Christian Advocate and Journal.*

"Reflecting, inquiring minds will love to study his pages, so full of fresh, original thought, and giving out a clear and mellow light on some of the grandest themes of Christian truth. His works need not our commendation."—*Newark Daily.*

"Such a work as the Miscellanies of Vinet is one of rare occurrence, and the translator and publisher have conferred an obligation on the part of the intelligent and thinking mind who may be disposed to profit by it. It is of great moment at the present time, and the importance of its elucidations and arguments, and the author's striking delineations of 'pure and undefiled religion,' should not fail to command the admiration and hearty concurrence of every reader."—*Farmer and Mechanic.*

"While he charms by his beauty and convinces by his persuasive power, he abounds in original views, and leads the mind into fresh channels of reflection and feeling. His writings abound in *the seeds of things*, and possess a remarkable power to quicken and expand the mind of the reader."—*Columbian and Great West.*

"Few among the continental writers on religious subjects have in this century had so wide a celebrity as Vinet. His works are characterized by a beauty and persuasive power which appeal to every reader of taste. They possess, too, a remarkable influence in quickening and expanding the mind, and can therefore be dwelt upon and studied. In many respects they remind us of the searching analysis and profound thought of Foster's Essays."—*Daily State Register.*

"Having said thus much we will add, that the volume is a valuable one, and that the Introduction and Notes increase its value. The translation appears to be well done, and the public have reason to thank Mr. Turnbull for bringing it into acquaintance with a writer of so much eminence as Vinet."—*Boston Christian Register.*

"Under this new title we are happy to perceive the main substance of a work by Dr. Vinet, translated by Mr. Turnbull some years ago, and truly called VITAL CHRISTIANITY. Causes not clearly explained, have induced him to issue the best part of that volume anew, with an enlarged Introduction, and several valuable pieces not found in the former. Among the latter are the articles from which this issue derives its name. We welcome it with sincere pleasure."—*Baptist Quarterly Record.*

GOSPEL STUDIES.

By Alexander Vinet, D.D., Author of Vital Christianity, with an Introduction by Dr. Baird.

"These discourses are remarkable for originality and beauty of thought and elegance of diction. They are unlike anything that we ever read—they are delightful."—*Daily Evening Traveller.*

"Vinet, beyond any writer of our day, was characterized by the perpetual progress from novelty to novelty. The originality of Vinet is his principal charm. He treats the most common topics of theology with a freshness which fascinates us like a discovery. In the conduct of his metaphors, he so fuses the thought in the illustration, as to give the most familiar truths the brilliancy of inventions; and by penetrating and profound analysis reveals new relations of truth which elude common sagacity, and are indeed so many new truths. We believe the perusal of this volume will be an excellent discipline for those whose religious views need enlivening; all here is full of nobleness, aspiring speculation, and enthusiastic love."—*Literary World.*

"They possess the peculiar characteristics of French sermonizing—lively, abrupt, strikingly beautiful in description, and artistically arranged."—*N. Y. Evangelist.*

"Vinet has been styled "the Chalmers of Switzerland," but his manner is different, although his thoughts are not less brilliant. In his style, Vinet is original. He was a profound thinker, and in communicating his ideas he knows how to make others think. No one can read these admirable discourses without entering into the spirit and feelings of the author, nor without gaining new and valuable ideas from him."—*Christian Secretary.*

"The writer had a most versatile as well as a most discriminating and powerful mind; and probably deserved, more than almost any other writer, to be called, in the best sense of the word, a philosophical Christian. He is equally at home in the heights and in the depths: and his range of thought seems illimitable."—*Albany Argus.*

"Gospel Studies" contains much that is adapted to stir the soul, to nourish piety, and to enlarge one's range of thoughts in certain directions."—*Watchman and Reflector.*

"Simplicity, beauty, original thought, and ardent piety, are the prominent attributes of the author's mind as developed in this work. There is a freshness in his views which will delight the intelligent reader."—*Christian Observer.*

"Such is the title of one of the best books on the subject of religion that we have seen for many a day. In an introduction of a few pages, Dr. Baird gives a short notice of the life of Dr. Vinet, whom he pronounces the greatest philosopher that the Continent, if not Europe, has produced in our times. He has been called the Chalmers of Switzerland, but not very correctly. He was rather the John Foster. But he had a mind far more clear and discriminating than that of the great British Essayist just named. It has a freshness about it, and is so removed from the usual style of an English or American mind that it awakens and excites attention at every step."—*Journal of Commerce.*

JOURNAL OF THREE YEARS' RESIDENCE IN ABYSSINIA.

BY REV. SAMUEL GOBAT, NOW BISHOP OF JERUSALEM. PRECEDED BY AN INTRODUCTION, GEOGRAPHICAL AND HISTORICAL, ON ABYSSINIA. Translated from the French by Rev. SERENO D. CLARK. Accompanied with a Biographical Sketch of Bishop GOBAT, by ROBERT BAIRD, D. D.

"This is probably the most complete and accurate work on Abyssinia accessible to the general reader in the English language. It is a valuable contribution to the literature of missions and to church history, and whoever desires to have a good library in either of these departments, will be sure to obtain it."—*Christian Intelligencer.*

"In an Introduction of a dozen pages, the Rev. Dr. Baird has given an interesting account of the early life, conversion, and subsequent history of Bishop Gobat—whom he pronounces to be as remarkable a man as Henry Martyn. We have no doubt that this book will do great good. It gives more valuable, reliable information respecting Abyssinia, than all other books in the English language put together. The first 120 pages, relating to the geography, manners, customs, and history of that country, will well reward a careful perusal."—*Jour. of Com.*

"Of what country not utterly unknown do we know so little as of Abyssinia? The work here presented to the public, has all the marks of genuine worth. Mr. Gobat was educated at a missionary school—or, more properly, a school for the training of missionaries, in Switzerland. His residence in Abyssinia was not long, amounting to only five or six years in all, but he has given more knowledge of the country, and of its inhabitants, than can be gleaned from all other books extant."—*Northern Christian Advocate.*

"Bishop Gobat's journal teems with interest."—*Commercial Advertiser.*

"The contents of this volume are of surpassing interest. They comprise a well-written biographical sketch of a man of extraordinary talents, learning, and piety; a graphic account of the remarkable country of Abyssinia, and its inhabitants; an historical view of the ancient Abyssinian Church; and Mr. Gobat's Journal of his travels and labors in this country, which occupies the larger portion of the volume."—*Christian Observer.*

"The volume before us abounds in information."—*Puritan Recorder.*

"The author's life is a romance, realized into experiments of bold adventure and comprehensive charity. In Abyssinia he was domiciled three years, visiting places altogether unexplored by any other European, and everywhere keeping his eyes and ears open to apprehend the true condition of the country. It is no wonder that such a man, in such a field, should be able to write a book 'to be as a light shining in a dark place.'"—*U. S. Gazette and N. Amer.*

"We have read this book with very great interest, as the only one of which we know, giving us any information with regard to Abyssinia. There is a novelty about his adventures which would arrest the attention of one who reads only for amusement; it is something so entirely out of the ordinary track of travel."—*Albany State Register.*

AN EARNEST MINISTRY,

THE WANT OF THE TIMES. BY JOHN ANGELL JAMES. WITH AN INTRODUCTION BY REV. J. B. CONDIT, D.D., OF NEWARK, N. J.

"There is a power in the very title of this book. It strikes home to he convictions of every mind that is wakeful to the condition and wants of the church. 'An Earnest Ministry.' The ear tingles with the sound, it stirs up thought; it lingers in the memory; it turns into prayer.

"'Has the evangelical pulpit lost, and is it likely to lose any of its power?' is the question with which the veteran preacher and author commences his discussion. In the progress of his own earnest mind through the several stages of this subject, he begins with the ministry of the Apostles, finding his the. .e in it; examines the nature of earnestness, and shows its appropriateness in him who handles the word of life, in respect to its matter, manner, and practice; illustrates his points by numerous quotations and biographical notices; and from the whole, gathers motives of great power to bear on the conscience of the professional reader.

"We wish that we could lay a copy on the table of every pastor, and put it into the portmanteau of every missionary in the land: we should feel quite sure that the Sabbath following, at least, would bear witness to its effect; and we should hope for still more enduring results. And we could scarcely imagine a more useful appropriation of money, than would be made by supplying the young men of our own Theological Seminaries, with each a copy of this exhibition of an 'earnest ministry.'"—*N. Y. Observer.*

"We read this work with the greatest interest. A more impressive, truth telling, pungent appeal to the ministry, we have never met with. This noble, stirring effort to infuse new life and energy into the ministry cannot be too highly praised. Without attempting an analysis of its contents, we beg to assure our brethren, that of all useful and able productions of this author, this is by far the most useful and able. There are hints, and appeals, and principles in it, of incalculable importance, and of most awakening interest."—*N. Y. Evangelist.*

"Every work of his we have read meets an exigency—in other words, is opportune to the state of the Church, and shows profound thought, thorough investigation, and withal, is given in a chaste and vigorous style. This last volume in no sense falls behind—there is a clearness, a comprehension, and a power in it, which makes it compare with anything he has written; and throughout it is an illustration of the very earnestness he commends. Dr. Condit of Newark, has written a very judicious introduction to the volume. We feel that Mr. James may well be taken by young men in Theological training, and ministers generally, as their oracle on the importance of earnestness in the ministry."—*Christian Intelligencer.*

"His specimens and illustrations, drawn from the most eminent divines of ancient and modern days, and of various countries, are extremely apt and interesting. By the method he has pursued, Mr. J. has given us a kind of biographical library of the ministry, in such a manner as to impress their excellencies upon the memory, and to inspire a wish to imitate them. The work is richly worthy of the perusal of the class for whom it is specially designed."—*Christian Review.*

"Not to make a book, but to do good, seems to have been the whole object in view. All our ministers, especially the younger, should give this book a reading, and we believe its circulation generally among our people would be productive of great benefit to the whole Church."—*Methodist Pulpit.*

THE HOME ALTAR.

An Appeal in Behalf of Family Worship, with Prayers and Hymns for Family Use, and a Calendar of Lessons in Reading the Bible for every day in the year. By Charles F. Deems, Editor of the Southern M. Pulpit. 12mo.

"We cheerfully say that as a plea for family worship it has but few superiors in ordinary circulation, and that as an aid in performing the duty it is equal to any now before the public."—*Watchman and Observer.*

"The Home Altar appears to us to be admirably arranged, and conspicuous throughout for that clearness of style, beauty, and strength, which Mr. Deem's productions combine in a remarkable degree."—*The Newbernian.*

"This work is adapted to be an efficient auxiliary in aid of family devotion, and of course in aid of domestic happiness. It contains a well-digested and forcible argument in favor of this duty, in connection with various prayers, and hymns, and scripture selections, well fitted to aid and guide in its performance. The writer has performed a service, the good effects of which will be felt much beyond the limits of his own communion."—*Albany Argus.*

"The appeal is in point—able and conclusive in argument—in style, clear and concise—in spirit, earnest, liberal and kind. It should be read by all, and especially by heads of families."—*The Weekly Review.*

"The style of the author is beautifully adapted to the design of the work, and the forms of prayers given breathe a truly humble and penitent spirit."—*Whig and Courier.*

"His selections, too, of scripture readings and hymns, is very judicious and suitable. This is a valuable manual of devotion, and we believe the cause of Christianity would be much advanced by its introduction into every Christian family in the land."—*The Patriot.*

"If the families now neglecting prayer, would adopt such a manual of devotion as the one before us, we cannot doubt but it would enure very much to their spiritual advantage."—*Christian Secretary.*

"This is an excellent work. The Appeal ought to be placed in every house which contains no family altar. It seems impossible to read it and continue delinquent in regard to the duty in question. The prayers are all catholic and scriptural."—*Sunday School [illegible]tor.*

"The pious object of the author is to promote one of the most influential, and delightful, and imperative of all religious exercises. And this he has ably done, by showing the grounds of the duty, meeting the objections to its performance, and offering such facilities as exigencies may require. The only part of the book which has even the appearance of a fault, is that which contains the forms of prayer. But this is a real recommendation, when the object of the author is considered, as the perusal will show. The style is characteristic; simple, perspicuous, neat and forcible; adapted to the nature of the subject. Several other works of a similar kind may be found, but none of which, we are aware, are better suited to its end."—*Quarterly Review of the Methodist Episcopal Church.*

APOSTOLIC BAPTISM.

FACTS AND EVIDENCES ON THE SUBJECTS AND MODES OF CHRISTIAN BAPTISM. BY C. TAYLOR, EDITOR OF CALMET'S DICTIONARY OF THE BIBLE. WITH 13 ENGRAVINGS. 12mo.

"We are glad to see a revised and stereotyped edition of this learned and valuable work on the baptismal controversy. It is not necessary, at this late day, to speak of its peculiar merits. We are not aware that these 'Facts and Evidences' here presented, have ever been invalidated, either in this country or in Great Britain, and if not, they are certainly entitled to no little weight in favor of the arguments of Pædobaptists, both as to the subjects of Christian baptism and the apostolic mode."—*Biblical Repository.*

"This work has given no little trouble to immersionists. The facts of Mr. Taylor have never been denied, to our knowledge; nor have his evidences ever been disproved. The work before us has acquired a reputation which our endorsement cannot materially increase."—*Princeton Review.*

"The American editor presents this volume to the American Churches, as the authentic delineation of original Christian Baptism—with the assured conviction, that an erudite polemic cannot be found who will seriously controvert Mr. Taylor's oracular position—'Baptism, from the day of Pentecost, was administered by the Apostles and Evangelists, to Infants, and not by submersion:' the Facts and Evidences sustaining this position, he regards as irrefutable, as the truth is in Jesus.

"The book displays wonderful research, and brings out the proof from philology and ecclesiastical history, with a distinctness and force perhaps never excelled. It even proves that the warrant for baptizing infants is more certain, or less open to cavils, than if that word had been employed in the command, or in the narration of examples of baptism—because a term is used of more certain meaning, which unquestionably includes little children. The work was published in England more than thirty years ago, and no Baptist author has yet attempted to disprove the facts, or to deny the evidences here adduced, in favor of Pædobaptist principles and practice."—*Christian Mirror.*

"This is a very curious book. It commences the argument in respect to baptism at the right starting point, and enforces it by reasoning of the most convincing character. It seeks to carry back the interpreter of the teachings of the Scriptures, to the time when the New Testament was written, and to enable him to read the passages under circumstances, like those under which they were originally heard. The engravings, which are copies of the oldest representations of the administration of the rite of baptism, in pictures, sculptures, and mosaics, speak forcibly to the eye and the mind."—*New Englander.*

"This is unquestionably the *greatest work* ever published on this question. It has been thirty years *challenging* examination, and no Baptist minister, so far as we know, has dared to touch it. No minister should be without it. Remember, it is a body of *Texts* and *Evidences*. The history of the book is interesting, but we have not room to give it. It ought to be in every Sunday school library. It has *thirteen engravings*, themselves, as evidences, worth the price. The book has had an immense circulation in Europe and America. We wish some plan could be devised to put it in every family of our church."—*Southern Methodist Pulpit.*

IS CHRISTIANITY FROM GOD?

OR A MANUAL OF BIBLE EVIDENCE FOR THE PEOPLE. BY REV. JOHN CUMMINGS, D.D., MINISTER OF THE SCOTTISH NATIONAL CHURCH IN LONDON. WITH AN INTRODUCTION BY HON. THEODORE FRELINGHUYSEN.

"Let no one neglect this volume because its subject is one that has been ably and unanswerably handled before. If we mistake not, it has some traits of superiority over any that has preceded it. As a manual of arguments against infidel assaults and sceptical insinuations we do not think of another that we should call its equal."

"Here is a book that we can heartily commend. Its title, "Is Christianity from God? or a Manual of Bible Evidence for the People," indicates the character of the work. The author attempts no new theory—no new and startling truths—for these are not found in the Bible; but with singular ability he has explored the old truths of revelation, and shown conclusively that the Bible is from God. * * *

"Its positions are taken with so much confidence, and held with so much quiet ease, that the reader can scarcely fail to feel a kind of contempt for the delirious twattling of upstarts, whose intellectual calibre is simply of the capacity to *doubt* what a manly intellect has established."—*Religious Recorder.*

"In an age like the present, when scepticism is so fashionable, a work like this cannot fail to produce a wholesome influence on the mind of the reader."—*Christian Secretary.*

"This work is an able one. It treats of very grave subjects, in an earnest and practical manner. The work will arrest the attention of earnest thinkers, whether sceptics or Christians. The Introduction by Mr. Frelinghuysen is brief, neat, pertinent, and highly commendatory of the body of the book."—*The Republican.*

"This is an able and valuable work on a most important subject, which the author has illustrated in a style and manner that cannot fail to interest that numerous class of readers for whom it was intended. It is a good standard book for the Christian family library."—*Christian Observer.*

"It is a work admirably calculated to enlighten the inquirer after truth, and to confirm the pious in the truth of the Christian Religion." —*Baltimore American.*

"For all classes this is an admirable summary—compendious but complete—of the evidences of Christianity. Its style is more polished, and its learning more profound than Nelson's; but it is well adapted to carry conviction to plain minds, and to suggest to the Christian arguments and facts for the defence of his faith. The moral argument is brought out with great strength; and also that from prophecy."—*The Independent.*

"We earnestly recommend the circulation of this volume. Where skepticism exists, here is strong argument, freshly presented, to settle the belief: where general confidence in the Bible exists, here are detailed proofs to give it corroboration."—*Princeton Review.*

THE FEMALE JESUIT; OR, THE SPY IN THE FAMILY.

"THE JESUIT. Such is the title of a work from the pen of a talented lady, wife of a valuable clergyman in London. It will be read with great interest. We are assured from the best authority that it is an authentic relation of facts."—*Christian Union.*

"THE FEMALE JESUIT; or, the Spy in the Family.—We took up this book for the purpose merely of seeing what it was about. It was late at night, but we became insensibly interested in the narrative, and we read on and on, into the small hours of the morning, until we had finished its 350 pages. As a book of interest, therefore, whether truth or fiction, we can commend it to our readers."—*Albany State Register.*

"If there is anything more dangerous than a Jesuit, says a French writer, it is a Jesuitess. Those who read this little book will think so. It opens a lower deep among the common deeps of human duplicity and degradation. The book should be read; and it would make Protestants careful of escaped nuns, Popish governesses fitted out in convents and Popish schools."—*Christian Intelligencer.*

"In the title of this book is condensed the substance of the story; and a most thrilling, startling, astounding story it is. A girl, professedly a convert from Romanism, obtains a place in a Protestant family, and remains there a considerable time, while yet she is as much a Romanist as ever, and is practising the deepest Jesuitism. Let those who have no fear of the influence of Romanism read this book; and if it does not awaken their apprehensions, it must be because they are more than half Romanists themselves. Let those who resort to fiction, because truth is not sufficiently exciting, read this book, and if it does not furnish all the excitement they wish, we know not whither they will look for more."—*N. Y. Observer.*

"The above is the title of a work recently published by Mr. Dodd which is, in some respects, one of the most strange and mysterious, in the nature and extent of the deceptions practised by one individual upon those with whom she associated herself, that we have ever seen. Indeed, were it not that it emanates from a highly respectable source and its authenticity is fully established, we could scarcely subscribe to its credibility. The developments of this volume strongly illustrate the correctness of the remark, that 'truth is stranger than fiction.' No one who glances at the work will be satisfied until the entire volume has been read."—*Farmer and Mechanic.*

"The truth of the narrative is vouched for, and the truth is sufficiently marvellous to excite astonishment and to puzzle one. The story is that of an accomplished young lady who introduced herself into the family of a clergyman in London as an escaped nun. She won the sympathy and friendship of the family and of many other persons, by her apparent artless simplicity of character, by her talents, and by her melancholy tale of hardships during a long residence in a convent. And yet with all her apparent innocence she was an impostor, and lived and acted a life of deceit."—*Bangor Whig and Courier.*

"The book is a recital of facts of the most engrossing character. It will be read with avidity, as it shows up the arch deceptions, which none but practised Jesuits have skill or depravity enough to palm off upon the world."—*Christian Times.*

CRUDEN'S COMPLETE CONCORDANCE.

A COMPLETE CONCORDANCE

TO THE

HOLY SCRIPTURES

OF THE

OLD AND NEW TESTAMENT;

OR, A

DICTIONARY AND ALPHABETICAL INDEX TO THE BIBLE:

Very useful to all Christians who seriously read and study the inspired writings.

IN TWO PARTS:

CONTAINING,

I. The Appellative or Common Words in so full and large a manner, that any verse may be readily found by looking for any material word in it. In this part the various significations of the principal words are given; by which the true meaning of many passages of Scripture is shown; an account of several Jewish Customs and Ceremonies is also added, which may serve to illustrate many parts of Scripture.

II. The Proper Names in the Scriptures. To this part is prefixed a Table, containing the signification of the words in the original languages from which they are derived.

TO WHICH IS ADDED

A CONCORDANCE TO THE BOOKS CALLED APOCRYPHA.

The whole digested in an easy and regular method: which, together with the various significations and other improvements now added, renders it more useful than any book of the kind hitherto published.

BY ALEXANDER CRUDEN, M.A.

From the Tenth London Edition, carefully revised and corrected by the Holy Scriptures.

TO WHICH IS ADDED

AN ORIGINAL LIFE OF THE AUTHOR.

"Ever since the first publication of Cruden's Concordance, in 1736, it has maintained the acknowledged reputation of being the very best work of the kind in the English language. Indeed, no other has ever deserved to be even compared to it. It maintains its superiority still; and probably will ever hold that pre-eminence.

"We speak of the *complete* edition, which is here presented to the public. A work in the market *called* Cruden's Concordance being only a compilation from the complete work, and wanting many of its most valuable features. To abridge this work of Cruden, as it came from his finishing hand, would be to make it nearly valueless to ninety-nine of every hundred who need a concordance. And of all aids to an accurate understanding of the Bible, we believe Cruden's complete Concordance to be the best."

"DEAR SIR:—I have carefully compared your edition of Cruden's Concordance with a fine English edition, and find it true to the original. Knowing, from many years' use, the value of Cruden, I cannot but be glad that you have thus presented a cheap edition of his invaluable work to the American public. I find in your copy an unimpaired, complete Cruden. This is not the case with another American edition, published last year. In that, great liberties are taken with the original work—such as abridgments, omissions, &c., greatly reducing the amount of its contents, and in the same proportion diminishing its value. A student of the Bible needs a concordance in which he can find *every* passage he wants. Your edition is just such an one."

"We know, from long use, this full and admirable reprint of the original Cruden's Concordance; and we think that the whole value of the work depends upon its being complete and entire; and that its great value would be impaired seriously by the omission of a single word or reference."

"The high price at which this gigantic work has been necessarily sold hitherto, has prevented thousands from purchasing it. A complete edition, with the very latest corrections, with the notes of the author and every line of the London edition faithfully given, is now published, as above, for only TWO DOLLARS. It is the best commentary on the Bible that was ever made: it is worth more to the diligent and devout student than the whole of Henry or Scott, or any other critic, and we would part with all our commentaries rather than with Cruden's Concordance. It ought to be in every intelligent family, and we presume that the low price at which it is now sold will be the means of putting it into the hands of many who would not otherwise have obtained it.'

THE PREACHER AND PASTOR;

A Collection of Standard Treatises on Preaching, and Pastoral Duties, containing Fenelon's Dialogues, on Eloquence, Herbert's Country Parson, Baxter's Reformed Pastor, Campbell's Lectures on Pulpit Eloquence, and other Essays of English Divines. Edited, with an Introductory Essay, by Professor Park, of Andover Seminary.

SERMONS, NOT BEFORE PUBLISHED, ON VARIOUS PRACTICAL SUBJECTS.

By the late Edward Dorr Griffin, D. D.

"Dr. Griffin may be regarded as having been a prince among the princes of the American pulpit. He left a large number of sermons carefully revised and ready for publication, part of which were published shortly after his death, but the *greater* portion of which constitute the present volume. They are doubtless among the ablest discourses of the present day, and are alike fitted to disturb the delusions of guilt, to quicken and strengthen, and comfort the Christian, and to serve as a model to the theological student, who would construct his discourses, in a way to render them at once the most impressive, and the most edifying."

A MEMOIR OF THE REV. LEGH RICHMOND, A. M.

Rector of Turvey, Bedfordshire. By Rev. T. S. Grimshaw, A. M., Rector of Burton-Latimer, &c. Seventh American from the last London Edition, with a handsome Portrait on Steel.

"We have here a beautiful reprint of one of the best books of it class, to be found in our language. Such beauty and symmetry of character, such manly intelligence and child-like simplicity, such official dignity and condescending meekness, such warmth of zeal united with a perception of fitness which always discerns the right thing to be done, and an almost faultless prudence in doing it,—are seldom found combined in the same person. It is a book for a minister, and a book for parishioners; a book for the lovers of nature, and a book for the friends of God and of his species. Never perhaps were the spirits and duties of a Christian Pastor more happily exemplified. Never did warmer or purer domestic affections throb in a human bosom, or exercise themselves more unceasingly and successfully for the comfort, the present well-being and final salvation of sons and daughters. From no heart probably, did ever good will flow out to men, in a fuller, warmer current. In a word, he was the author of the 'Dairyman's Daughter, and the 'Young Cottager.'

"The engraved likeness of Mr. Richmond alone is worth the cost of the work; as illustrative of the uncommon benignity that adorned and endeared the man to his friends and the world."

UNCLE BARNABY;

Or Recollections of his Character and Opinions, pp. 316.

"The religion of this book is good—the morality excellent, and the mode of exhibiting their important lessons can hardly be surpassed in anything calculated to make them attractive to the young, or successful in correcting anything bad in their habits or morals. There are some twenty chapters on as many common sayings and maxims, occurrences and incidents—in this respect bearing a resemblance to 'the Prompter, a somewhat oracular book forty or fifty years ago. It is an excellent book to keep in a family, and may be alike beneficial to parents and children."

THE BOOK THAT WILL SUIT YOU;

Or a Word for Every One. By Rev. James Smith, Author of "Believer's Daily Remembrancer," &c.

"An elegant little hand book of some 300 pages 16mo., and by an English author. Its contents are a rare selection of topics, treated briefly to suit the circumstances of those who have fifteen or twenty minutes to spend in reading, which it would be wicked to throw away, and yet discouraging to commence a heavier volume. 'The Successful Mourner,' 'The Child's Guide,' 'The Husband's example,' 'The Wife's Rule,'—these are some of the topics taken promiscuously from the book; and they show the author's mind to be travelling in the right direction, viz.: towards the theory of life's daily practice. We hope that the time is near when Christian parlors will be emptied of 'The Book of Fashion,' 'Somebody's Lady's Book,' etc., etc., made up of love stories mawkishly told, and other drivelling nonsense; and their places supplied with works like the 'Book that will Suit you'—no less pleasing, and far more useful."

GRACE ABOUNDING TO THE CHIEF OF SINNERS,

In a faithful account of the Life and death of John Bunyan, pp. 176.

"We are pleased to see a very handsome edition of this admirable treatise. It is just published, and will be eagerly sought after by all who admire the spirit and genius of this remarkable man whose 'Pilgrims Progress' stands nearly if not quite at the head of religious literature."

KIND WORDS FOR THE KITCHEN;

Or Illustrations of Humble Life. By Mrs. Copley.

"This admirable little volume is the production of Mrs. Esther Copley, (late Mrs. Hewlett,) whose popularity as an authoress has long been established upon both sides of the Atlantic. The welfare of that interesting and important part of society who discharge the domestic duties of life has long engaged the attention of this distinguished and accomplished lady.

"We have read the 'Kind Words for the Kitchen,' with a firm conviction that it is the best work we have ever seen in so small a compass for its designed purpose; it suggests all that a sense of duty would lead the head of a well regulated household to advise, and having loaned the book to ladies distinguished for their judgment and skill as heads of well-governed families, they have urged its publication with a few omissions of matter deemed inappropriate to our country.

"We believe almost every Christian lady will be glad to place such a manual of sound instruction in the hands of her domestics, and that which is *kindly* bestowed will generally be *gratefully* received. With an assurance that the general diffusion of this book would accomplish a most valuable service in binding together more closely the interests of the employer and the employed, and softening down the asperities which so frequently grow out of the ill performed duties of the household sphere, we should rejoice to know that this little volume was placed by the side of the Bible in every kitchen of our country."

PURITAN HEROES;

OR, SKETCHES OF THEIR CHARACTER AND TIMES. BY JOHN STOUGHTON. WITH AN INTRODUCTORY LETTER BY JOEL HAWES, D.D.

"This is a well-printed duodecimo volume, wherein is given a series of admirable sketches of those noble minded men whose renunciations of existing glaring evils subjected them to so great a degree of suffering and calumniation. The present volume is not a continuous nor a prosy history. It is more; for while the best and standard authorities, old MSS., and curious tracts, have been consulted in its compilation, it abounds with vivid and life-like pictures of the principal characters and events in the time of the Puritans and Nonconformists. No portion of English History can be more interesting than this, and none better deserves deep and earnest study."—*N. Y. Tribune.*

"The perusal of this volume has awakened in our heart more than our former love for the Puritans of the olden times, and given us a burning desire that every American citizen may possess, individually, as intense a regard for the memory of those men whose principles, refined like gold in the fires of intolerance and persecution, laid the foundation on which the glorious superstructure of our Temple of Liberty has been erected. The pen of Stoughton has given to these records of Puritan days all the vividness, power, and glory of life, and Mr. Dodd has published them in a style of beauty and elegance worthy of much commendation."—*Albany Spectator.*

"The author has evidently written so as to adapt his style to the young, and thereby secure their attention to the toils and struggles of the early advocates of Truth, then imperfectly known, against ecclesiastical domination and spiritual tyranny. This we have no doubt he will have accomplished. The book is one of the most readable that has been issued from the religious press for years. We mean that it possesses a captivation, both from the style and the subject, which is rarely found."—*Methodist Protestant.*

"This book commemorates, in a thrilling and powerful manner, some of the greatest spirits of perhaps the most interesting period of British history. It shows us the struggles and heaviness of the free spirit as it was coming forth to ripen upon the earth. It is history, the most interesting—but not continuous history. It is highly and most justly recommended by Dr. Hawes."—*Albany Express.*

"This work relates to a period when great truths were struggling into birth—when soul-liberty was asserted and maintained at the expense of fortune, reputation, friends, everything:—a liberty which has long blessed our happy land; and which is extending a like boon to other nations."—*The Trojan.*

"This book is of decided interest. The times to which it relates, the characters it describes; the stirring events which it sketches; and the noble sentiments which it illustrates, lend to it a peculiar charm."—*Biblical Repository.*

"The volume before us gives an admirable insight into the character and times of the Puritans. It is not a dry history, like Neal's: it is a spirit-stirring review of the men and the age, in which every character and every scene lives before us. Here we may worship with 'the Islington Congregation' in the woods: here we may follow Barrow and Greenwood, and Perry, to the gallows: here we may witness the embarkation of the Pilgrim Fathers: here we may sit by the death-bed of Owen, and Baxter, and Howe; and walk among the graves of men of whom the world is not worthy."—*The Independent.*

www.ingramcontent.com/pod-product-compliance
Lightning Source LLC
LaVergne TN
LVHW021135110826
845150LV00005B/1034

* 9 7 8 1 4 2 5 5 4 9 4 0 4 *